Haruka

-Beyond the Stream of Time-

4

Story & Art by **Tohko Mizuno**

Haruka
-Beyond the Stream of Time-

4

CONTENTS

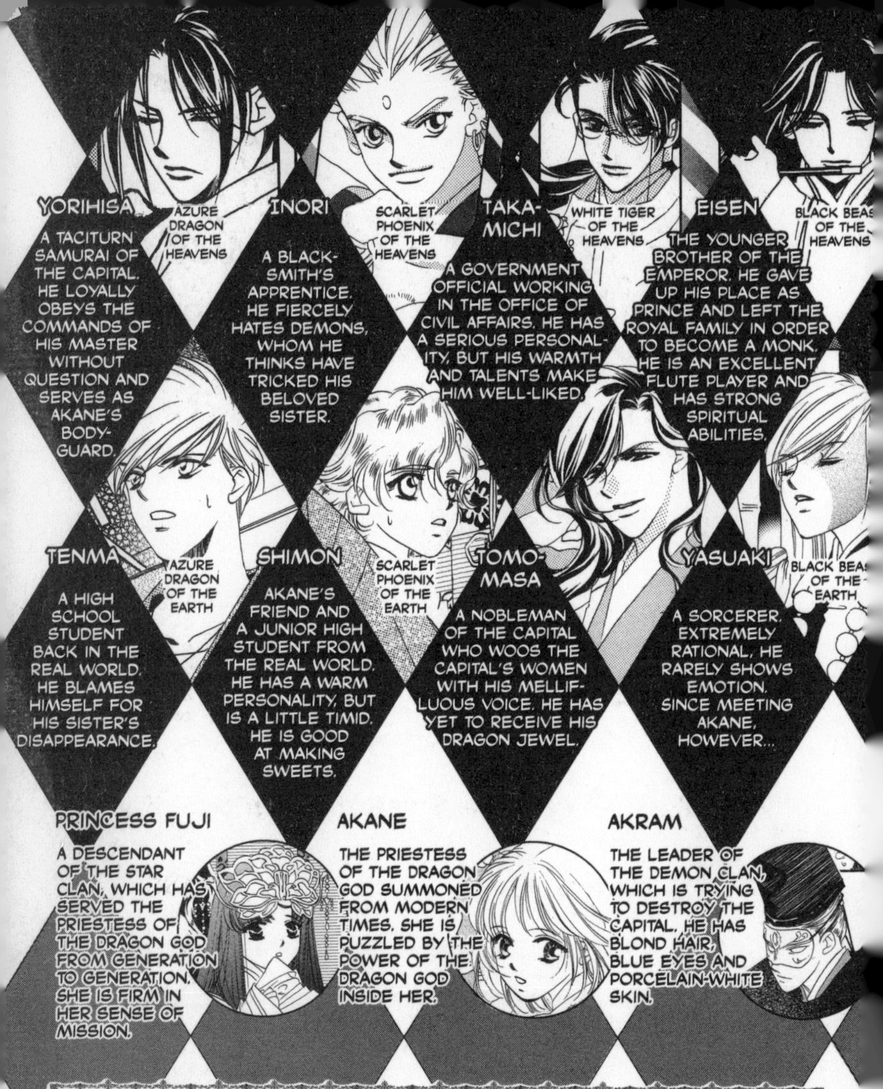
YORIHISA
AZURE DRAGON OF THE HEAVENS
A TACITURN SAMURAI OF THE CAPITAL. HE LOYALLY OBEYS THE COMMANDS OF HIS MASTER WITHOUT QUESTION AND SERVES AS AKANE'S BODY-GUARD.
INORI
SCARLET PHOENIX OF THE HEAVENS
A BLACK-SMITH'S APPRENTICE. HE FIERCELY HATES DEMONS, WHOM HE THINKS HAVE TRICKED HIS BELOVED SISTER.
TAKA-MICHI
WHITE TIGER OF THE HEAVENS
A GOVERNMENT OFFICIAL WORKING IN THE OFFICE OF CIVIL AFFAIRS. HE HAS A SERIOUS PERSONAL-ITY, BUT HIS WARMTH AND TALENTS MAKE HIM WELL-LIKED.
EISEN
BLACK BEAS OF THE HEAVENS
THE YOUNGER BROTHER OF THE EMPEROR. HE GAVE UP HIS PLACE AS PRINCE AND LEFT THE ROYAL FAMILY IN ORDER TO BECOME A MONK. HE IS AN EXCELLENT FLUTE PLAYER AND HAS STRONG SPIRITUAL ABILITIES.
TENMA
AZURE DRAGON OF THE EARTH
A HIGH SCHOOL STUDENT BACK IN THE REAL WORLD. HE BLAMES HIMSELF FOR HIS SISTER'S DISAPPEARANCE.
SHIMON
SCARLET PHOENIX OF THE EARTH
AKANE'S FRIEND AND A JUNIOR HIGH STUDENT FROM THE REAL WORLD. HE HAS A WARM PERSONALITY, BUT IS A LITTLE TIMID. HE IS GOOD AT MAKING SWEETS.
TOMO-MASA
A NOBLEMAN OF THE CAPITAL WHO WOOS THE CAPITAL'S WOMEN WITH HIS MELLIF-LUOUS VOICE. HE HAS YET TO RECEIVE HIS DRAGON JEWEL.
YASUAKI
BLACK BEAS OF THE EARTH
A SORCERER. EXTREMELY RATIONAL, HE RARELY SHOWS EMOTION. SINCE MEETING AKANE, HOWEVER...
PRINCESS FUJI
A DESCENDANT OF THE STAR CLAN, WHICH HAS SERVED THE PRIESTESS OF THE DRAGON GOD FROM GENERATION TO GENERATION. SHE IS FIRM IN HER SENSE OF MISSION.
AKANE
THE PRIESTESS OF THE DRAGON GOD SUMMONED FROM MODERN TIMES. SHE IS PUZZLED BY THE POWER OF THE DRAGON GOD INSIDE HER.
AKRAM
THE LEADER OF THE DEMON CLAN, WHICH IS TRYING TO DESTROY THE CAPITAL. HE HAS BLOND HAIR, BLUE EYES AND PORCELAIN-WHITE SKIN.

THE STORY SO FAR

AKANE IS JUST A TYPICAL MODERN-DAY HIGH SCHOOL STUDENT. BUT ONE DAY, SHE AND HER FRIENDS TENMA AND SHIMON ARE PULLED INTO A MYSTERIOUS WORLD THAT RESEMBLES HEIAN ERA JAPAN. THE DEMON CLAN, WHICH HOLDS A GRUDGE AGAINST HUMANS, IS PLOTTING THE CAPITAL'S DESTRUCTION. AKRAM, THE DEMON CLAN'S LEADER, SUMMONED AKANE (THE FATED PRIESTESS OF THE DRAGON GOD) TO THE CAPITAL IN THE HOPES OF HARNESSING THE DRAGON GOD'S POWERS AGAINST THE CAPITAL'S RESIDENTS.

USING THE DRAGON GOD'S POWER IS THE CAPITAL'S ONLY HOPE OF SURVIVING THE DEMON CLAN'S SIEGE. PRINCESS FUJI PLEADS WITH AKANE TO DEFEND THE PEOPLE OF THE CAPITAL AS PRIESTESS, AND TELLS HER THAT EIGHT GUARDIANS WILL GATHER TO PROTECT HER.

TENMA DISCOVERS THAT HIS LONG-LOST SISTER RAN WAS ALSO SUMMONED BY AKRAM YEARS AGO AND HAS LOST ALL HER MEMORY OF THE MODERN WORLD. AKANE PLUNGES INTO A VOID TO SAVE RAN AND THE GUARDIANS RUSH AFTER HER. IN THE BATTLE THAT FOLLOWS, TENMA SLASHES AKRAM'S ARM WITH ONE STROKE OF THE FAMED SWORD DEMONSLAYER. AKRAM RETREATS, AND AKANE AND RAN ARE SAFE...FOR NOW.

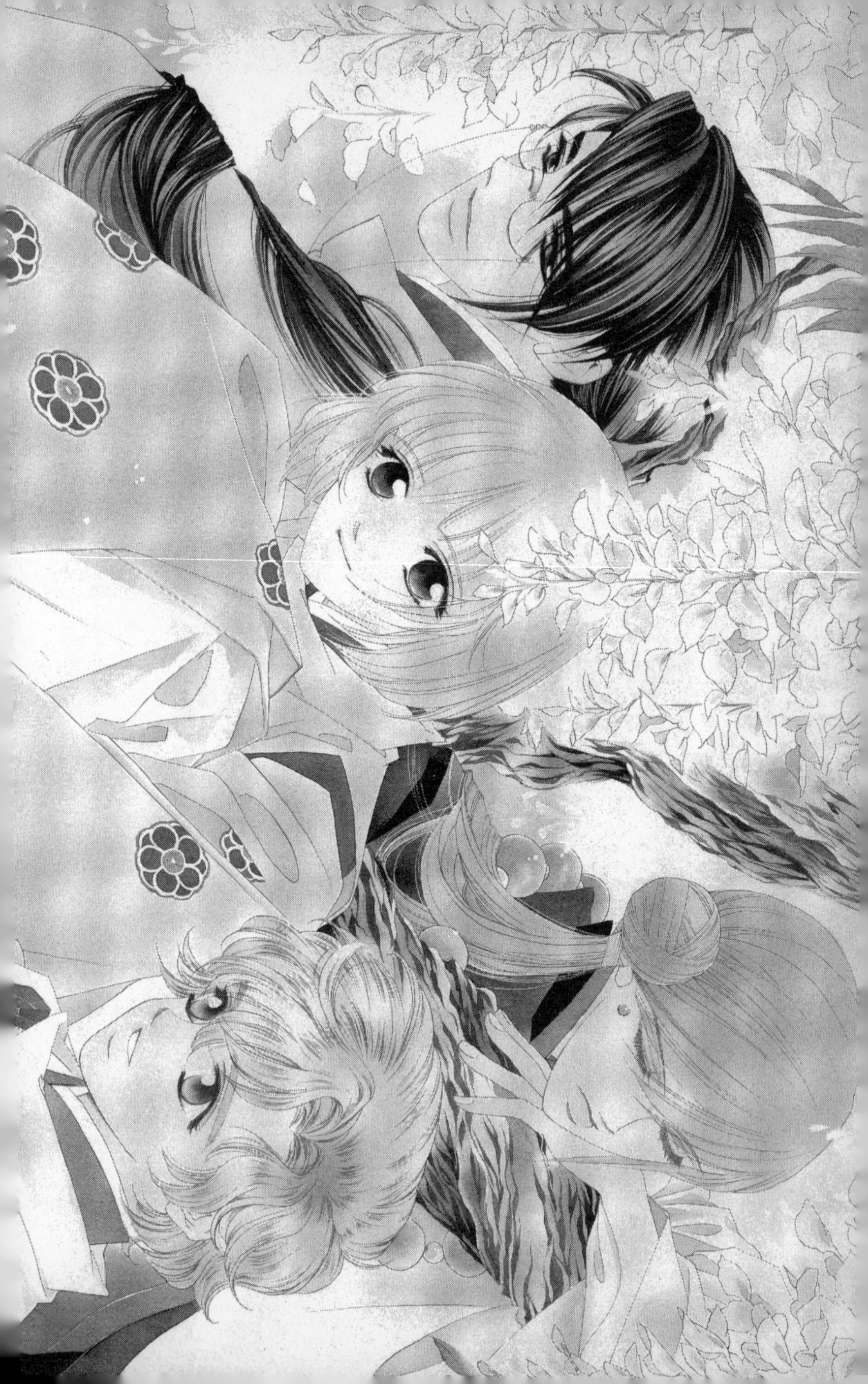

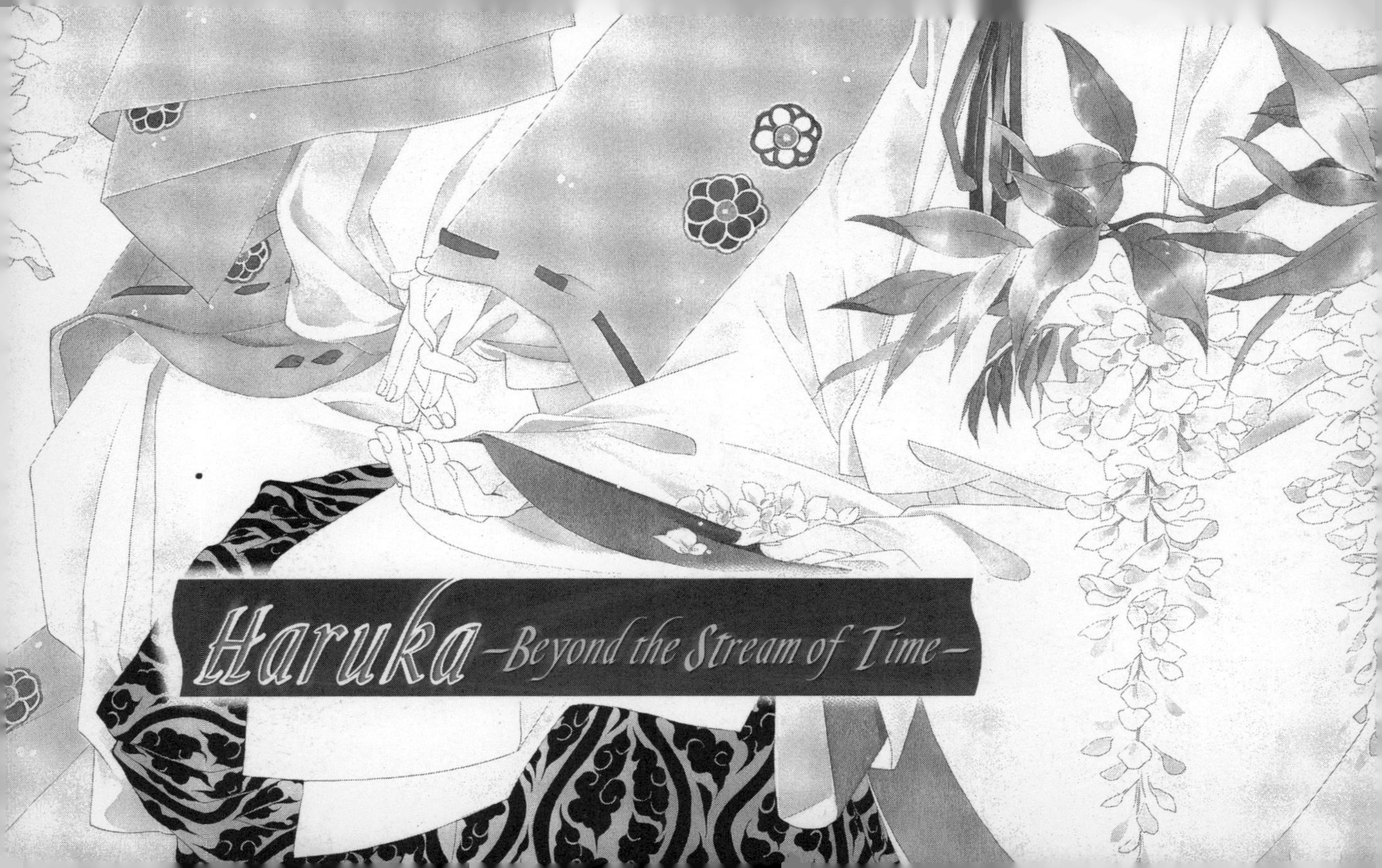
Haruka -Beyond the Stream of Time-

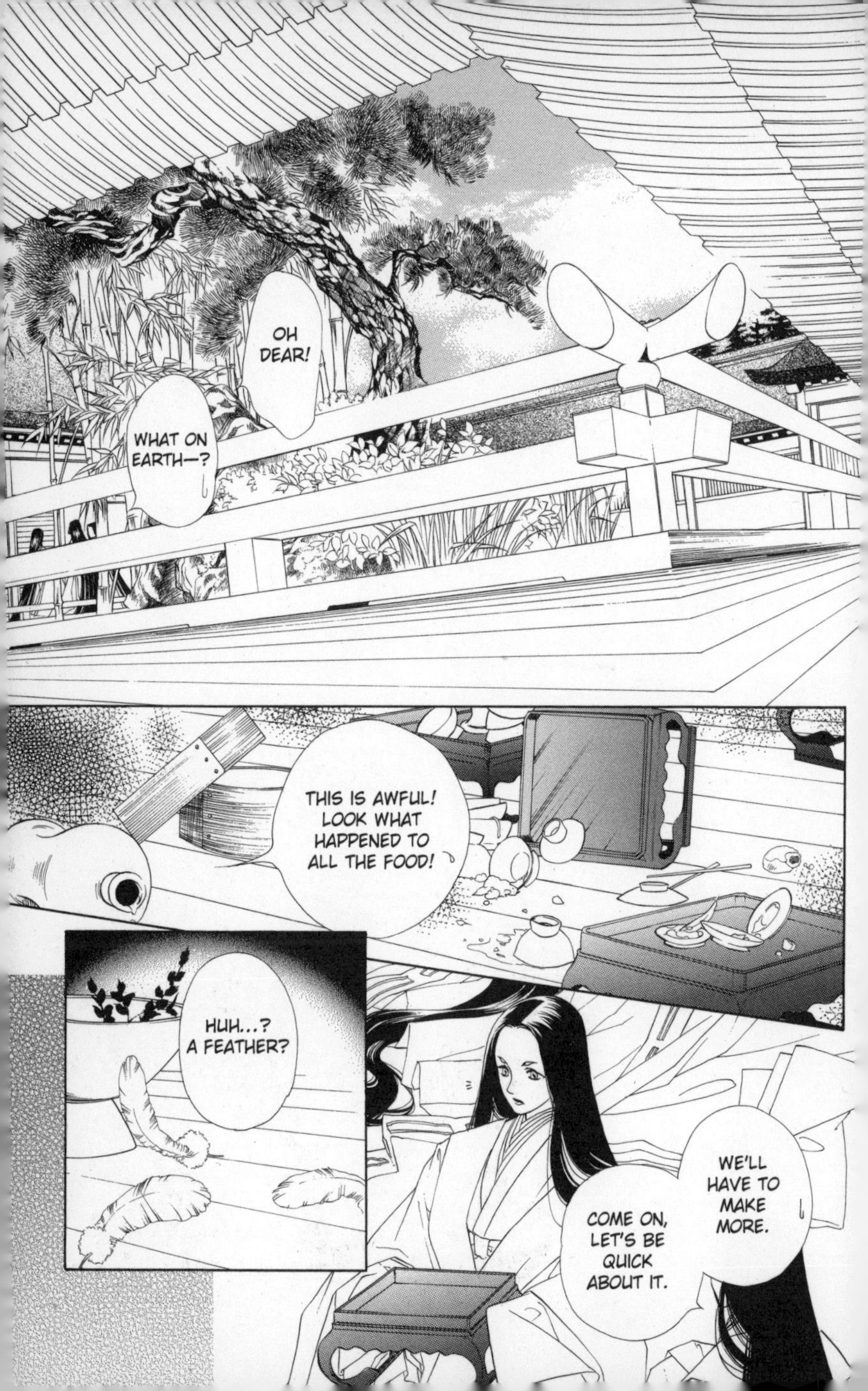
OH DEAR!
WHAT ON EARTH—?
THIS IS AWFUL! LOOK WHAT HAPPENED TO ALL THE FOOD!
WE'LL HAVE TO MAKE MORE.
COME ON, LET'S BE QUICK ABOUT IT.
HUH...? A FEATHER?

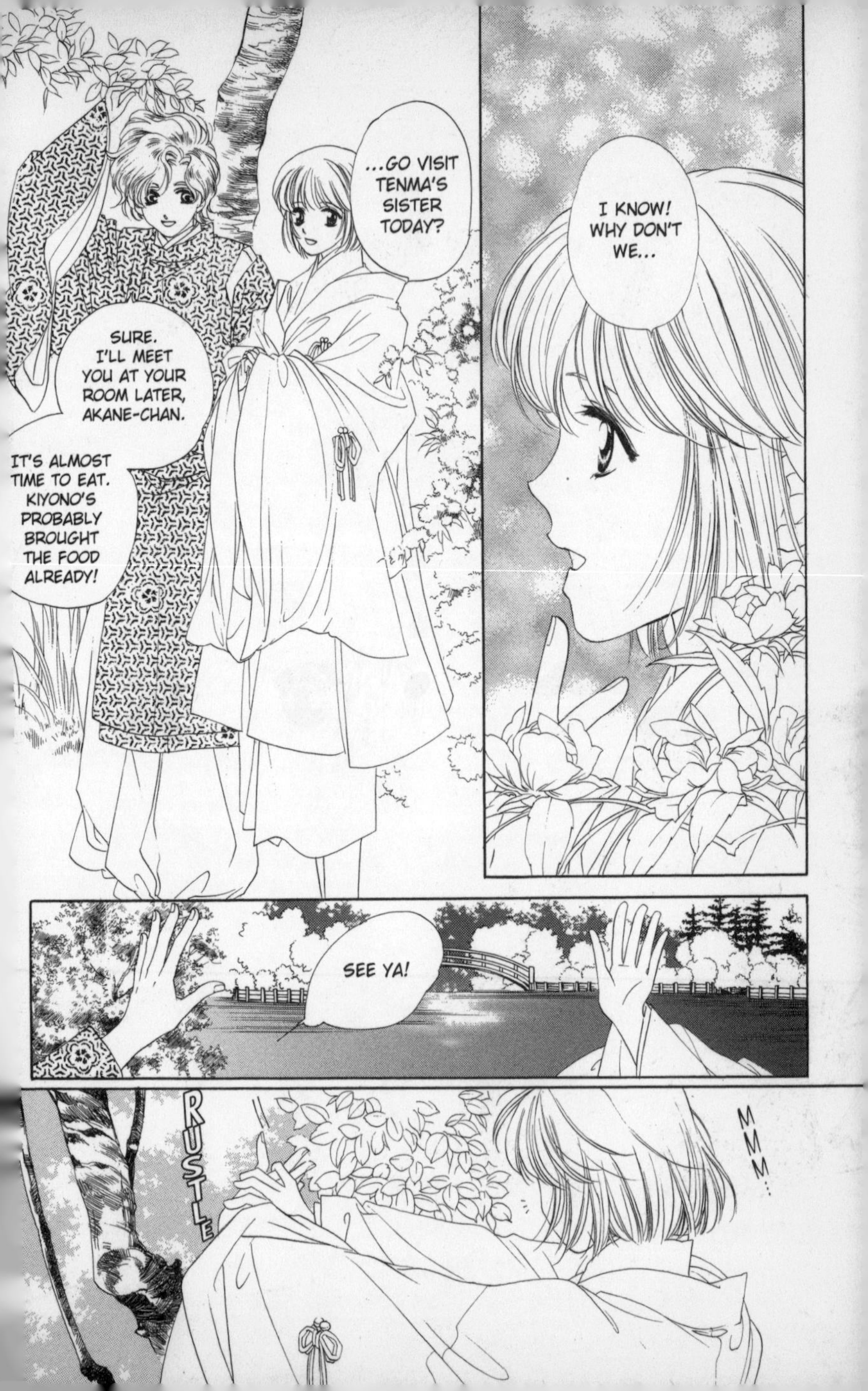
I KNOW! WHY DON'T WE...
...GO VISIT TENMA'S SISTER TODAY?
SURE. I'LL MEET YOU AT YOUR ROOM LATER, AKANE-CHAN.
IT'S ALMOST TIME TO EAT. KIYONO'S PROBABLY BROUGHT THE FOOD ALREADY!
SEE YA!
MMM...
RUSTLE

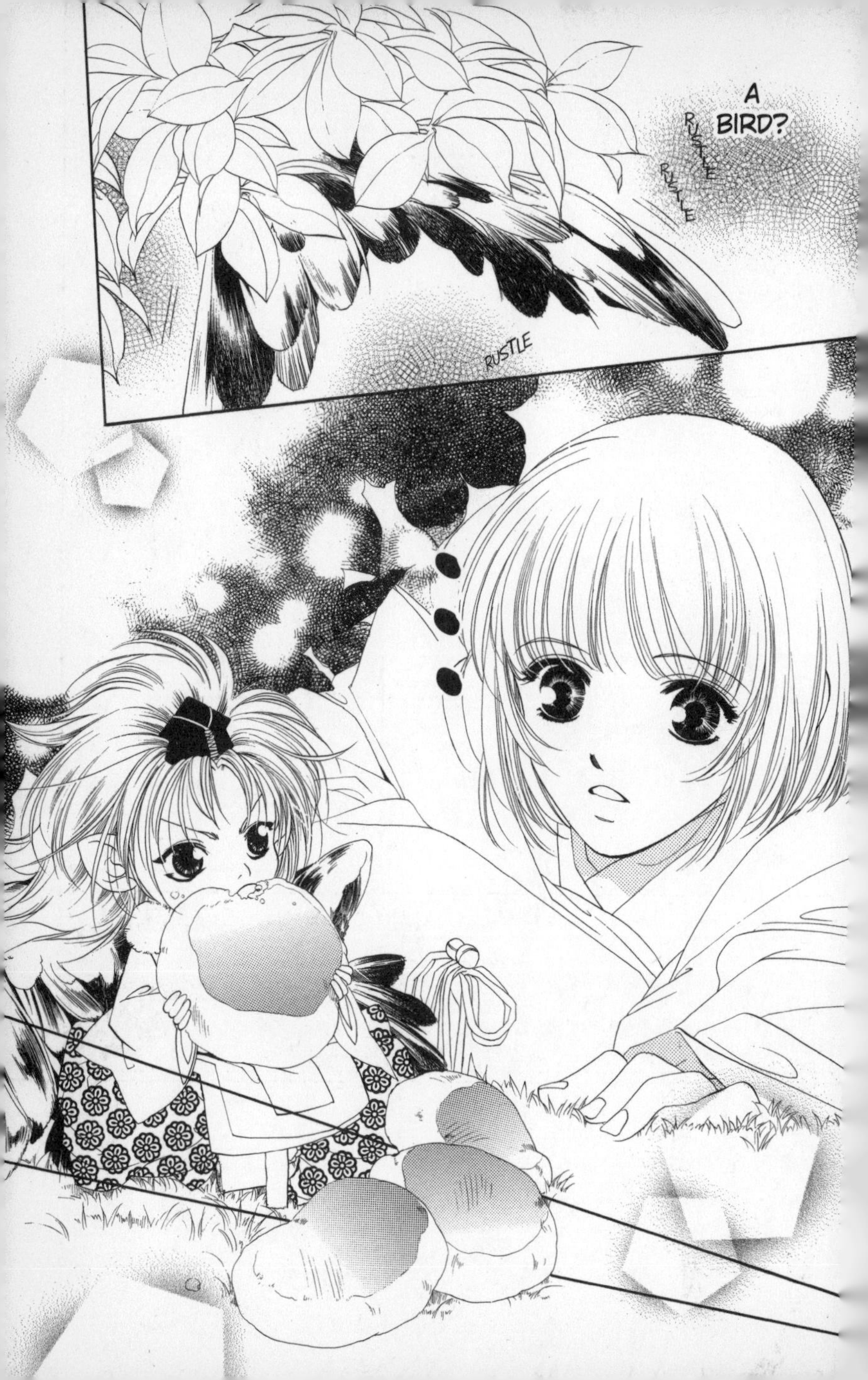
A BIRD?
RUSTLE
RUSTLE
RUSTLE

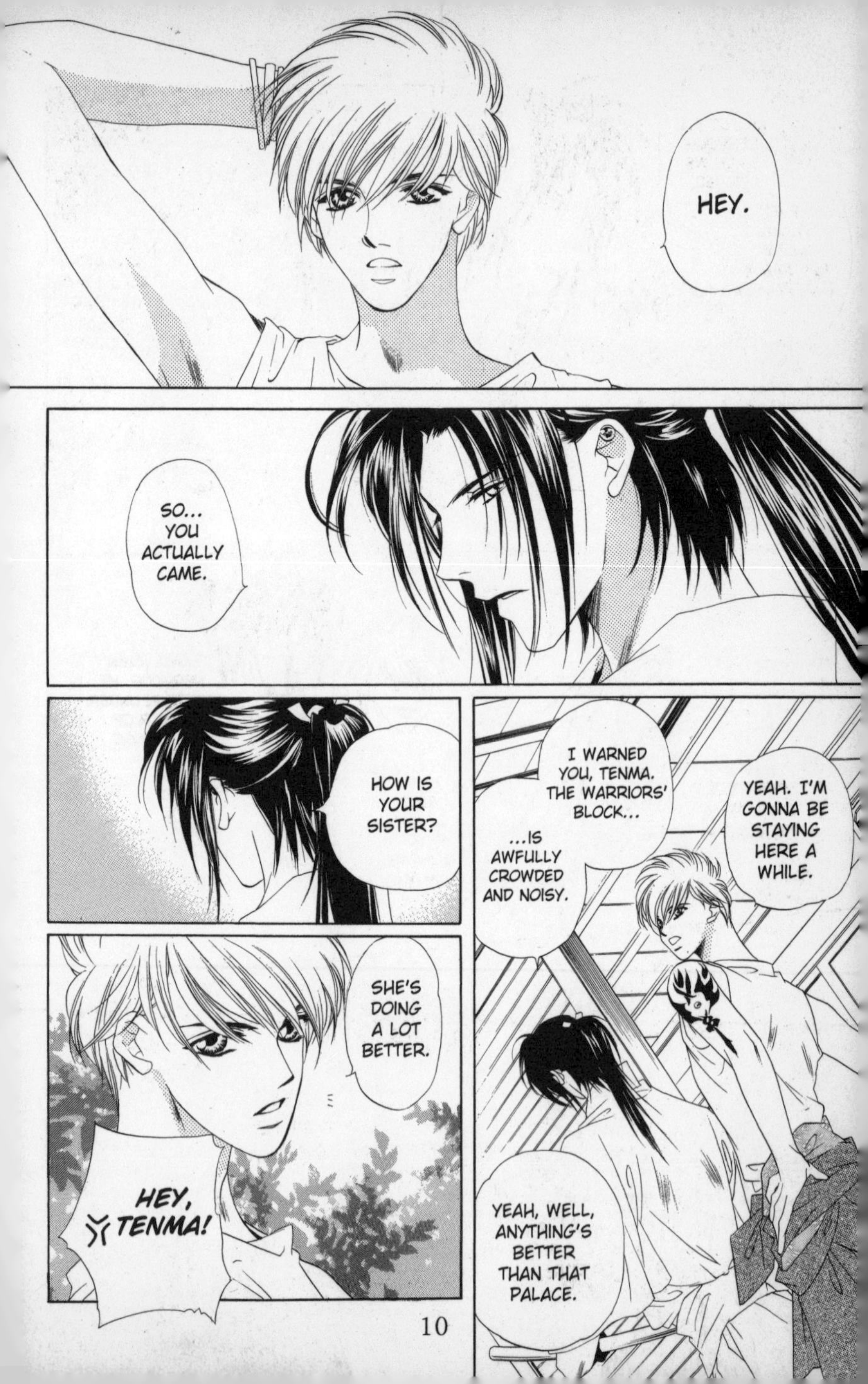
HEY.
SO... YOU ACTUALLY CAME.
YEAH. I'M GONNA BE STAYING HERE A WHILE.
I WARNED YOU, TENMA. THE WARRIORS' BLOCK...
...IS AWFULLY CROWDED AND NOISY.
YEAH, WELL, ANYTHING'S BETTER THAN THAT PALACE.
HOW IS YOUR SISTER?
SHE'S DOING A LOT BETTER.
HEY, TENMA!

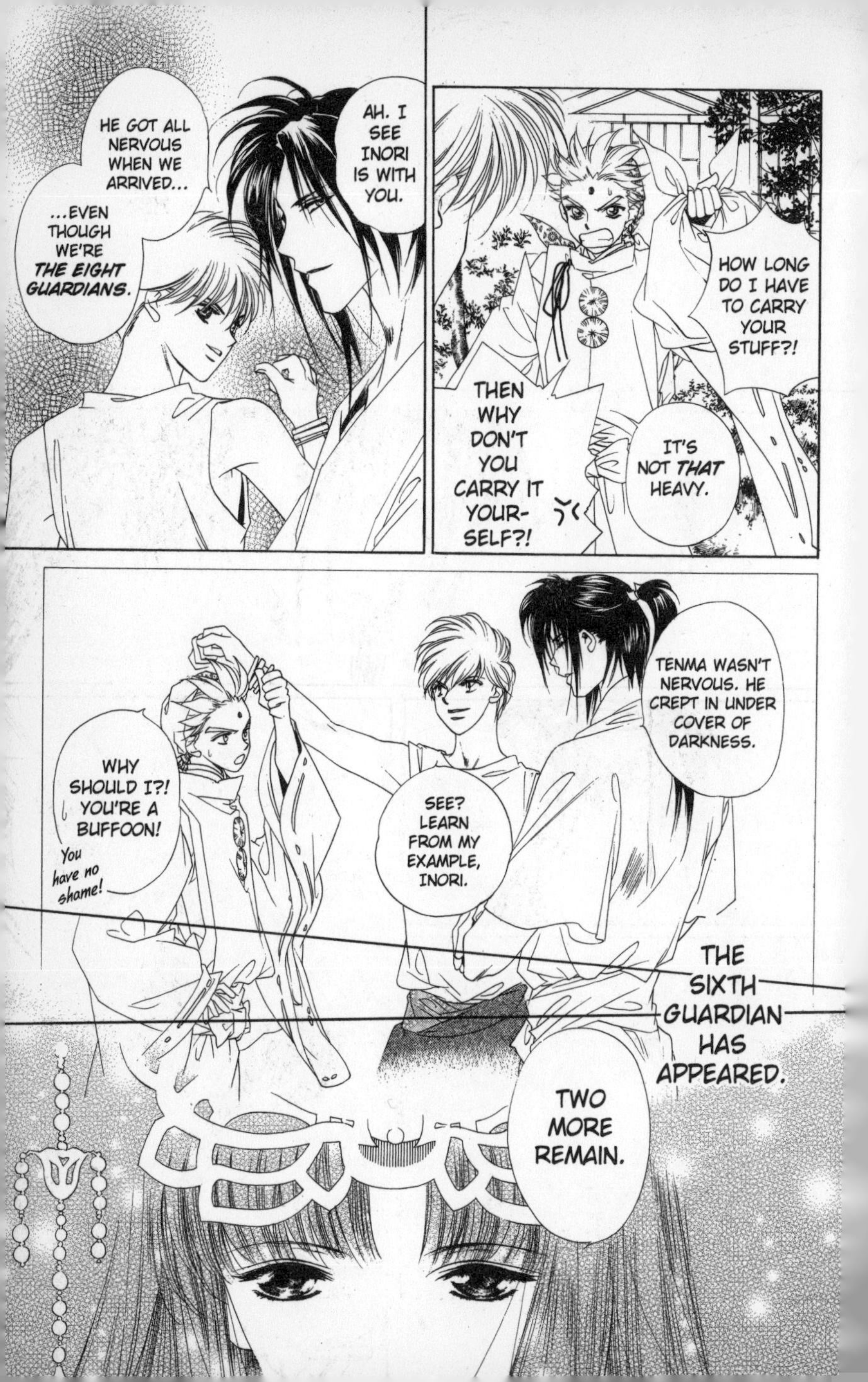
HOW LONG DO I HAVE TO CARRY YOUR STUFF?!
IT'S NOT *THAT* HEAVY.
THEN WHY DON'T YOU CARRY IT YOUR-SELF?!
AH. I SEE INORI IS WITH YOU.
HE GOT ALL NERVOUS WHEN WE ARRIVED...
...EVEN THOUGH WE'RE *THE EIGHT GUARDIANS*.
TENMA WASN'T NERVOUS. HE CREPT IN UNDER COVER OF DARKNESS.
SEE? LEARN FROM MY EXAMPLE, INORI.
WHY SHOULD I?! YOU'RE A BUFFOON!
You have no shame!
THE SIXTH GUARDIAN HAS APPEARED.
TWO MORE REMAIN.

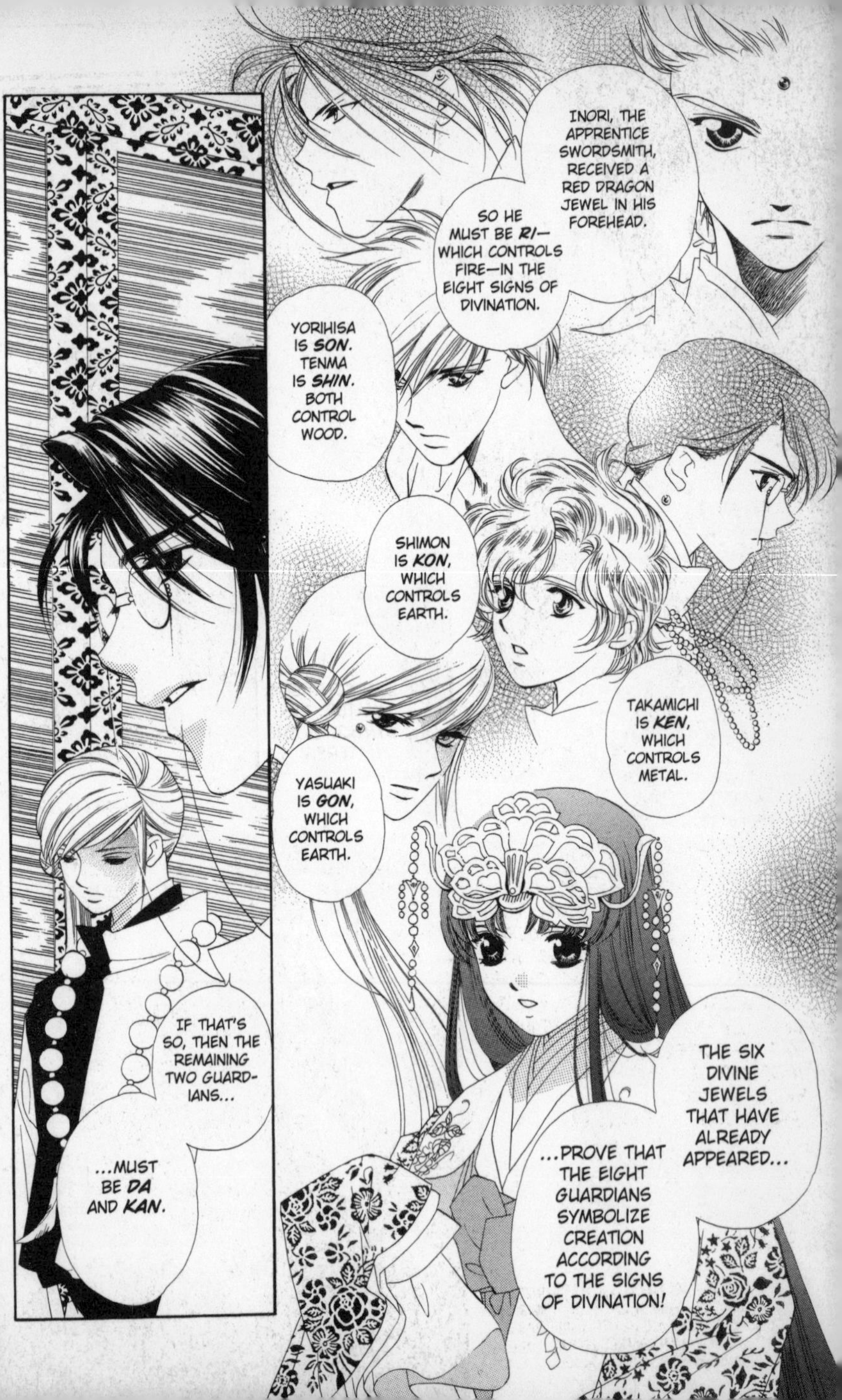
INORI, THE APPRENTICE SWORDSMITH, RECEIVED A RED DRAGON JEWEL IN HIS FOREHEAD.
SO HE MUST BE *RI*—WHICH CONTROLS FIRE—IN THE EIGHT SIGNS OF DIVINATION.
YORIHISA IS *SON*. TENMA IS *SHIN*. BOTH CONTROL WOOD.
SHIMON IS *KON*, WHICH CONTROLS EARTH.
TAKAMICHI IS *KEN*, WHICH CONTROLS METAL.
YASUAKI IS *GON*, WHICH CONTROLS EARTH.
THE SIX DIVINE JEWELS THAT HAVE ALREADY APPEARED...
...PROVE THAT THE EIGHT GUARDIANS SYMBOLIZE CREATION ACCORDING TO THE SIGNS OF DIVINATION!
IF THAT'S SO, THEN THE REMAINING TWO GUARD-IANS...
...MUST BE *DA* AND *KAN*.

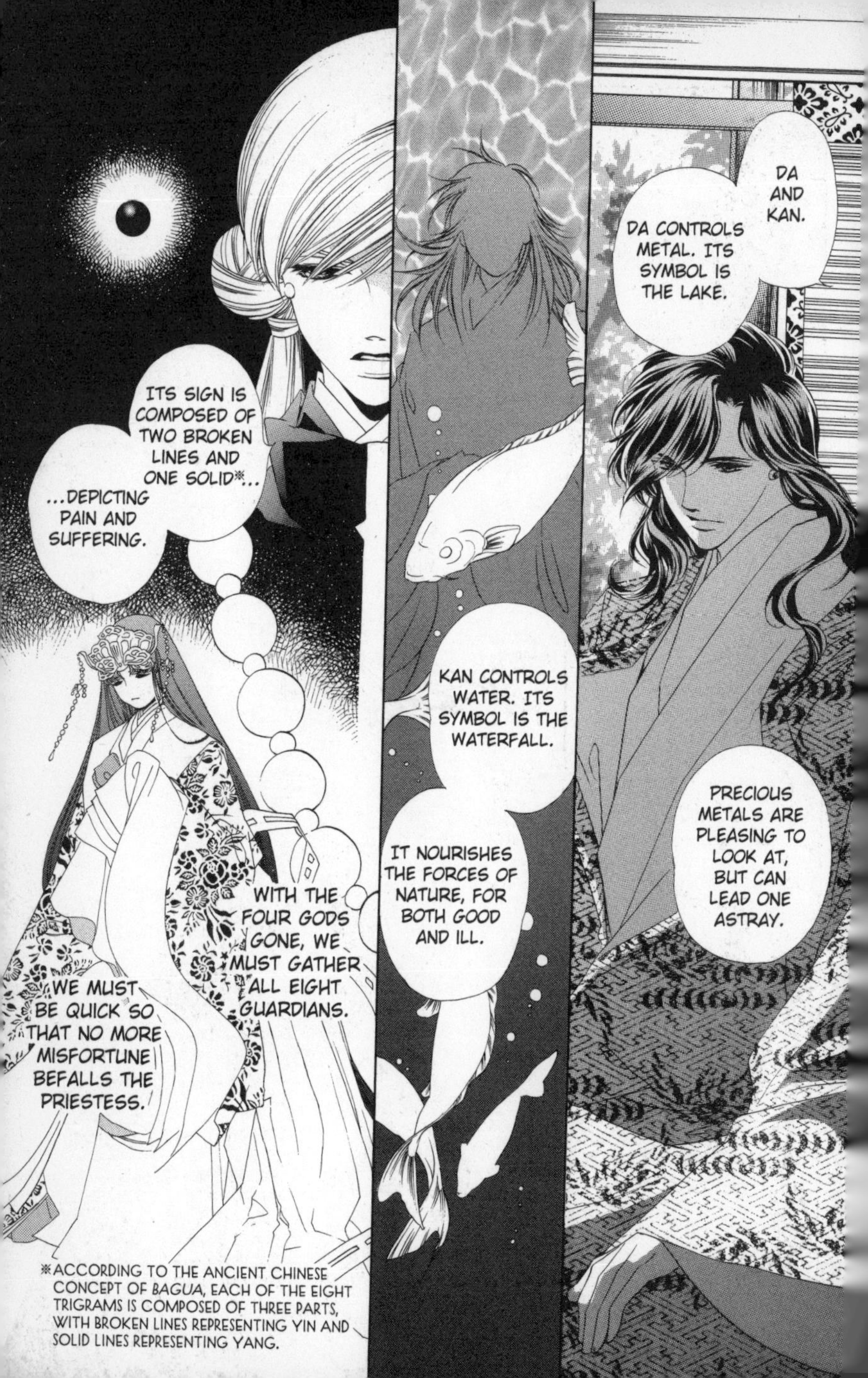
DA AND KAN.
DA CONTROLS METAL. ITS SYMBOL IS THE LAKE.
PRECIOUS METALS ARE PLEASING TO LOOK AT, BUT CAN LEAD ONE ASTRAY.
KAN CONTROLS WATER. ITS SYMBOL IS THE WATERFALL.
IT NOURISHES THE FORCES OF NATURE, FOR BOTH GOOD AND ILL.
ITS SIGN IS COMPOSED OF TWO BROKEN LINES AND ONE SOLID※...
...DEPICTING PAIN AND SUFFERING.
WITH THE FOUR GODS GONE, WE MUST GATHER ALL EIGHT GUARDIANS.
WE MUST BE QUICK SO THAT NO MORE MISFORTUNE BEFALLS THE PRIESTESS.

※According to the ancient Chinese concept of *Bagua*, each of the eight trigrams is composed of three parts, with broken lines representing yin and solid lines representing yang.

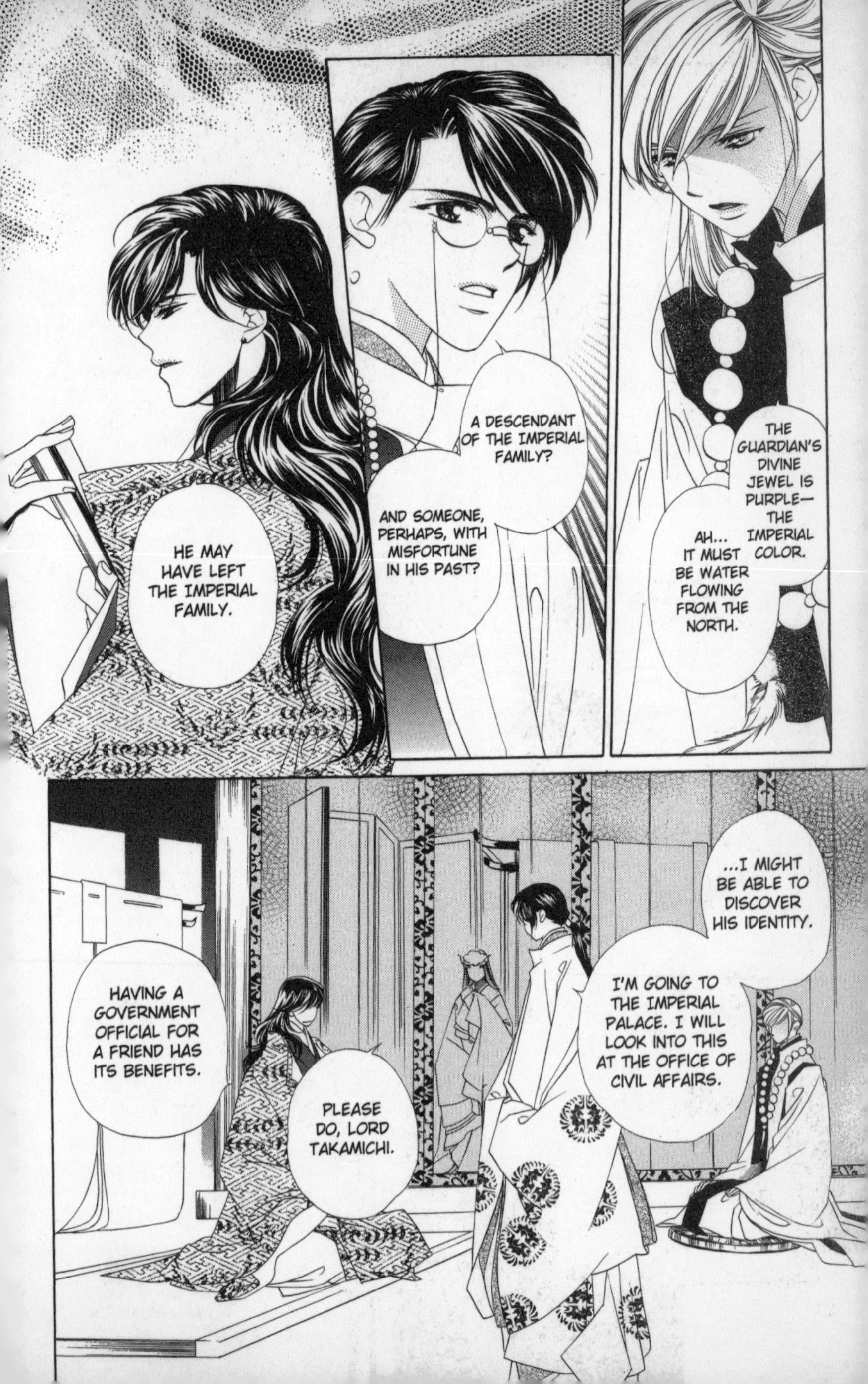
THE GUARDIAN'S DIVINE JEWEL IS PURPLE— THE IMPERIAL COLOR.
AH... IT MUST BE WATER FLOWING FROM THE NORTH.
A DESCENDANT OF THE IMPERIAL FAMILY?
AND SOMEONE, PERHAPS, WITH MISFORTUNE IN HIS PAST?
HE MAY HAVE LEFT THE IMPERIAL FAMILY.
...I MIGHT BE ABLE TO DISCOVER HIS IDENTITY.
I'M GOING TO THE IMPERIAL PALACE. I WILL LOOK INTO THIS AT THE OFFICE OF CIVIL AFFAIRS.
PLEASE DO, LORD TAKAMICHI.
HAVING A GOVERNMENT OFFICIAL FOR A FRIEND HAS ITS BENEFITS.

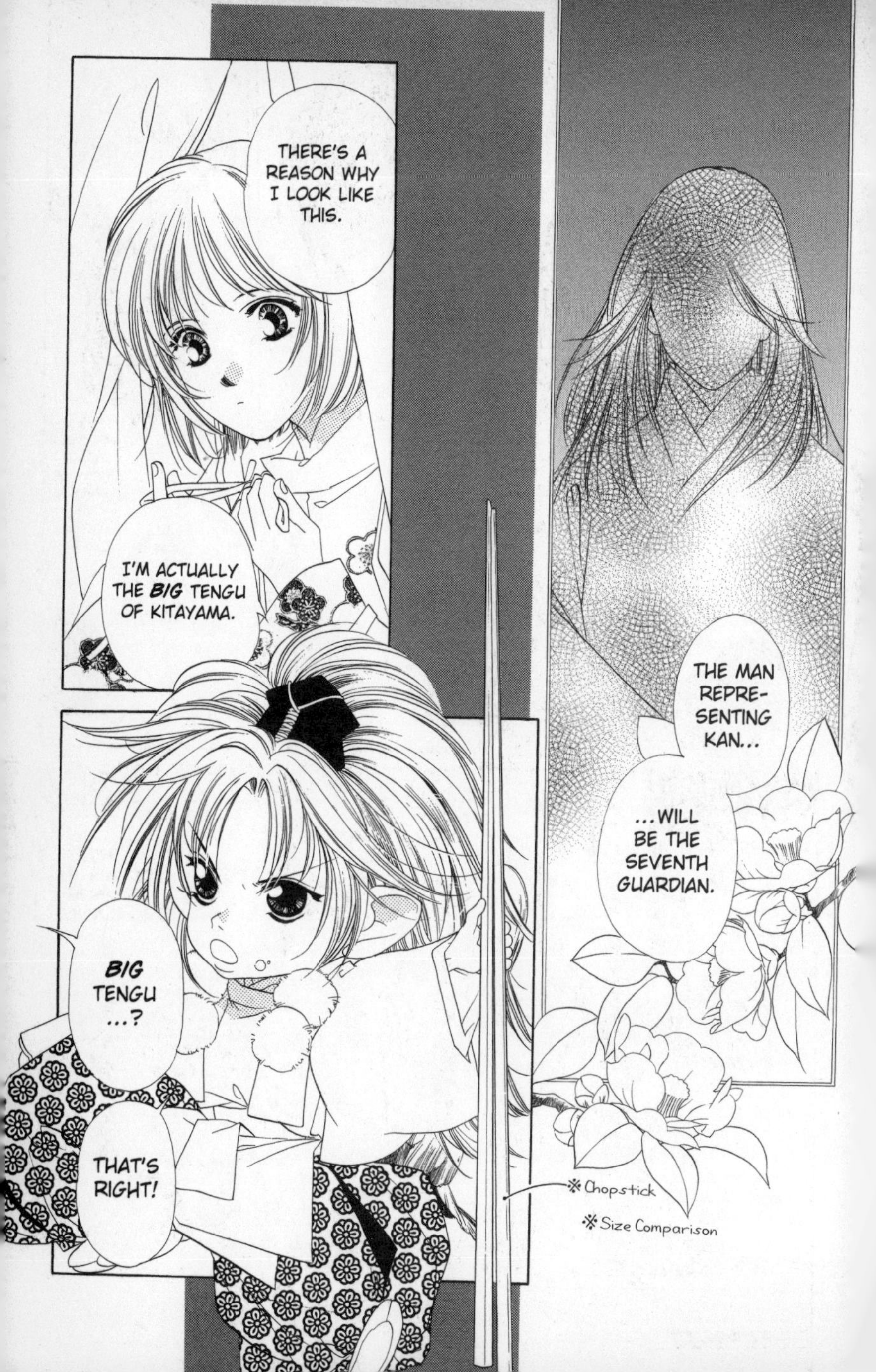
THE MAN REPRESENTING KAN...
...WILL BE THE SEVENTH GUARDIAN.
THERE'S A REASON WHY I LOOK LIKE THIS.
I'M ACTUALLY THE *BIG* TENGU OF KITAYAMA.
BIG TENGU ...?
THAT'S RIGHT!
※Chopstick
※Size Comparison

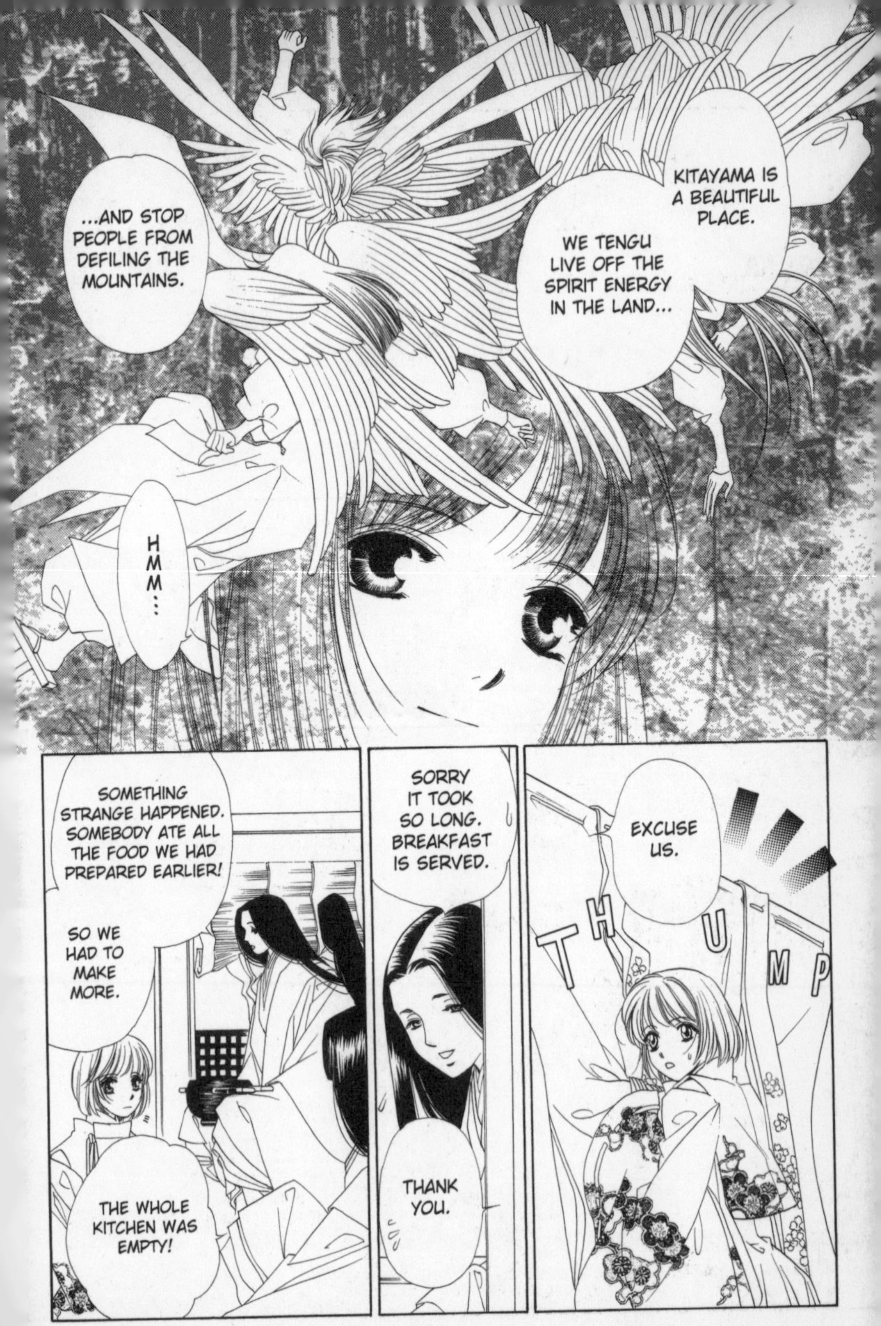
KITAYAMA IS A BEAUTIFUL PLACE.
WE TENGU LIVE OFF THE SPIRIT ENERGY IN THE LAND...
...AND STOP PEOPLE FROM DEFILING THE MOUNTAINS.
HMM...
EXCUSE US.
THUMP
SORRY IT TOOK SO LONG. BREAKFAST IS SERVED.
THANK YOU.
SOMETHING STRANGE HAPPENED. SOMEBODY ATE ALL THE FOOD WE HAD PREPARED EARLIER!
SO WE HAD TO MAKE MORE.
THE WHOLE KITCHEN WAS EMPTY!

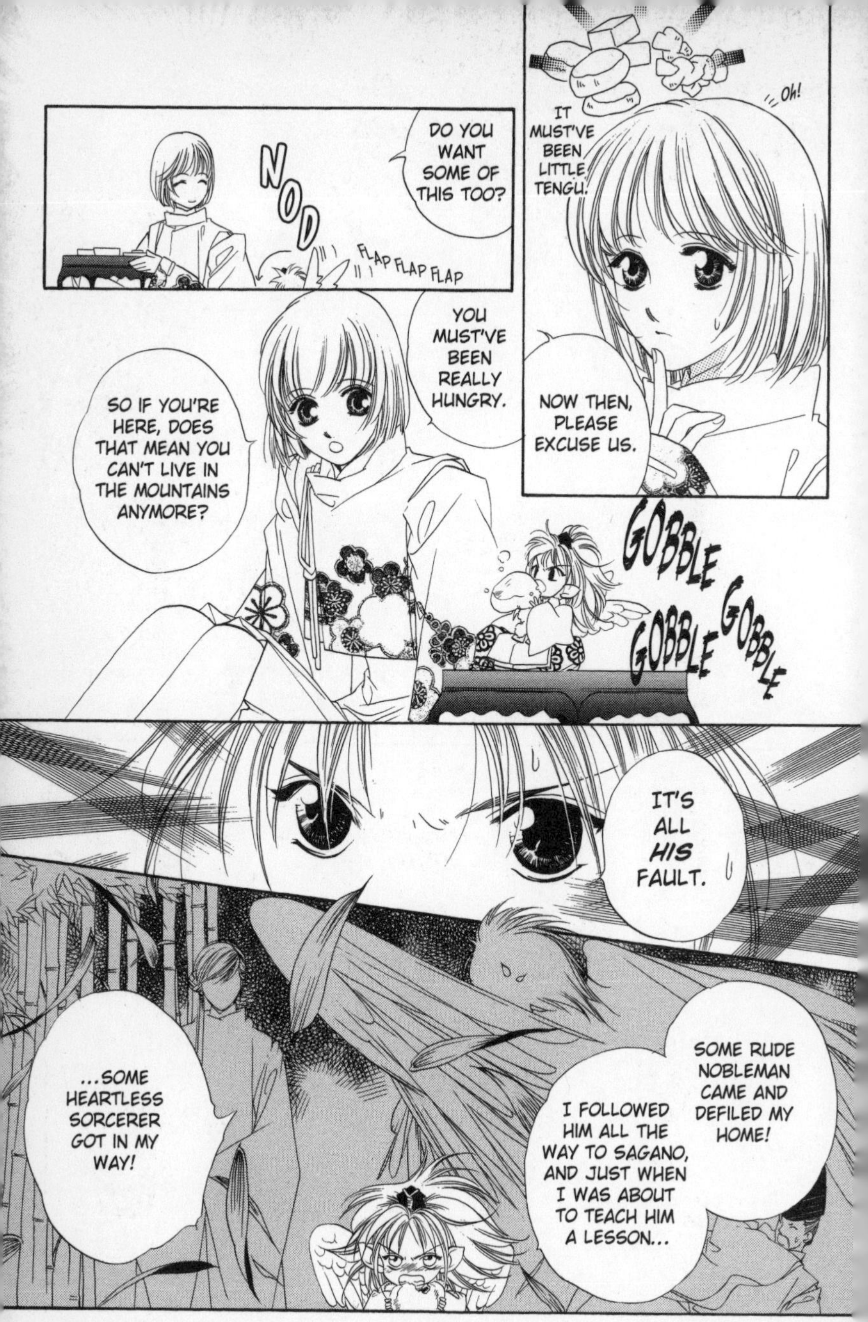
Oh!
IT MUST'VE BEEN LITTLE TENGU.
NOW THEN, PLEASE EXCUSE US.
DO YOU WANT SOME OF THIS TOO?
NOD
FLAP FLAP FLAP
YOU MUST'VE BEEN REALLY HUNGRY.
SO IF YOU'RE HERE, DOES THAT MEAN YOU CAN'T LIVE IN THE MOUNTAINS ANYMORE?
GOBBLE GOBBLE GOBBLE
IT'S ALL *HIS* FAULT.
SOME RUDE NOBLEMAN CAME AND DEFILED MY HOME!
I FOLLOWED HIM ALL THE WAY TO SAGANO, AND JUST WHEN I WAS ABOUT TO TEACH HIM A LESSON...
...SOME HEARTLESS SORCERER GOT IN MY WAY!

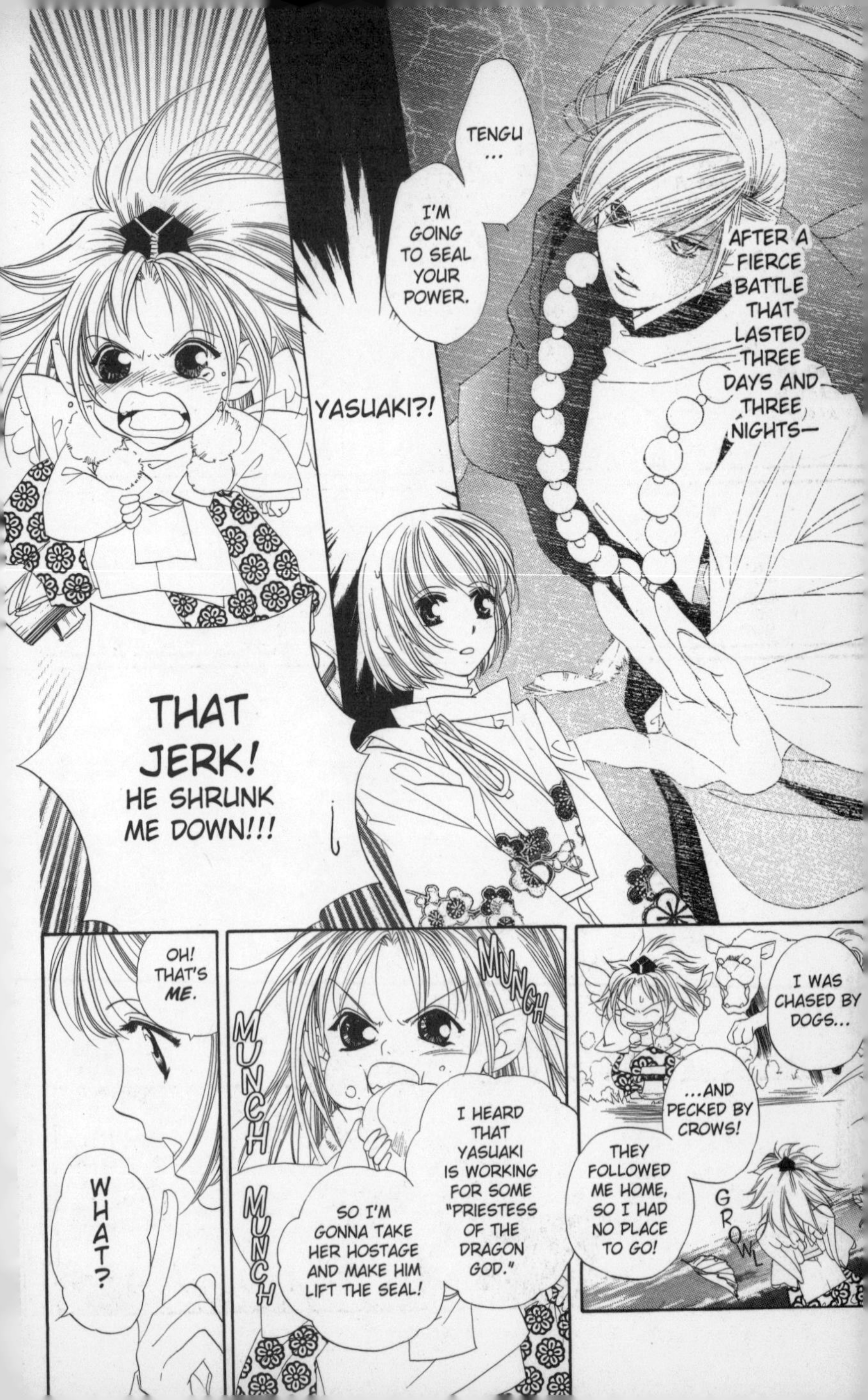
AFTER A FIERCE BATTLE THAT LASTED THREE DAYS AND THREE NIGHTS—
TENGU ...
I'M GOING TO SEAL YOUR POWER.
YASUAKI?!
THAT JERK! HE SHRUNK ME DOWN!!!
I WAS CHASED BY DOGS...
...AND PECKED BY CROWS!
THEY FOLLOWED ME HOME, SO I HAD NO PLACE TO GO!
GROWL
MUNCH
MUNCH
MUNCH
I HEARD THAT YASUAKI IS WORKING FOR SOME "PRIESTESS OF THE DRAGON GOD."
SO I'M GONNA TAKE HER HOSTAGE AND MAKE HIM LIFT THE SEAL!
MUNCH
OH! THAT'S *ME*.
WHAT?

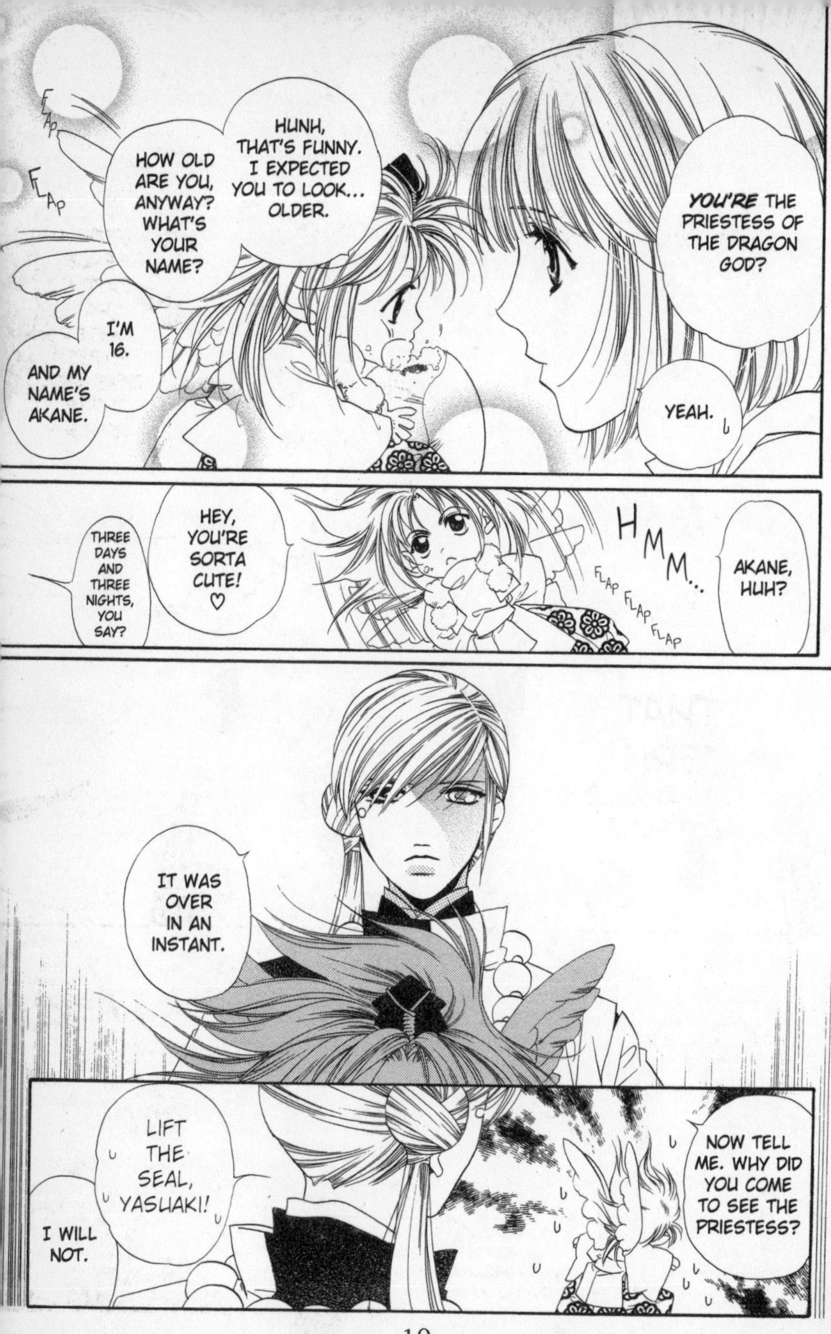
YOU'RE THE PRIESTESS OF THE DRAGON GOD?
YEAH.
HUNH, THAT'S FUNNY. I EXPECTED YOU TO LOOK... OLDER.
HOW OLD ARE YOU, ANYWAY? WHAT'S YOUR NAME?
FLAP
FLAP
I'M 16.
AND MY NAME'S AKANE.
AKANE, HUH?
HMM...
FLAP FLAP FLAP
HEY, YOU'RE SORTA CUTE! ♡
THREE DAYS AND THREE NIGHTS, YOU SAY?
IT WAS OVER IN AN INSTANT.
NOW TELL ME. WHY DID YOU COME TO SEE THE PRIESTESS?
LIFT THE SEAL, YASUAKI!
I WILL NOT.

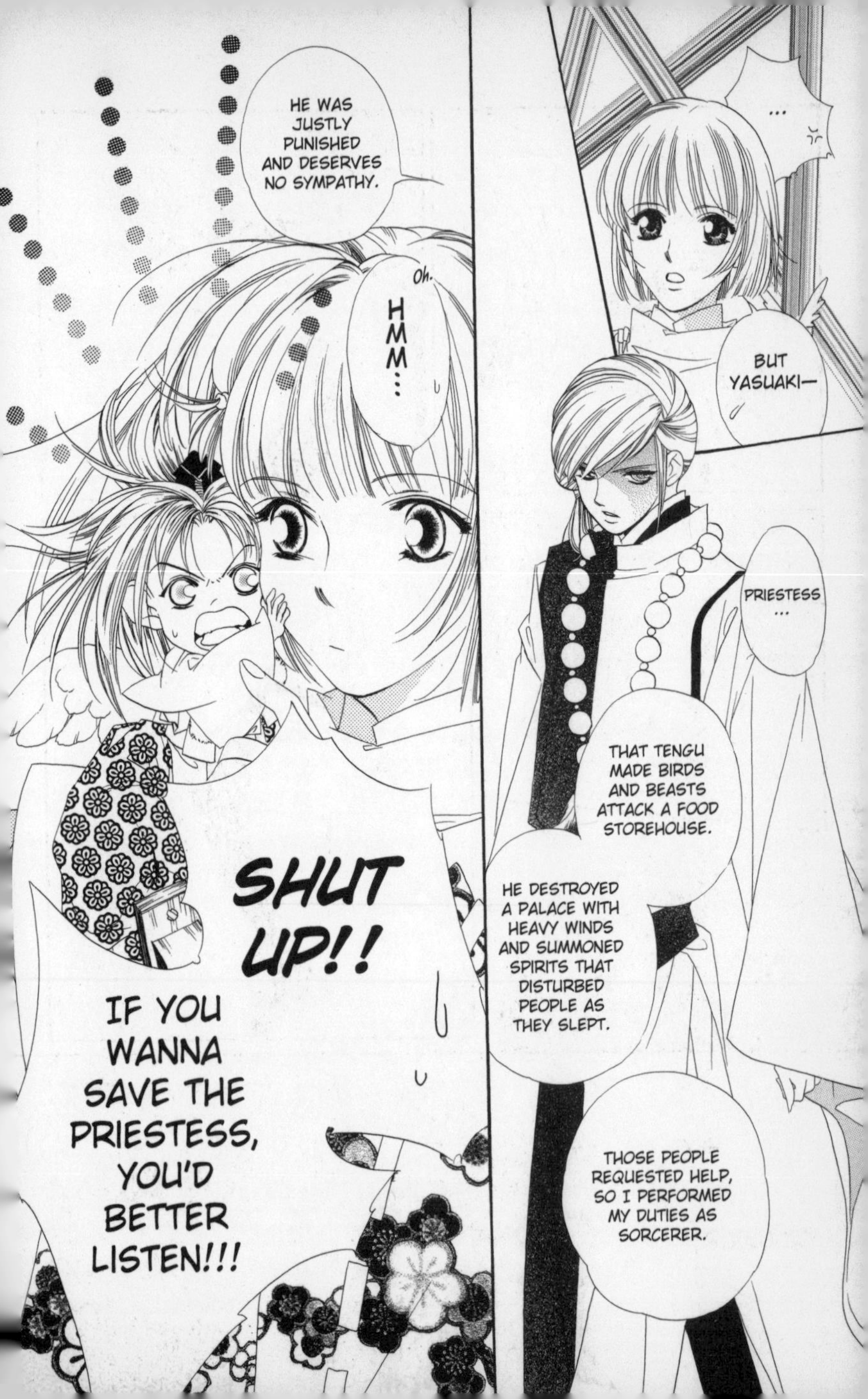
...
BUT YASUAKI—
PRIESTESS...
THAT TENGU MADE BIRDS AND BEASTS ATTACK A FOOD STOREHOUSE.
HE DESTROYED A PALACE WITH HEAVY WINDS AND SUMMONED SPIRITS THAT DISTURBED PEOPLE AS THEY SLEPT.
THOSE PEOPLE REQUESTED HELP, SO I PERFORMED MY DUTIES AS SORCERER.
HE WAS JUSTLY PUNISHED AND DESERVES NO SYMPATHY.
Oh.
HMM...
SHUT UP!!
IF YOU WANNA SAVE THE PRIESTESS, YOU'D BETTER LISTEN!!!

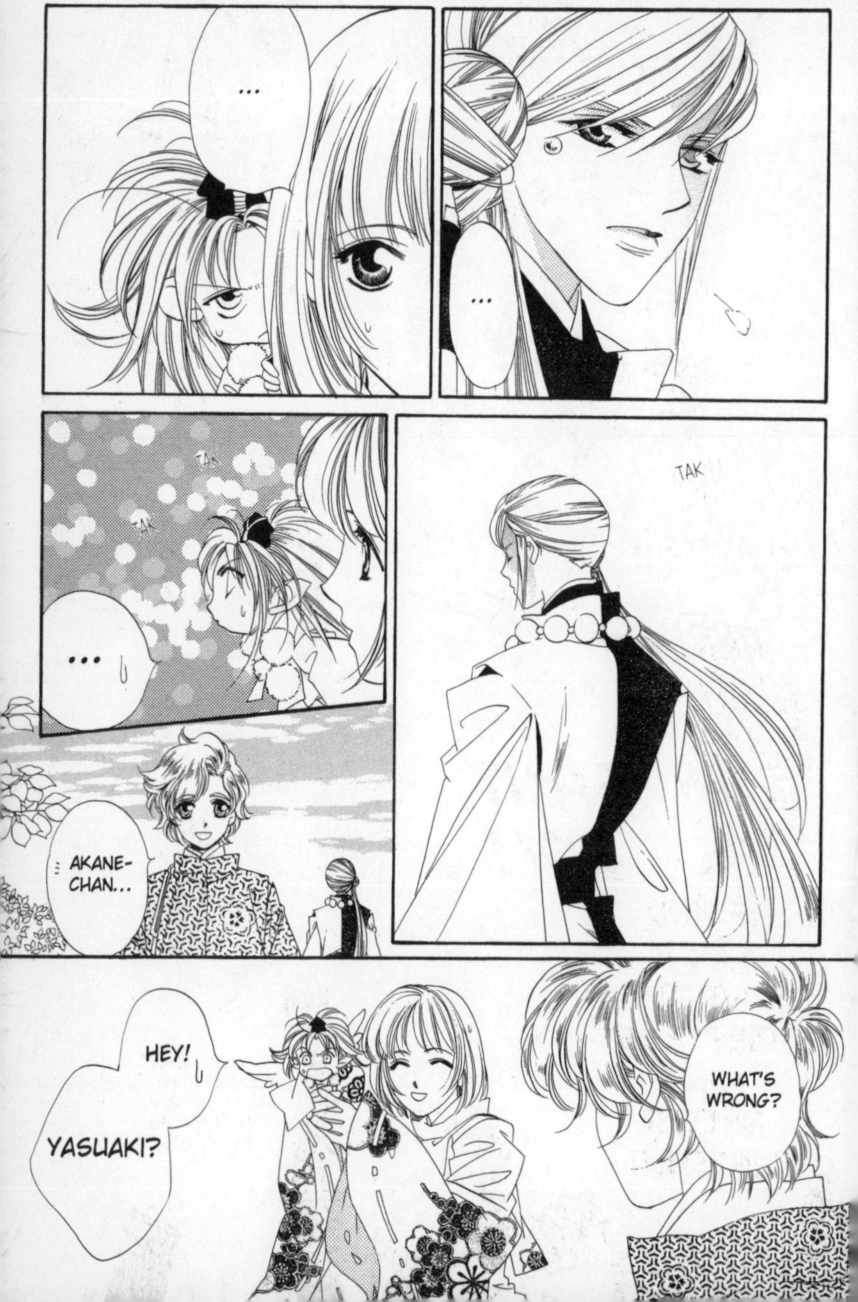
...
...
TAK
TAK
TAK
...
AKANE-CHAN...
WHAT'S WRONG?
HEY!
YASUAKI?

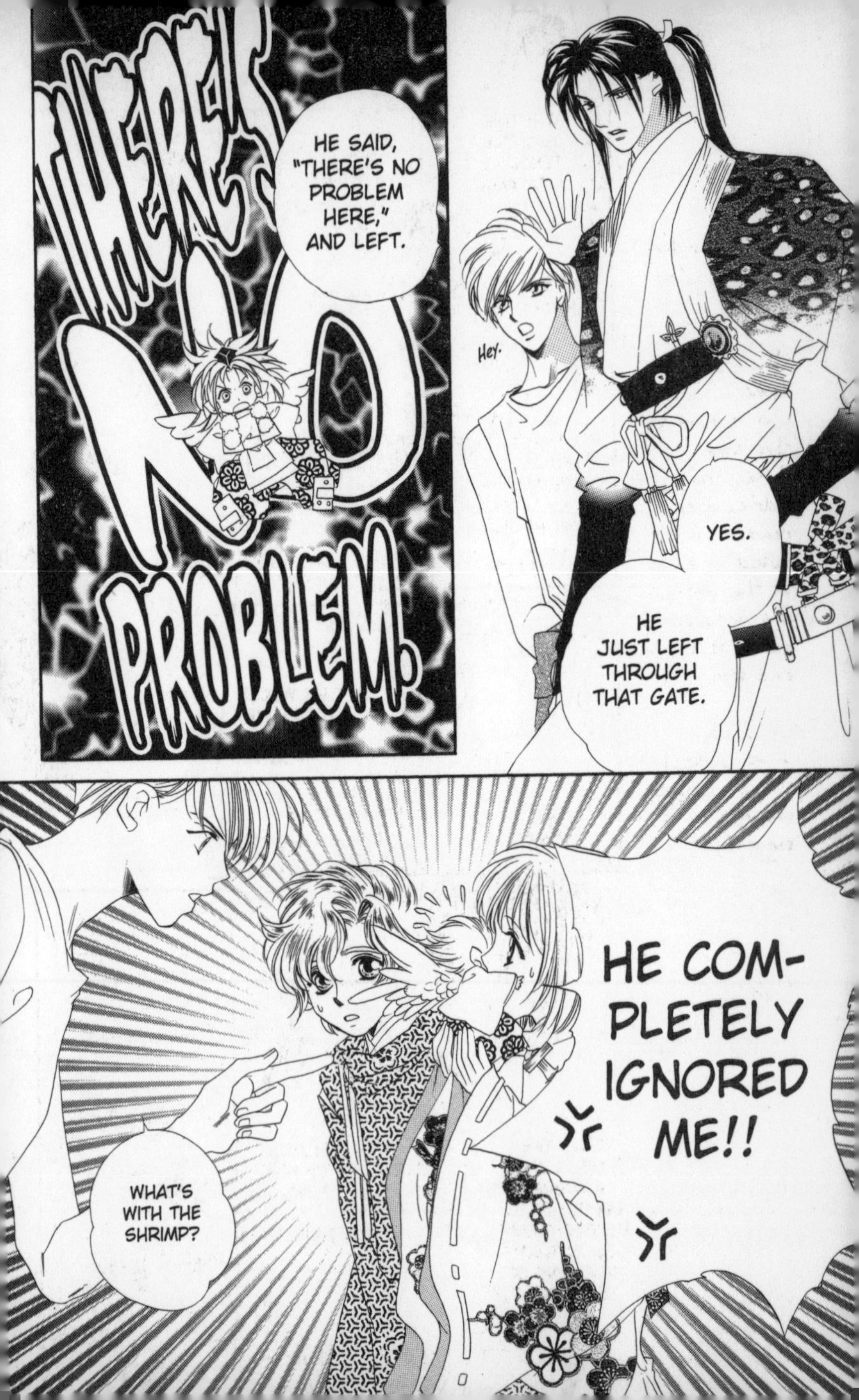
Hey.
YES.
HE JUST LEFT THROUGH THAT GATE.
THERE'S NO PROBLEM.
HE SAID, "THERE'S NO PROBLEM HERE," AND LEFT.
HE COMPLETELY IGNORED ME!!
WHAT'S WITH THE SHRIMP?

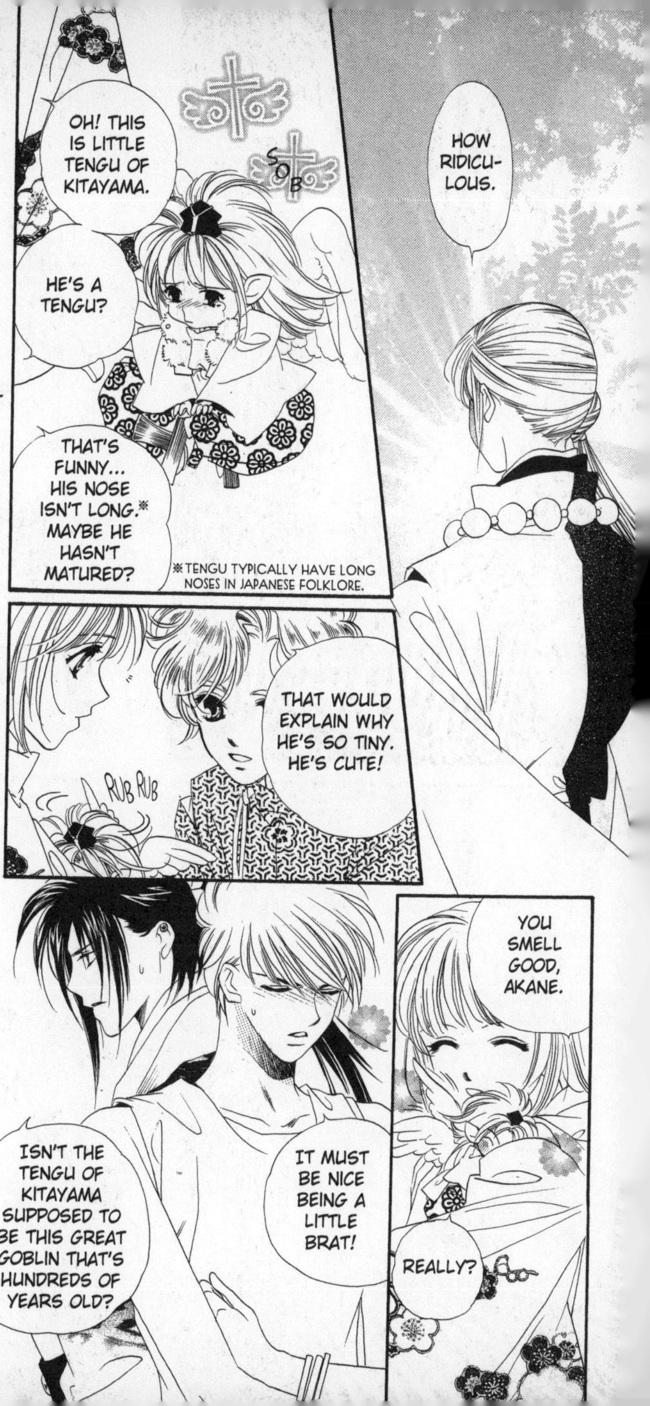
HOW RIDICULOUS.
OH! THIS IS LITTLE TENGU OF KITAYAMA.
SOB
HE'S A TENGU?
THAT'S FUNNY... HIS NOSE ISN'T LONG.※ MAYBE HE HASN'T MATURED?
※TENGU TYPICALLY HAVE LONG NOSES IN JAPANESE FOLKLORE.
THAT WOULD EXPLAIN WHY HE'S SO TINY. HE'S CUTE!
RUB RUB
YOU SMELL GOOD, AKANE.
REALLY?
IT MUST BE NICE BEING A LITTLE BRAT!
ISN'T THE TENGU OF KITAYAMA SUPPOSED TO BE THIS GREAT GOBLIN THAT'S HUNDREDS OF YEARS OLD?

An Explanation, Just In Case

The name for Kiyono, a character who appears in this volume, was chosen from many entries sent in by readers. I consulted my editor on the phone, who decided she should be a calm and sober girl.

I would like to thank everyone who sent in their suggestions!

Mizuno

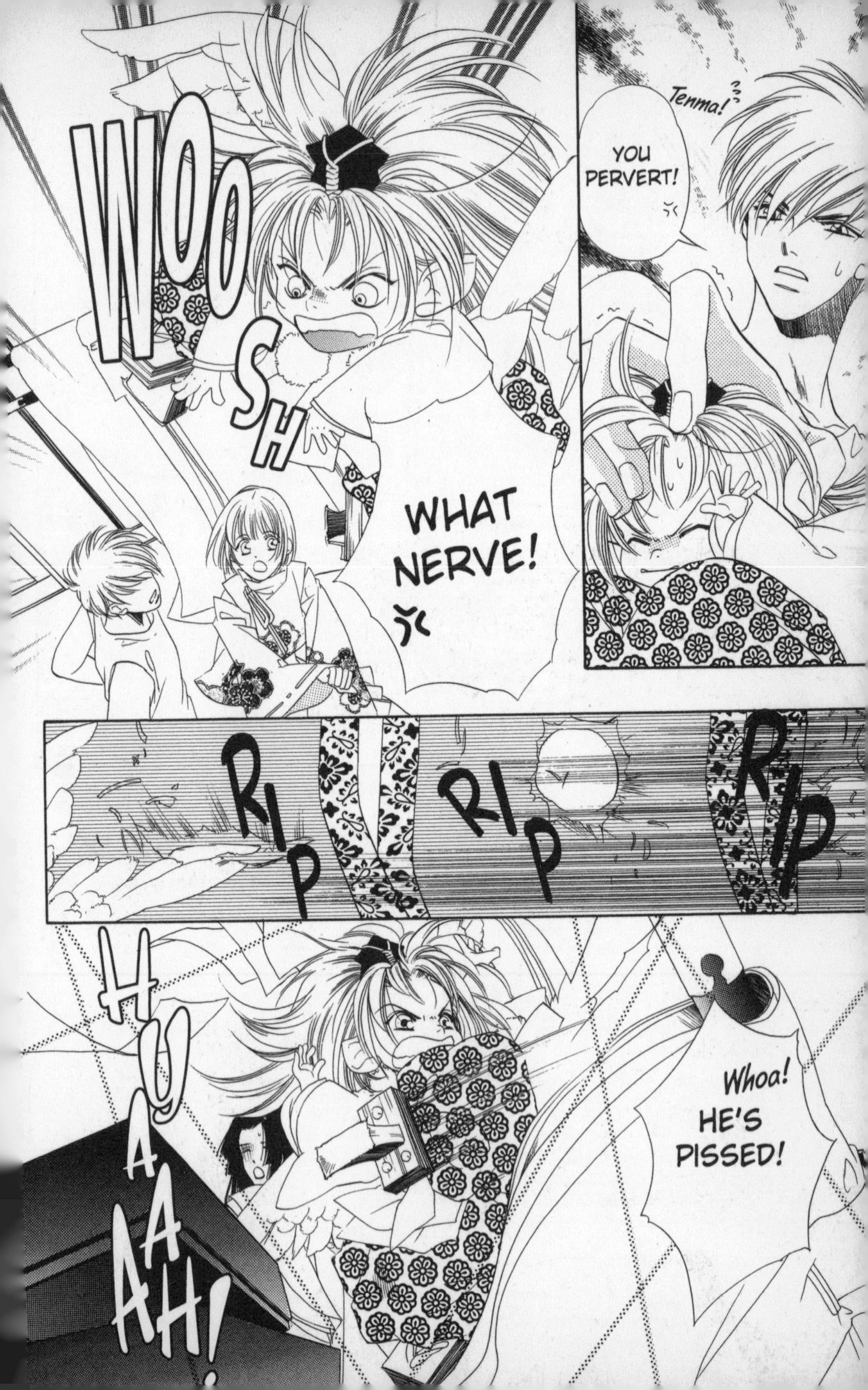
Tenma!
YOU PERVERT!
WOOSH
WHAT NERVE!
RIP
RIP
RIP
Whoa!
HE'S PISSED!
HUYAAAAH!

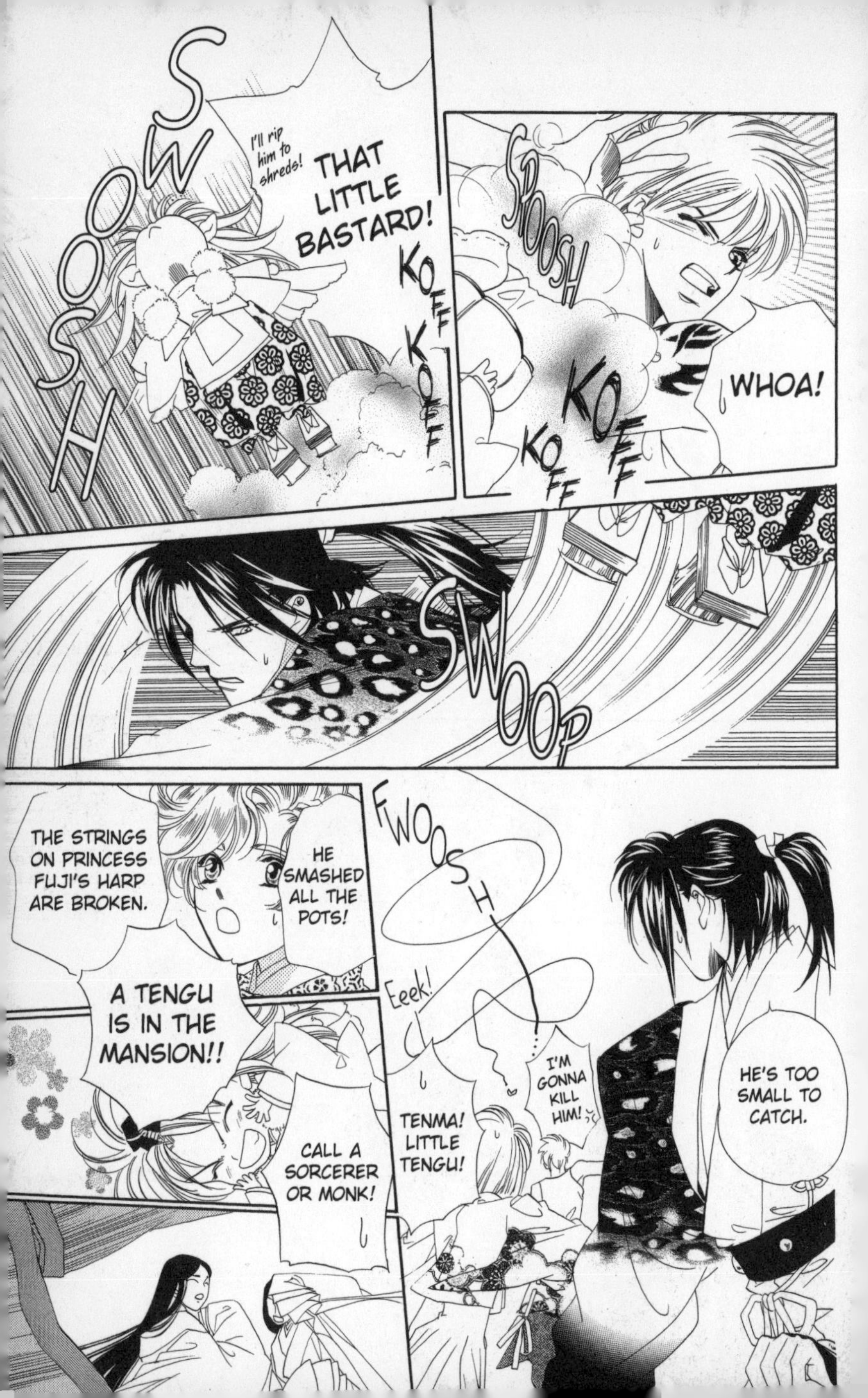
SPOOSH
WHOA!
KOFF
KOFF
SWOOSH
I'll rip him to shreds!
THAT LITTLE BASTARD!
KOFF
KOFF
KOFF
SWOOP
FWOOSH
HE'S TOO SMALL TO CATCH.
I'M GONNA KILL HIM!
TENMA! LITTLE TENGU!
Eeek!
HE SMASHED ALL THE POTS!
THE STRINGS ON PRINCESS FUJI'S HARP ARE BROKEN.
A TENGU IS IN THE MANSION!!
CALL A SORCERER OR MONK!

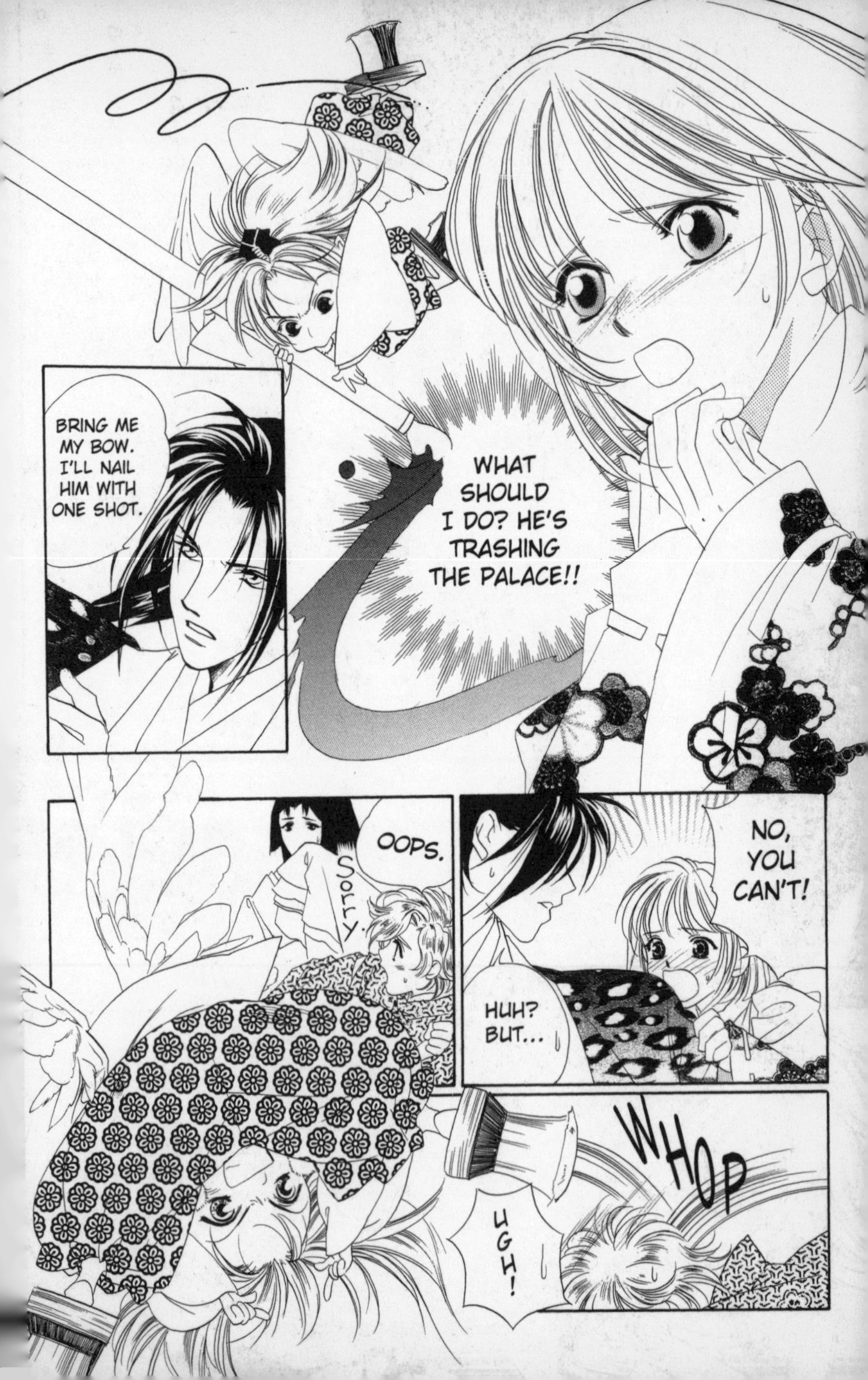
WHAT SHOULD I DO? HE'S TRASHING THE PALACE!!
BRING ME MY BOW. I'LL NAIL HIM WITH ONE SHOT.
NO, YOU CAN'T!
HUH? BUT...
OOPS.
Sorry
WHOP
UGH!

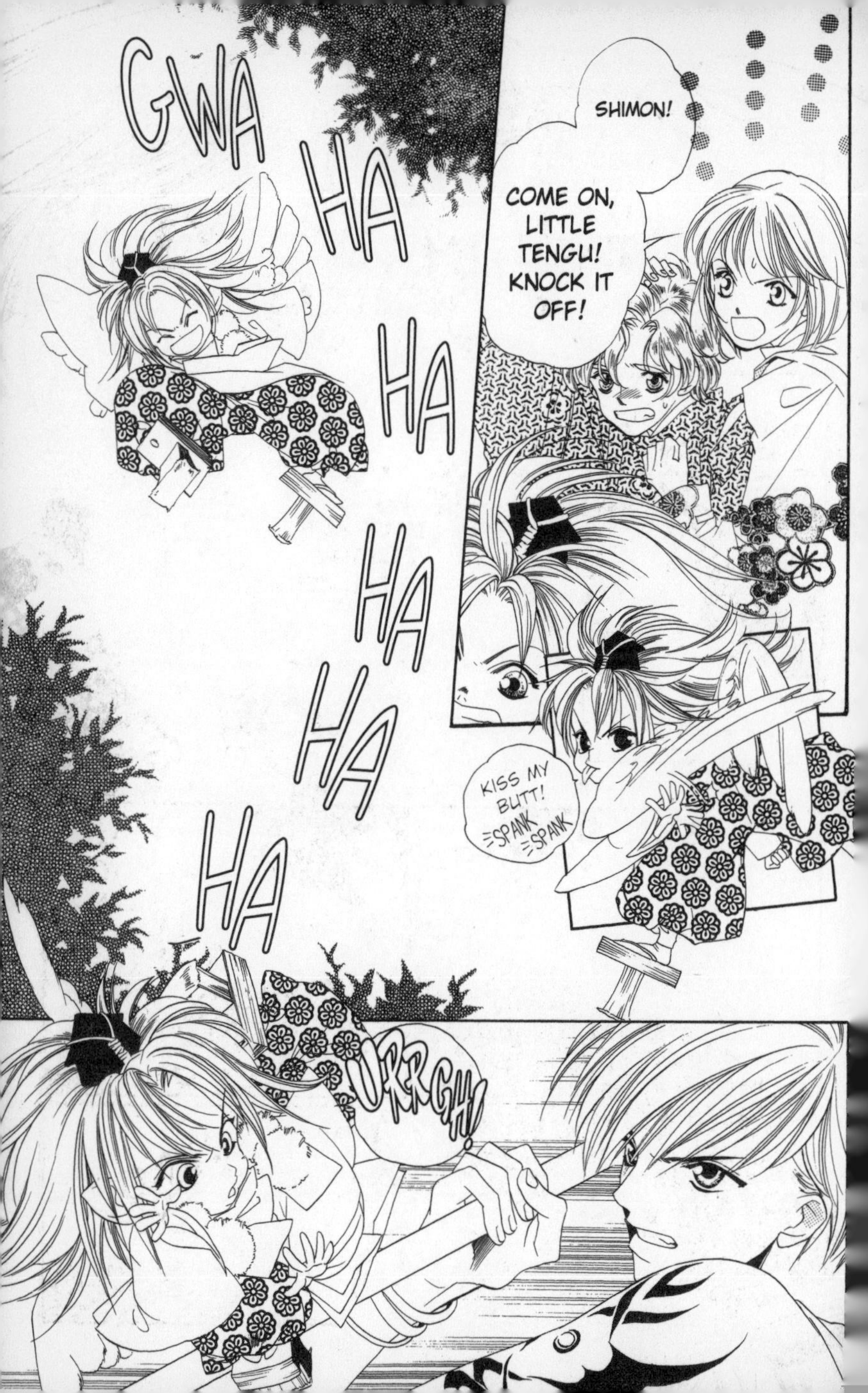
SHIMON!
COME ON, LITTLE TENGU! KNOCK IT OFF!
GWA HA HA HA HA HA
KISS MY BUTT!
SPANK SPANK
URRGH!

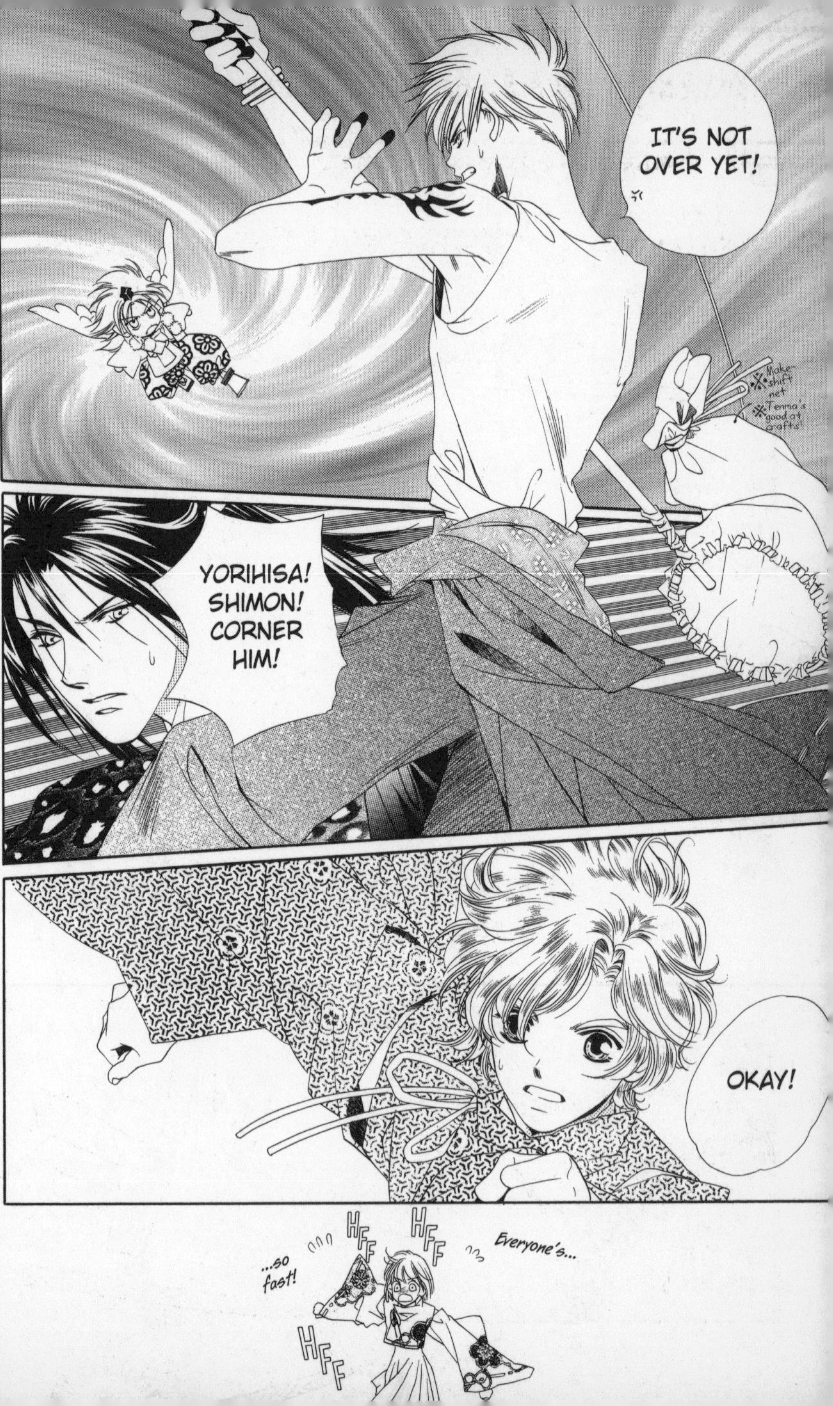
IT'S NOT OVER YET!
※Make-shift net
※Tenma's good at crafts!
YORIHISA! SHIMON! CORNER HIM!
OKAY!
HFF
HFF
Everyone's...
...so fast!
HFF

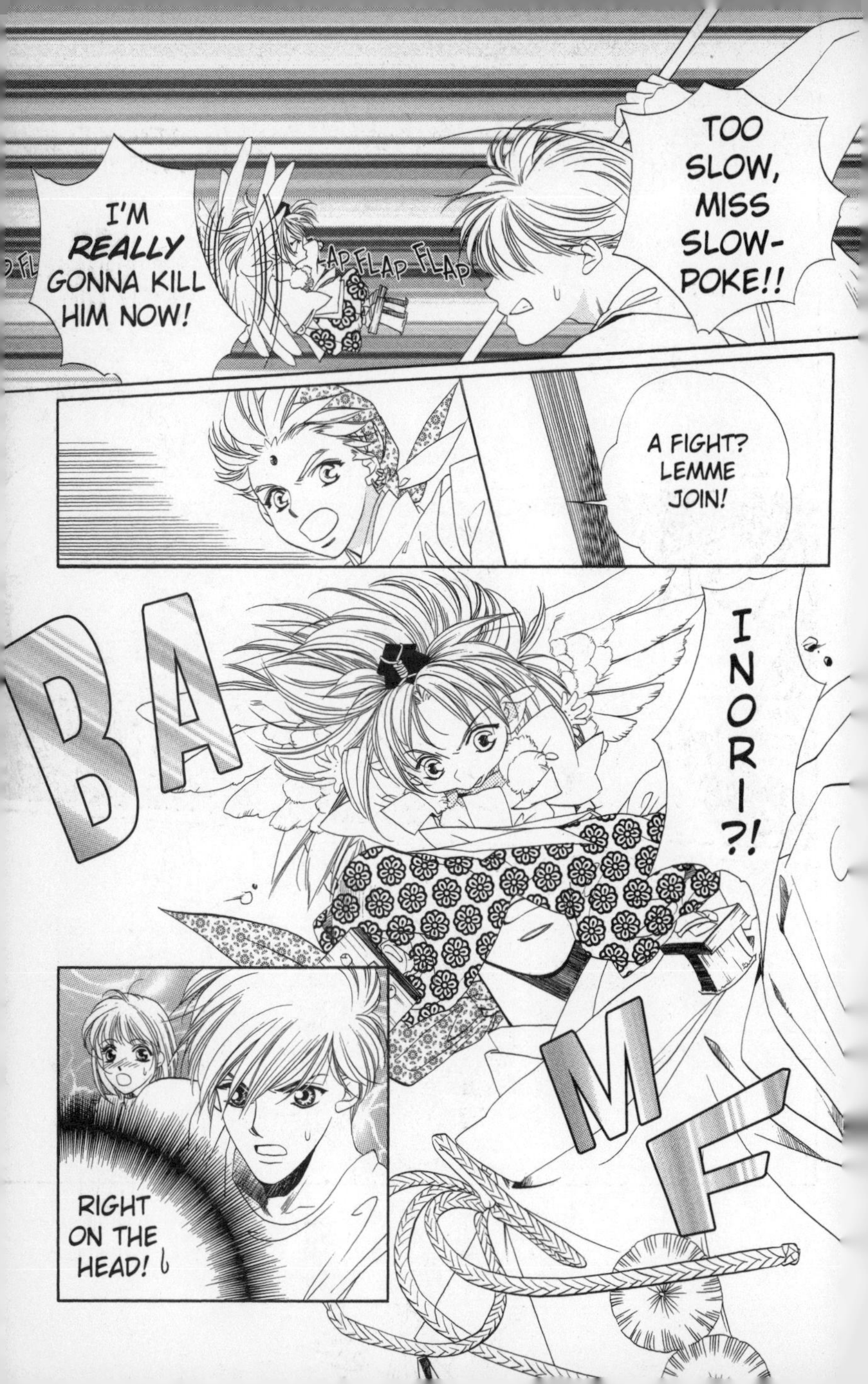
TOO SLOW, MISS SLOW-POKE!!
FLAP FLAP FLAP
I'M *REALLY* GONNA KILL HIM NOW!
A FIGHT? LEMME JOIN!
INORI?!
BAMF
RIGHT ON THE HEAD!

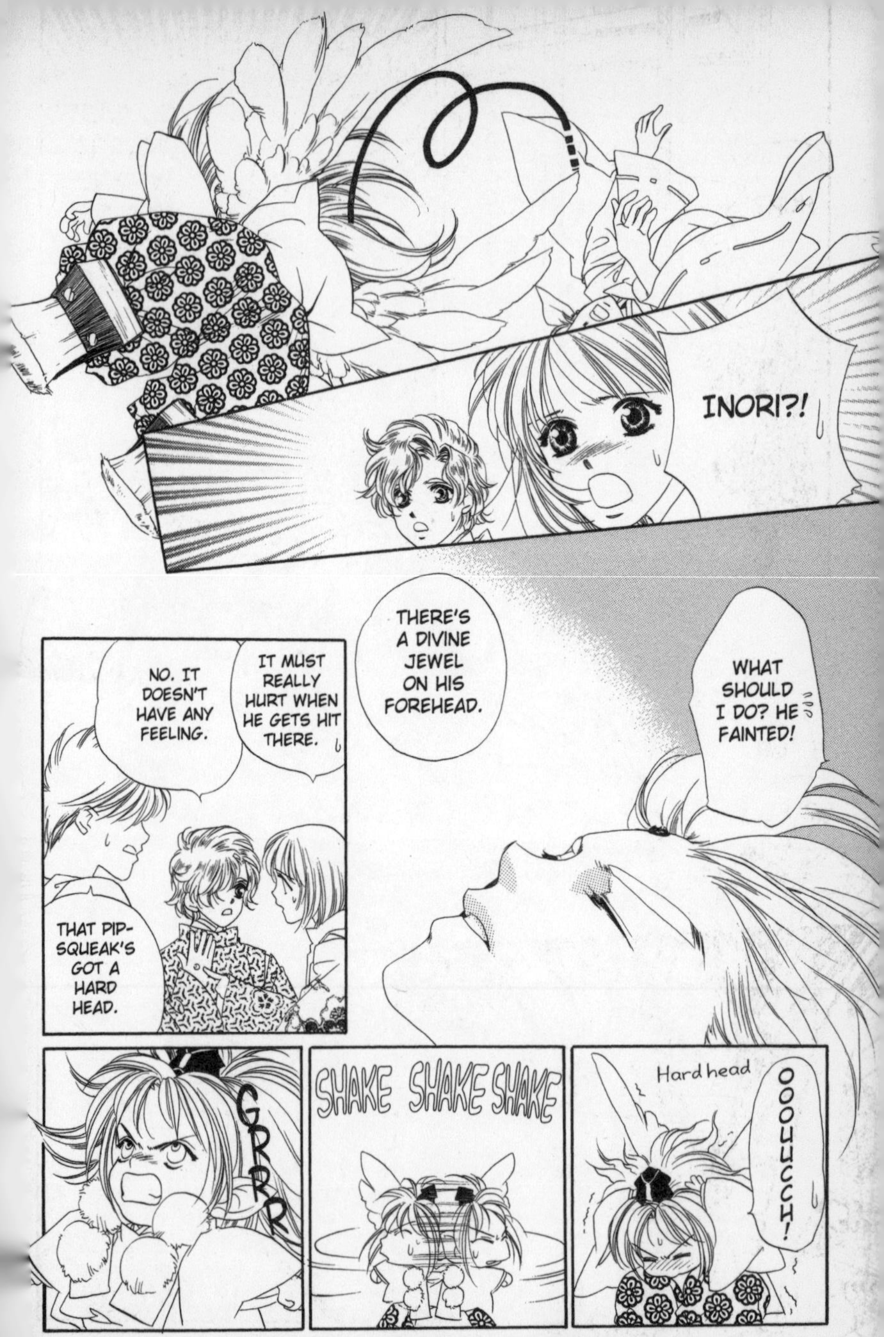
INORI?!
WHAT SHOULD I DO? HE FAINTED!
THERE'S A DIVINE JEWEL ON HIS FOREHEAD.
IT MUST REALLY HURT WHEN HE GETS HIT THERE.
NO. IT DOESN'T HAVE ANY FEELING.
THAT PIP-SQUEAK'S GOT A HARD HEAD.
OOOUUCCH!
Hard head
SHAKE SHAKE SHAKE
GRRR

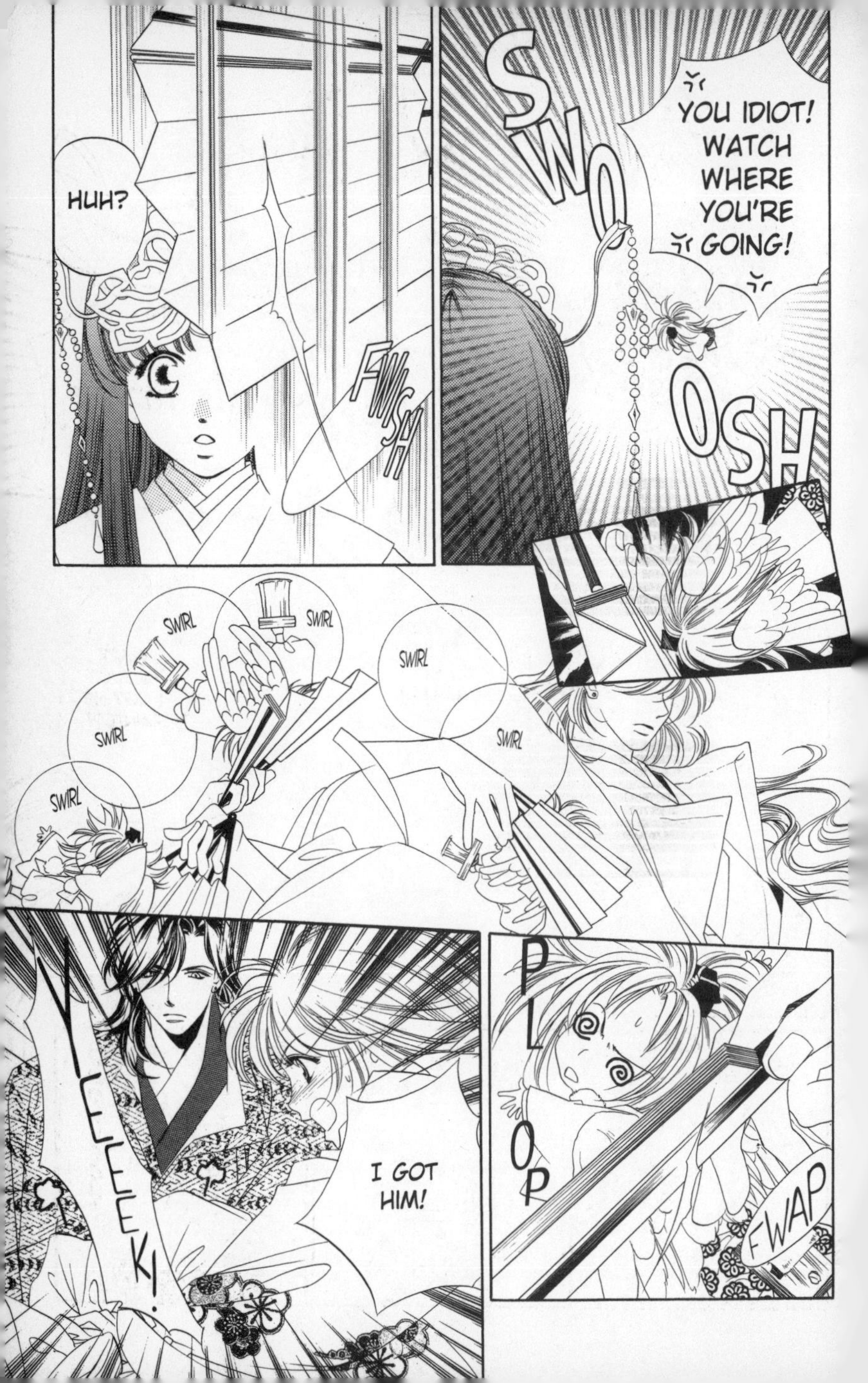
SWOOSH
YOU IDIOT! WATCH WHERE YOU'RE GOING!
HUH?
FWISH
SWIRL
SWIRL
SWIRL
SWIRL
SWIRL
SWIRL
PLOP
FWAP
EEEEEK!
I GOT HIM!

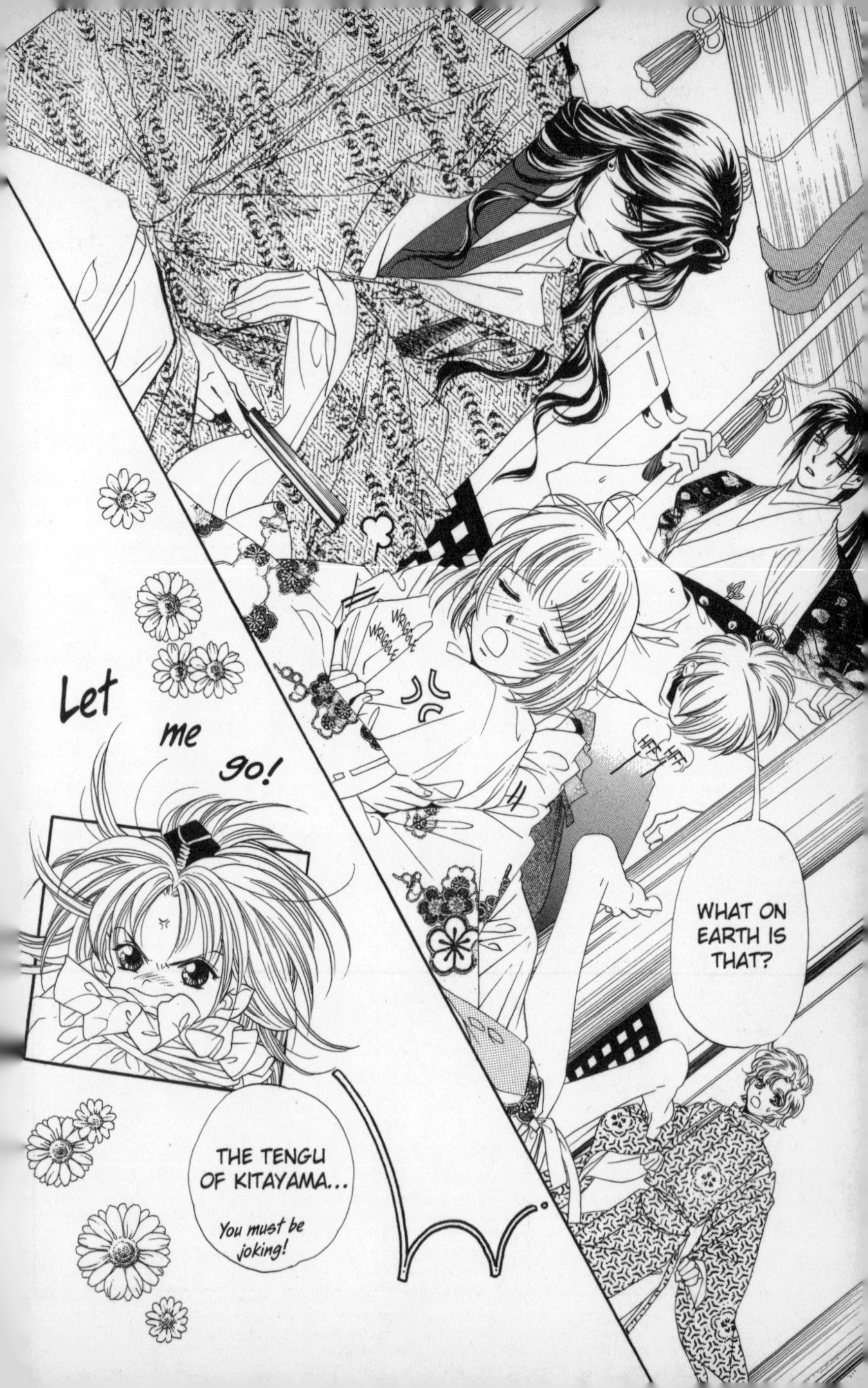
WRIGGLE WRIGGLE
HFF HFF
WHAT ON EARTH IS THAT?
Let me go!
THE TENGU OF KITAYAMA...
You must be joking!

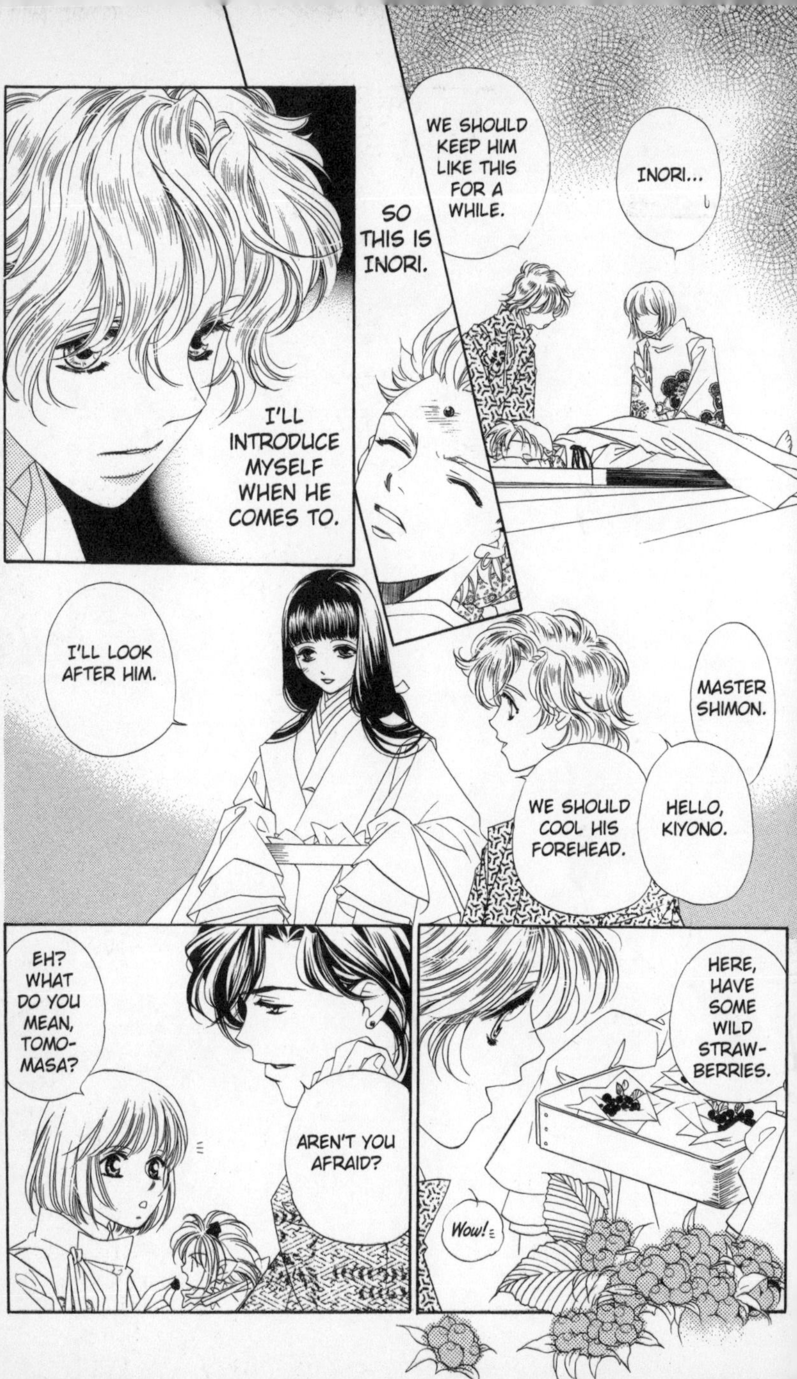
INORI...
WE SHOULD KEEP HIM LIKE THIS FOR A WHILE.
SO THIS IS INORI.
I'LL INTRODUCE MYSELF WHEN HE COMES TO.
MASTER SHIMON.
HELLO, KIYONO.
WE SHOULD COOL HIS FOREHEAD.
I'LL LOOK AFTER HIM.
HERE, HAVE SOME WILD STRAW-BERRIES.
Wow!
AREN'T YOU AFRAID?
EH? WHAT DO YOU MEAN, TOMO-MASA?

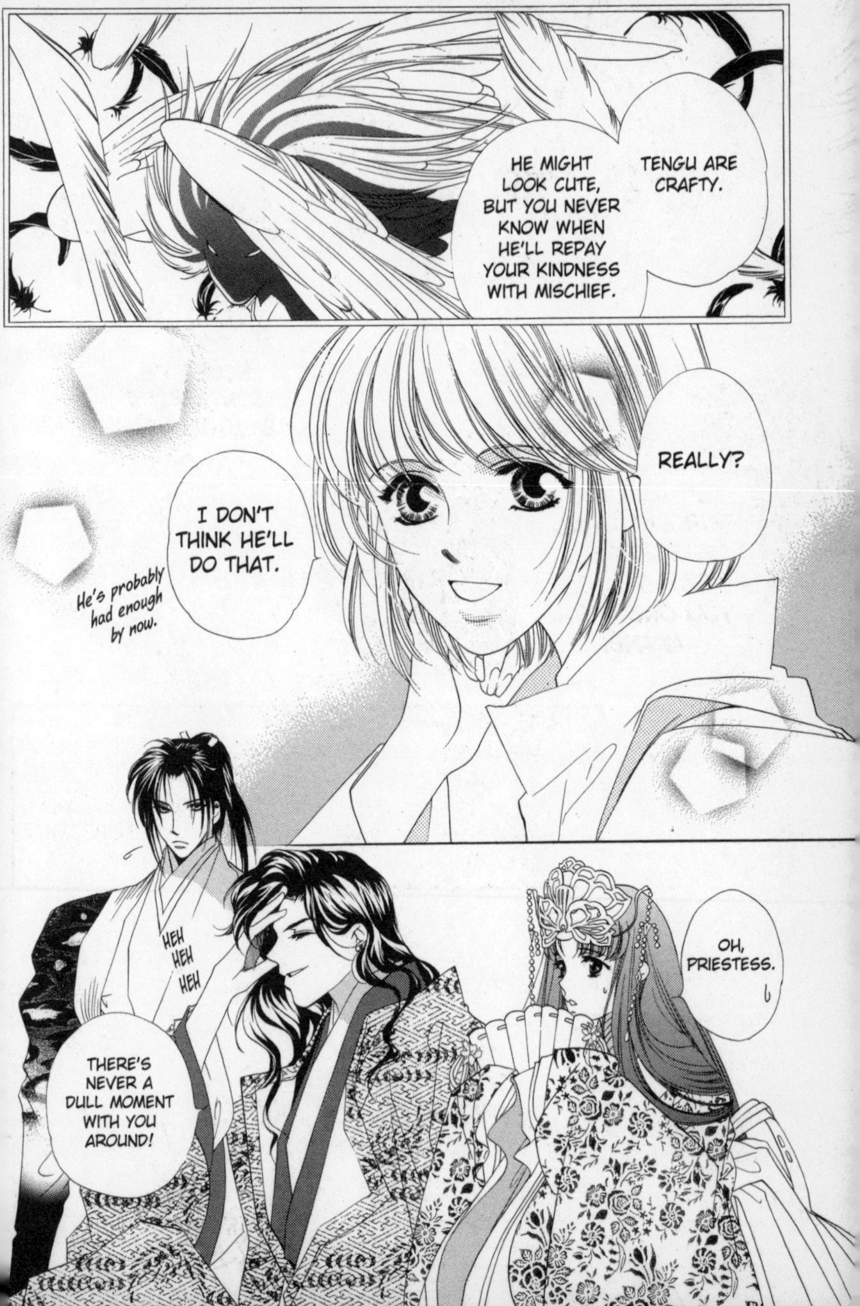
TENGU ARE CRAFTY.
HE MIGHT LOOK CUTE, BUT YOU NEVER KNOW WHEN HE'LL REPAY YOUR KINDNESS WITH MISCHIEF.
REALLY?
I DON'T THINK HE'LL DO THAT.
He's probably had enough by now.
OH, PRIESTESS.
HEH HEH HEH
THERE'S NEVER A DULL MOMENT WITH YOU AROUND!

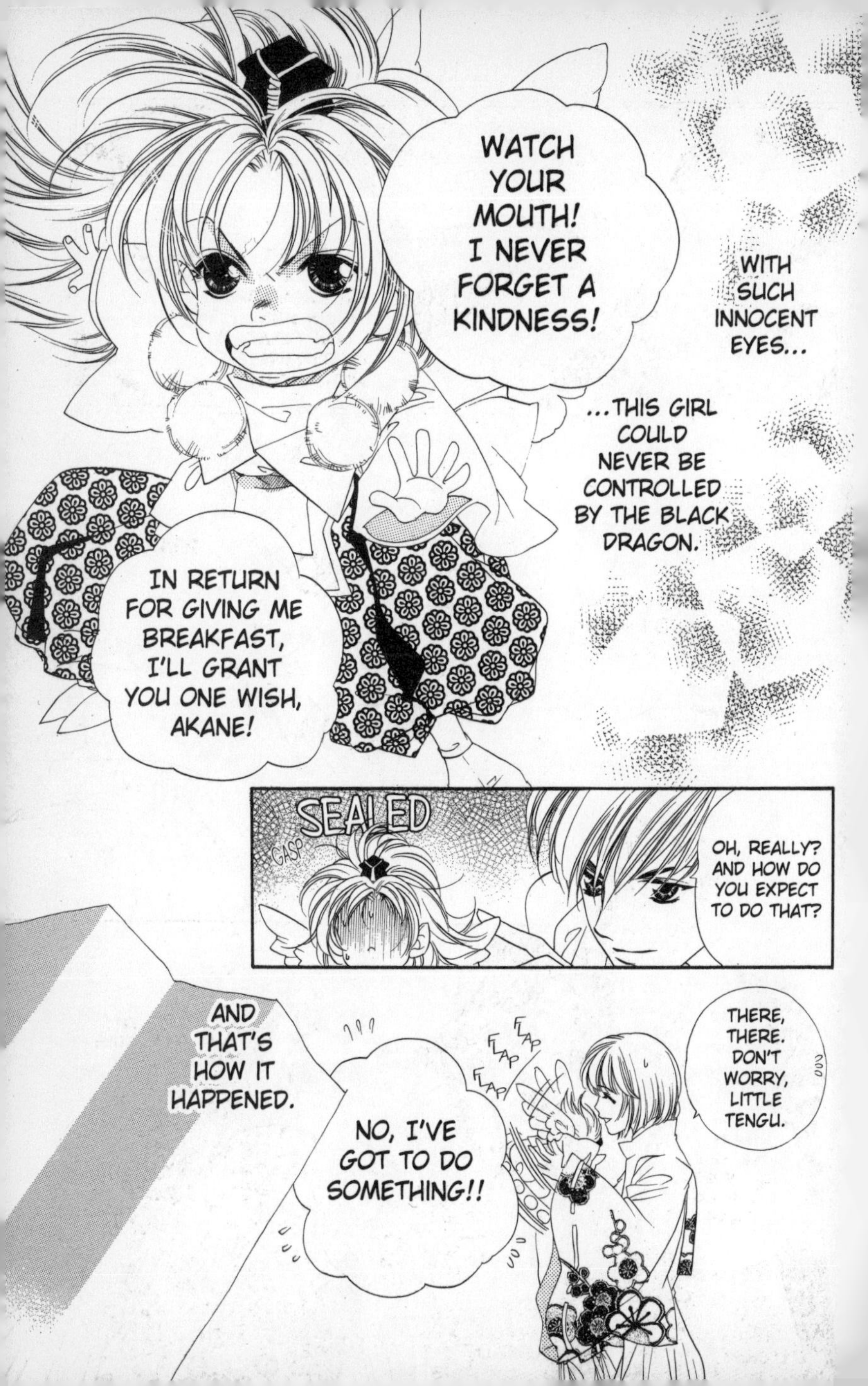
WITH SUCH INNOCENT EYES...
...THIS GIRL COULD NEVER BE CONTROLLED BY THE BLACK DRAGON.
WATCH YOUR MOUTH! I NEVER FORGET A KINDNESS!
IN RETURN FOR GIVING ME BREAKFAST, I'LL GRANT YOU ONE WISH, AKANE!
OH, REALLY? AND HOW DO YOU EXPECT TO DO THAT?
SEALED
GASP
THERE, THERE. DON'T WORRY, LITTLE TENGU.
FLAP FLAP FLAP
NO, I'VE GOT TO DO SOMETHING!!
AND THAT'S HOW IT HAPPENED.

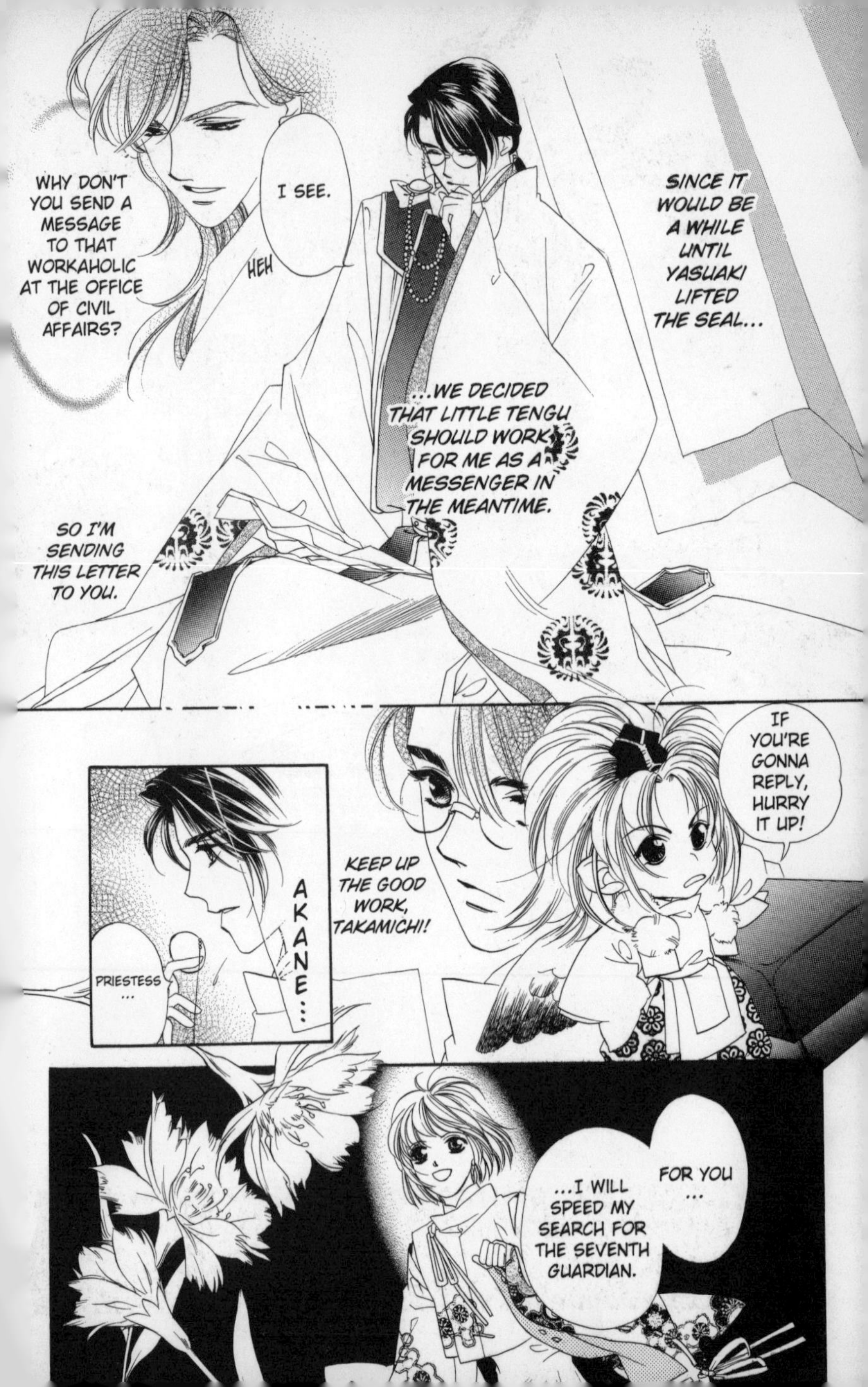
SINCE IT WOULD BE A WHILE UNTIL YASUAKI LIFTED THE SEAL...
...WE DECIDED THAT LITTLE TENGU SHOULD WORK FOR ME AS A MESSENGER IN THE MEANTIME.
I SEE.
HEH
WHY DON'T YOU SEND A MESSAGE TO THAT WORKAHOLIC AT THE OFFICE OF CIVIL AFFAIRS?
SO I'M SENDING THIS LETTER TO YOU.
IF YOU'RE GONNA REPLY, HURRY IT UP!
KEEP UP THE GOOD WORK, TAKAMICHI!
AKANE...
PRIESTESS...
FOR YOU...
...I WILL SPEED MY SEARCH FOR THE SEVENTH GUARDIAN.

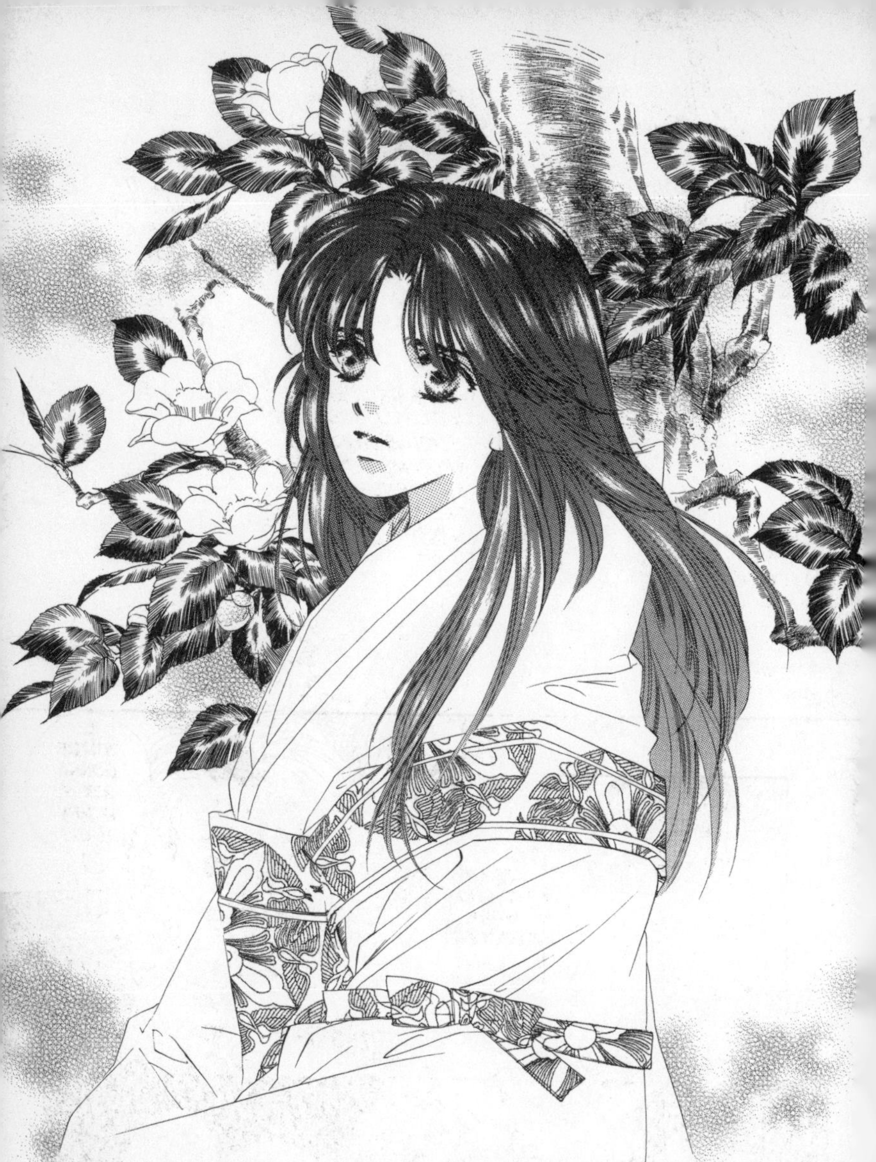

Haruka -Beyond the Stream of Time-

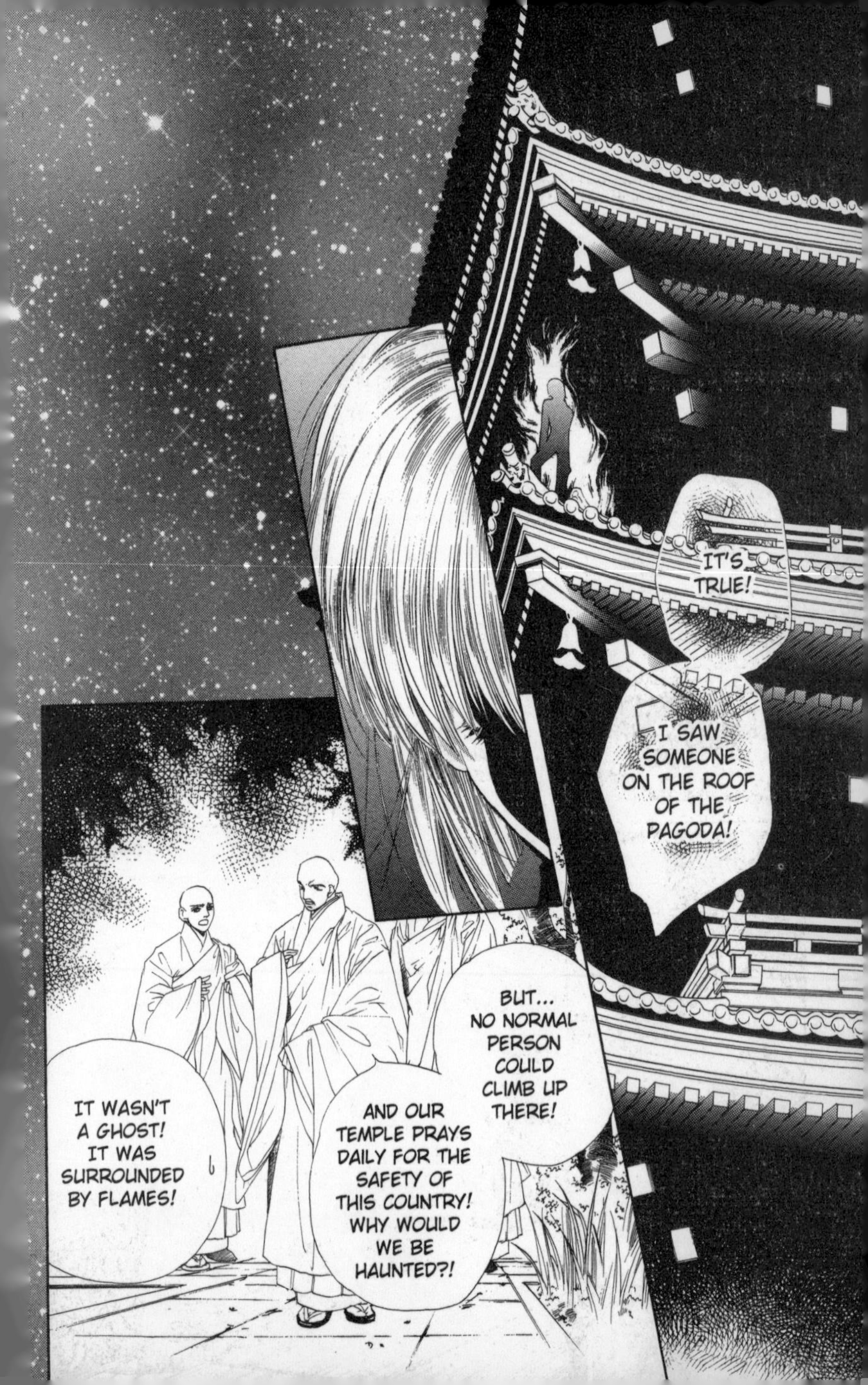
IT'S TRUE!
I SAW SOMEONE ON THE ROOF OF THE PAGODA!
BUT... NO NORMAL PERSON COULD CLIMB UP THERE!
AND OUR TEMPLE PRAYS DAILY FOR THE SAFETY OF THIS COUNTRY! WHY WOULD WE BE HAUNTED?!
IT WASN'T A GHOST! IT WAS SURROUNDED BY FLAMES!

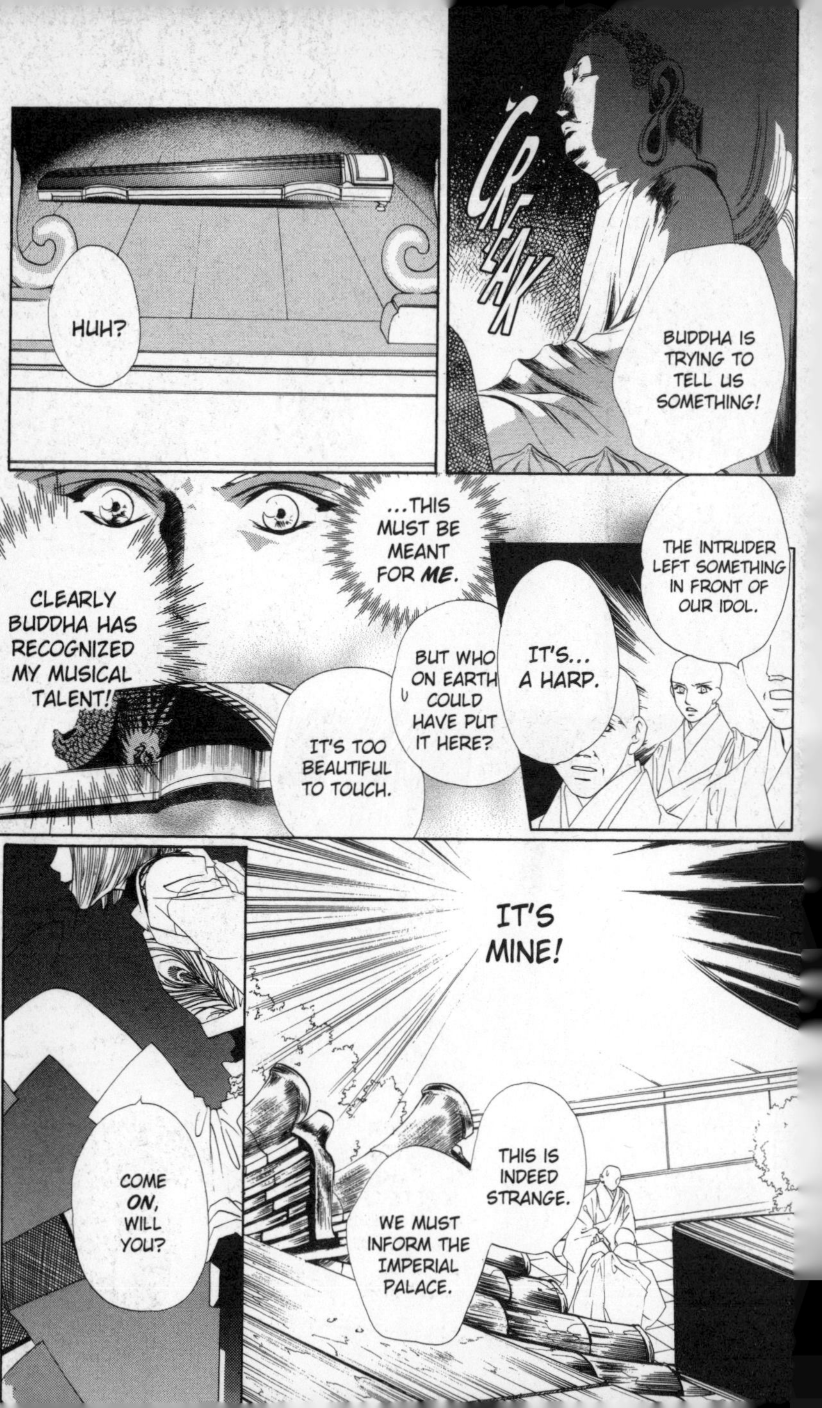
CREAK
BUDDHA IS TRYING TO TELL US SOMETHING!
HUH?
THE INTRUDER LEFT SOMETHING IN FRONT OF OUR IDOL.
IT'S... A HARP.
BUT WHO ON EARTH COULD HAVE PUT IT HERE?
IT'S TOO BEAUTIFUL TO TOUCH.
...THIS MUST BE MEANT FOR *ME*.
CLEARLY BUDDHA HAS RECOGNIZED MY MUSICAL TALENT!
IT'S MINE!
THIS IS INDEED STRANGE.
WE MUST INFORM THE IMPERIAL PALACE.
COME *ON*, WILL YOU?

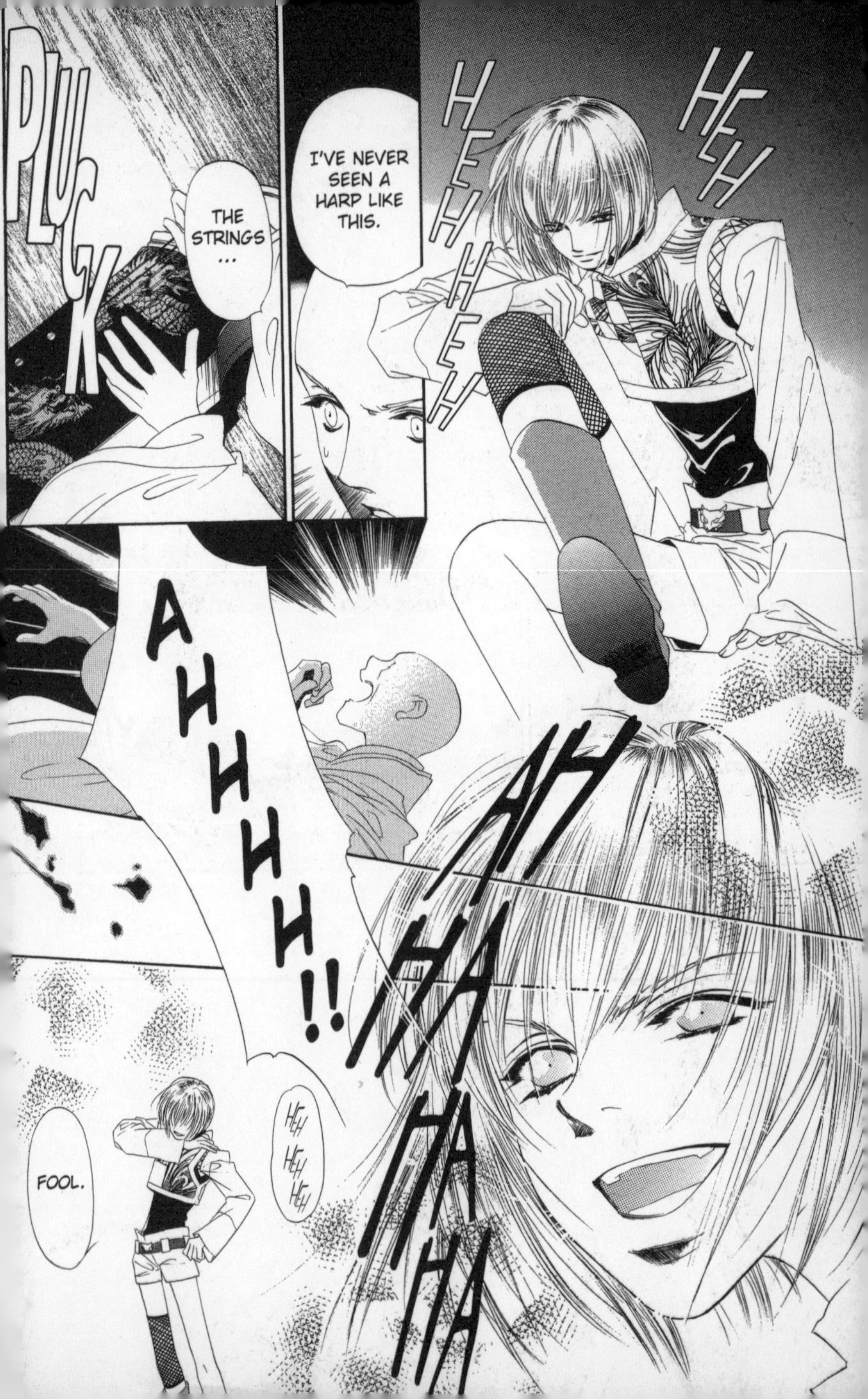
HEH
HEH HEH HEH
I'VE NEVER SEEN A HARP LIKE THIS.
THE STRINGS ...
PLUCK
AHHHH!!
AH HA HA HA HA
HEH HEH HEH
FOOL.

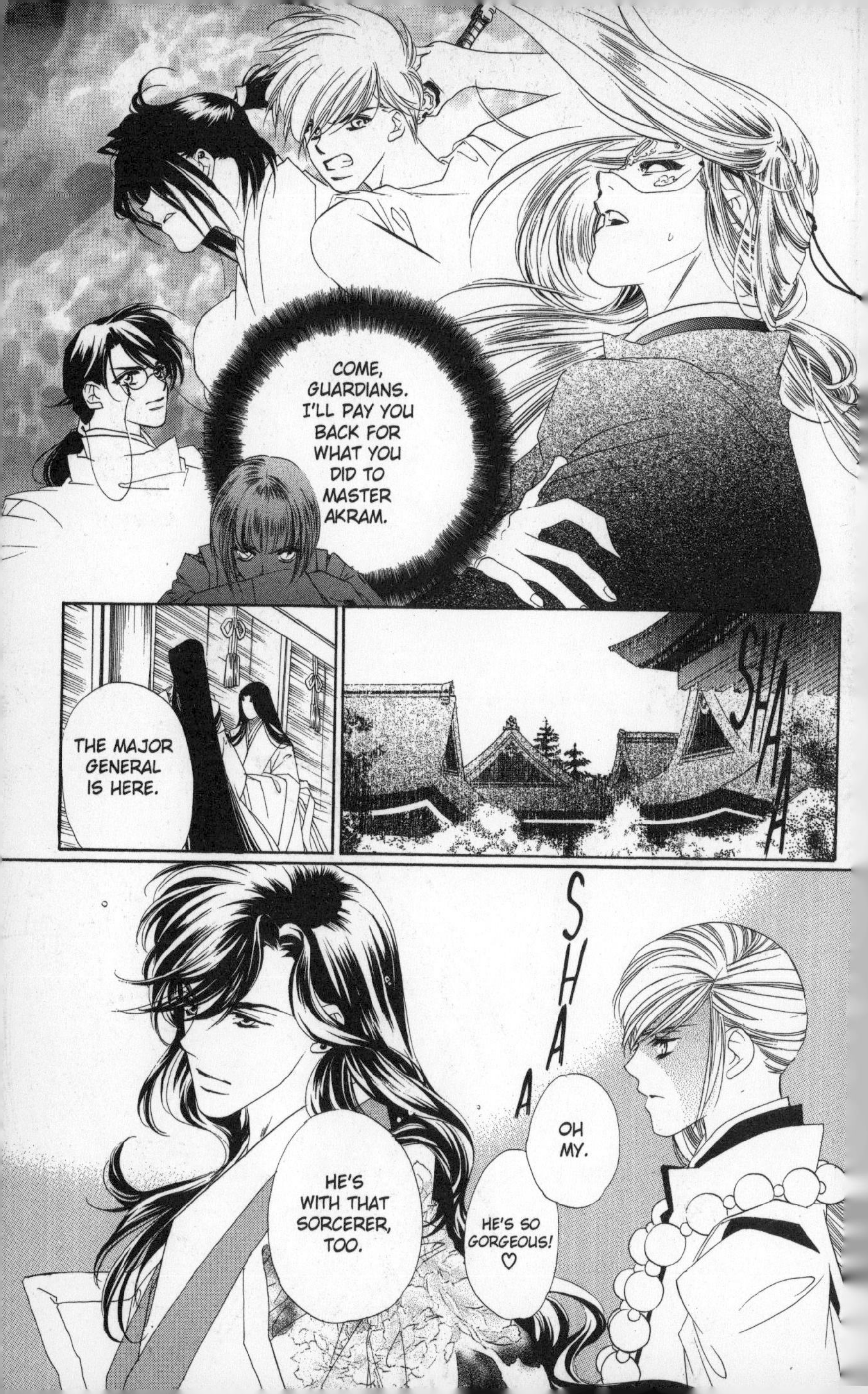
COME, GUARDIANS. I'LL PAY YOU BACK FOR WHAT YOU DID TO MASTER AKRAM.
SHAA
THE MAJOR GENERAL IS HERE.
SHAA
OH MY.
HE'S SO GORGEOUS! ♡
HE'S WITH THAT SORCERER, TOO.

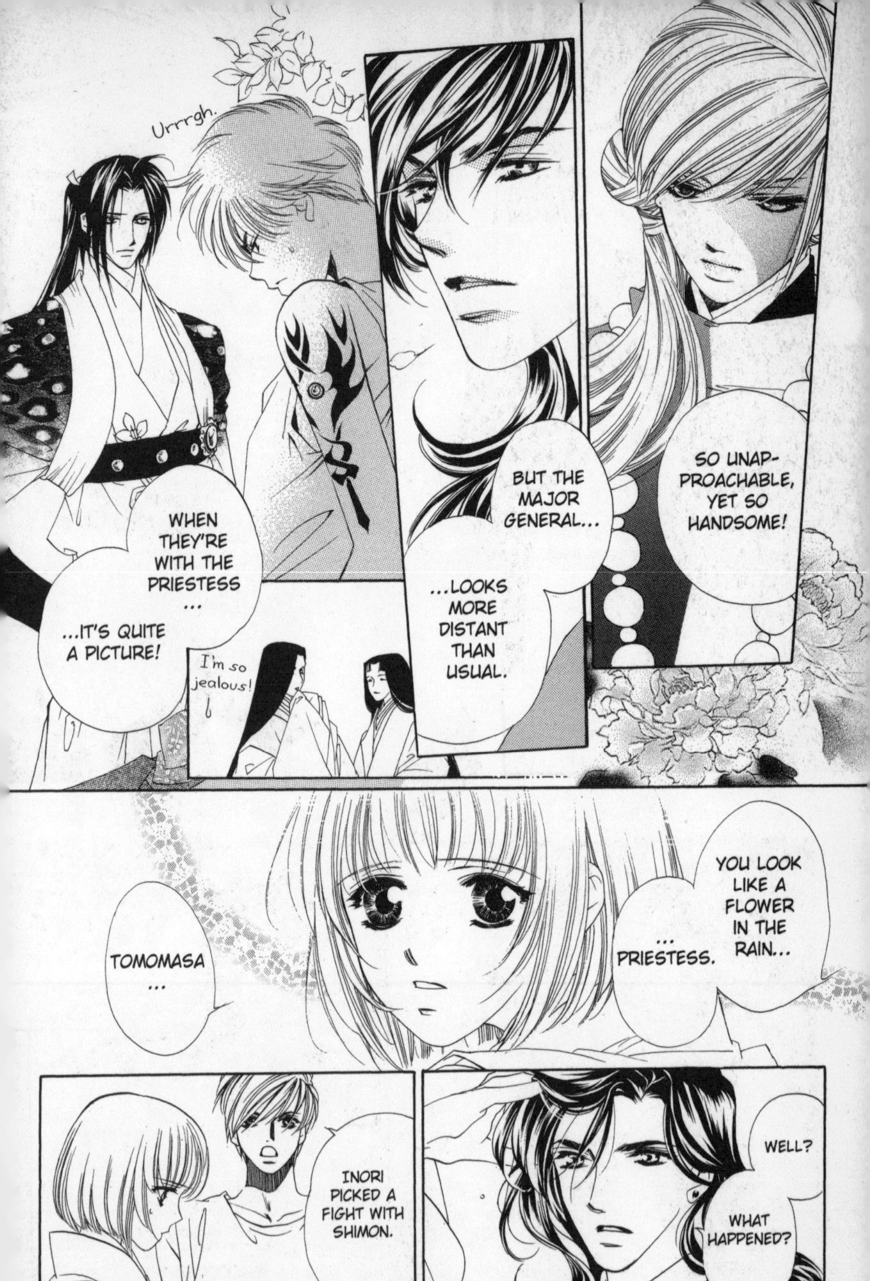
SO UNAP-PROACHABLE, YET SO HANDSOME!
BUT THE MAJOR GENERAL...
...LOOKS MORE DISTANT THAN USUAL.
Urrrgh.
WHEN THEY'RE WITH THE PRIESTESS...
...IT'S QUITE A PICTURE!
I'm so jealous!
YOU LOOK LIKE A FLOWER IN THE RAIN...
...PRIESTESS.
TOMOMASA...
WELL?
WHAT HAPPENED?
INORI PICKED A FIGHT WITH SHIMON.

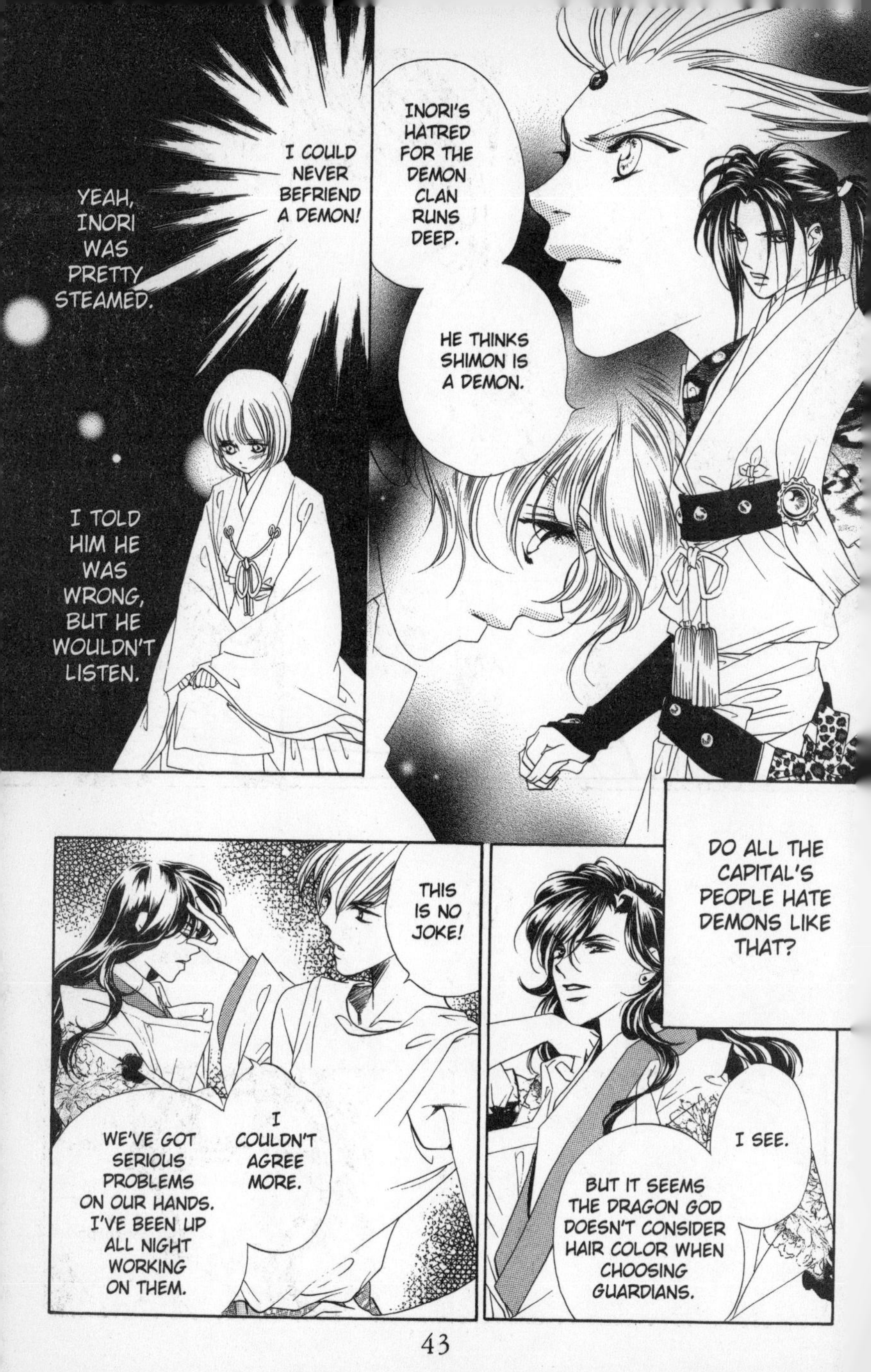
INORI'S HATRED FOR THE DEMON CLAN RUNS DEEP.
HE THINKS SHIMON IS A DEMON.
I COULD NEVER BEFRIEND A DEMON!
YEAH, INORI WAS PRETTY STEAMED.
I TOLD HIM HE WAS WRONG, BUT HE WOULDN'T LISTEN.
DO ALL THE CAPITAL'S PEOPLE HATE DEMONS LIKE THAT?
I SEE.
BUT IT SEEMS THE DRAGON GOD DOESN'T CONSIDER HAIR COLOR WHEN CHOOSING GUARDIANS.
THIS IS NO JOKE!
I COULDN'T AGREE MORE.
WE'VE GOT SERIOUS PROBLEMS ON OUR HANDS. I'VE BEEN UP ALL NIGHT WORKING ON THEM.

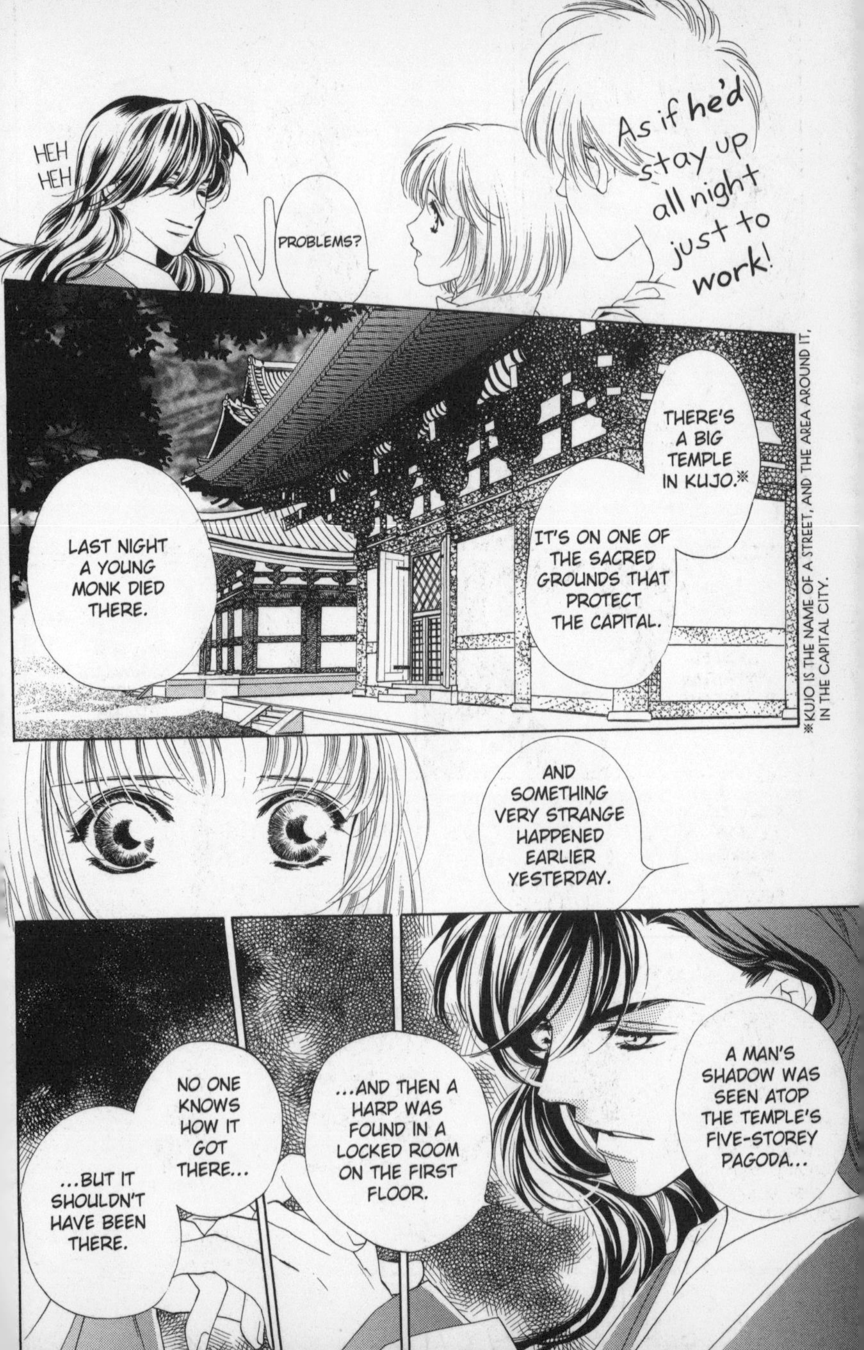
As if he'd stay up all night just to work!
PROBLEMS?
HEH HEH
THERE'S A BIG TEMPLE IN KUJO.※
IT'S ON ONE OF THE SACRED GROUNDS THAT PROTECT THE CAPITAL.
LAST NIGHT A YOUNG MONK DIED THERE.
AND SOMETHING VERY STRANGE HAPPENED EARLIER YESTERDAY.
A MAN'S SHADOW WAS SEEN ATOP THE TEMPLE'S FIVE-STOREY PAGODA...
...AND THEN A HARP WAS FOUND IN A LOCKED ROOM ON THE FIRST FLOOR.
NO ONE KNOWS HOW IT GOT THERE...
...BUT IT SHOULDN'T HAVE BEEN THERE.

※KUJO IS THE NAME OF A STREET, AND THE AREA AROUND IT, IN THE CAPITAL CITY.

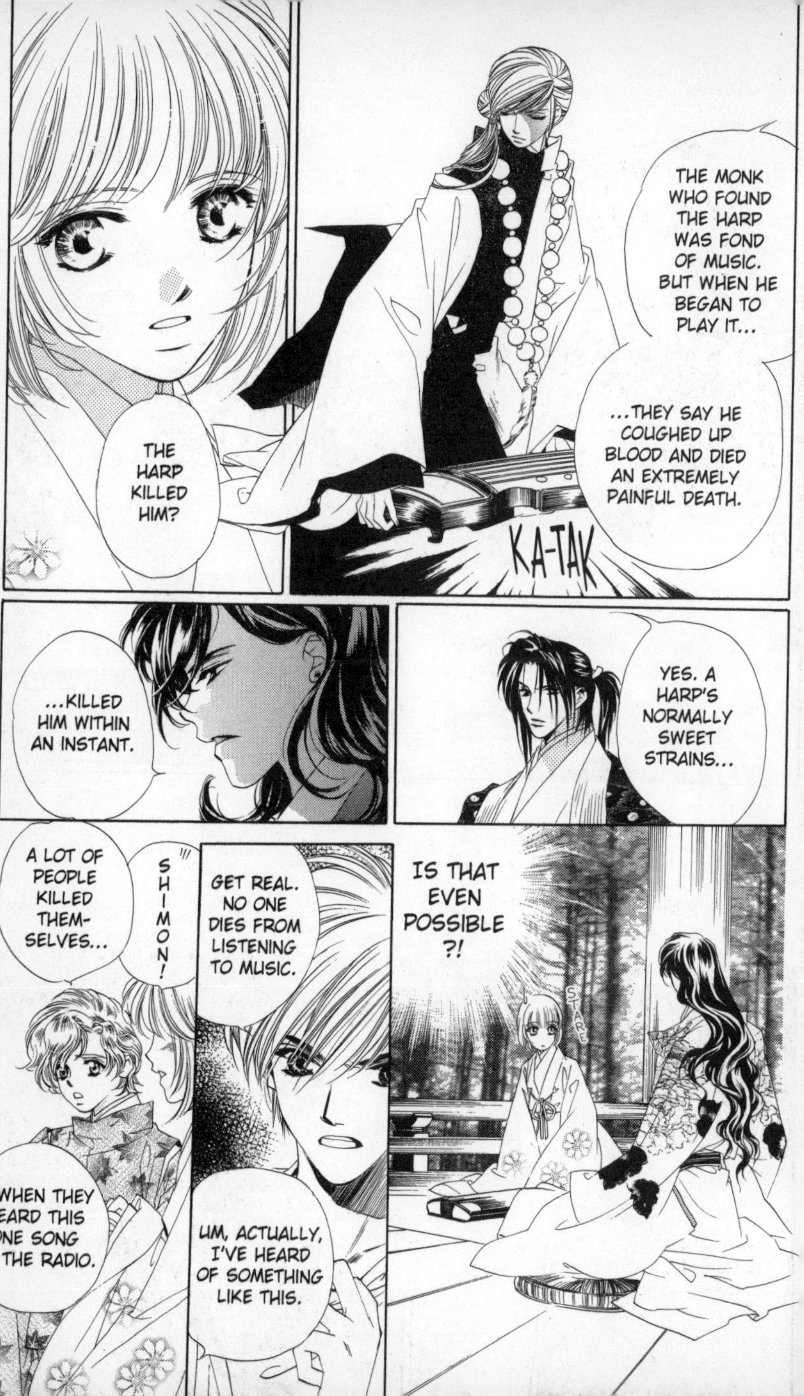
THE MONK WHO FOUND THE HARP WAS FOND OF MUSIC. BUT WHEN HE BEGAN TO PLAY IT...
...THEY SAY HE COUGHED UP BLOOD AND DIED AN EXTREMELY PAINFUL DEATH.
KA-TAK
THE HARP KILLED HIM?
YES. A HARP'S NORMALLY SWEET STRAINS...
...KILLED HIM WITHIN AN INSTANT.
IS THAT EVEN POSSIBLE?!
STARE
GET REAL. NO ONE DIES FROM LISTENING TO MUSIC.
UM, ACTUALLY, I'VE HEARD OF SOMETHING LIKE THIS.
SHIMON!
A LOT OF PEOPLE KILLED THEM-SELVES...
...WHEN THEY HEARD THIS ONE SONG ON THE RADIO.

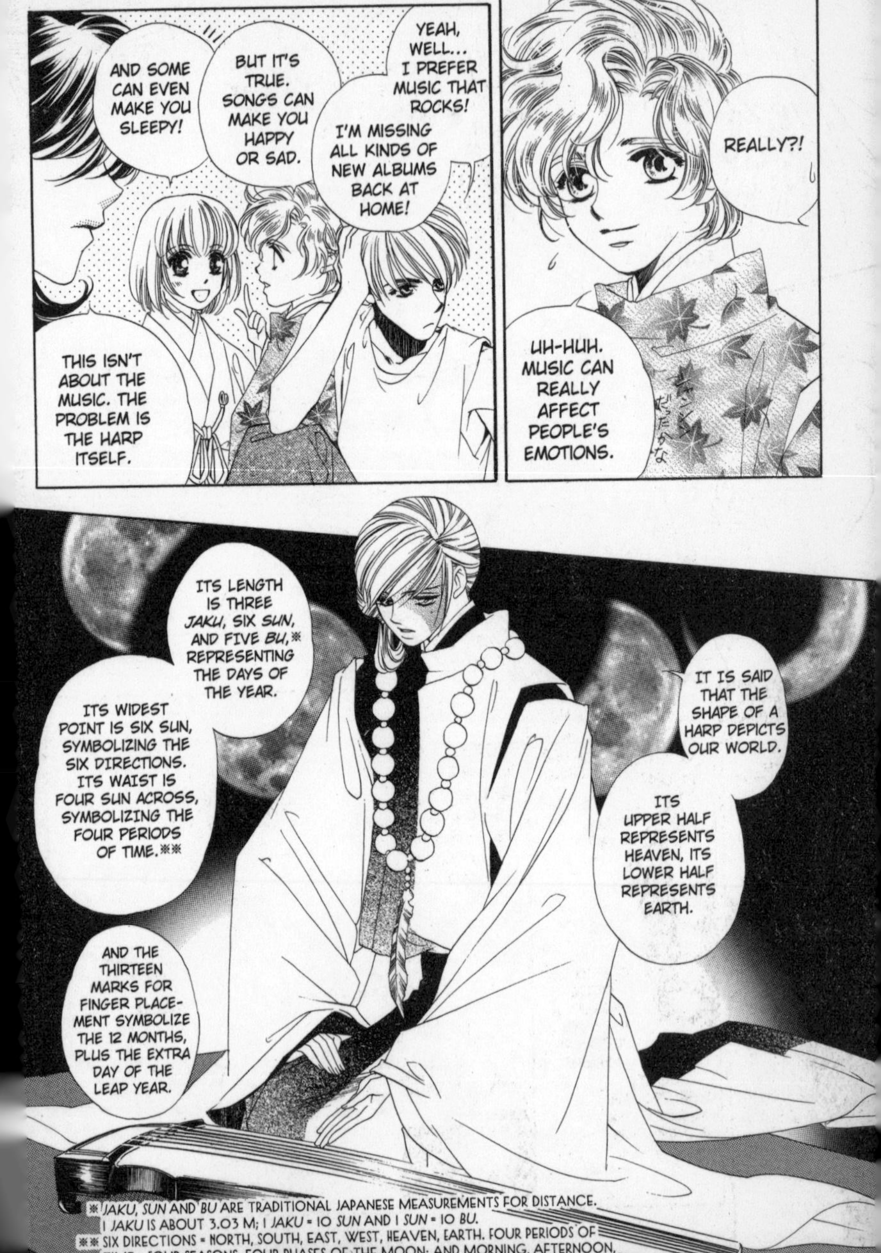
REALLY?!
UH-HUH. MUSIC CAN REALLY AFFECT PEOPLE'S EMOTIONS.
YEAH, WELL... I PREFER MUSIC THAT ROCKS!
I'M MISSING ALL KINDS OF NEW ALBUMS BACK AT HOME!
BUT IT'S TRUE. SONGS CAN MAKE YOU HAPPY OR SAD.
AND SOME CAN EVEN MAKE YOU SLEEPY!
THIS ISN'T ABOUT THE MUSIC. THE PROBLEM IS THE HARP ITSELF.
IT IS SAID THAT THE SHAPE OF A HARP DEPICTS OUR WORLD.
ITS UPPER HALF REPRESENTS HEAVEN, ITS LOWER HALF REPRESENTS EARTH.
ITS LENGTH IS THREE *JAKU*, SIX *SUN*, AND FIVE *BU*,※ REPRESENTING THE DAYS OF THE YEAR.
ITS WIDEST POINT IS SIX SUN, SYMBOLIZING THE SIX DIRECTIONS. ITS WAIST IS FOUR SUN ACROSS, SYMBOLIZING THE FOUR PERIODS OF TIME.※※
AND THE THIRTEEN MARKS FOR FINGER PLACEMENT SYMBOLIZE THE 12 MONTHS, PLUS THE EXTRA DAY OF THE LEAP YEAR.

※ *JAKU*, *SUN* AND *BU* ARE TRADITIONAL JAPANESE MEASUREMENTS FOR DISTANCE. 1 *JAKU* IS ABOUT 3.03 M; 1 *JAKU* = 10 *SUN* AND 1 *SUN* = 10 *BU*.

※※ SIX DIRECTIONS = NORTH, SOUTH, EAST, WEST, HEAVEN, EARTH. FOUR PERIODS OF TIME = FOUR SEASONS; FOUR PHASES OF THE MOON; AND MORNING, AFTERNOON, EVENING, AND NIGHT.

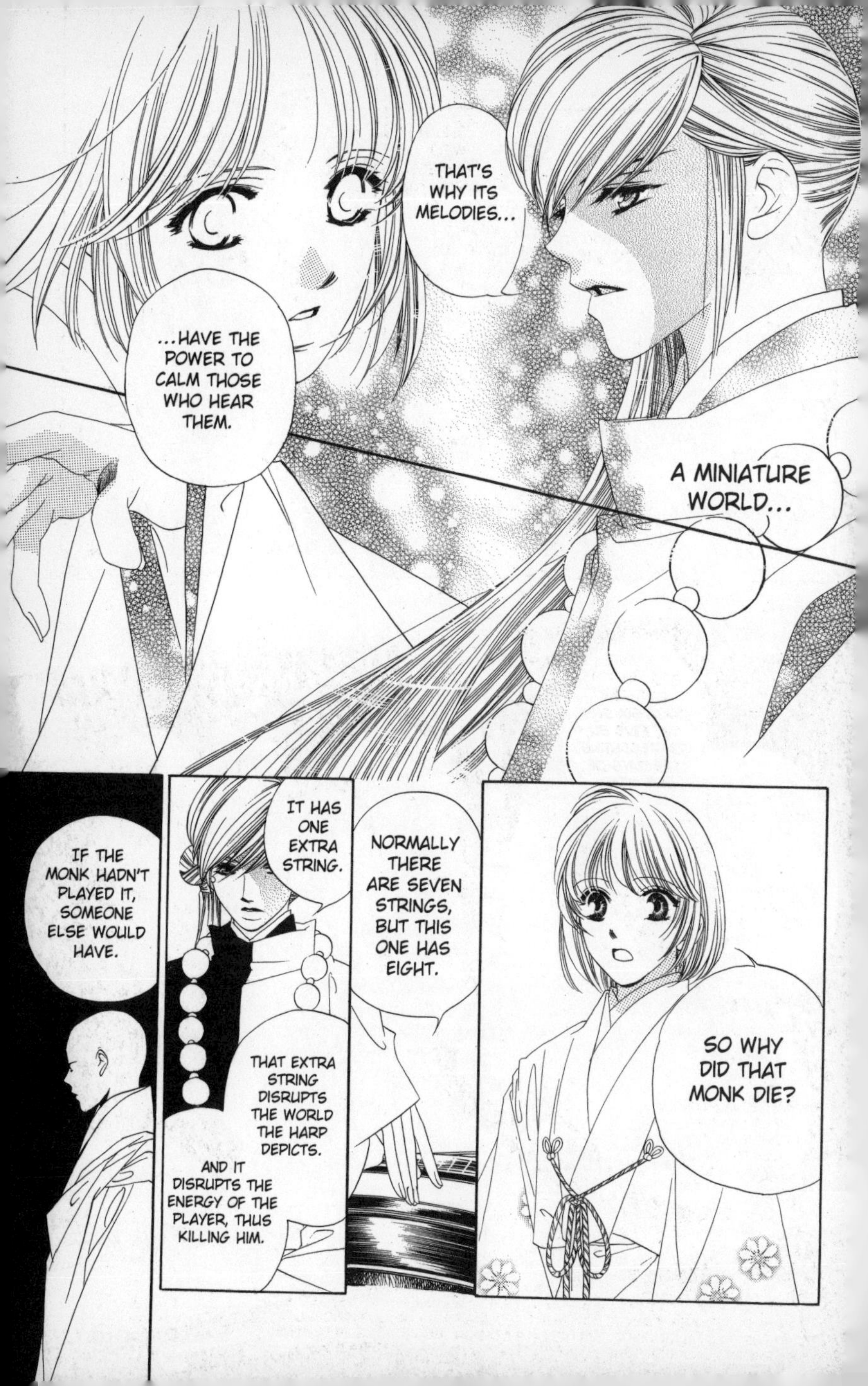
THAT'S WHY ITS MELODIES...
...HAVE THE POWER TO CALM THOSE WHO HEAR THEM.
A MINIATURE WORLD...
SO WHY DID THAT MONK DIE?
IT HAS ONE EXTRA STRING.
NORMALLY THERE ARE SEVEN STRINGS, BUT THIS ONE HAS EIGHT.
THAT EXTRA STRING DISRUPTS THE WORLD THE HARP DEPICTS.
AND IT DISRUPTS THE ENERGY OF THE PLAYER, THUS KILLING HIM.
IF THE MONK HADN'T PLAYED IT, SOMEONE ELSE WOULD HAVE.

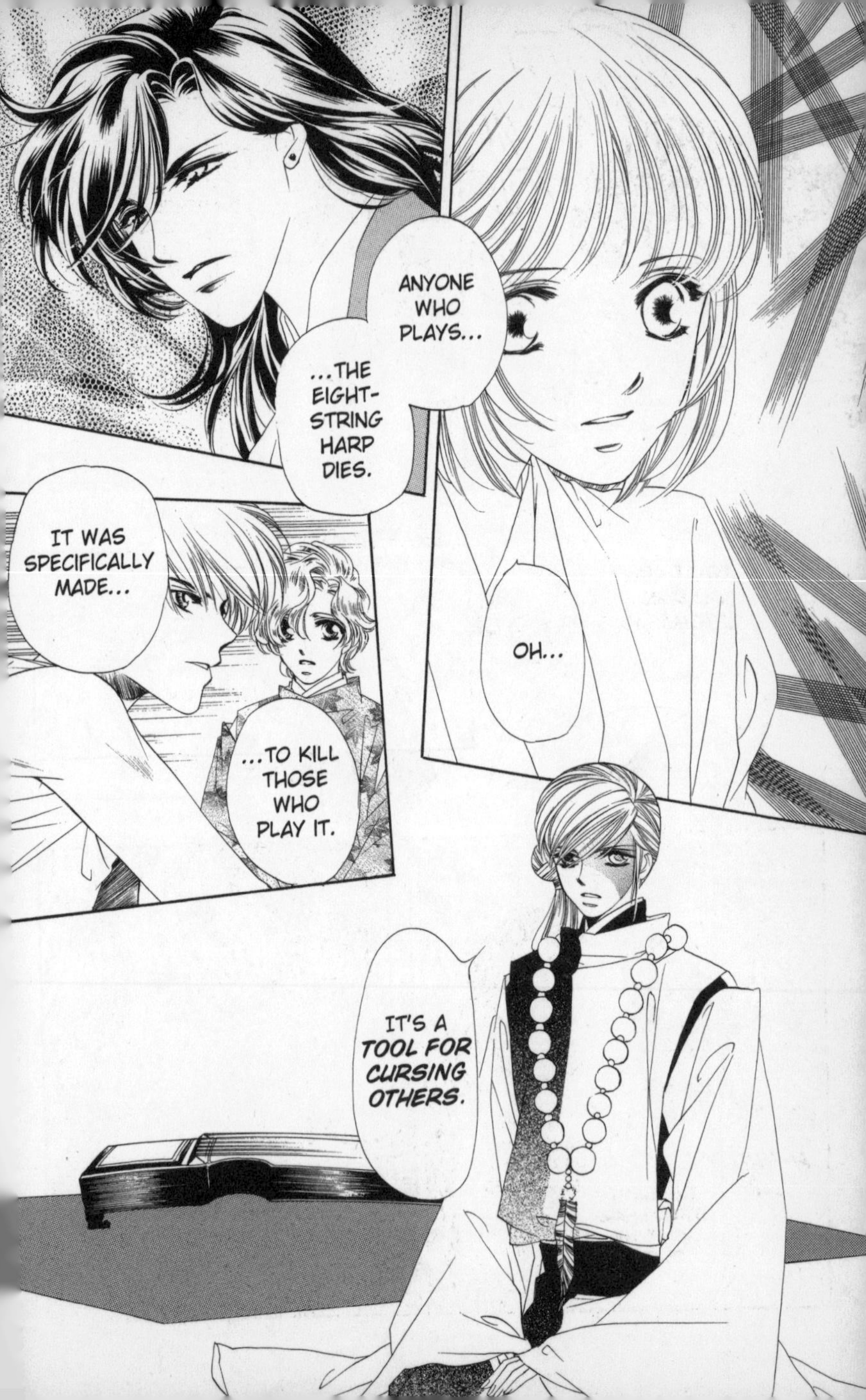
ANYONE WHO PLAYS...
...THE EIGHT-STRING HARP DIES.
OH...
IT WAS SPECIFICALLY MADE...
...TO KILL THOSE WHO PLAY IT.
IT'S A *TOOL FOR CURSING OTHERS.*

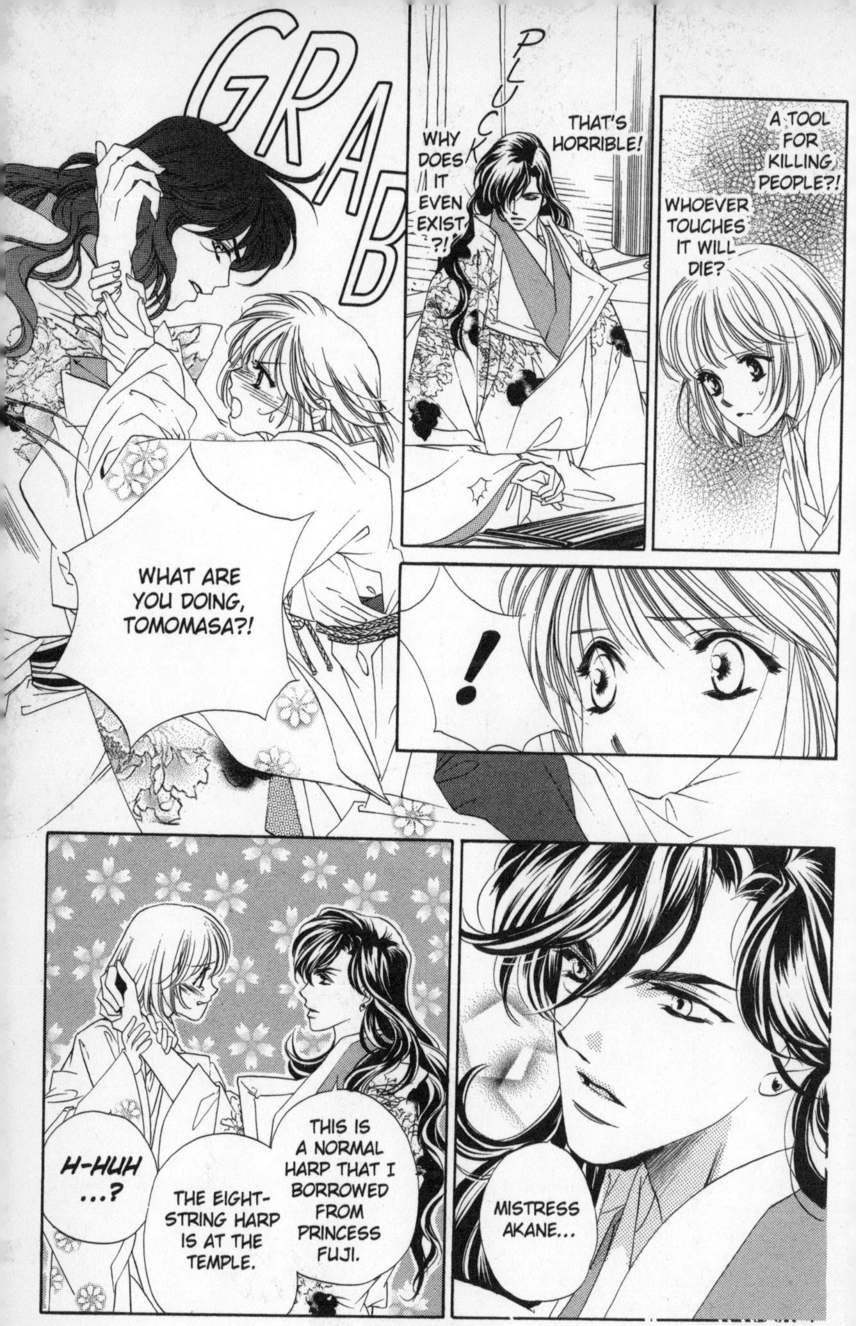
A TOOL FOR KILLING PEOPLE?!
WHOEVER TOUCHES IT WILL DIE?
THAT'S HORRIBLE!
PLUCK
WHY DOES IT EVEN EXIST?!
!
GRAB
WHAT ARE YOU DOING, TOMOMASA?!
MISTRESS AKANE...
THIS IS A NORMAL HARP THAT I BORROWED FROM PRINCESS FUJI.
THE EIGHT-STRING HARP IS AT THE TEMPLE.
H-HUH ...?

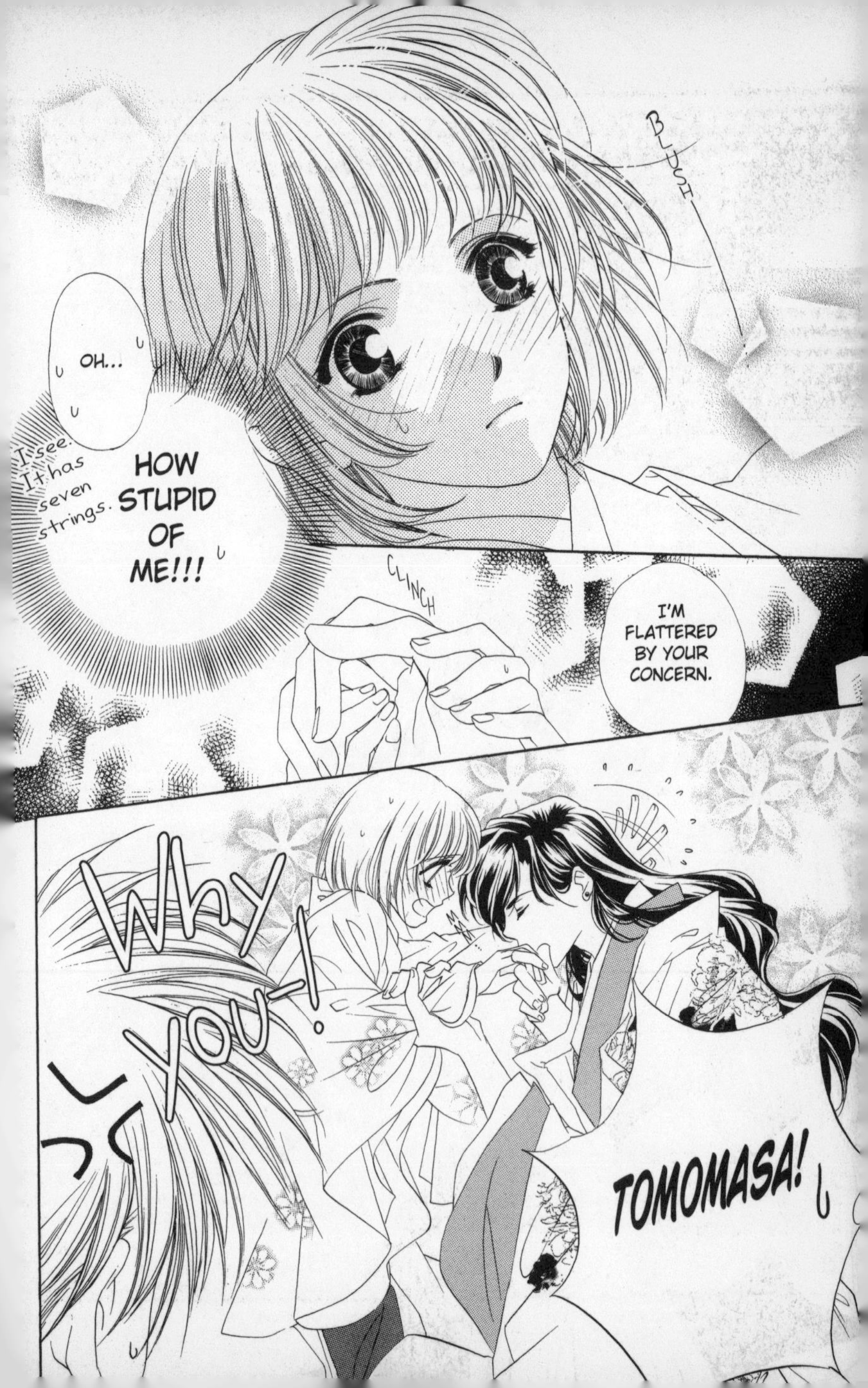
BLUSH
OH...
I see. It has seven strings.
HOW STUPID OF ME!!!
I'M FLATTERED BY YOUR CONCERN.
CLINCH
TOMOMASA!
Why you-!

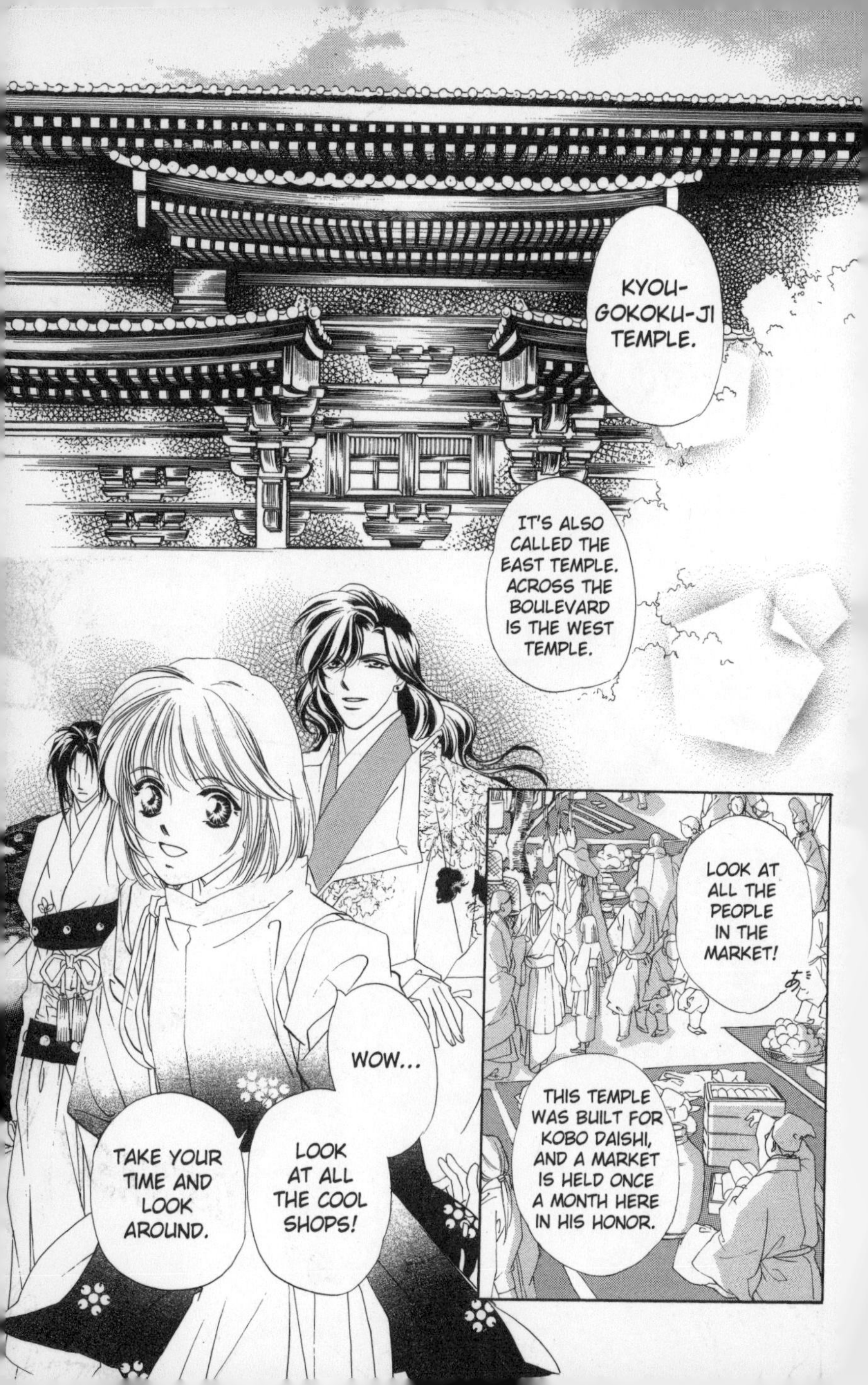
KYOU-GOKOKU-JI TEMPLE.
IT'S ALSO CALLED THE EAST TEMPLE. ACROSS THE BOULEVARD IS THE WEST TEMPLE.
LOOK AT ALL THE PEOPLE IN THE MARKET!
THIS TEMPLE WAS BUILT FOR KOBO DAISHI, AND A MARKET IS HELD ONCE A MONTH HERE IN HIS HONOR.
WOW...
LOOK AT ALL THE COOL SHOPS!
TAKE YOUR TIME AND LOOK AROUND.

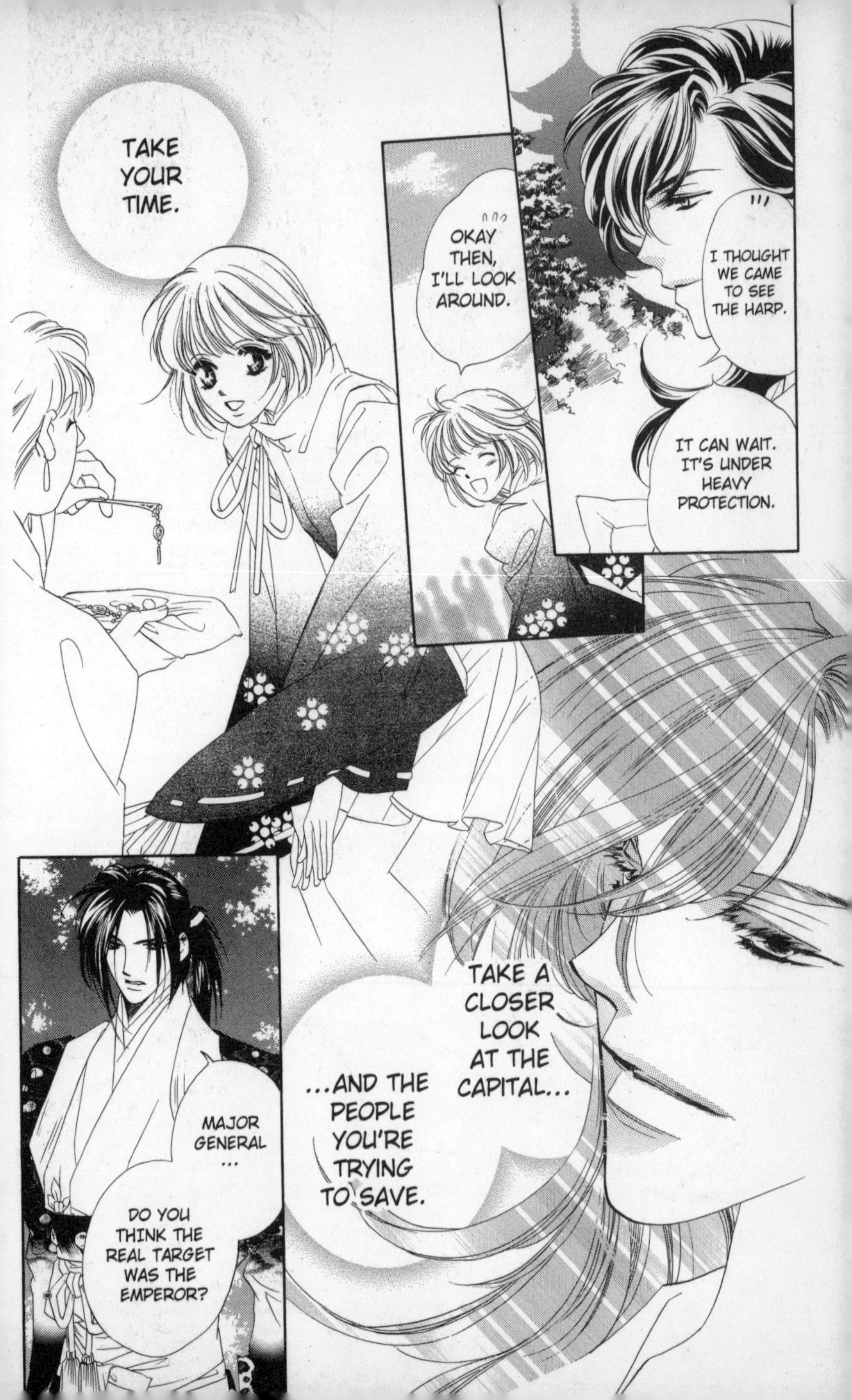
I THOUGHT WE CAME TO SEE THE HARP.
IT CAN WAIT. IT'S UNDER HEAVY PROTECTION.
OKAY THEN, I'LL LOOK AROUND.
TAKE YOUR TIME.
TAKE A CLOSER LOOK AT THE CAPITAL...
...AND THE PEOPLE YOU'RE TRYING TO SAVE.
MAJOR GENERAL ...
DO YOU THINK THE REAL TARGET WAS THE EMPEROR?

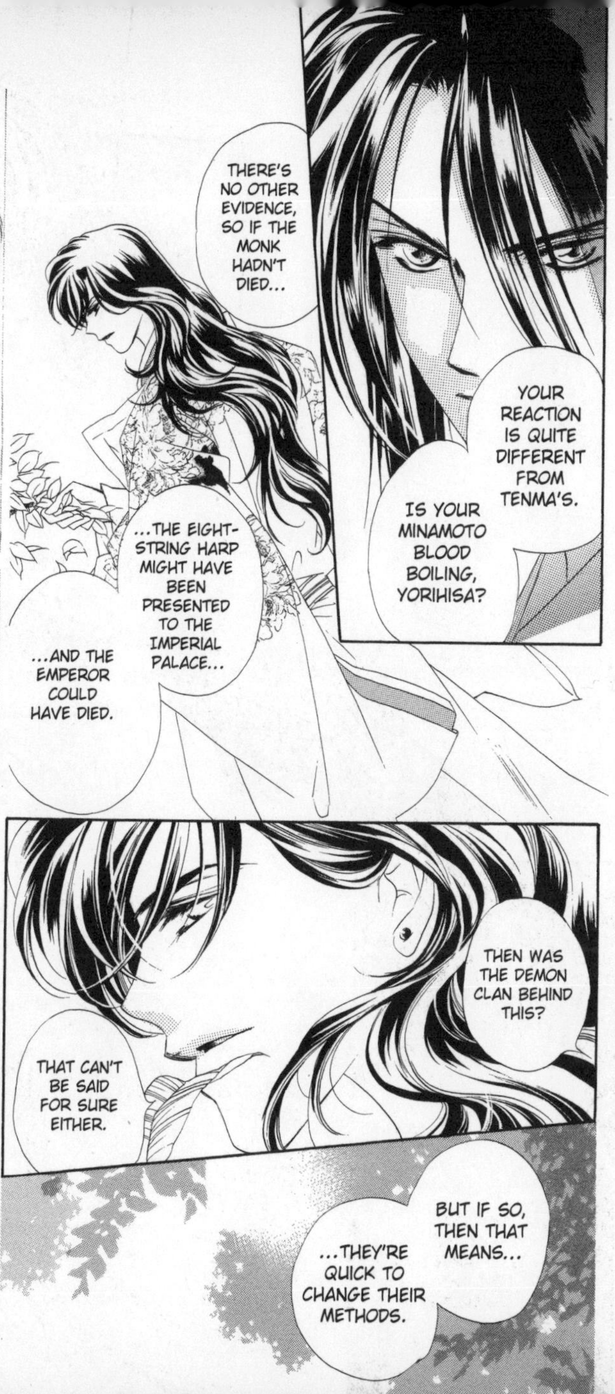
YOUR REACTION IS QUITE DIFFERENT FROM TENMA'S.
IS YOUR MINAMOTO BLOOD BOILING, YORIHISA?
THERE'S NO OTHER EVIDENCE, SO IF THE MONK HADN'T DIED...
...THE EIGHT-STRING HARP MIGHT HAVE BEEN PRESENTED TO THE IMPERIAL PALACE...
...AND THE EMPEROR COULD HAVE DIED.
THEN WAS THE DEMON CLAN BEHIND THIS?
THAT CAN'T BE SAID FOR SURE EITHER.
BUT IF SO, THEN THAT MEANS...
...THEY'RE QUICK TO CHANGE THEIR METHODS.
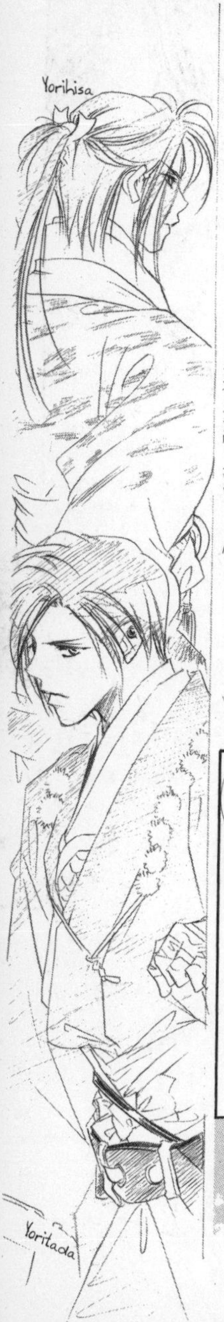
Yorihisa
Yoritada

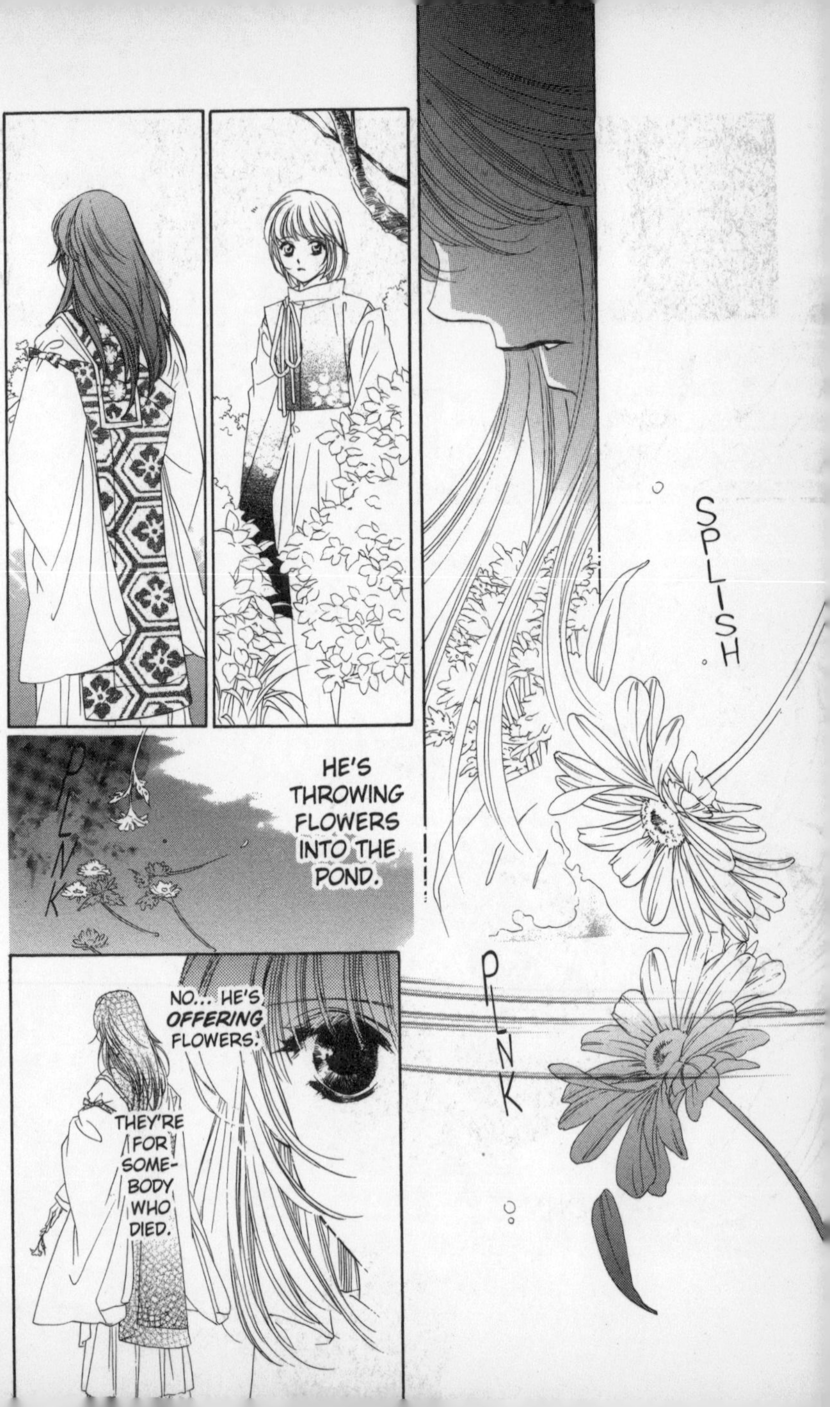
SPLISH
PLINK
PLINK
HE'S THROWING FLOWERS INTO THE POND.
NO... HE'S *OFFERING* FLOWERS.
THEY'RE FOR SOME-BODY WHO DIED.

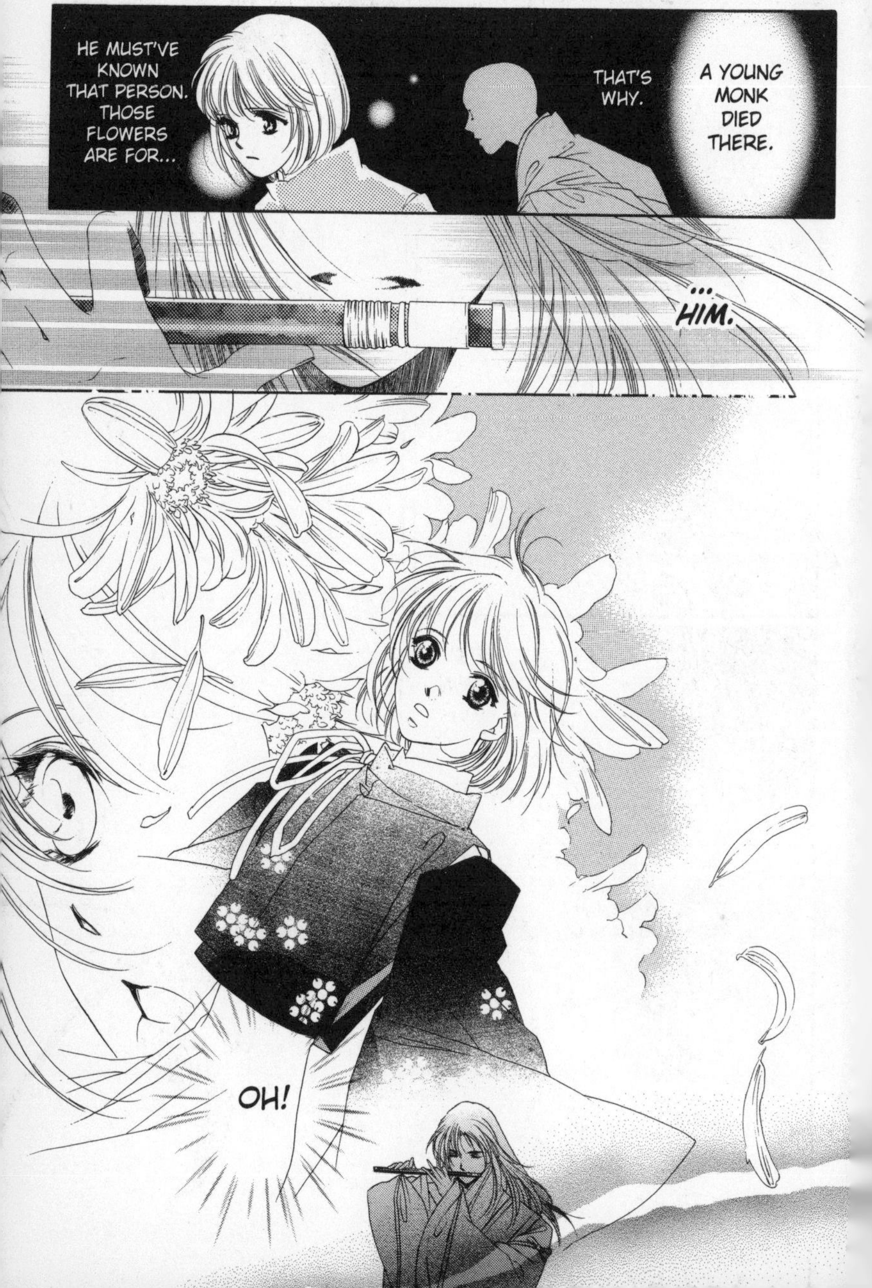
A YOUNG MONK DIED THERE.
THAT'S WHY.
HE MUST'VE KNOWN THAT PERSON. THOSE FLOWERS ARE FOR...
...HIM.
OH!

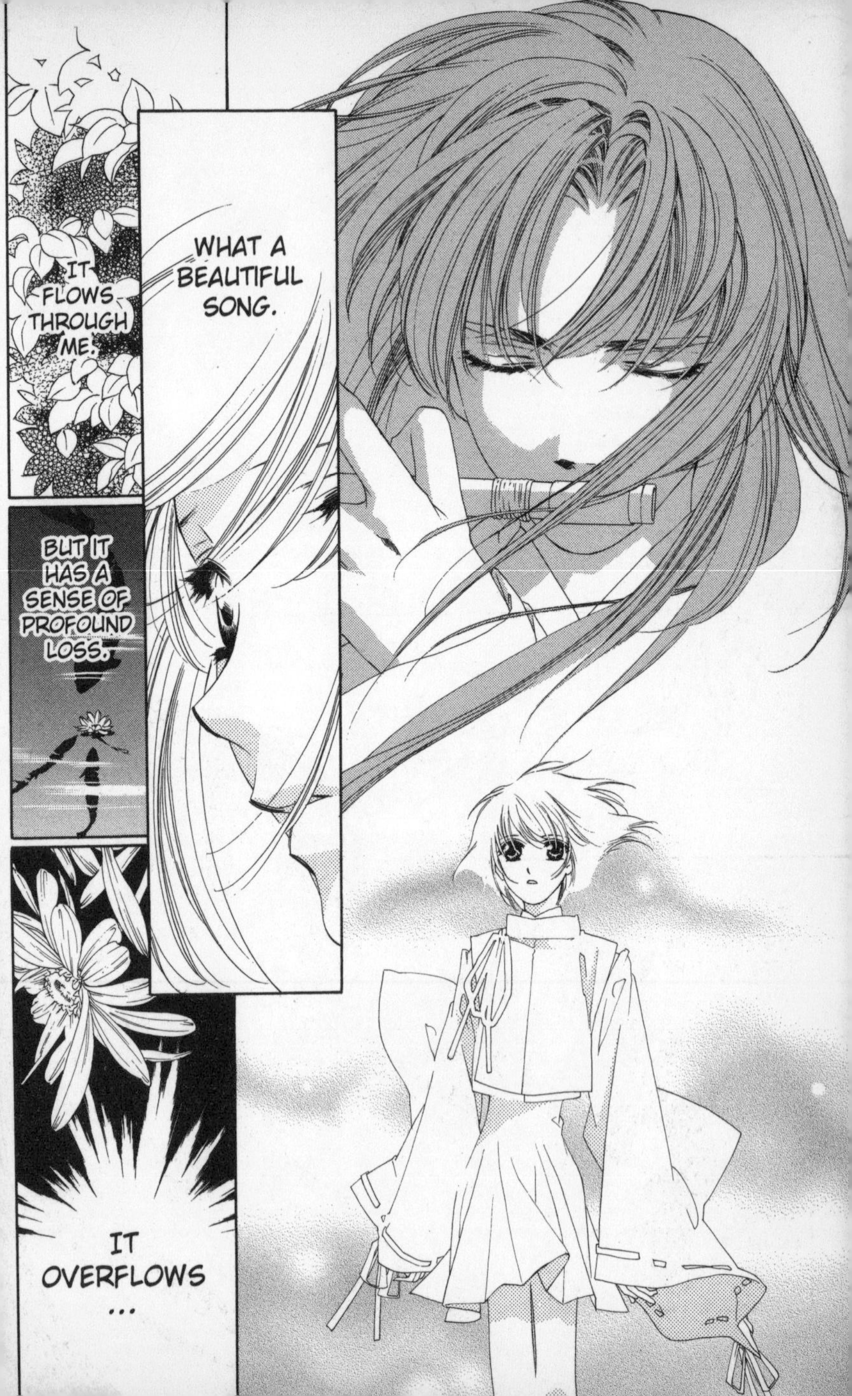
WHAT A BEAUTIFUL SONG.
IT FLOWS THROUGH ME.
BUT IT HAS A SENSE OF PROFOUND LOSS.
IT OVERFLOWS ...

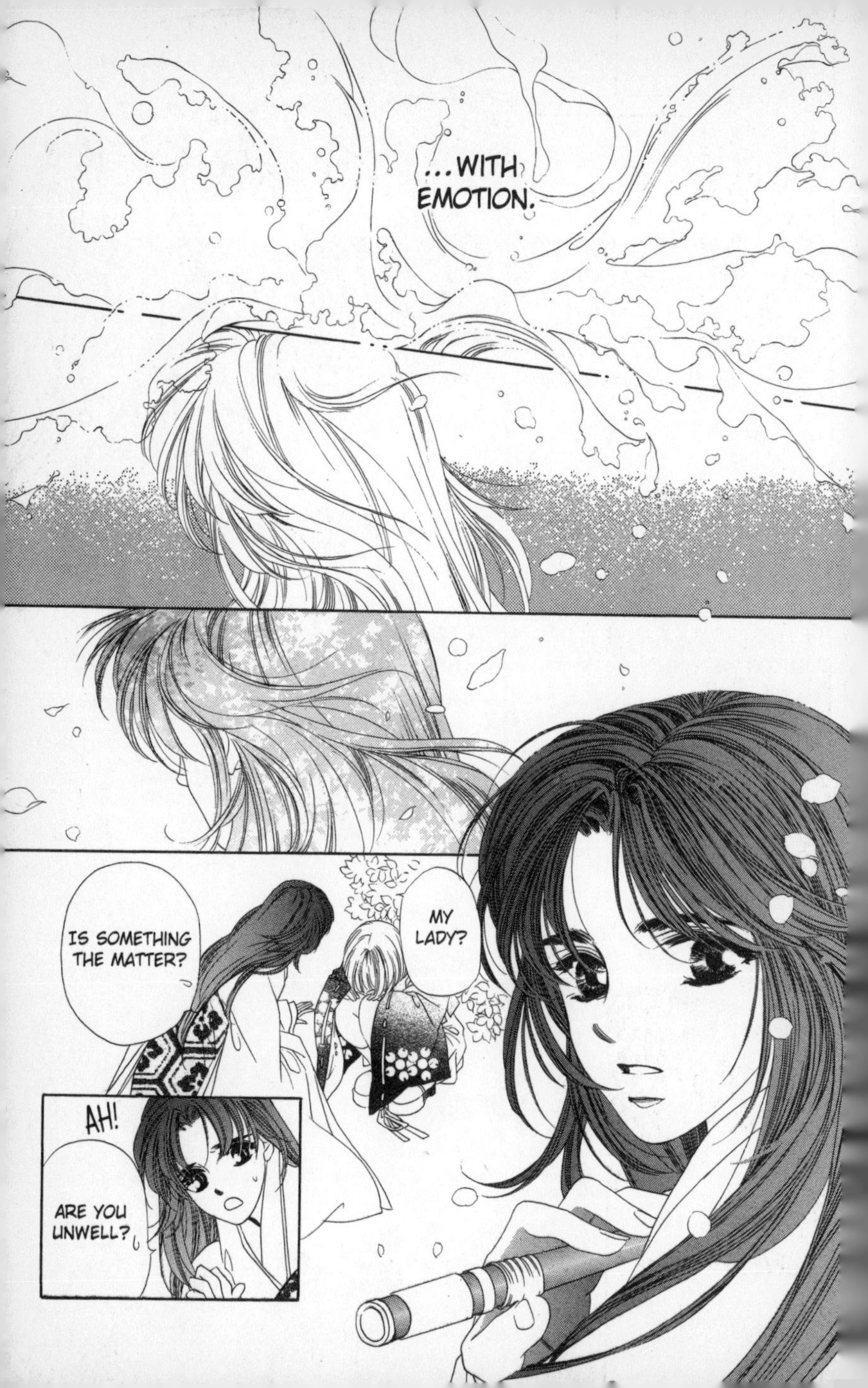
...WITH EMOTION.
MY LADY?
IS SOMETHING THE MATTER?
AH!
ARE YOU UNWELL?

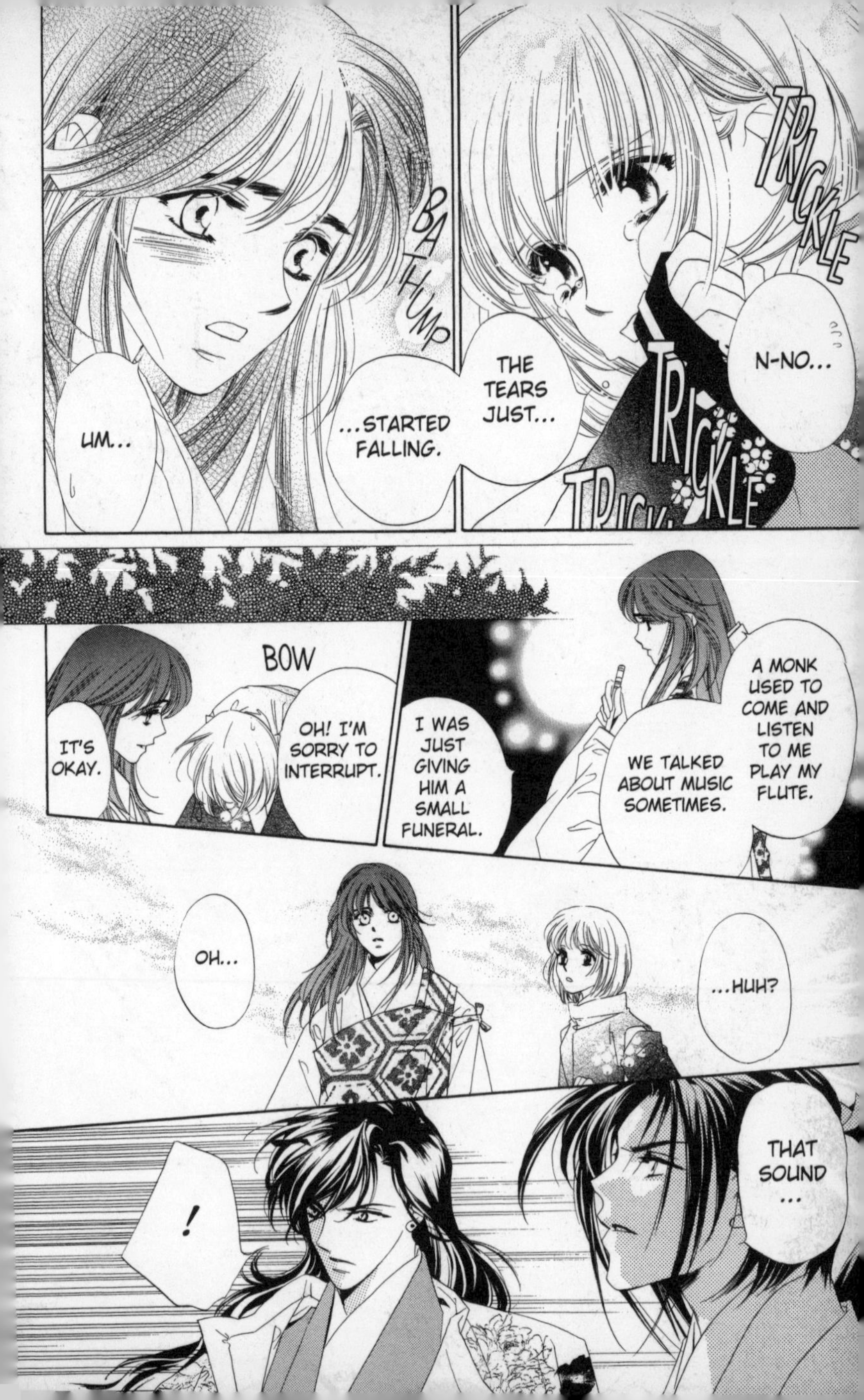
TRICKLE
N-NO...
THE TEARS JUST...
TRICKLE
...STARTED FALLING.
BATHUMP
UM...
A MONK USED TO COME AND LISTEN TO ME PLAY MY FLUTE.
WE TALKED ABOUT MUSIC SOMETIMES.
I WAS JUST GIVING HIM A SMALL FUNERAL.
OH! I'M SORRY TO INTERRUPT.
BOW
IT'S OKAY.
...HUH?
OH...
THAT SOUND...
!

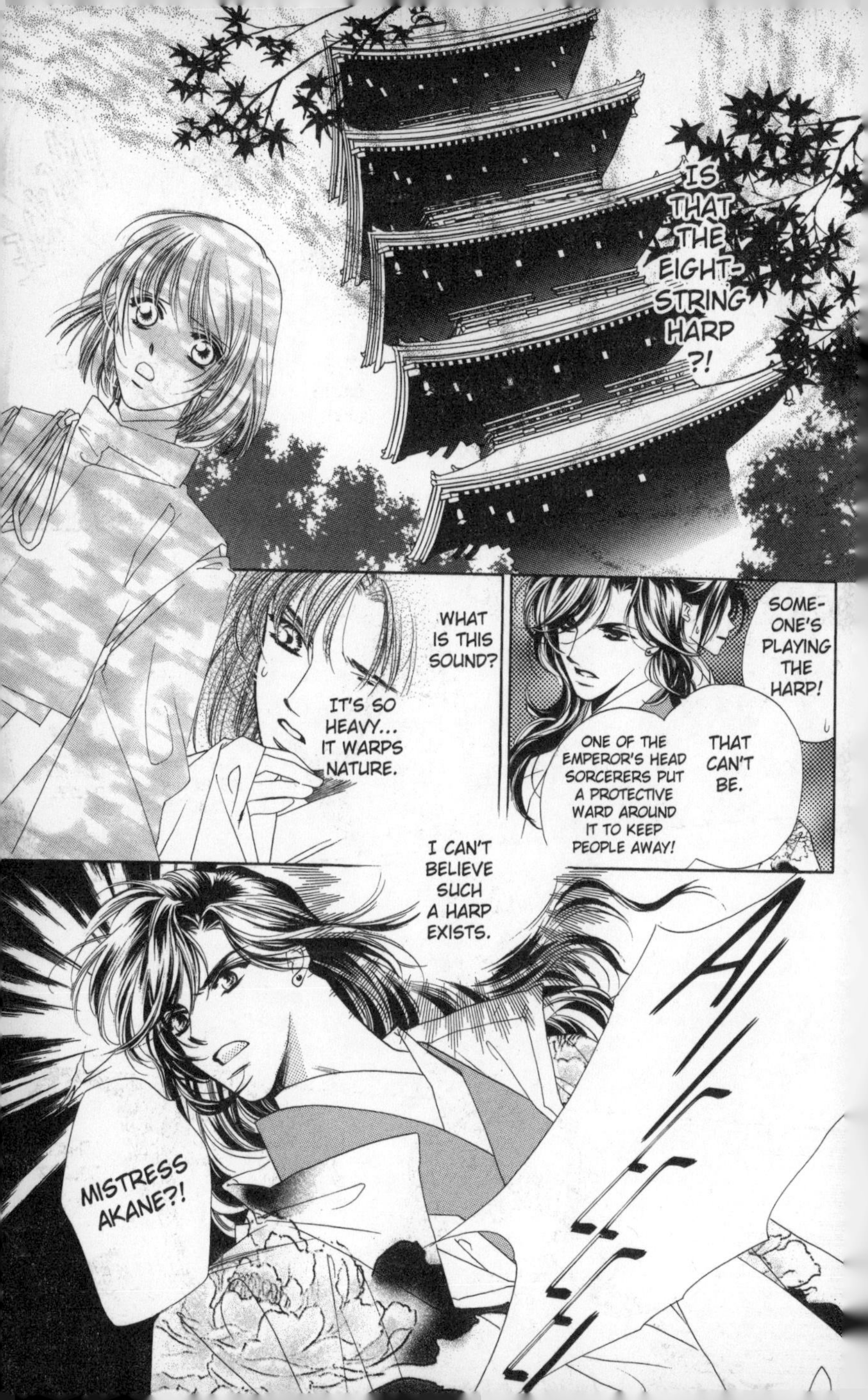
IS THAT THE EIGHT-STRING HARP?!
SOME-ONE'S PLAYING THE HARP!
THAT CAN'T BE.
ONE OF THE EMPEROR'S HEAD SORCERERS PUT A PROTECTIVE WARD AROUND IT TO KEEP PEOPLE AWAY!
WHAT IS THIS SOUND?
IT'S SO HEAVY... IT WARPS NATURE.
I CAN'T BELIEVE SUCH A HARP EXISTS.
MISTRESS AKANE?!

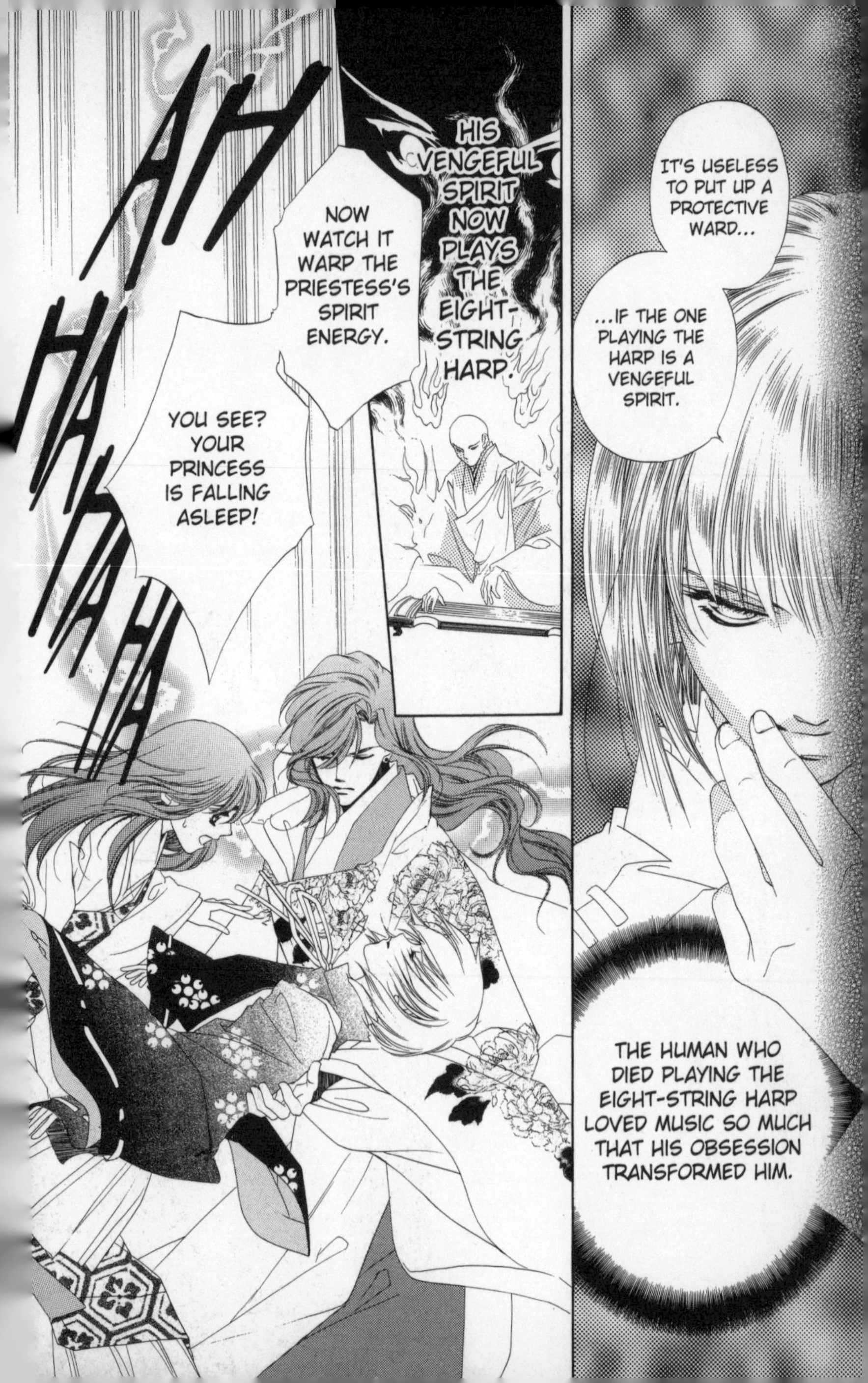
IT'S USELESS TO PUT UP A PROTECTIVE WARD...
...IF THE ONE PLAYING THE HARP IS A VENGEFUL SPIRIT.
THE HUMAN WHO DIED PLAYING THE EIGHT-STRING HARP LOVED MUSIC SO MUCH THAT HIS OBSESSION TRANSFORMED HIM.
HIS VENGEFUL SPIRIT NOW PLAYS THE EIGHT-STRING HARP.
NOW WATCH IT WARP THE PRIESTESS'S SPIRIT ENERGY.
AH HA HA HA HA HA HA
YOU SEE? YOUR PRINCESS IS FALLING ASLEEP!

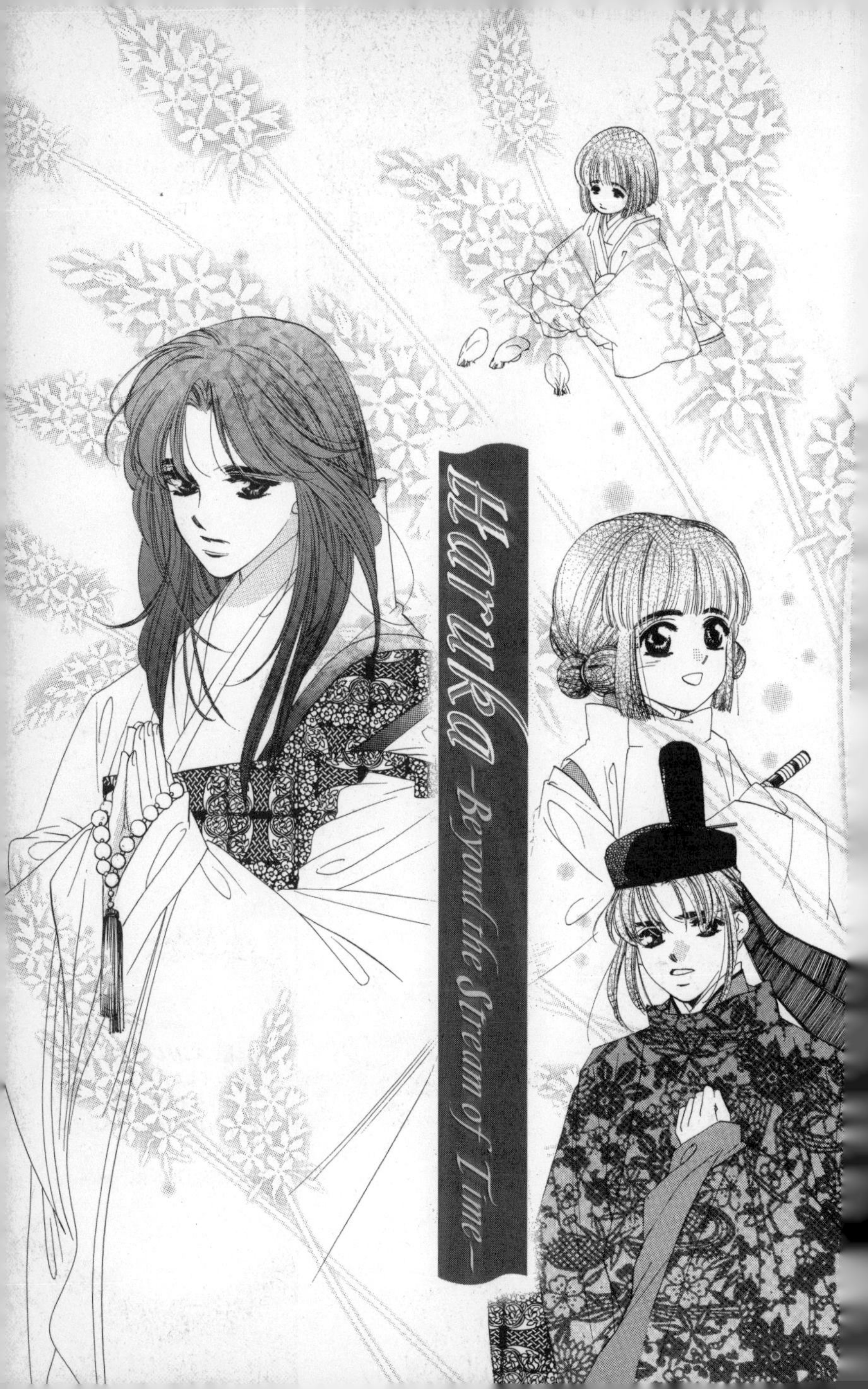
Haruka -Beyond the Stream of Time-

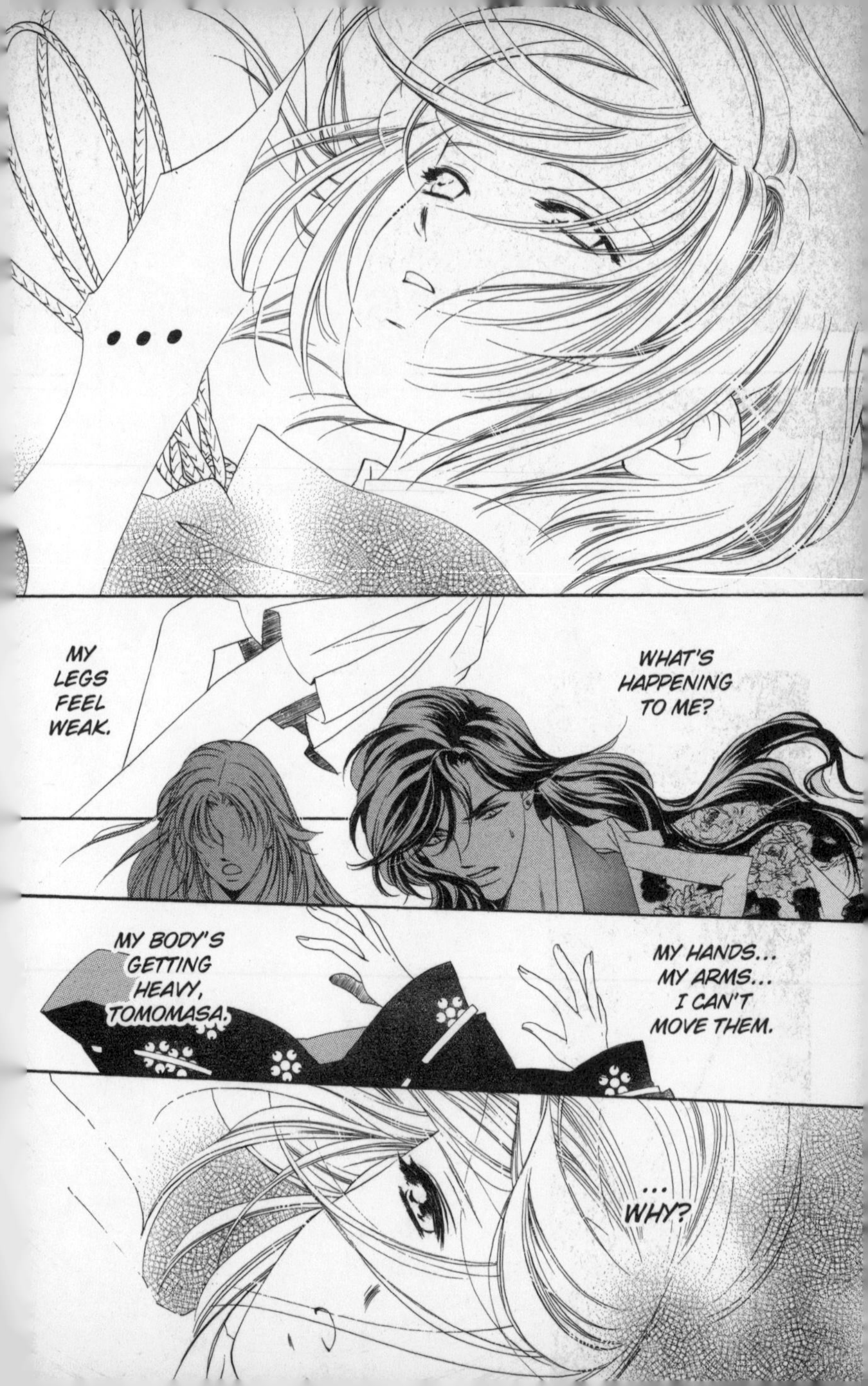
...
WHAT'S HAPPENING TO ME?
MY LEGS FEEL WEAK.
MY HANDS... MY ARMS... I CAN'T MOVE THEM.
MY BODY'S GETTING HEAVY, TOMOMASA.
... WHY?

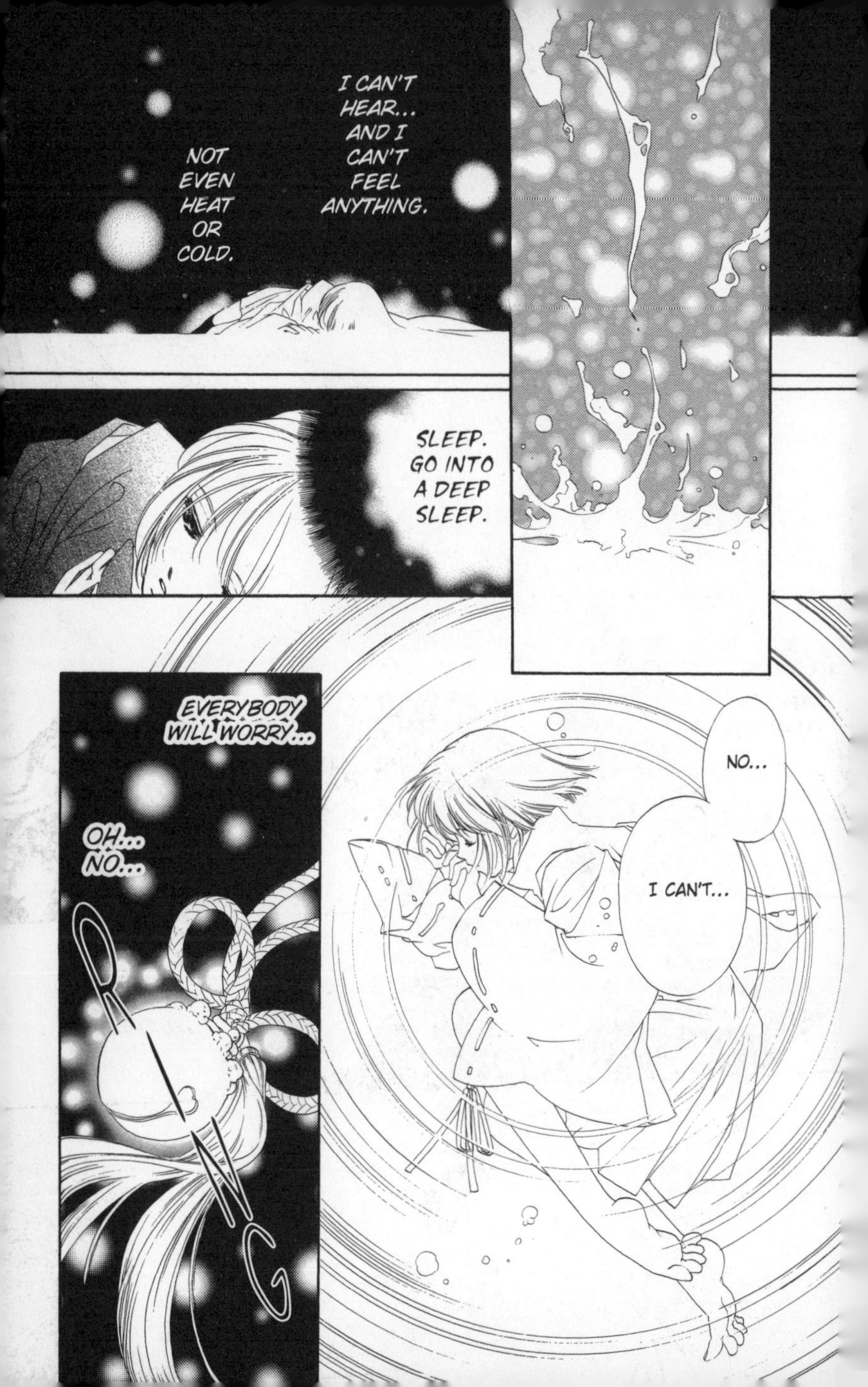
I CAN'T HEAR... AND I CAN'T FEEL ANYTHING.
NOT EVEN HEAT OR COLD.
SLEEP. GO INTO A DEEP SLEEP.
NO...
I CAN'T...
EVERYBODY WILL WORRY...
OH... NO...
RING

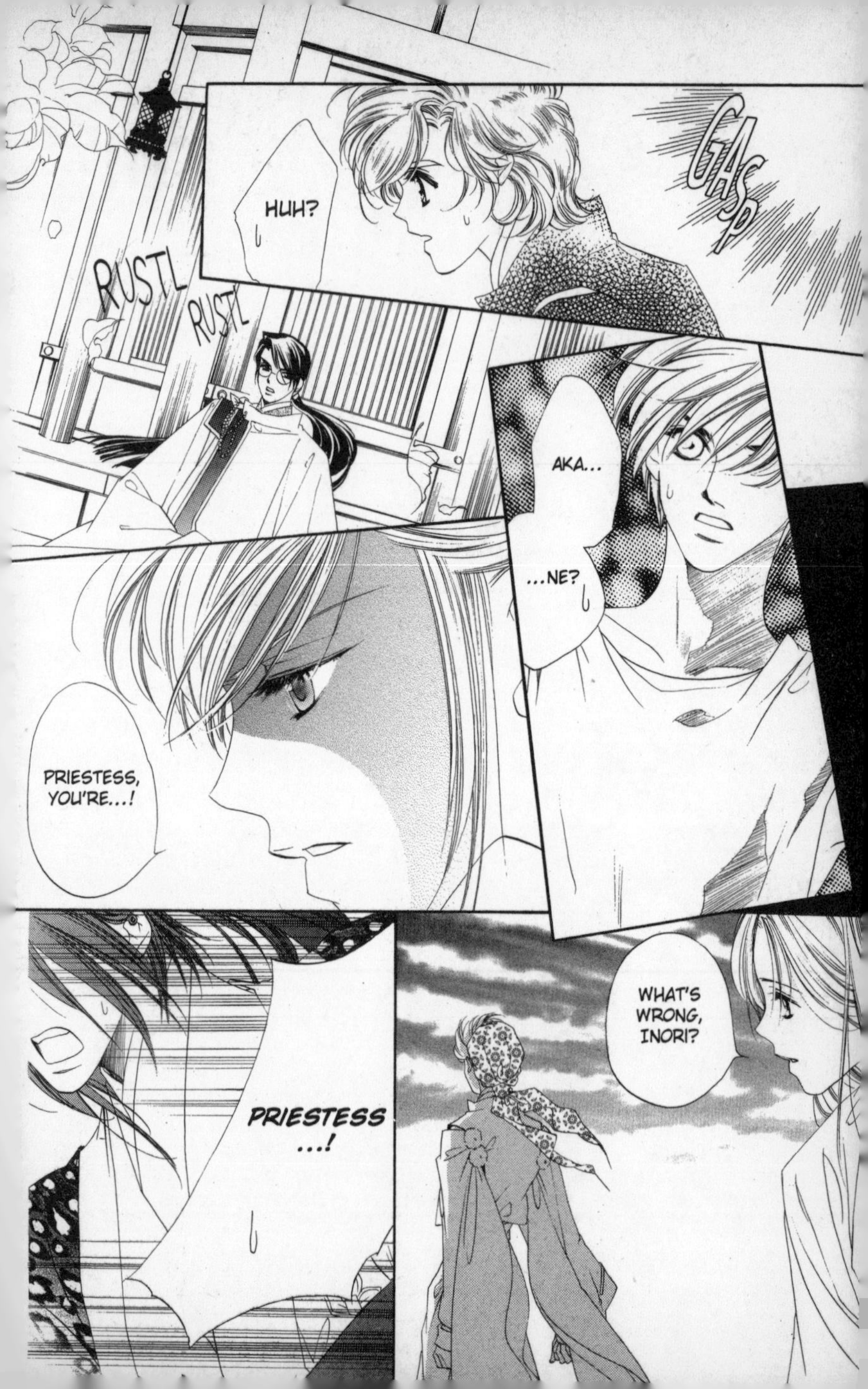
GASP
HUH?
AKA...
...NE?
RUSTL
RUSTL
PRIESTESS, YOU'RE...!
WHAT'S WRONG, INORI?
PRIESTESS ...!

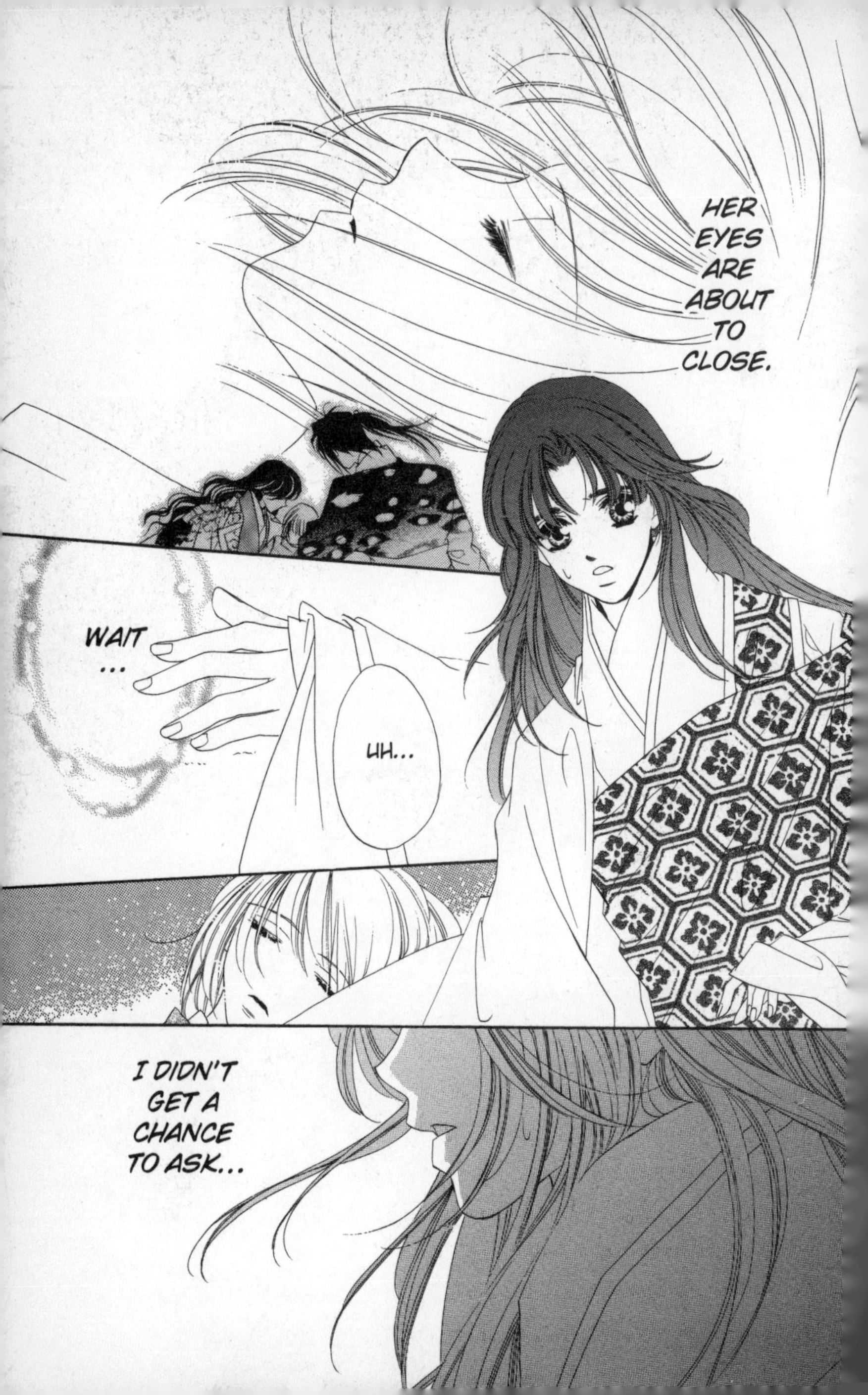
HER EYES ARE ABOUT TO CLOSE.
UH...
WAIT ...
I DIDN'T GET A CHANCE TO ASK...

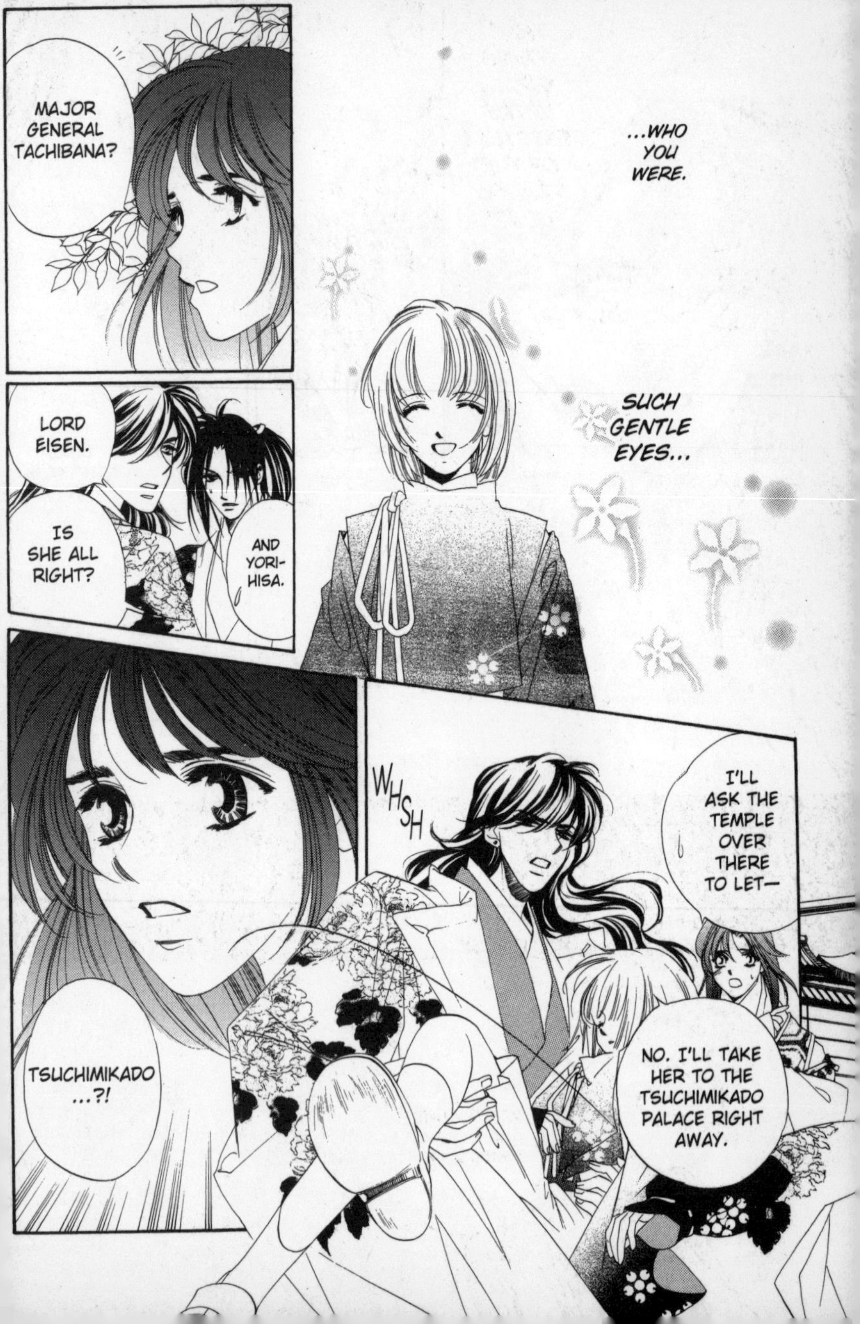
...WHO YOU WERE.
SUCH GENTLE EYES...
MAJOR GENERAL TACHIBANA?
LORD EISEN.
AND YORIHISA.
IS SHE ALL RIGHT?
WHSH
I'LL ASK THE TEMPLE OVER THERE TO LET—
NO. I'LL TAKE HER TO THE TSUCHIMIKADO PALACE RIGHT AWAY.
TSUCHIMIKADO ...?!

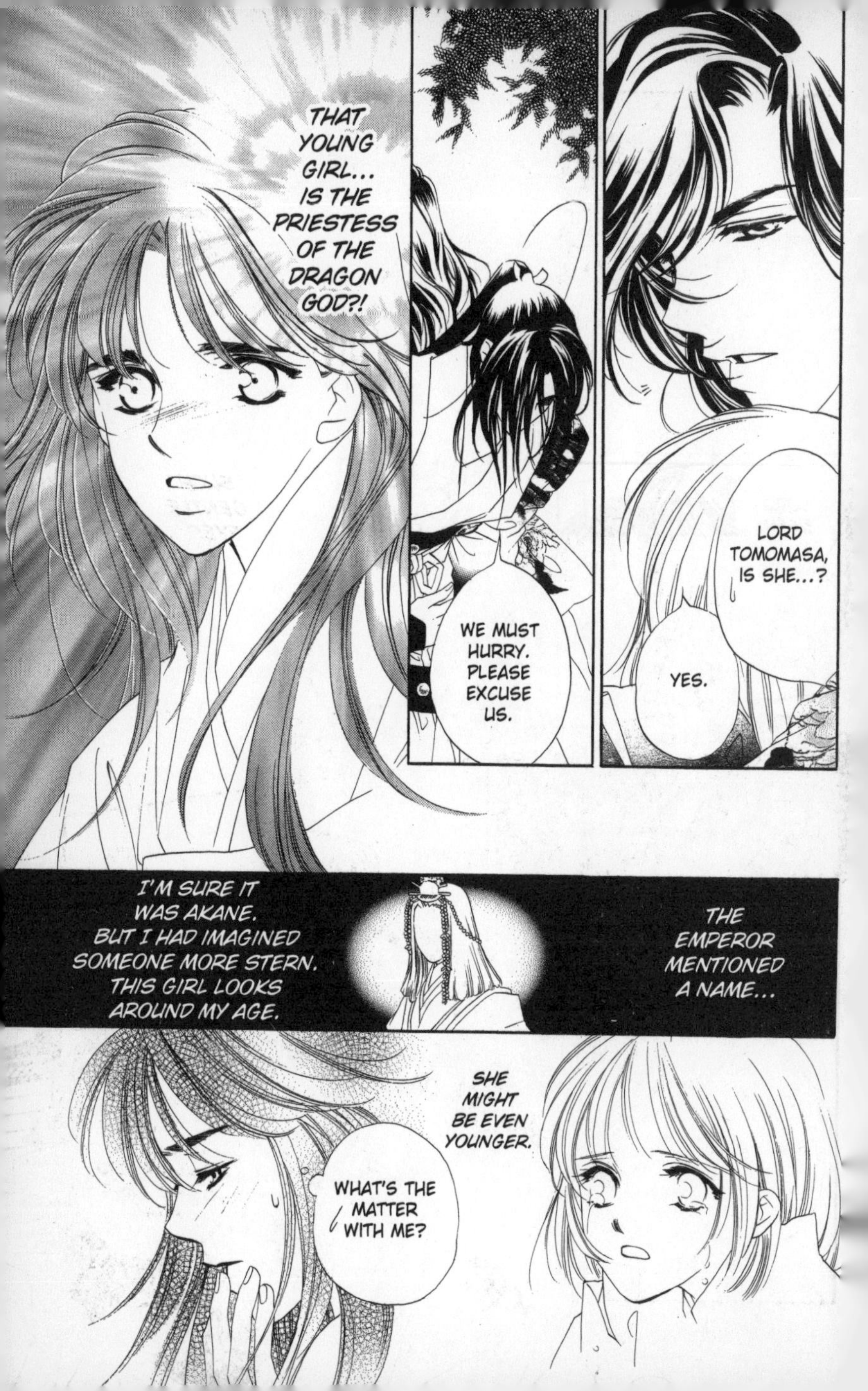
LORD TOMOMASA, IS SHE...?
YES.
WE MUST HURRY. PLEASE EXCUSE US.
THAT YOUNG GIRL... IS THE PRIESTESS OF THE DRAGON GOD?!
THE EMPEROR MENTIONED A NAME...
I'M SURE IT WAS AKANE. BUT I HAD IMAGINED SOMEONE MORE STERN. THIS GIRL LOOKS AROUND MY AGE.
SHE MIGHT BE EVEN YOUNGER.
WHAT'S THE MATTER WITH ME?

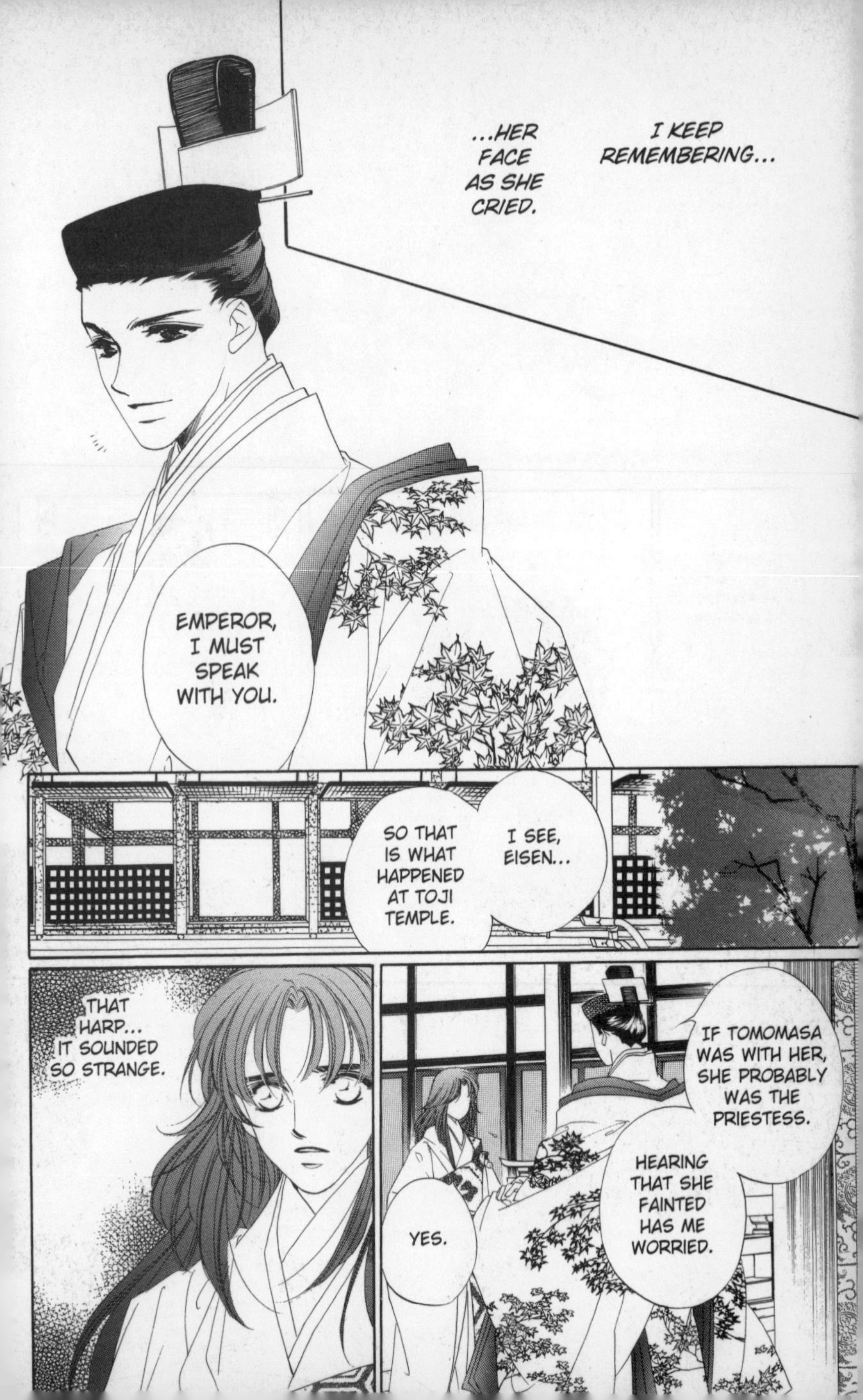
I KEEP REMEMBERING...
...HER FACE AS SHE CRIED.
EMPEROR, I MUST SPEAK WITH YOU.
I SEE, EISEN...
SO THAT IS WHAT HAPPENED AT TOJI TEMPLE.
IF TOMOMASA WAS WITH HER, SHE PROBABLY WAS THE PRIESTESS.
HEARING THAT SHE FAINTED HAS ME WORRIED.
YES.
THAT HARP... IT SOUNDED SO STRANGE.

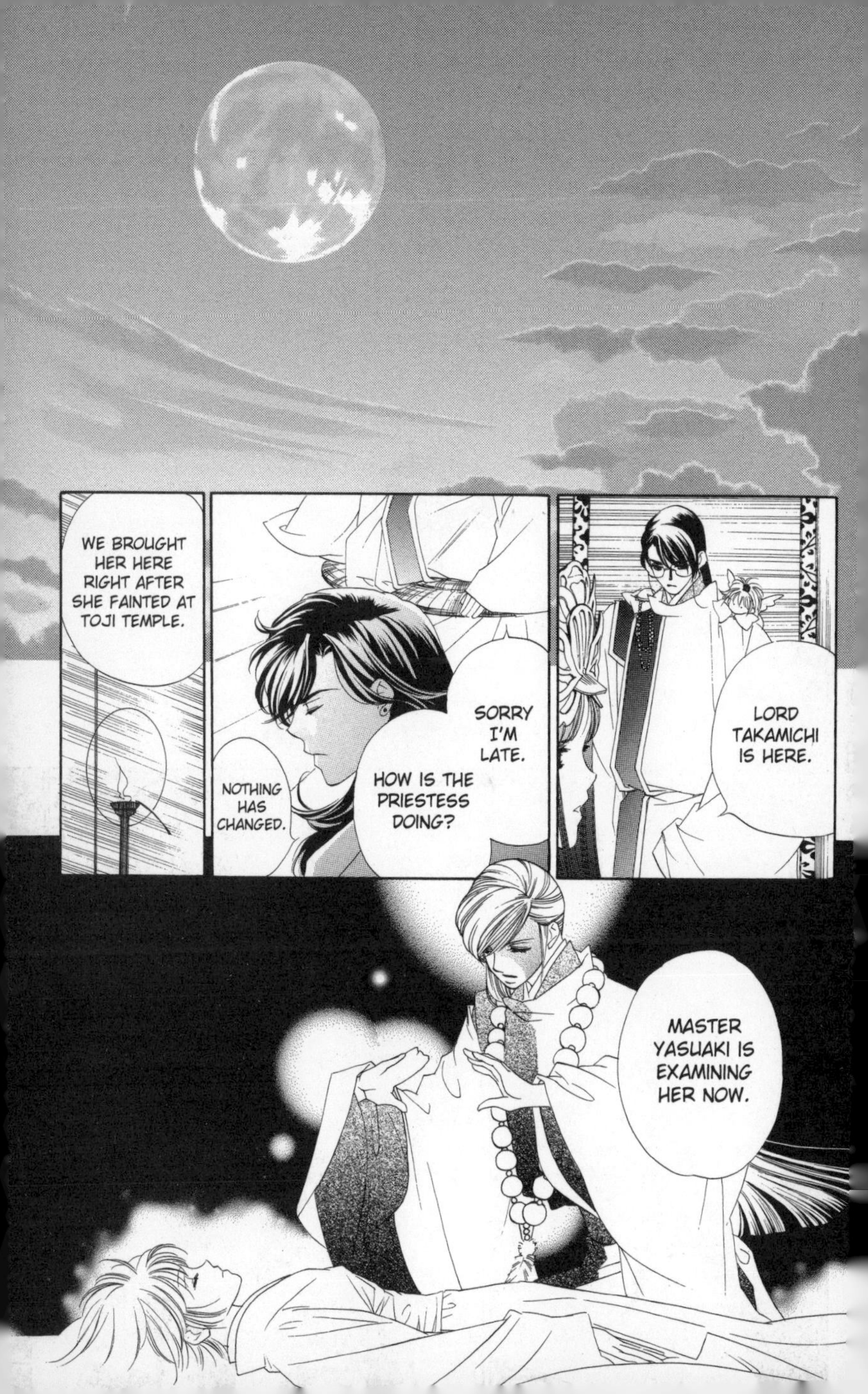
LORD TAKAMICHI IS HERE.
SORRY I'M LATE.
HOW IS THE PRIESTESS DOING?
NOTHING HAS CHANGED.
WE BROUGHT HER HERE RIGHT AFTER SHE FAINTED AT TOJI TEMPLE.
MASTER YASUAKI IS EXAMINING HER NOW.

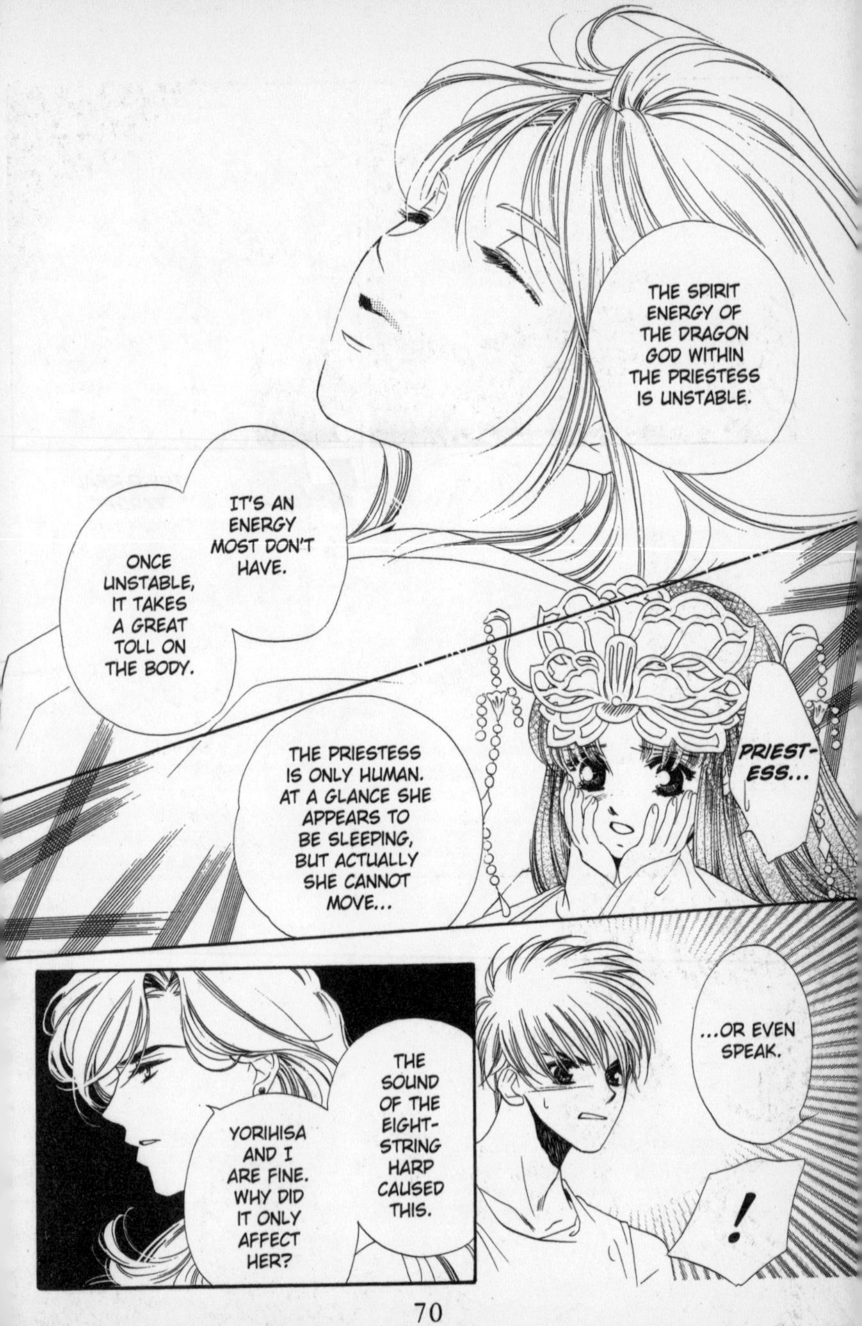
THE SPIRIT ENERGY OF THE DRAGON GOD WITHIN THE PRIESTESS IS UNSTABLE.
IT'S AN ENERGY MOST DON'T HAVE.
ONCE UNSTABLE, IT TAKES A GREAT TOLL ON THE BODY.
PRIEST-ESS...
THE PRIESTESS IS ONLY HUMAN. AT A GLANCE SHE APPEARS TO BE SLEEPING, BUT ACTUALLY SHE CANNOT MOVE...
...OR EVEN SPEAK.
!
THE SOUND OF THE EIGHT-STRING HARP CAUSED THIS.
YORIHISA AND I ARE FINE. WHY DID IT ONLY AFFECT HER?

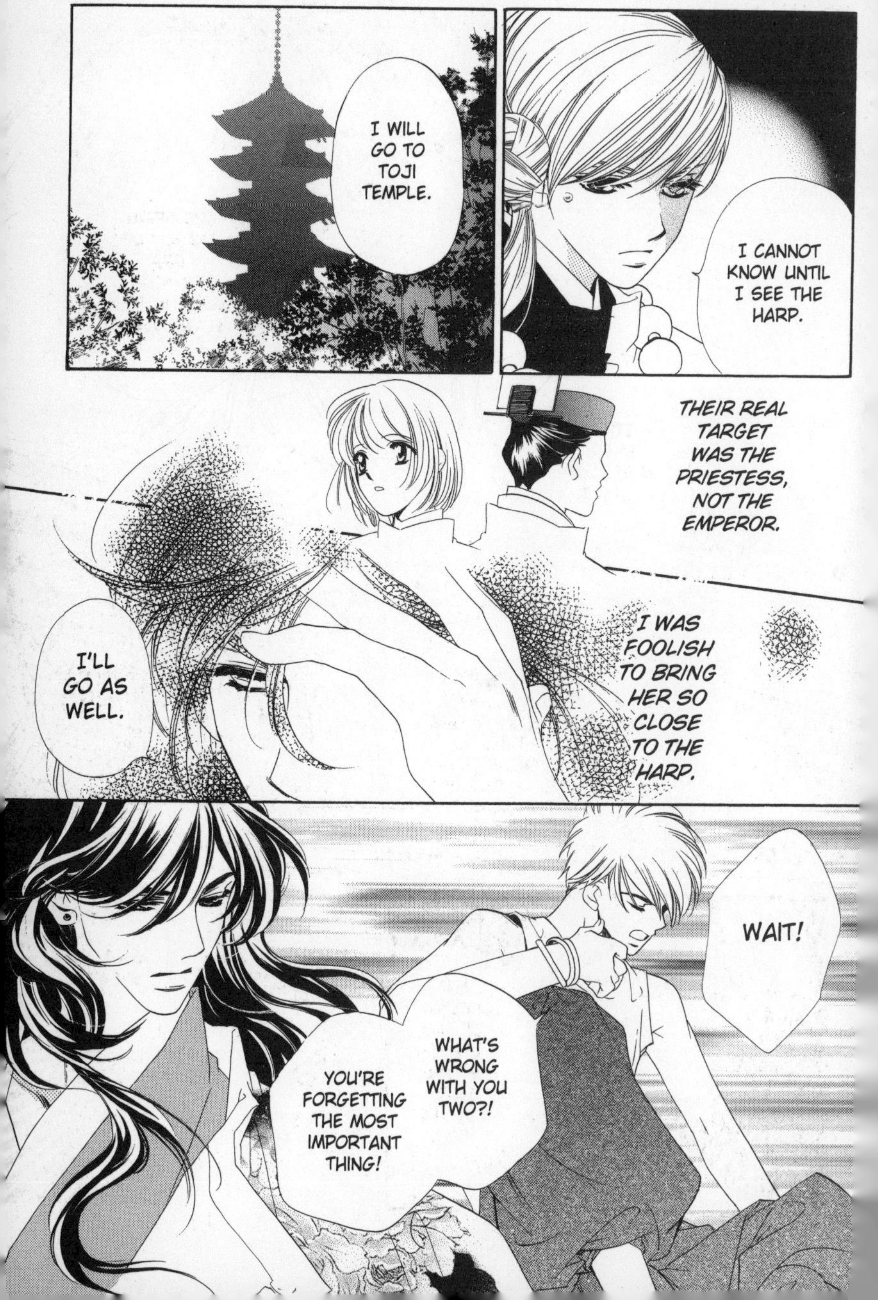
I CANNOT KNOW UNTIL I SEE THE HARP.
I WILL GO TO TOJI TEMPLE.
THEIR REAL TARGET WAS THE PRIESTESS, NOT THE EMPEROR.
I WAS FOOLISH TO BRING HER SO CLOSE TO THE HARP.
I'LL GO AS WELL.
WAIT!
WHAT'S WRONG WITH YOU TWO?!
YOU'RE FORGETTING THE MOST IMPORTANT THING!

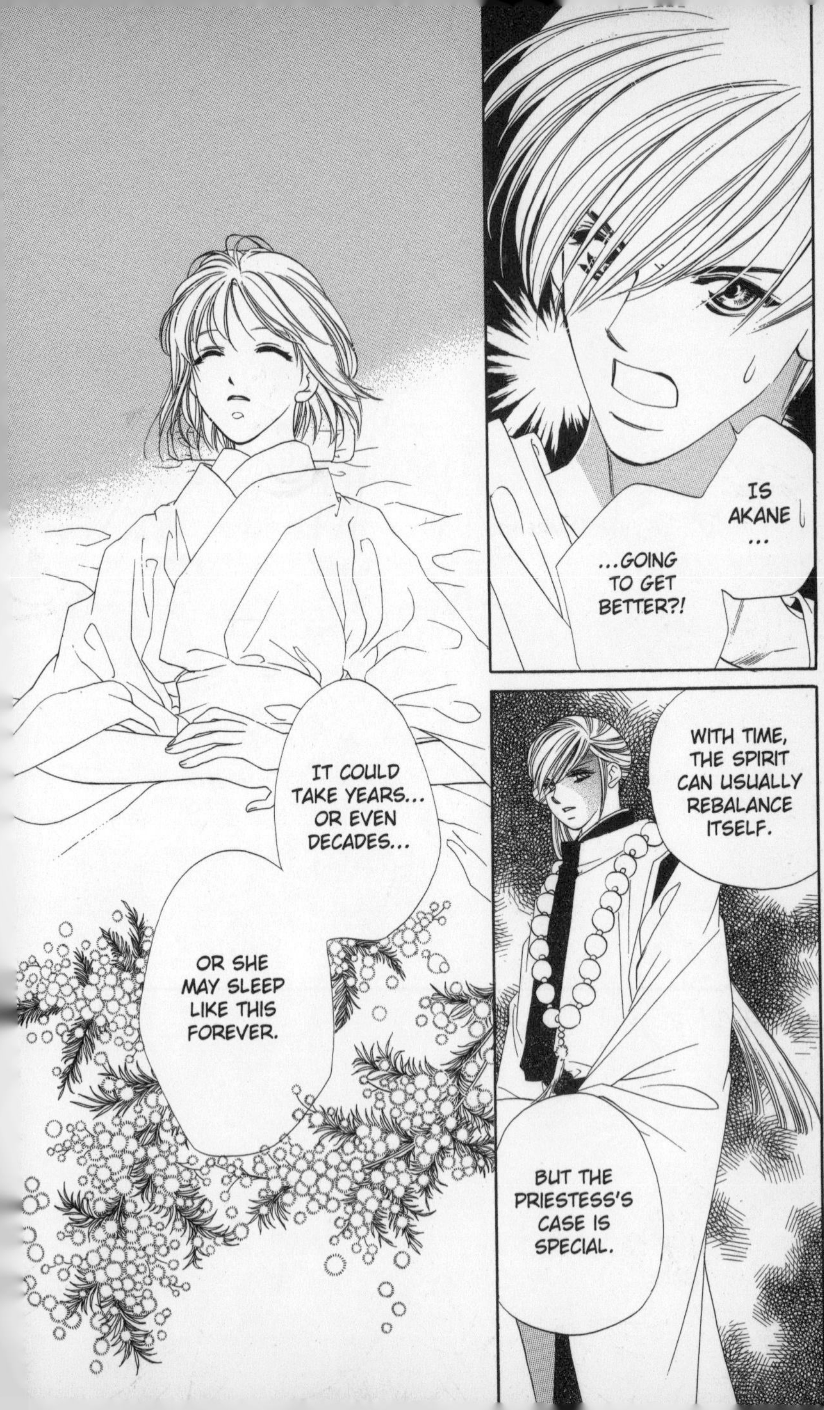
IS AKANE ...
...GOING TO GET BETTER?!
WITH TIME, THE SPIRIT CAN USUALLY REBALANCE ITSELF.
BUT THE PRIESTESS'S CASE IS SPECIAL.
IT COULD TAKE YEARS... OR EVEN DECADES...
OR SHE MAY SLEEP LIKE THIS FOREVER.

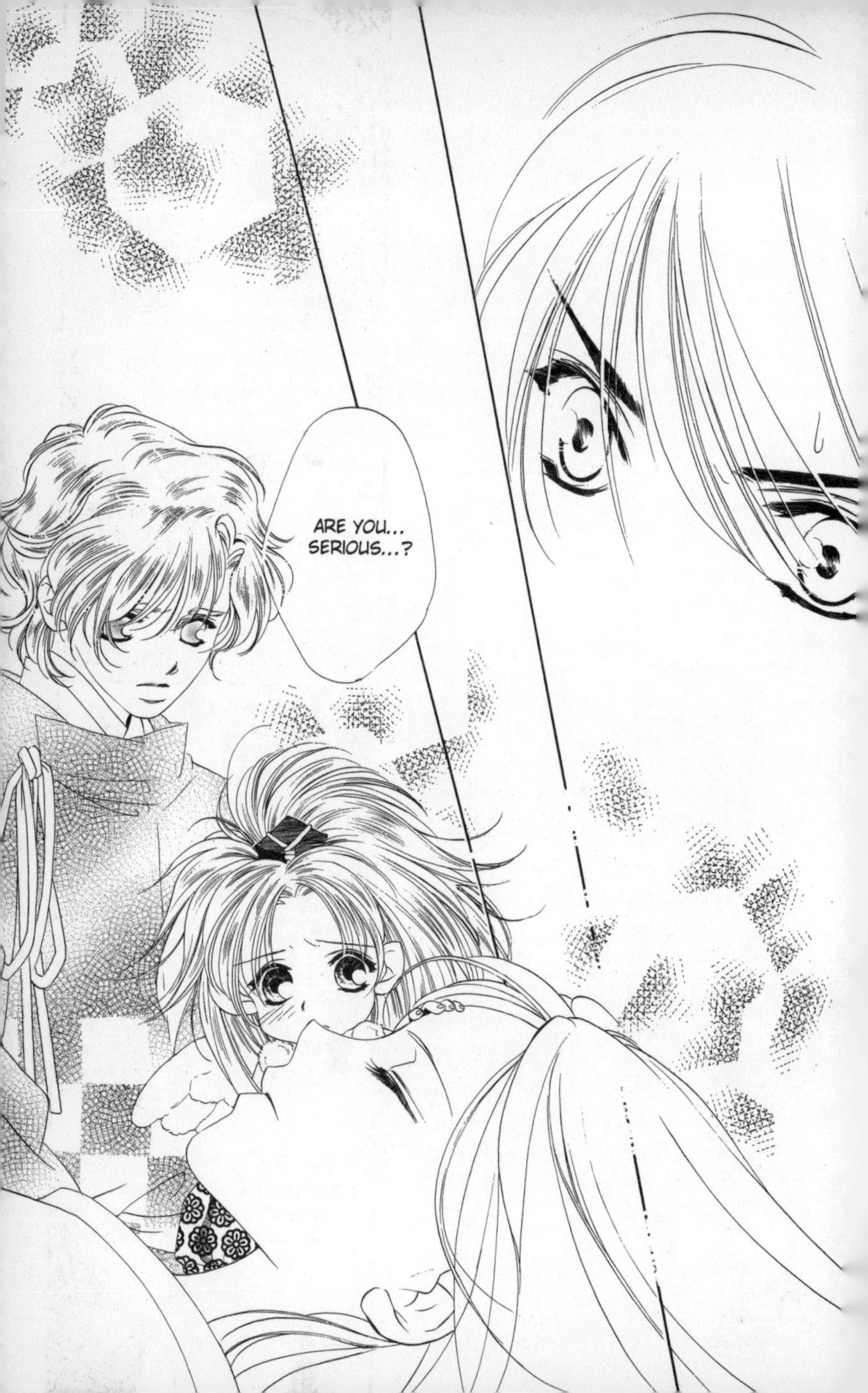
ARE YOU... SERIOUS...?

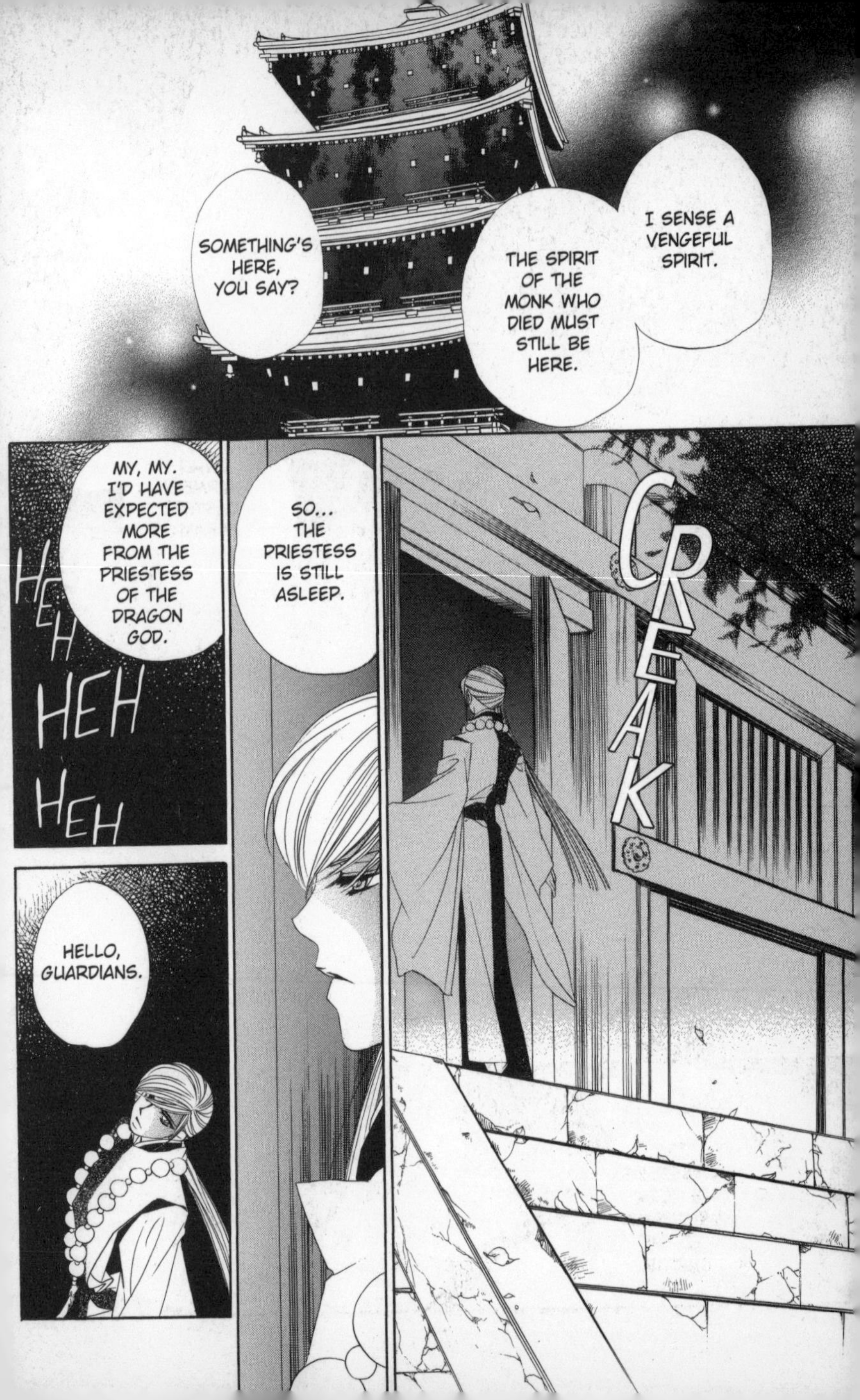
I SENSE A VENGEFUL SPIRIT.
THE SPIRIT OF THE MONK WHO DIED MUST STILL BE HERE.
SOMETHING'S HERE, YOU SAY?
CREAK
SO... THE PRIESTESS IS STILL ASLEEP.
MY, MY. I'D HAVE EXPECTED MORE FROM THE PRIESTESS OF THE DRAGON GOD.
HEH HEH HEH
HELLO, GUARDIANS.

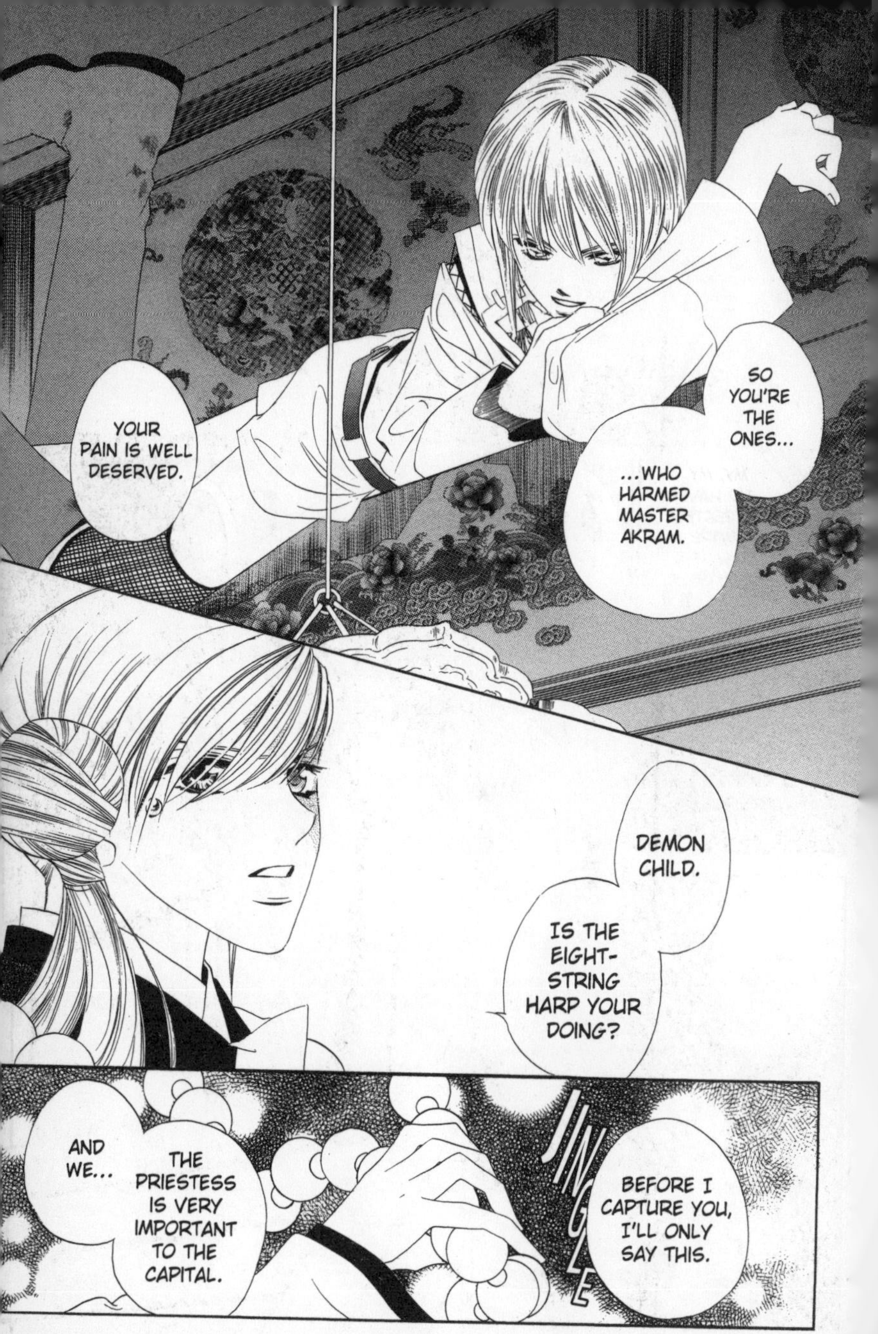
SO YOU'RE THE ONES...
...WHO HARMED MASTER AKRAM.
YOUR PAIN IS WELL DESERVED.
DEMON CHILD.
IS THE EIGHT-STRING HARP YOUR DOING?
BEFORE I CAPTURE YOU, I'LL ONLY SAY THIS.
JINGLE
THE PRIESTESS IS VERY IMPORTANT TO THE CAPITAL.
AND WE...

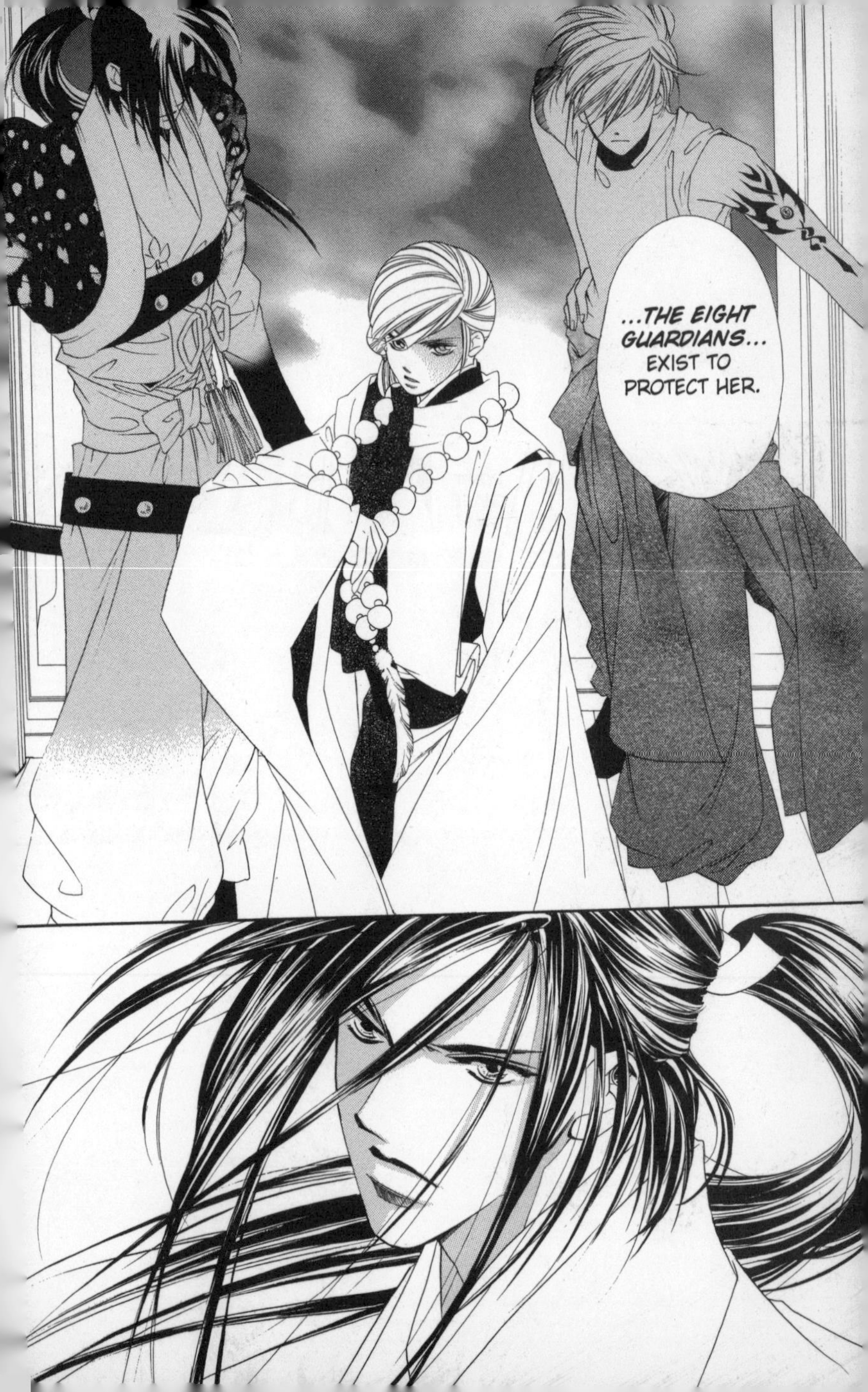
...THE EIGHT GUARDIANS... EXIST TO PROTECT HER.

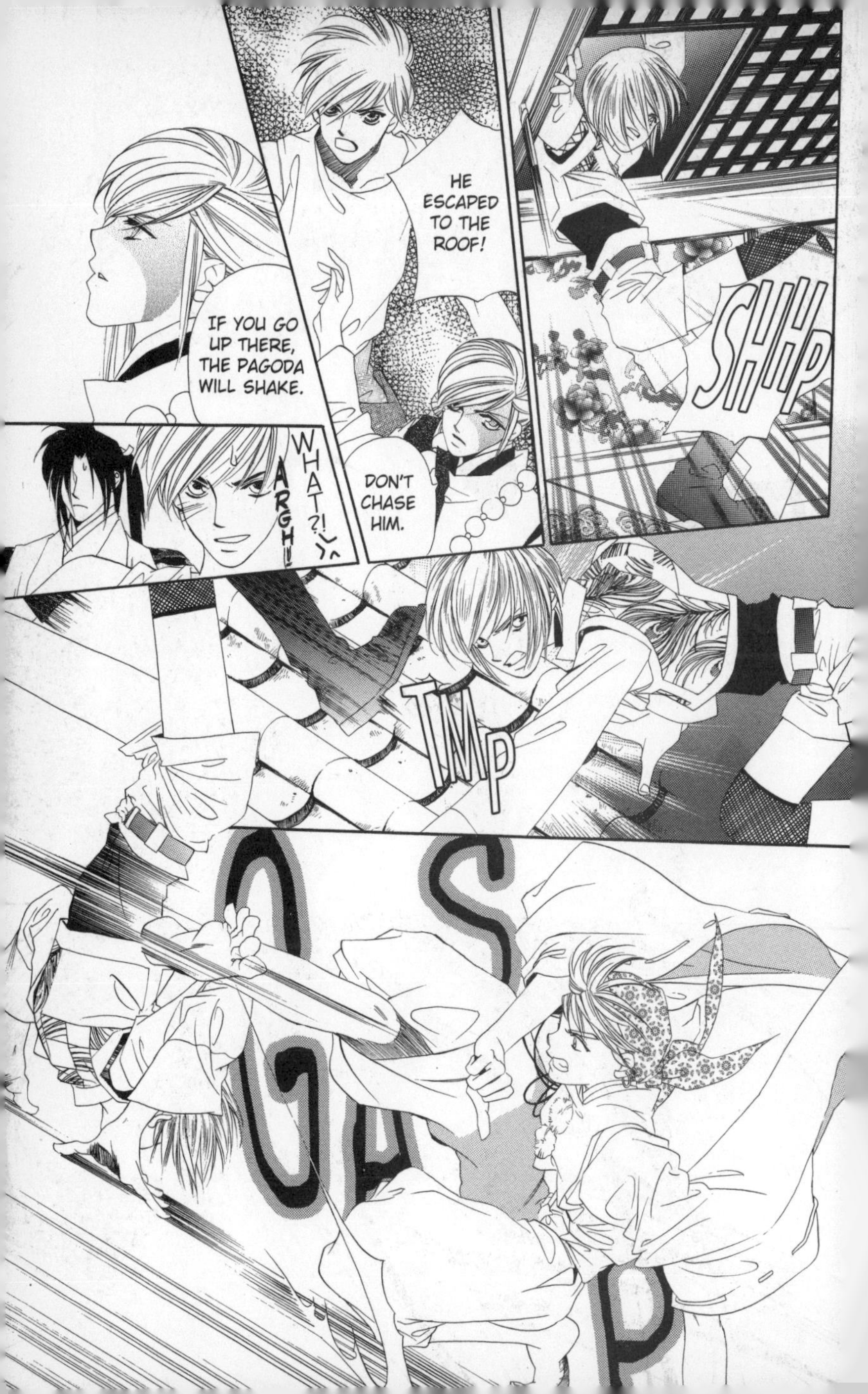
SHHP
HE ESCAPED TO THE ROOF!
DON'T CHASE HIM.
IF YOU GO UP THERE, THE PAGODA WILL SHAKE.
WHAT?!
ARGH!
TMP

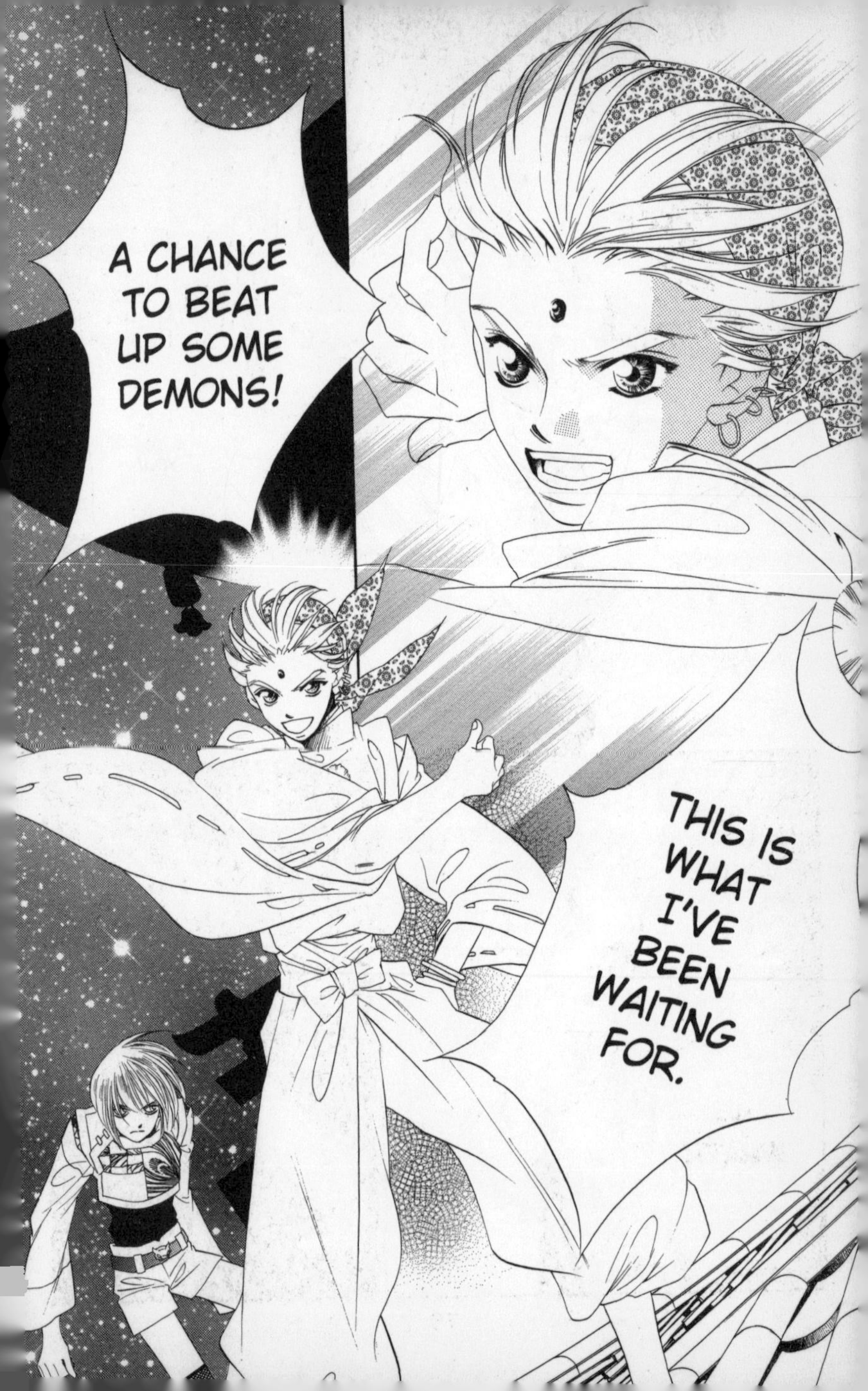
A CHANCE TO BEAT UP SOME DEMONS!
THIS IS WHAT I'VE BEEN WAITING FOR.

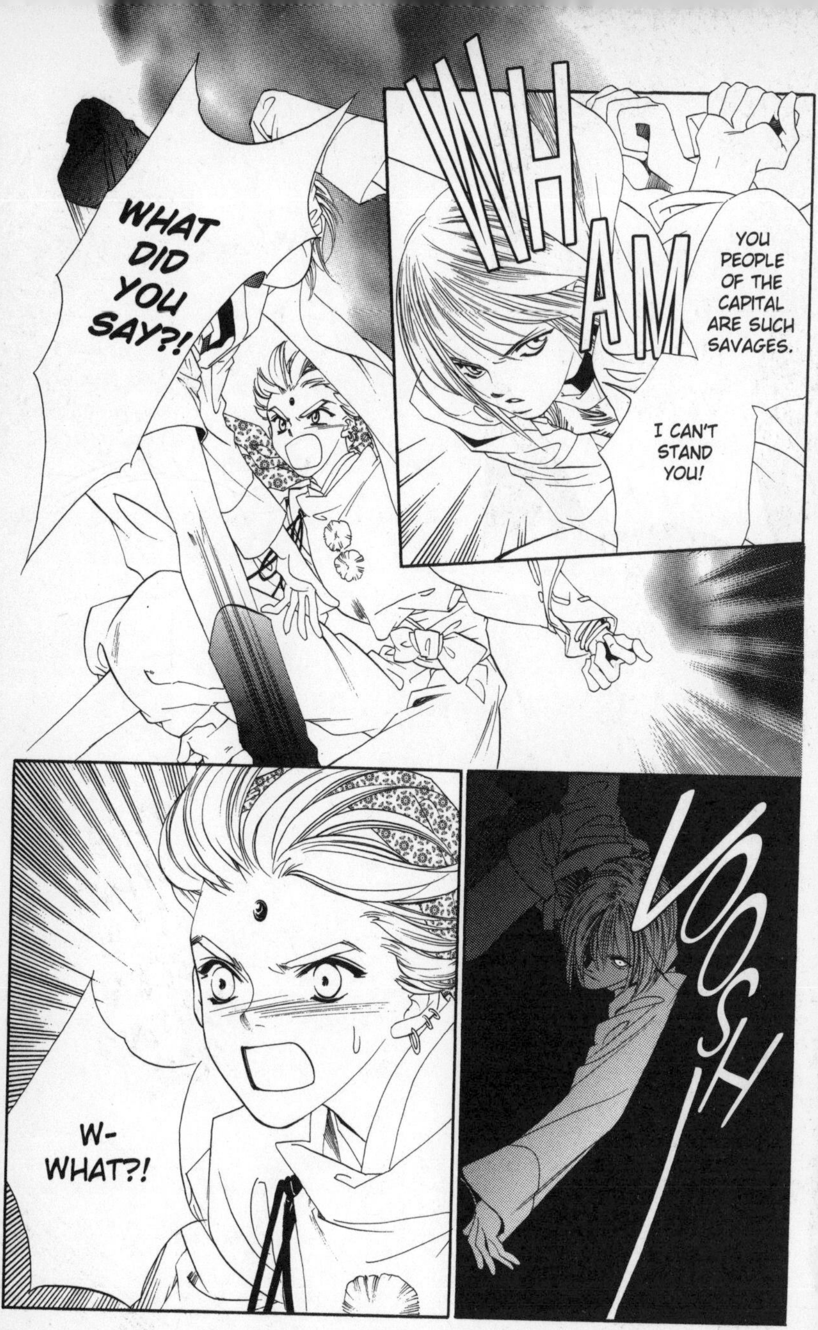
WHAM
YOU PEOPLE OF THE CAPITAL ARE SUCH SAVAGES.
I CAN'T STAND YOU!
WHAT DID YOU SAY?!
VOOSH
W-WHAT?!

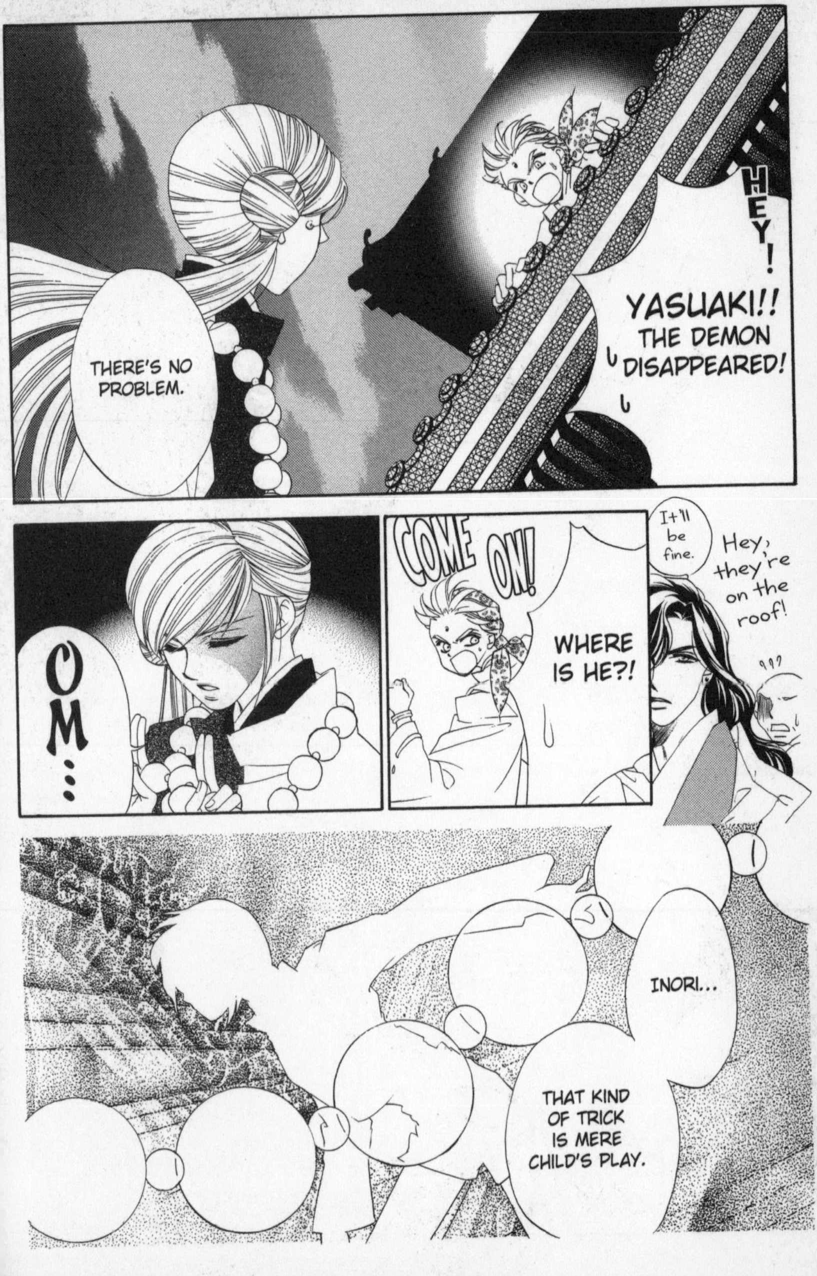
HEY!
YASUAKI!! THE DEMON DISAPPEARED!
THERE'S NO PROBLEM.
Hey, they're on the roof!
It'll be fine.
COME ON!
WHERE IS HE?!
OM...
INORI...
THAT KIND OF TRICK IS MERE CHILD'S PLAY.

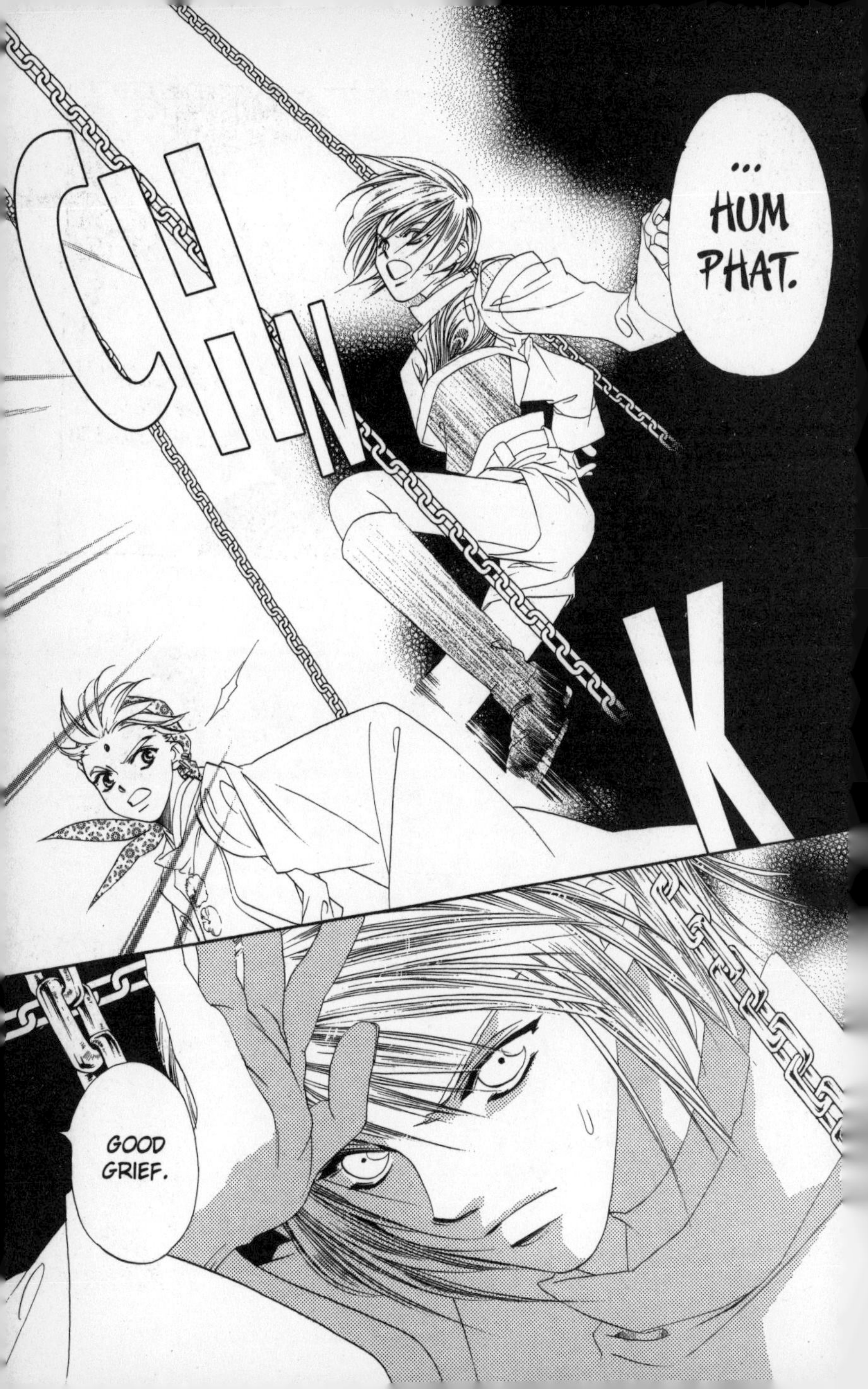
... HUM PHAT.
CHINK
GOOD GRIEF.

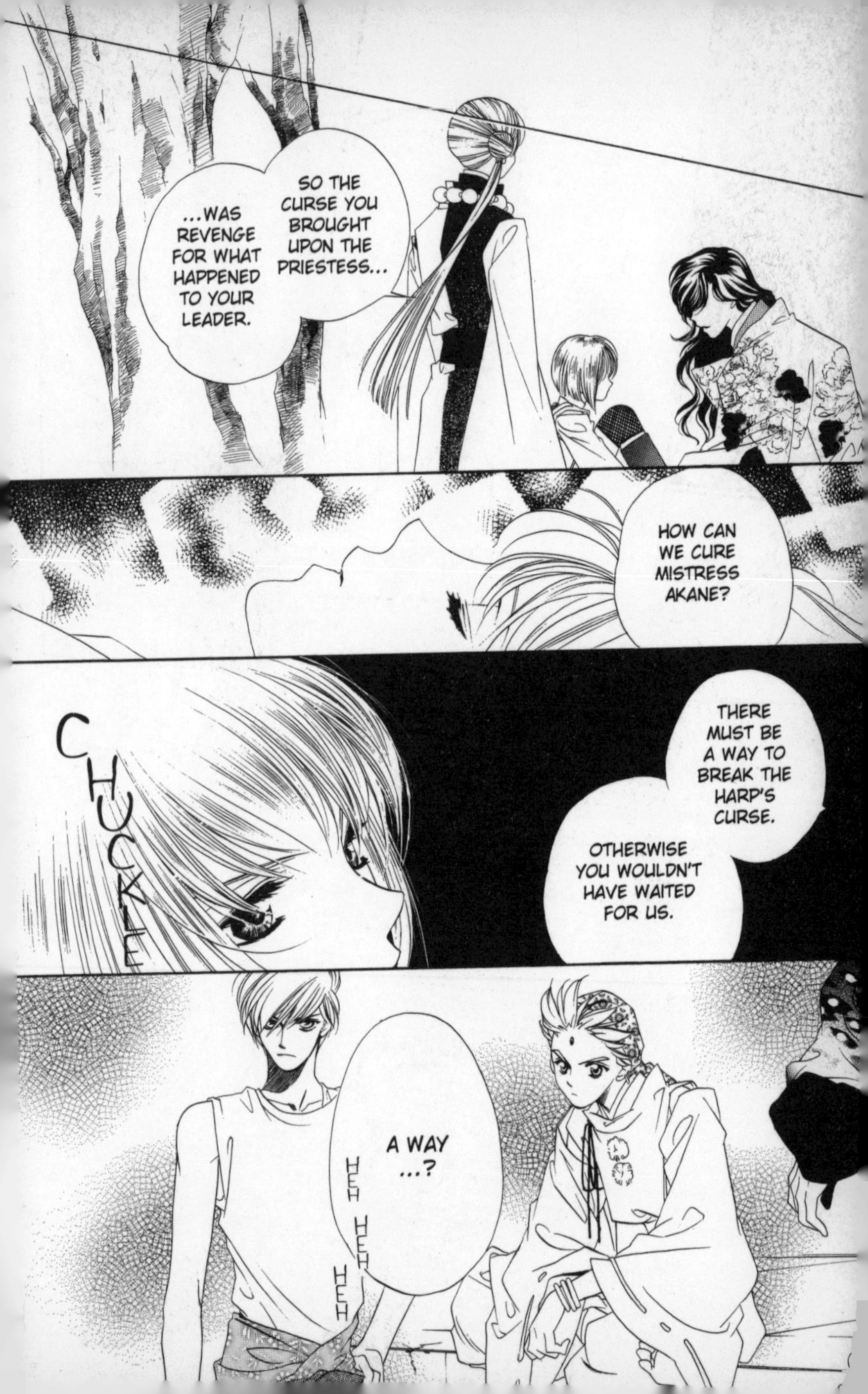
SO THE CURSE YOU BROUGHT UPON THE PRIESTESS...
...WAS REVENGE FOR WHAT HAPPENED TO YOUR LEADER.
HOW CAN WE CURE MISTRESS AKANE?
THERE MUST BE A WAY TO BREAK THE HARP'S CURSE.
OTHERWISE YOU WOULDN'T HAVE WAITED FOR US.
CHUCKLE
A WAY ...?
HEH HEH HEH

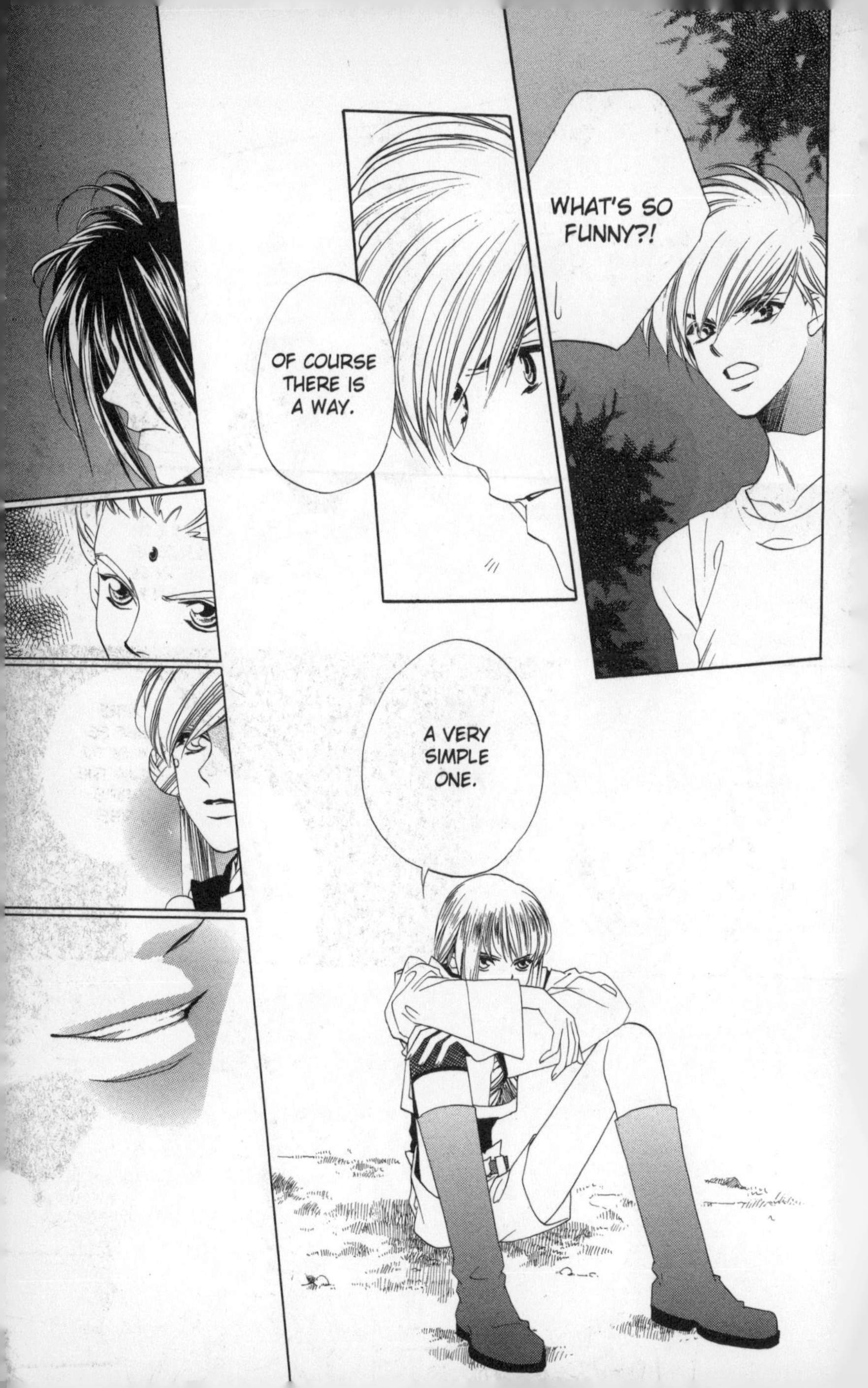
WHAT'S SO FUNNY?!
OF COURSE THERE IS A WAY.
A VERY SIMPLE ONE.

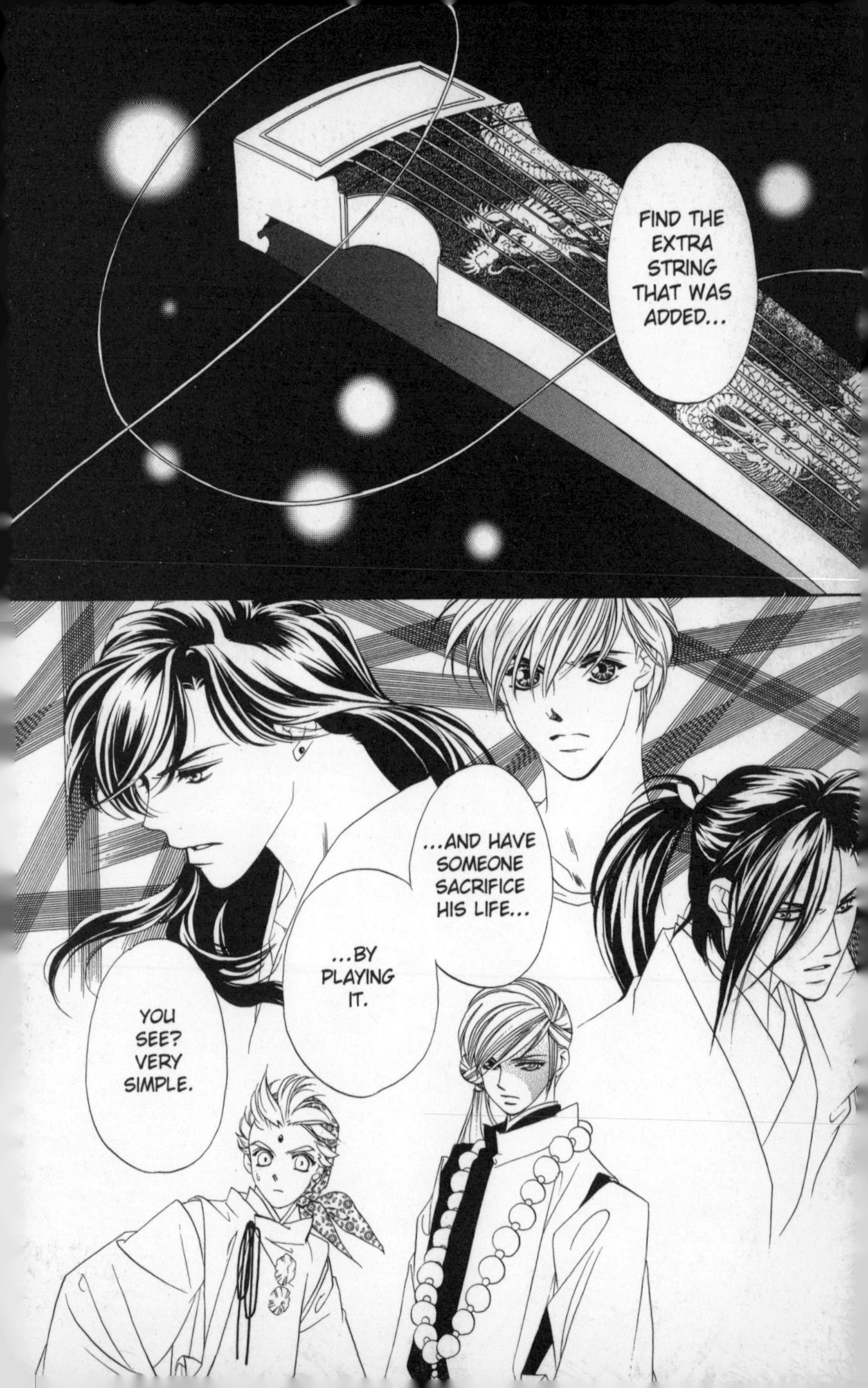
FIND THE EXTRA STRING THAT WAS ADDED...
...AND HAVE SOMEONE SACRIFICE HIS LIFE...
...BY PLAYING IT.
YOU SEE? VERY SIMPLE.

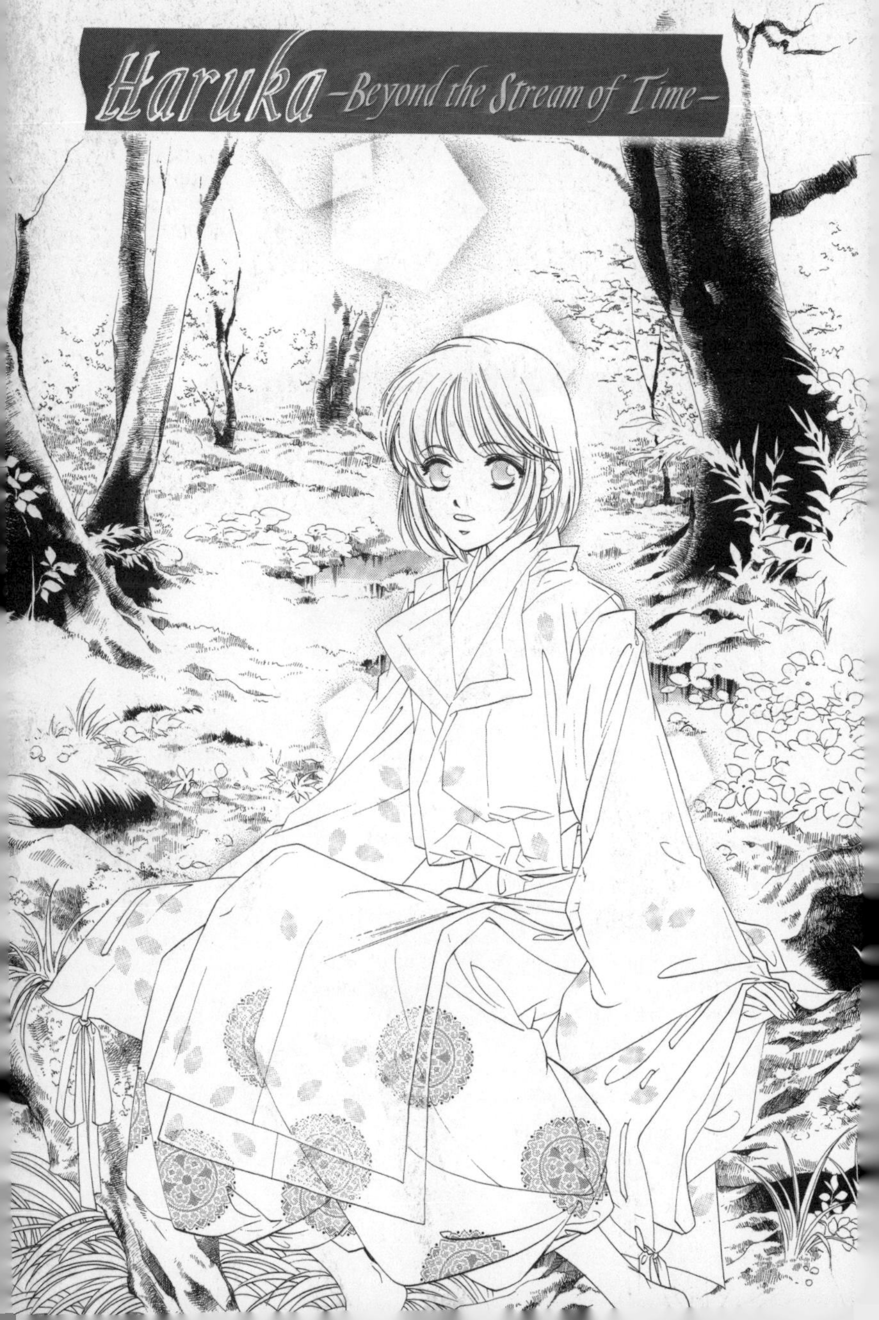
Haruka -Beyond the Stream of Time-

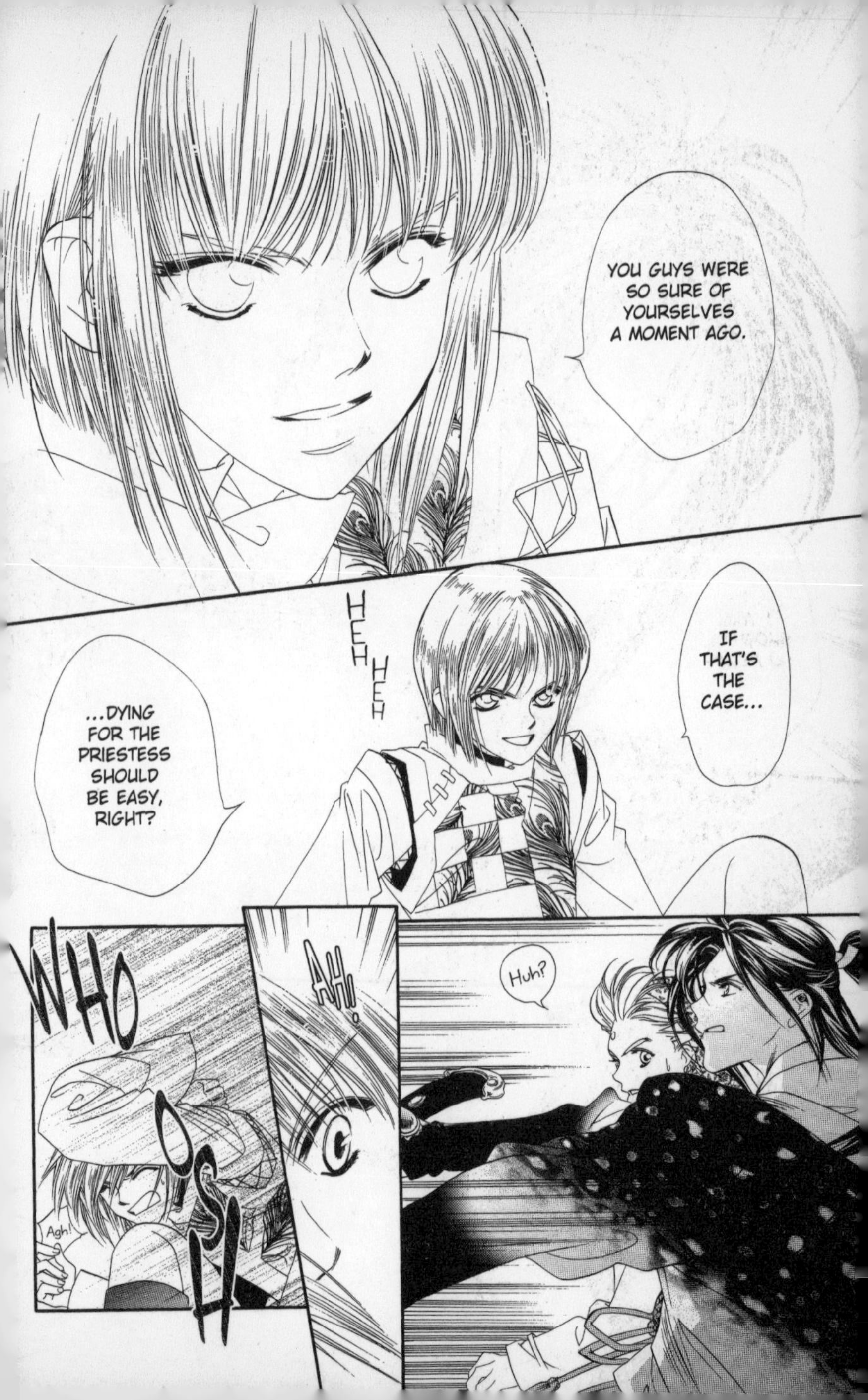
YOU GUYS WERE SO SURE OF YOURSELVES A MOMENT AGO.
IF THAT'S THE CASE...
HEH HEH
...DYING FOR THE PRIESTESS SHOULD BE EASY, RIGHT?
Huh?
AH!
WHOOSH
Agh!

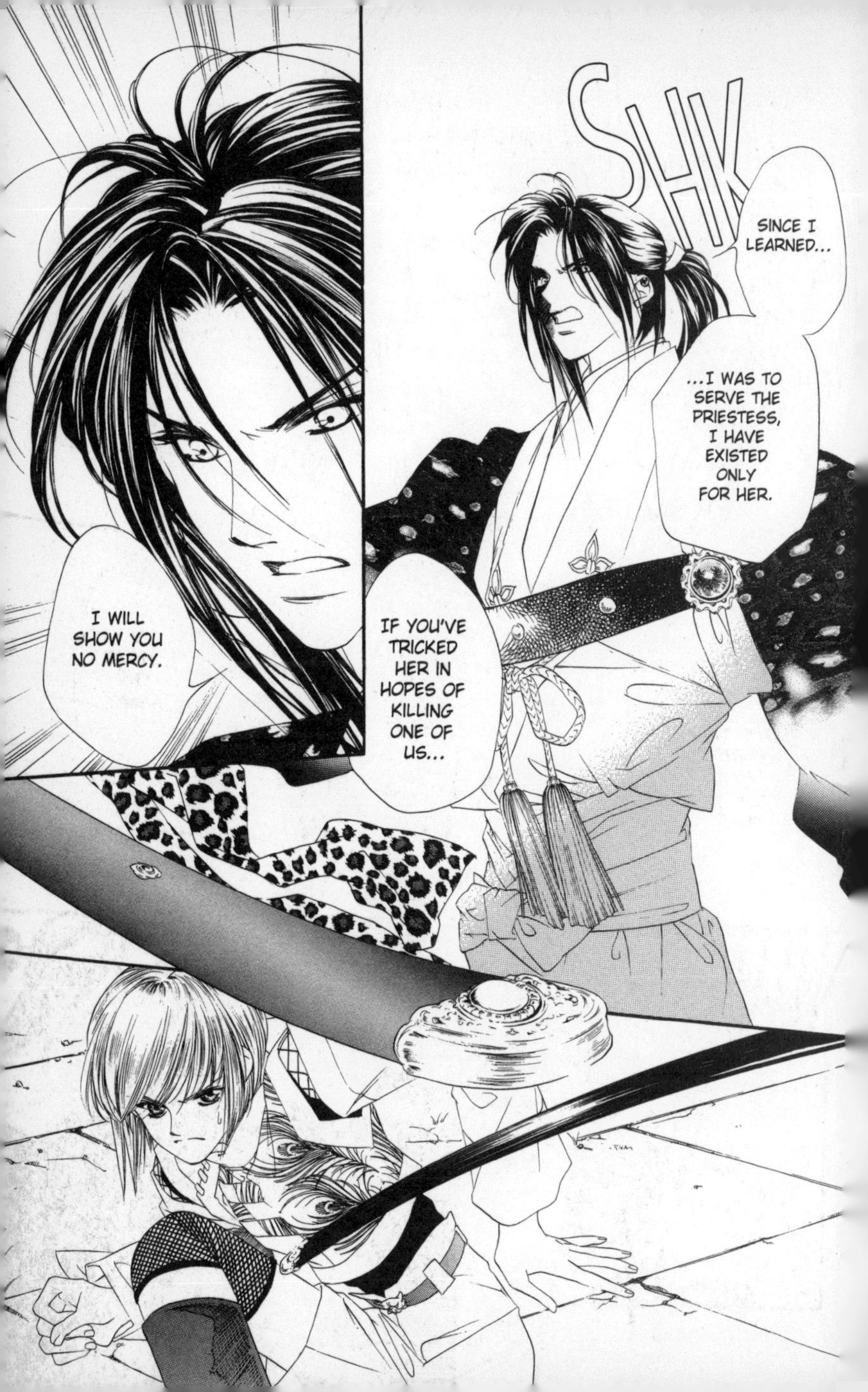
SHK
SINCE I LEARNED...
...I WAS TO SERVE THE PRIESTESS, I HAVE EXISTED ONLY FOR HER.
IF YOU'VE TRICKED HER IN HOPES OF KILLING ONE OF US...
I WILL SHOW YOU NO MERCY.

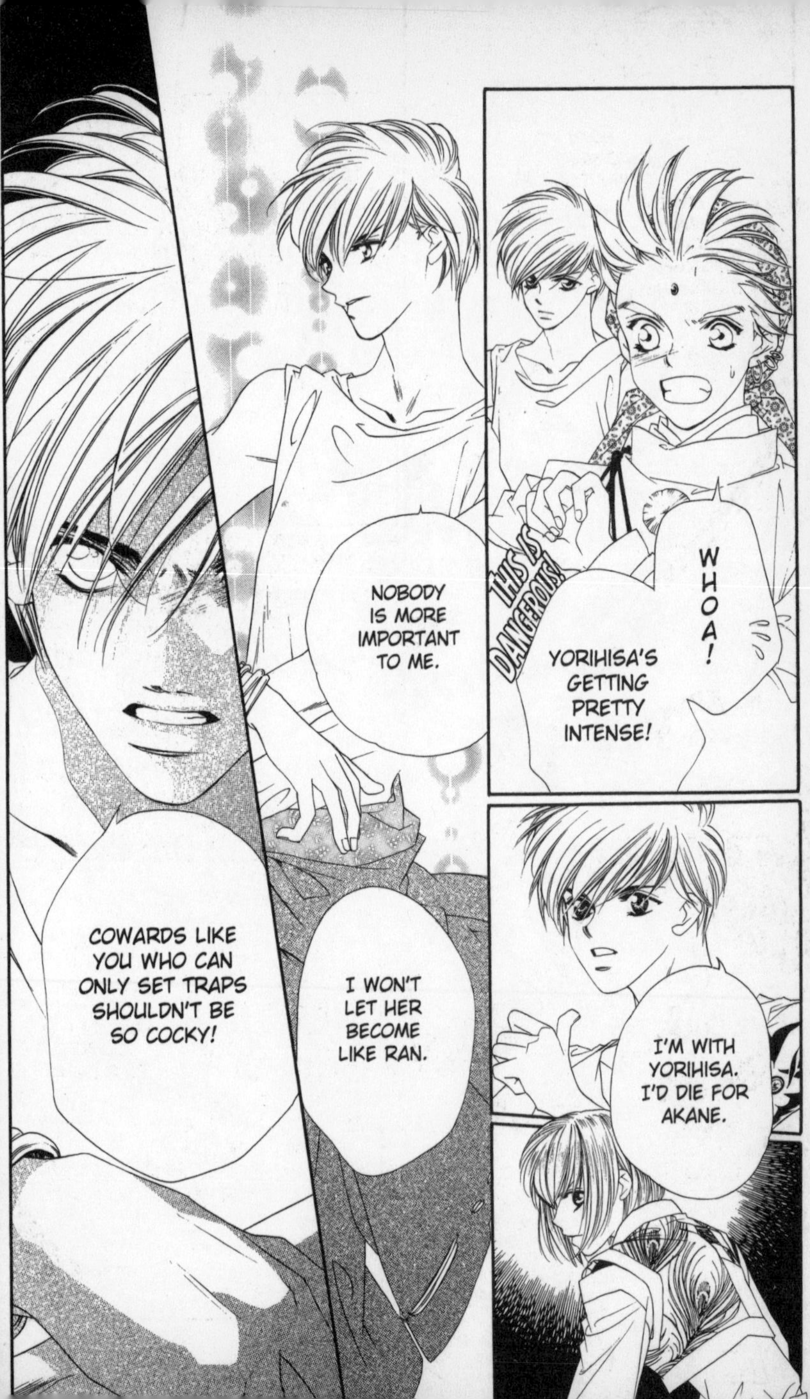
WHOA!
YORIHISA'S GETTING PRETTY INTENSE!
THIS IS DANGEROUS!
I'M WITH YORIHISA. I'D DIE FOR AKANE.
NOBODY IS MORE IMPORTANT TO ME.
I WON'T LET HER BECOME LIKE RAN.
COWARDS LIKE YOU WHO CAN ONLY SET TRAPS SHOULDN'T BE SO COCKY!

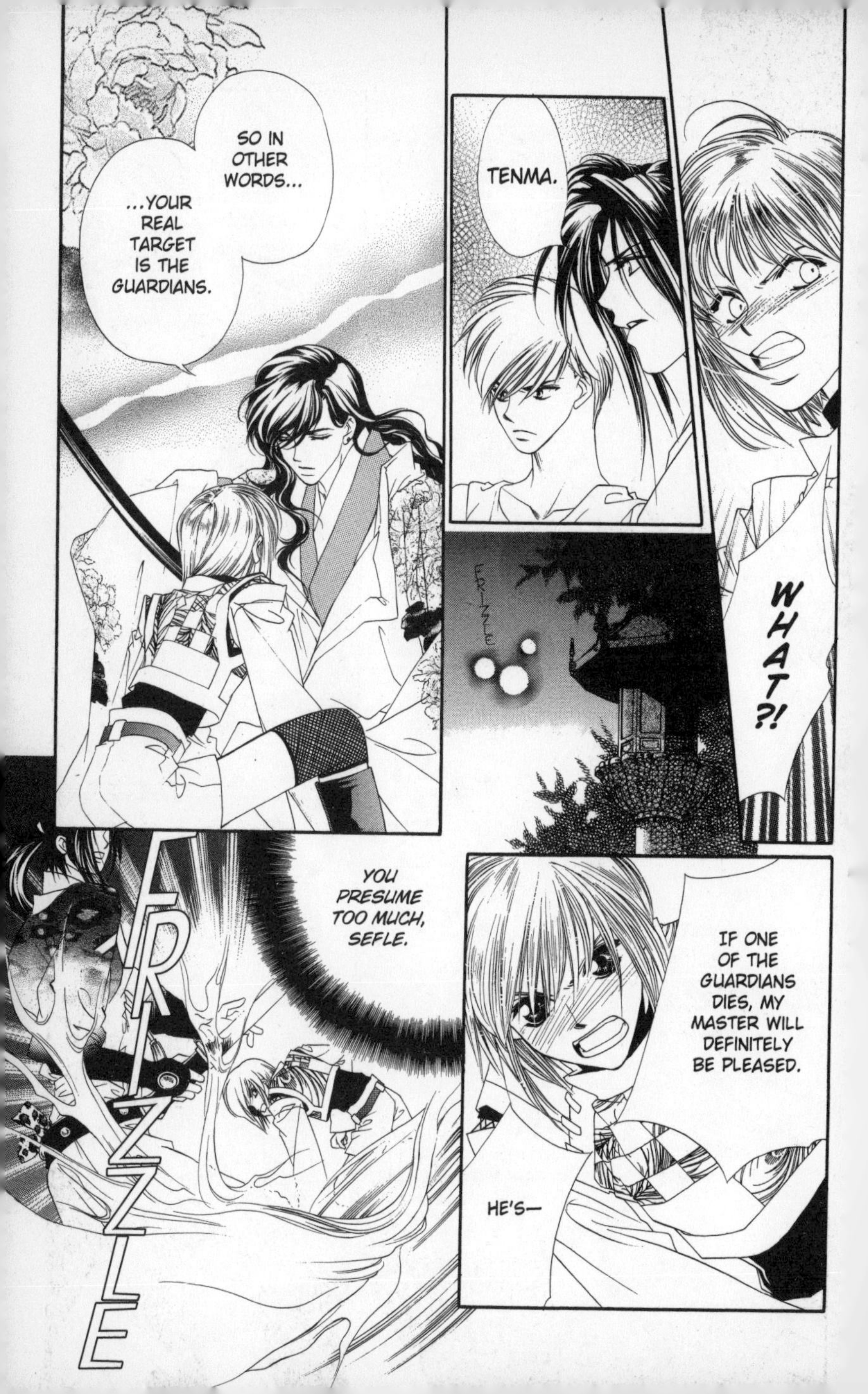
WHAT?!
TENMA.
FRIZZLE
SO IN OTHER WORDS...
...YOUR REAL TARGET IS THE GUARDIANS.
IF ONE OF THE GUARDIANS DIES, MY MASTER WILL DEFINITELY BE PLEASED.
HE'S—
YOU PRESUME TOO MUCH, SEFLE.
FRIZZLE

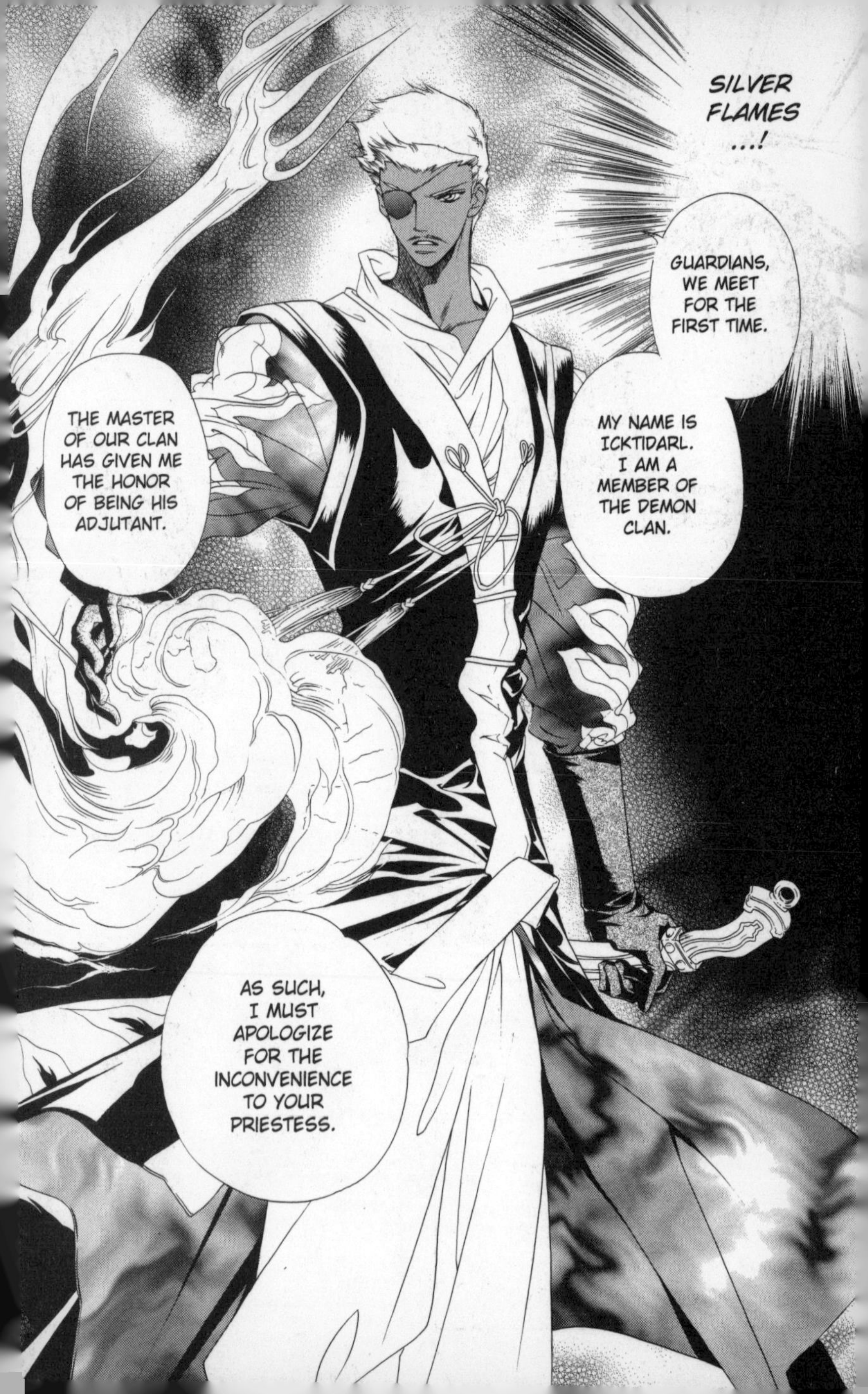
SILVER FLAMES ...!
GUARDIANS, WE MEET FOR THE FIRST TIME.
MY NAME IS ICKTIDARL. I AM A MEMBER OF THE DEMON CLAN.
THE MASTER OF OUR CLAN HAS GIVEN ME THE HONOR OF BEING HIS ADJUTANT.
AS SUCH, I MUST APOLOGIZE FOR THE INCONVENIENCE TO YOUR PRIESTESS.

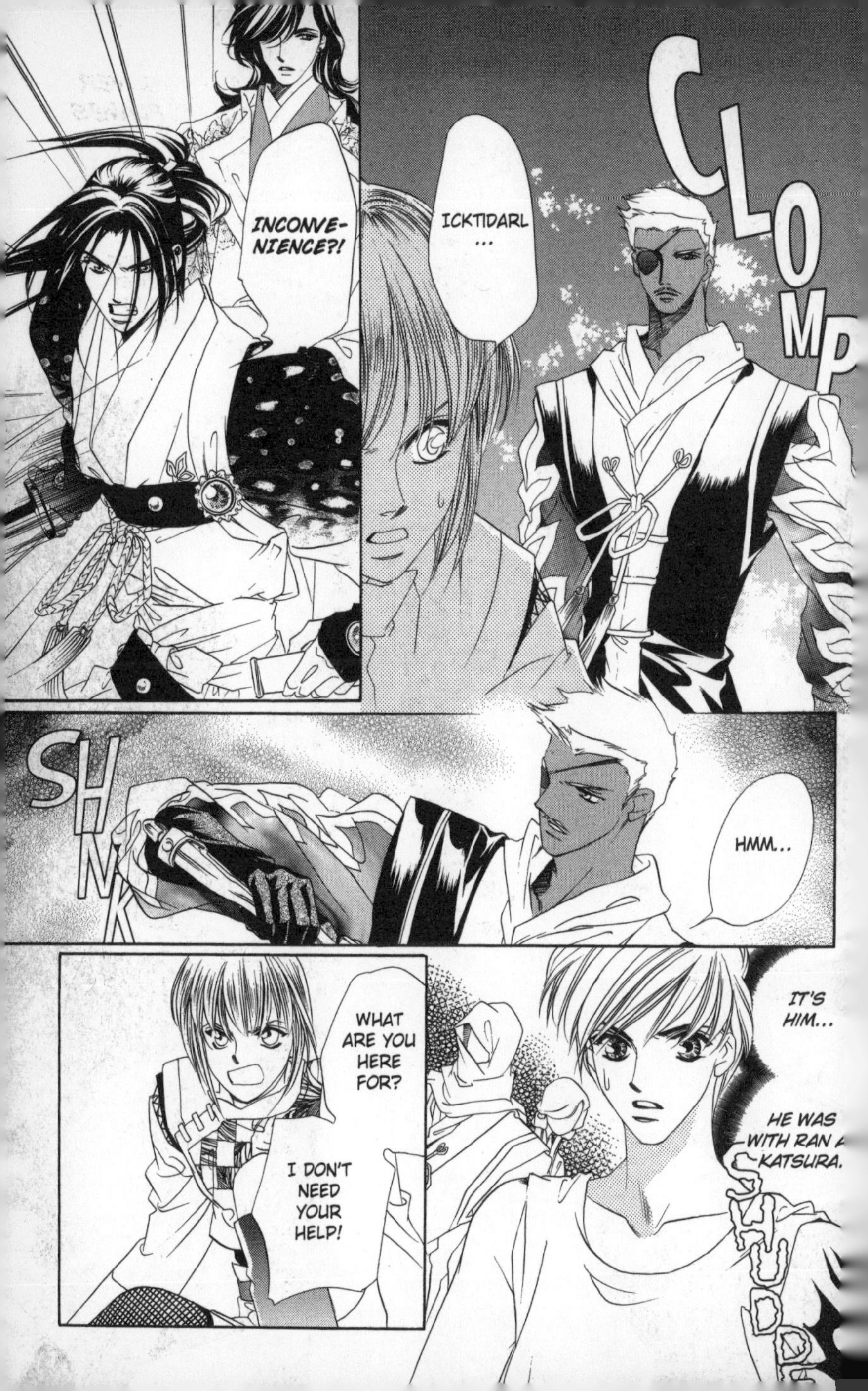
CLOMP
ICKTIDARL ...
INCONVE-NIENCE?!
HMM...
SHNK
IT'S HIM...
HE WAS WITH RAN AND KATSURA.
SHUDDER
WHAT ARE YOU HERE FOR?
I DON'T NEED YOUR HELP!

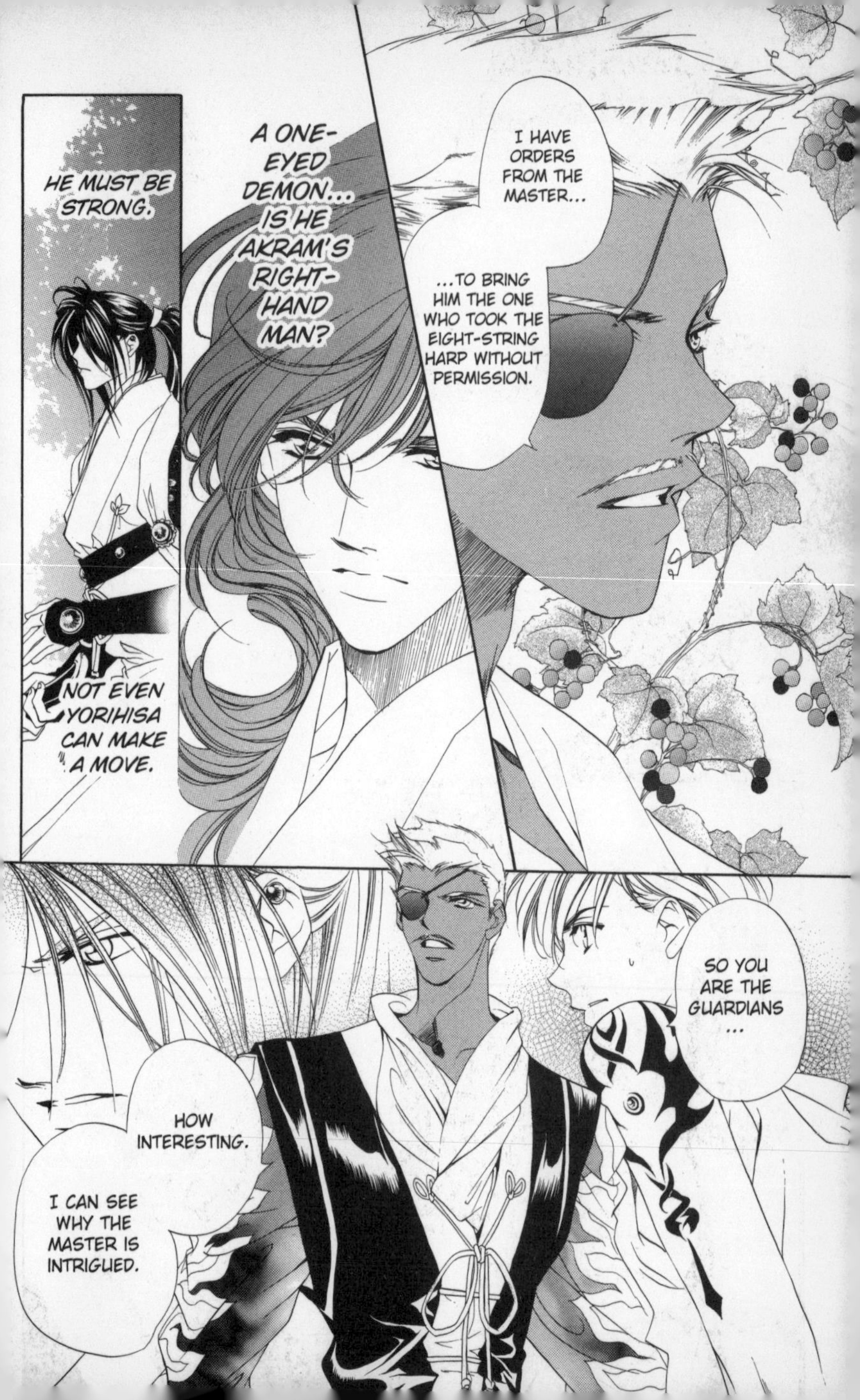
I HAVE ORDERS FROM THE MASTER...
...TO BRING HIM THE ONE WHO TOOK THE EIGHT-STRING HARP WITHOUT PERMISSION.
A ONE-EYED DEMON... IS HE AKRAM'S RIGHT-HAND MAN?
HE MUST BE STRONG.
NOT EVEN YORIHISA CAN MAKE A MOVE.
SO YOU ARE THE GUARDIANS...
HOW INTERESTING.
I CAN SEE WHY THE MASTER IS INTRIGUED.

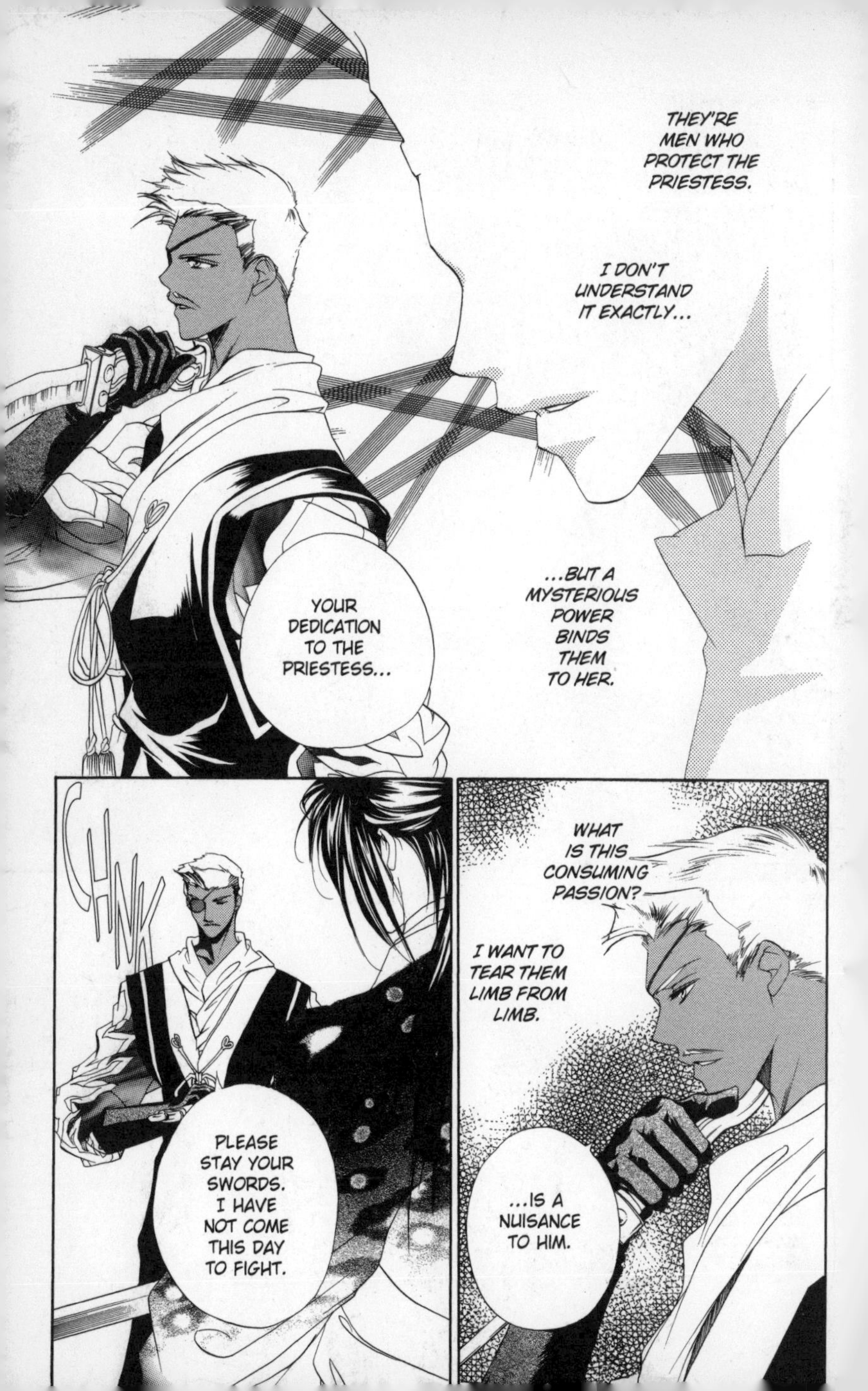
THEY'RE MEN WHO PROTECT THE PRIESTESS.
I DON'T UNDERSTAND IT EXACTLY...
...BUT A MYSTERIOUS POWER BINDS THEM TO HER.
YOUR DEDICATION TO THE PRIESTESS...
WHAT IS THIS CONSUMING PASSION?
I WANT TO TEAR THEM LIMB FROM LIMB.
...IS A NUISANCE TO HIM.
CHNK
PLEASE STAY YOUR SWORDS. I HAVE NOT COME THIS DAY TO FIGHT.

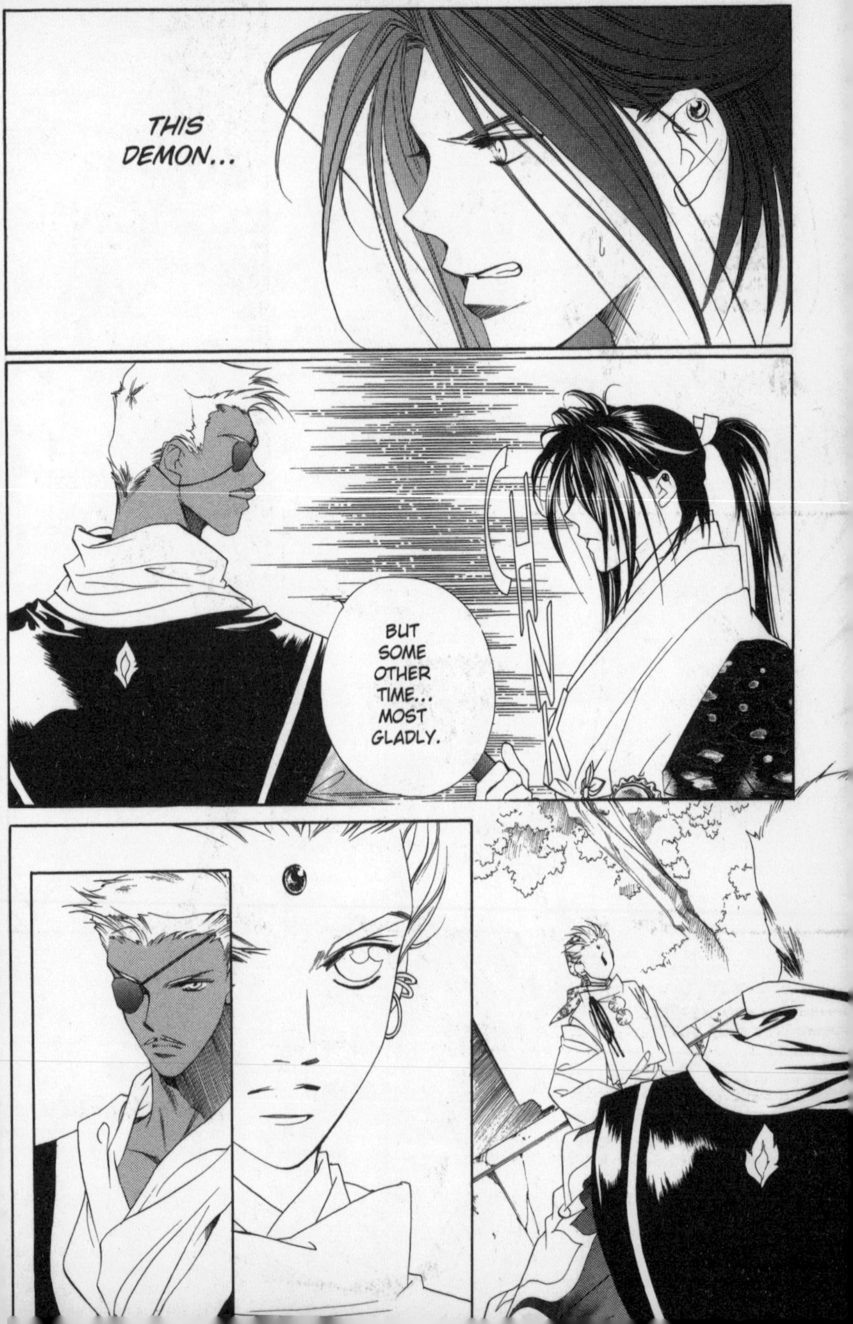
THIS DEMON...
BUT SOME OTHER TIME... MOST GLADLY.

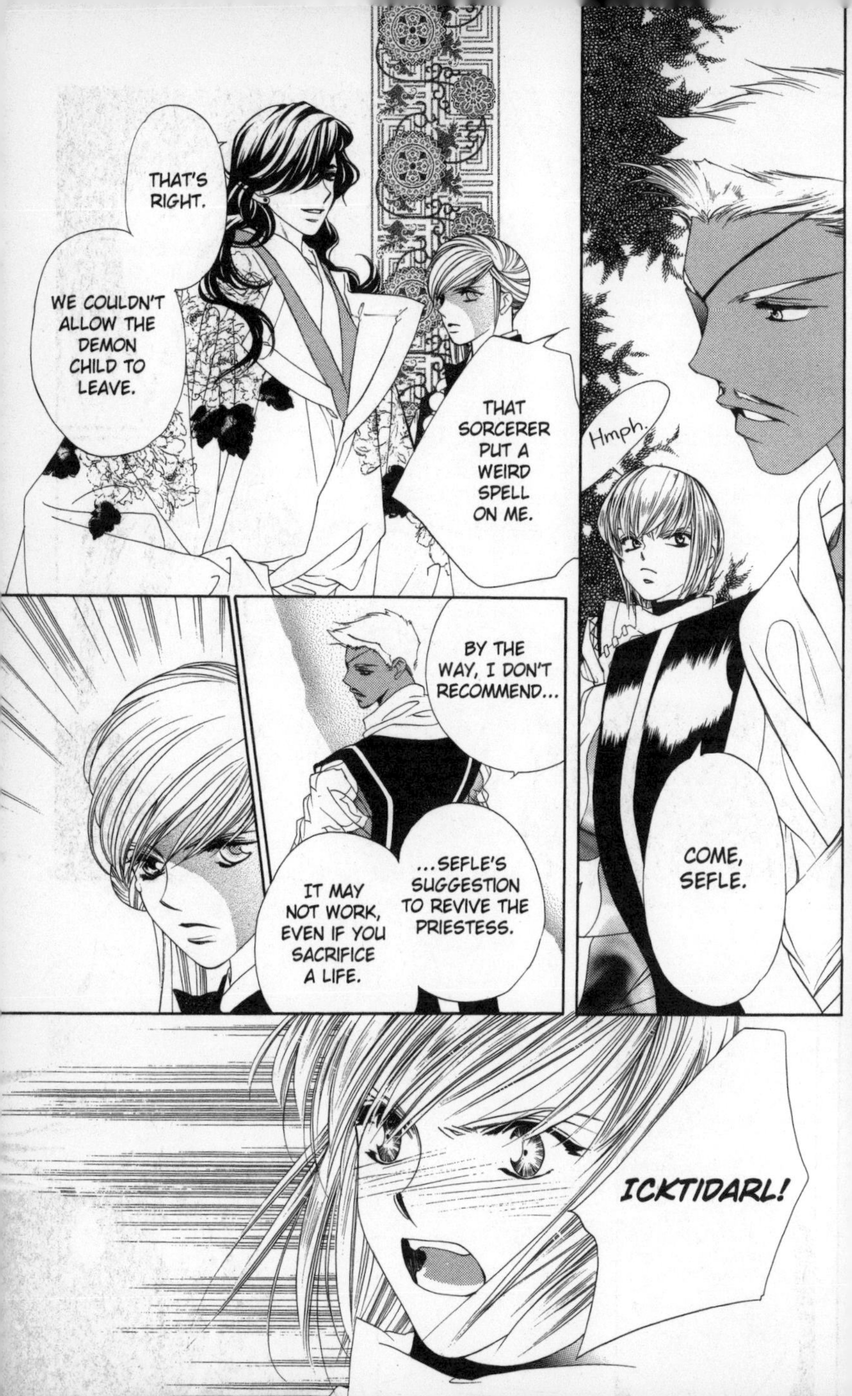
Hmph.
COME, SEFLE.
THAT SORCERER PUT A WEIRD SPELL ON ME.
THAT'S RIGHT.
WE COULDN'T ALLOW THE DEMON CHILD TO LEAVE.
BY THE WAY, I DON'T RECOMMEND...
...SEFLE'S SUGGESTION TO REVIVE THE PRIESTESS.
IT MAY NOT WORK, EVEN IF YOU SACRIFICE A LIFE.
ICKTIDARL!

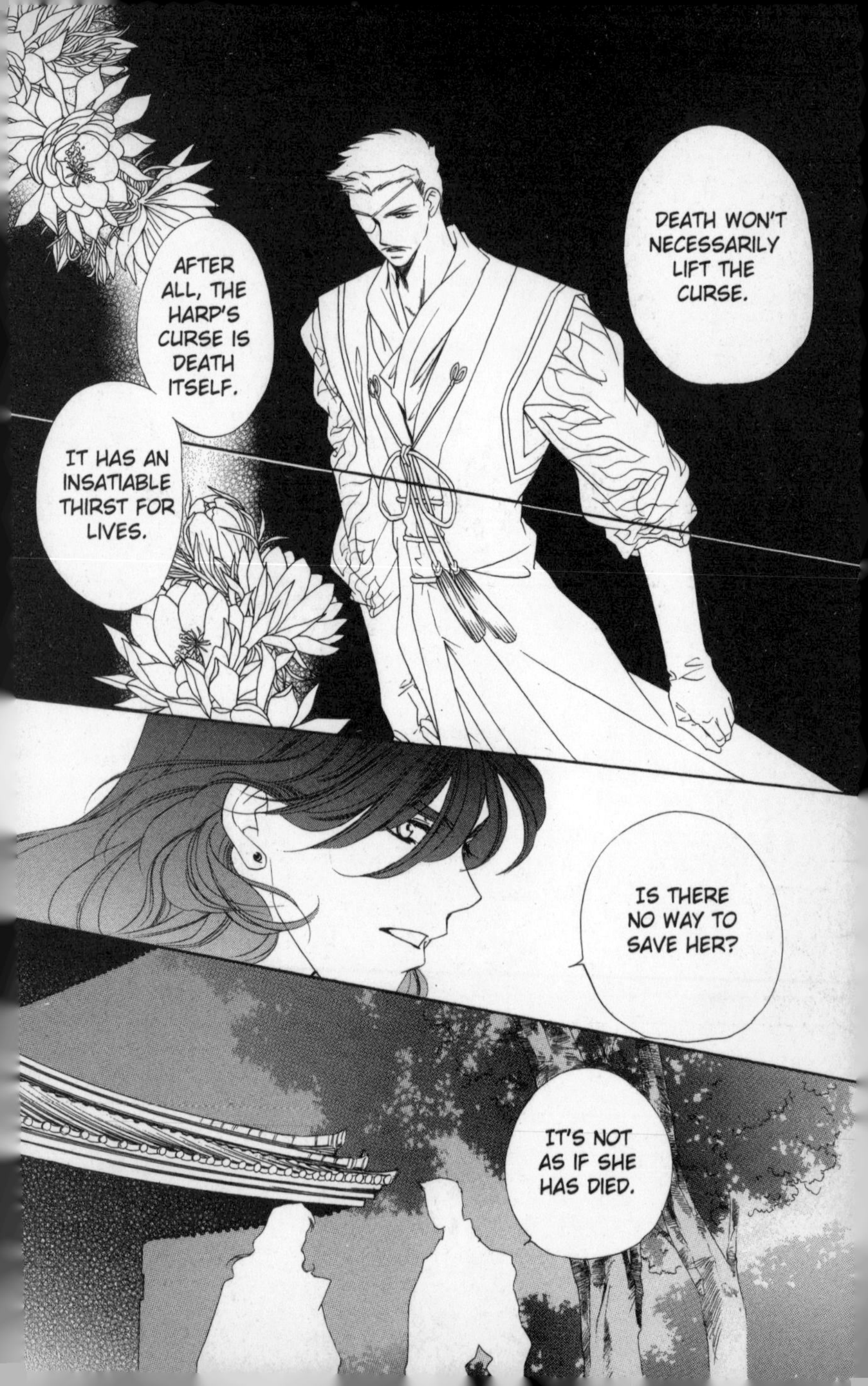
DEATH WON'T NECESSARILY LIFT THE CURSE.
AFTER ALL, THE HARP'S CURSE IS DEATH ITSELF.
IT HAS AN INSATIABLE THIRST FOR LIVES.
IS THERE NO WAY TO SAVE HER?
IT'S NOT AS IF SHE HAS DIED.

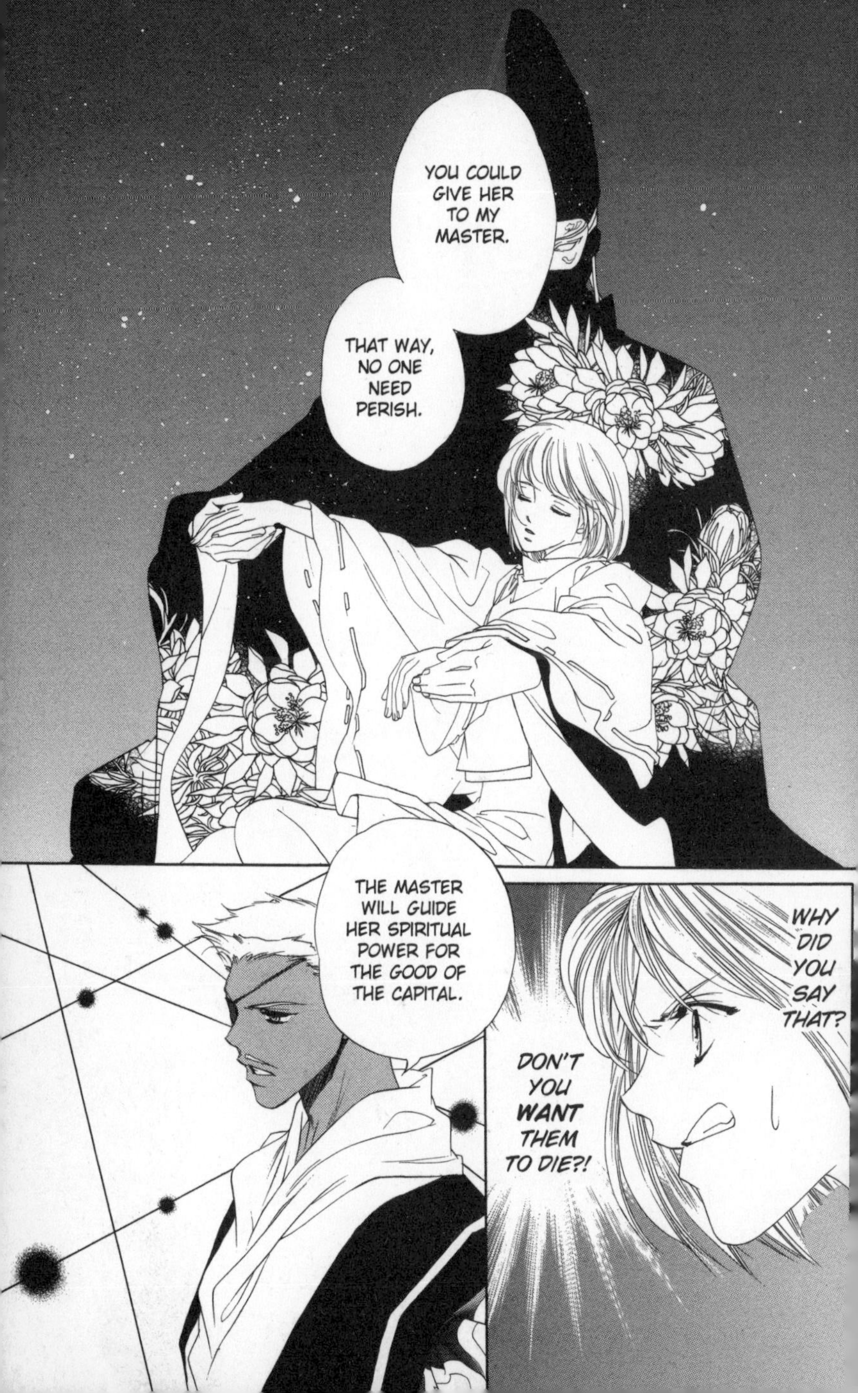
YOU COULD GIVE HER TO MY MASTER.
THAT WAY, NO ONE NEED PERISH.
WHY DID YOU SAY THAT?
DON'T YOU *WANT* THEM TO DIE?!
THE MASTER WILL GUIDE HER SPIRITUAL POWER FOR THE GOOD OF THE CAPITAL.

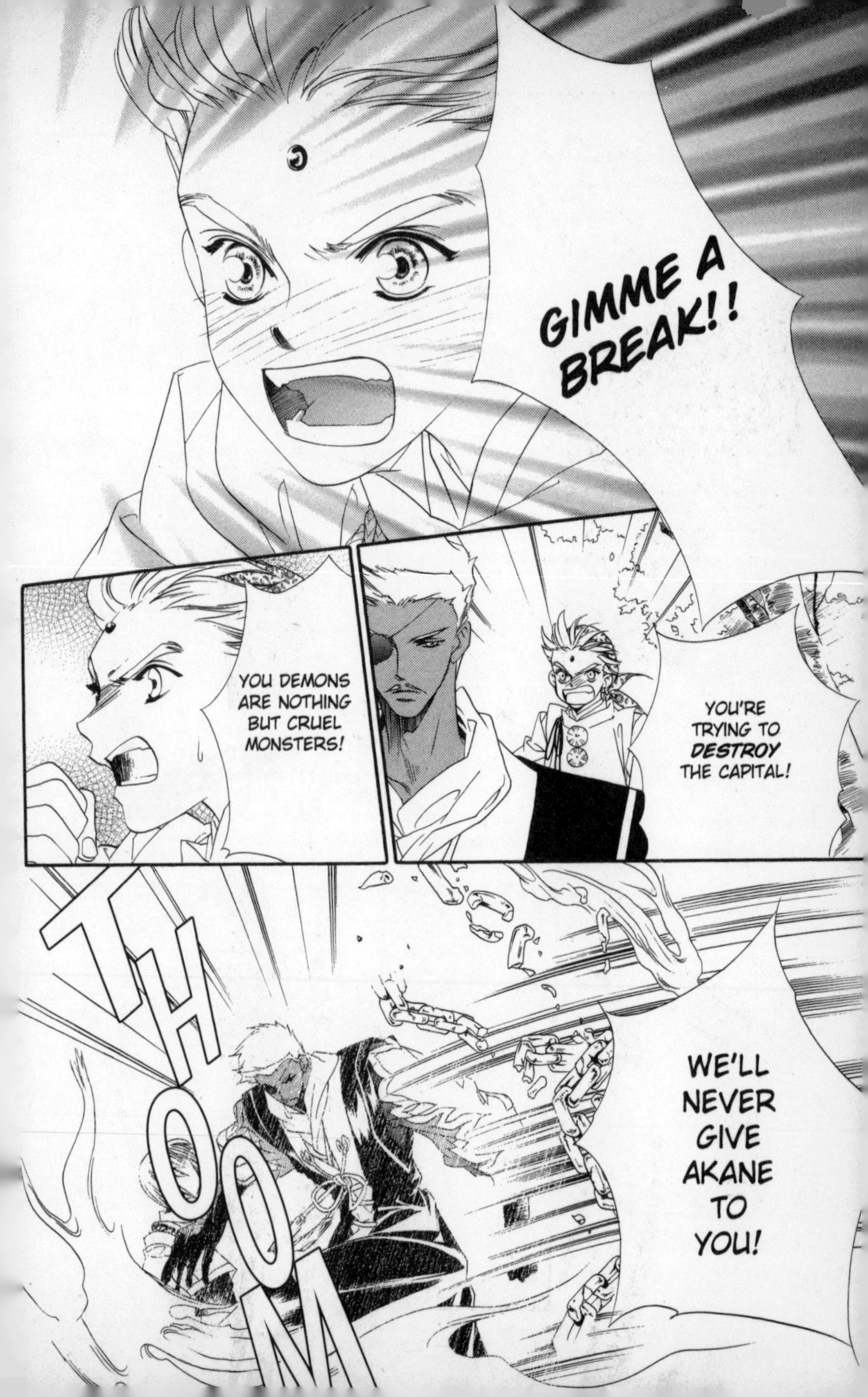
GIMME A BREAK!!
YOU'RE TRYING TO DESTROY THE CAPITAL!
YOU DEMONS ARE NOTHING BUT CRUEL MONSTERS!
WE'LL NEVER GIVE AKANE TO YOU!
THOOOM

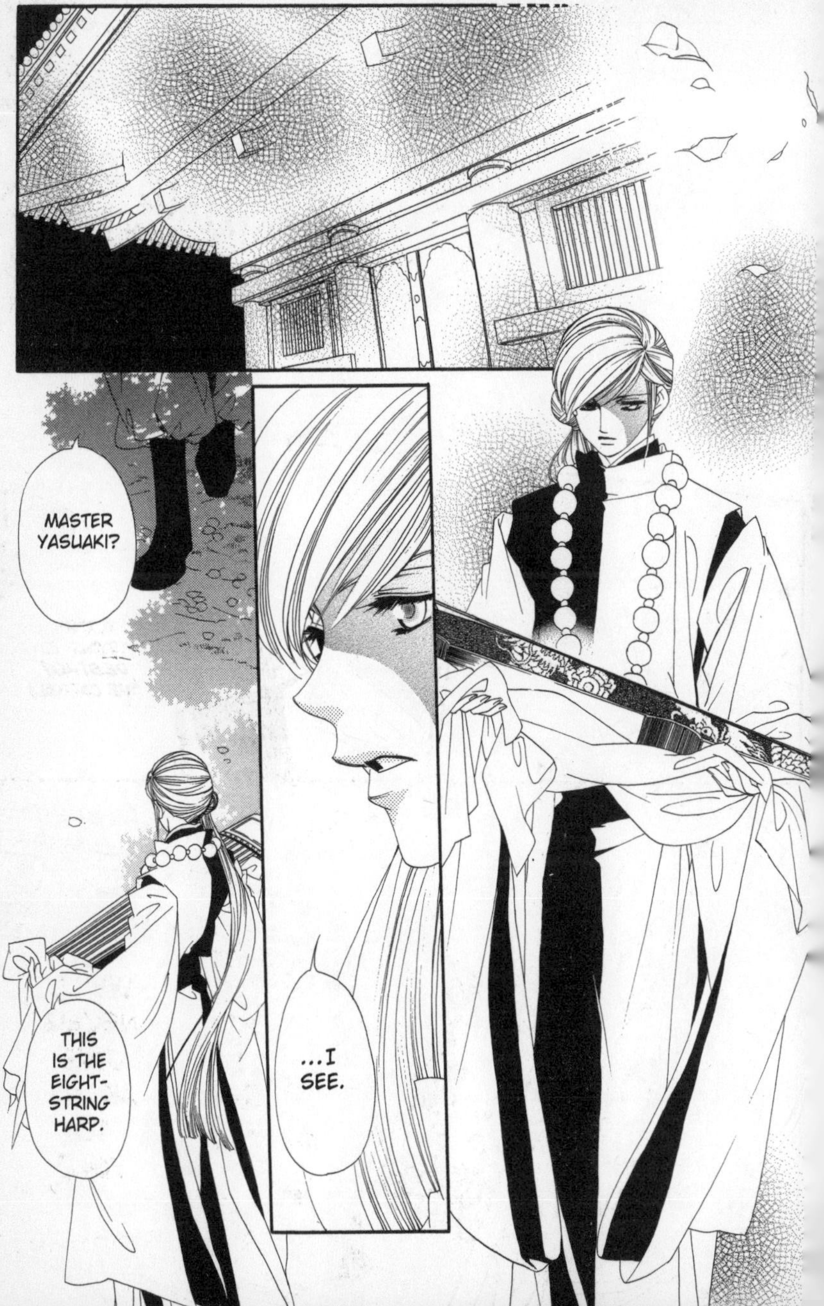
...I SEE.
MASTER YASUAKI?
THIS IS THE EIGHT-STRING HARP.

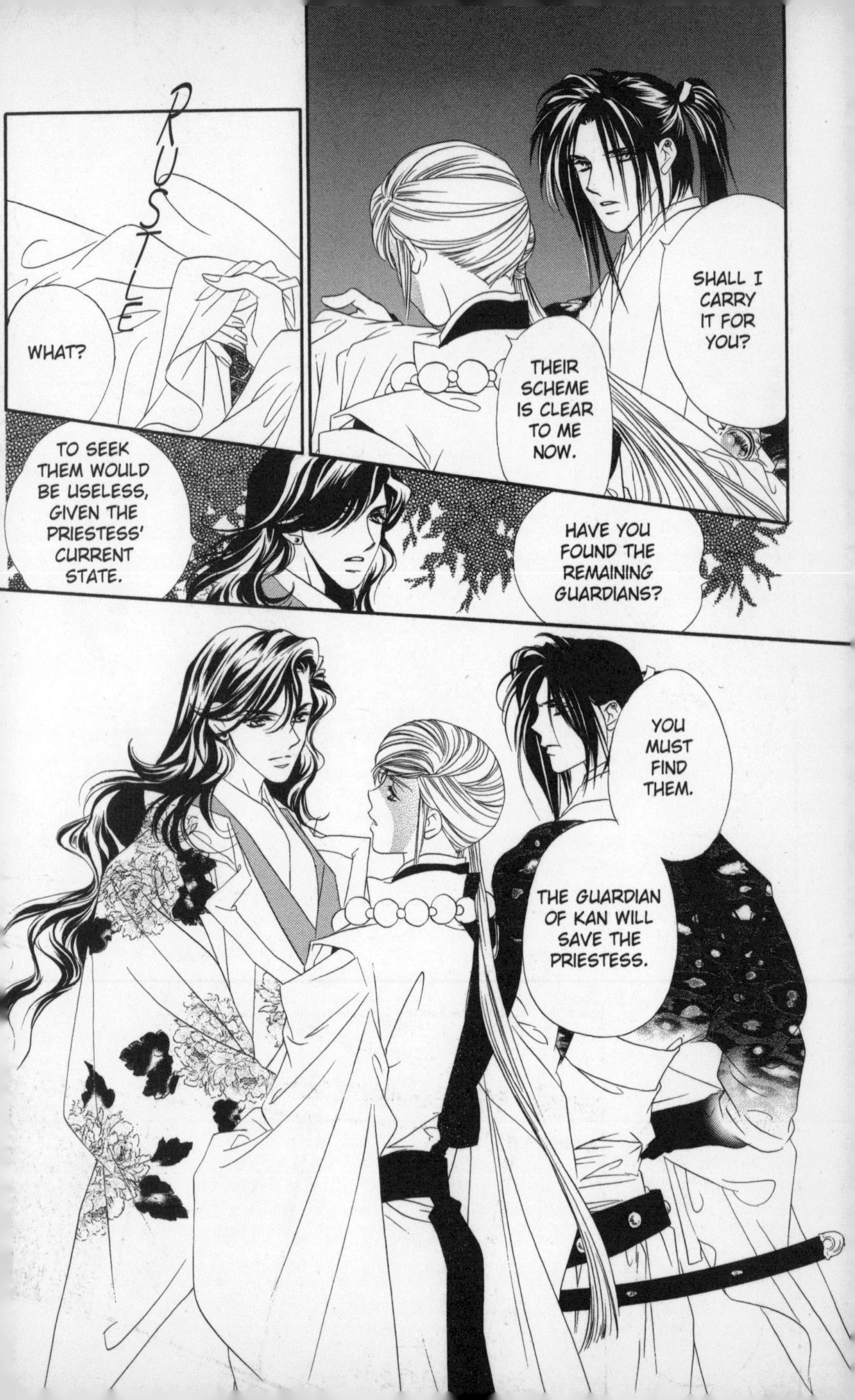
SHALL I CARRY IT FOR YOU?
THEIR SCHEME IS CLEAR TO ME NOW.
RUSTLE
WHAT?
HAVE YOU FOUND THE REMAINING GUARDIANS?
TO SEEK THEM WOULD BE USELESS, GIVEN THE PRIESTESS' CURRENT STATE.
YOU MUST FIND THEM.
THE GUARDIAN OF KAN WILL SAVE THE PRIESTESS.

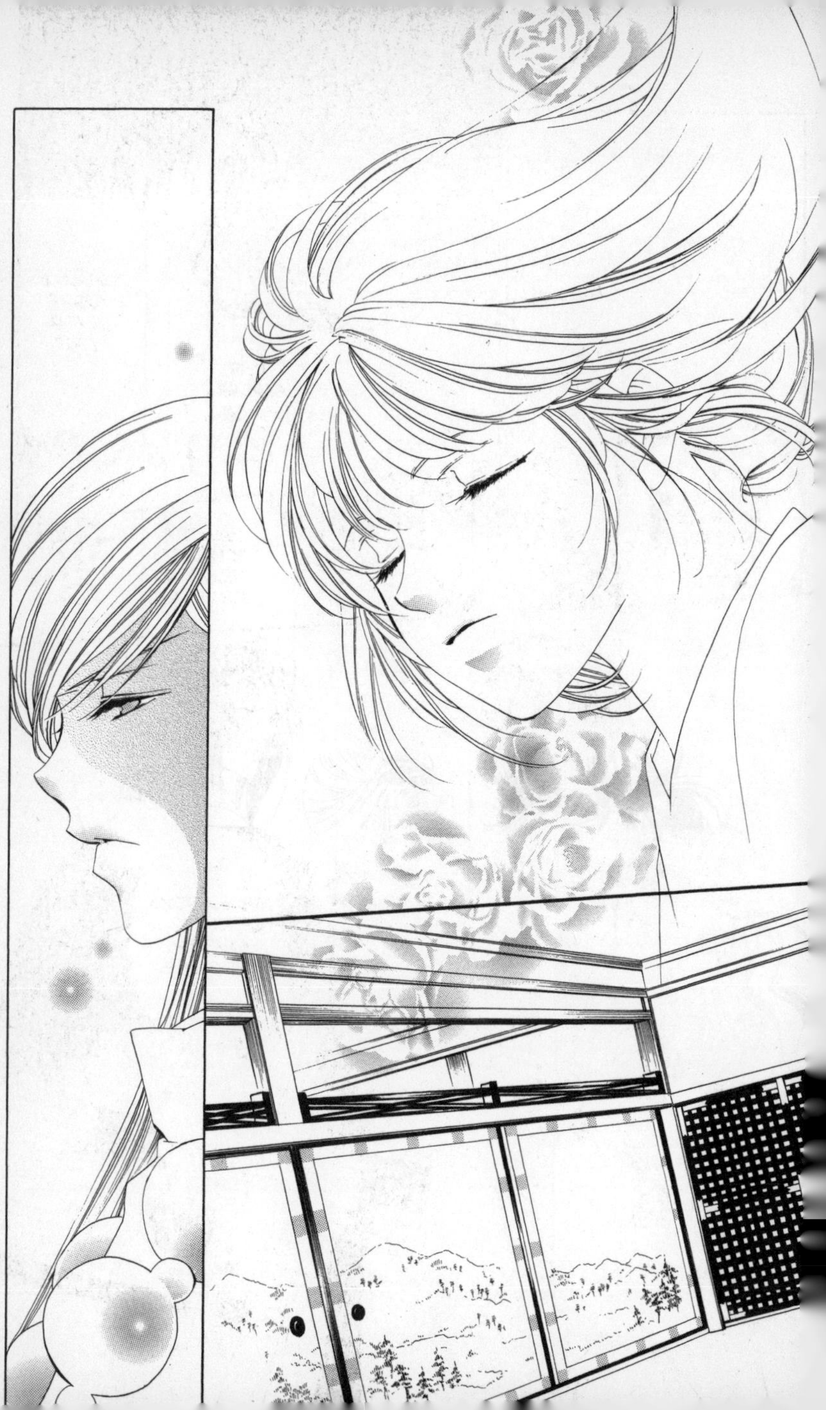

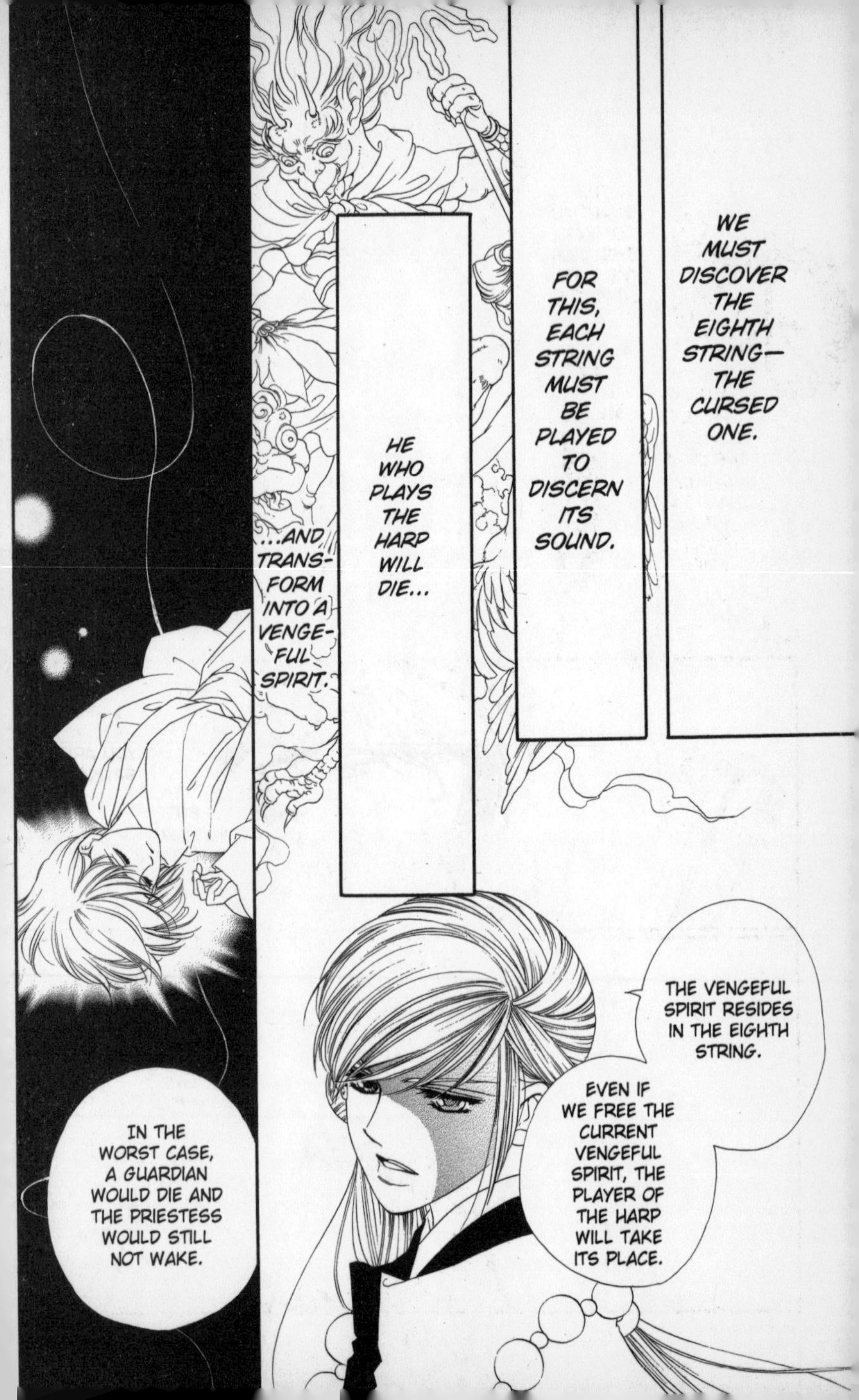
WE MUST DISCOVER THE EIGHTH STRING—THE CURSED ONE.
FOR THIS, EACH STRING MUST BE PLAYED TO DISCERN ITS SOUND.
HE WHO PLAYS THE HARP WILL DIE...
...AND TRANS-FORM INTO A VENGE-FUL SPIRIT.
THE VENGEFUL SPIRIT RESIDES IN THE EIGHTH STRING.
EVEN IF WE FREE THE CURRENT VENGEFUL SPIRIT, THE PLAYER OF THE HARP WILL TAKE ITS PLACE.
IN THE WORST CASE, A GUARDIAN WOULD DIE AND THE PRIESTESS WOULD STILL NOT WAKE.

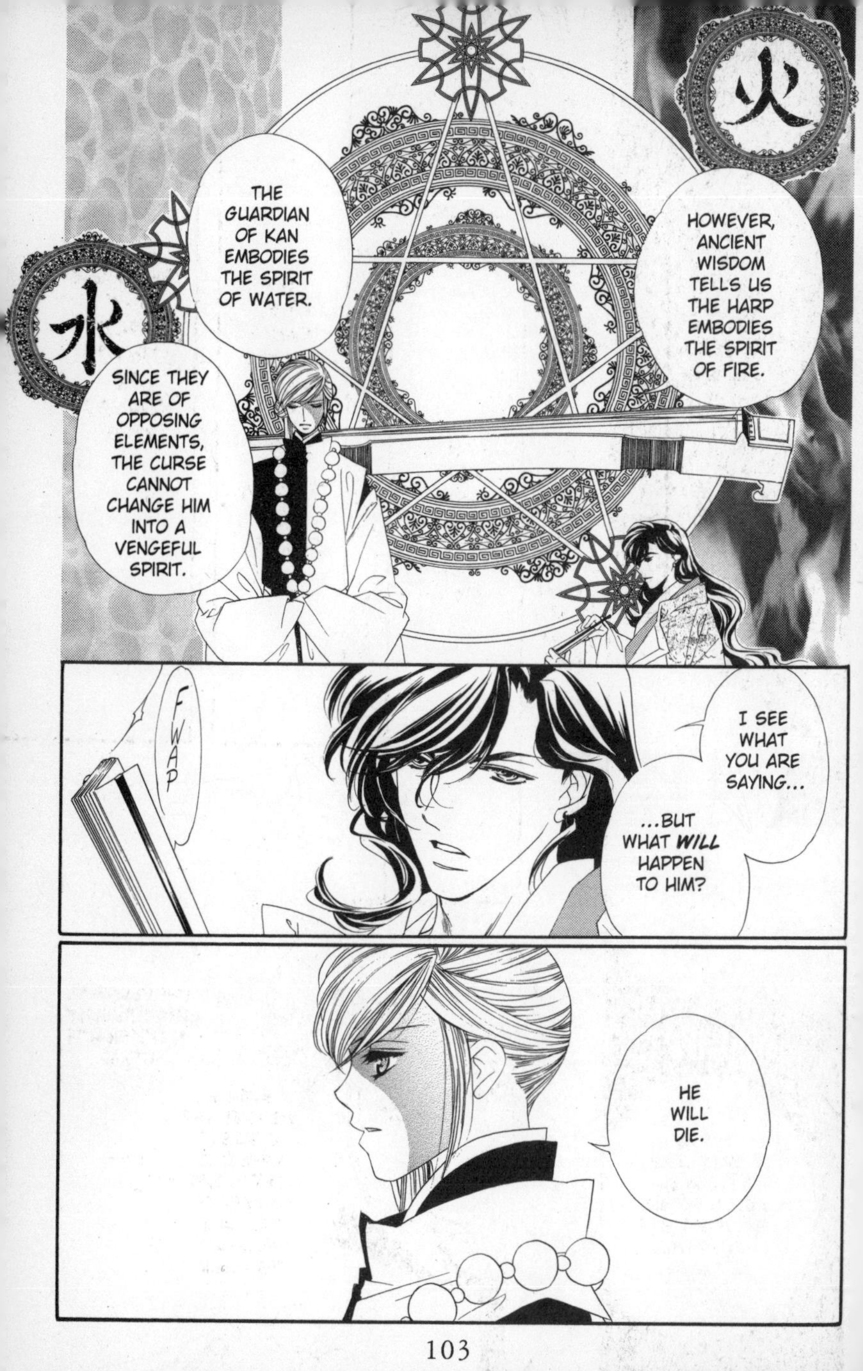

火
THE GUARDIAN OF KAN EMBODIES THE SPIRIT OF WATER.
HOWEVER, ANCIENT WISDOM TELLS US THE HARP EMBODIES THE SPIRIT OF FIRE.
水
SINCE THEY ARE OF OPPOSING ELEMENTS, THE CURSE CANNOT CHANGE HIM INTO A VENGEFUL SPIRIT.
I SEE WHAT YOU ARE SAYING...
...BUT WHAT *WILL* HAPPEN TO HIM?
FWAP
HE WILL DIE.

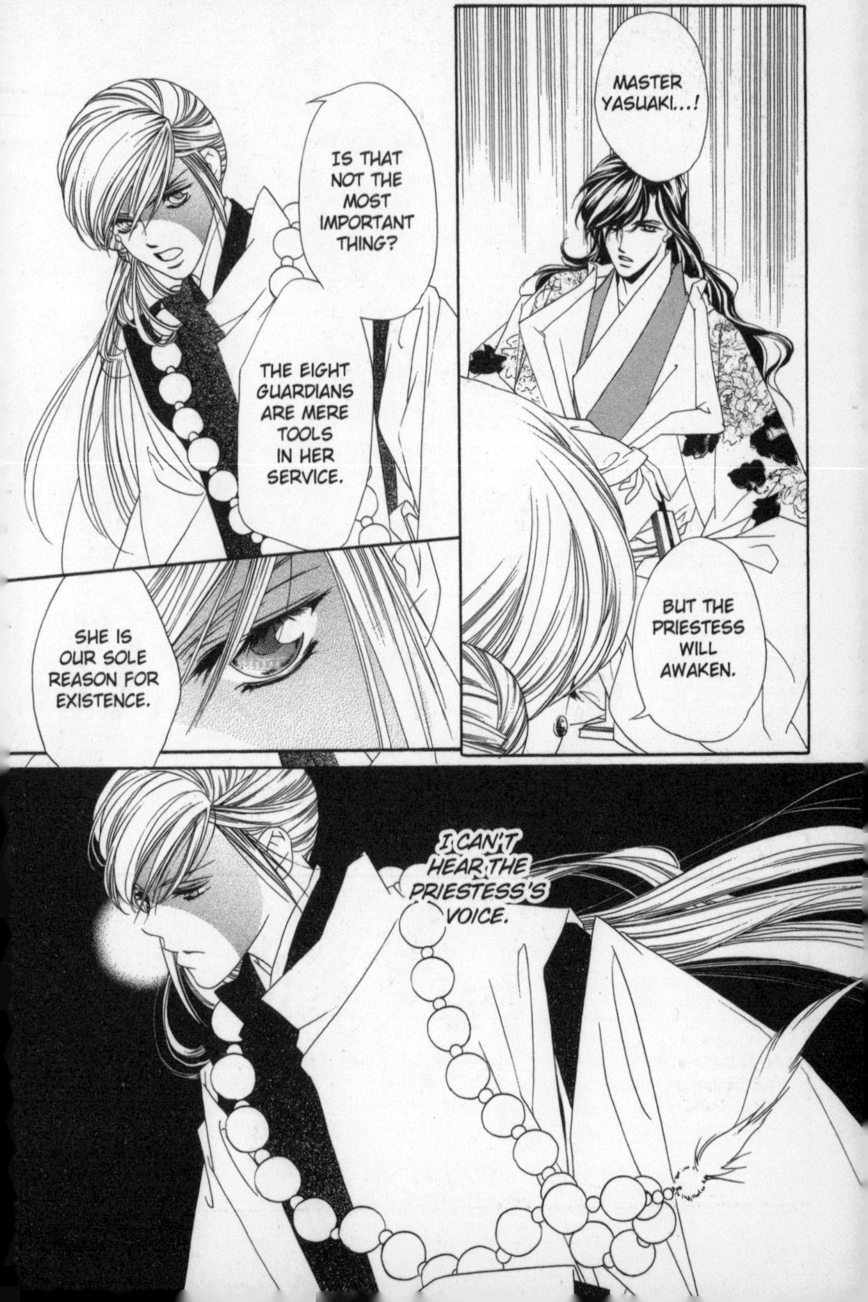
MASTER YASUAKI...!
BUT THE PRIESTESS WILL AWAKEN.
IS THAT NOT THE MOST IMPORTANT THING?
THE EIGHT GUARDIANS ARE MERE TOOLS IN HER SERVICE.
SHE IS OUR SOLE REASON FOR EXISTENCE.
I CAN'T HEAR THE PRIESTESS'S VOICE.

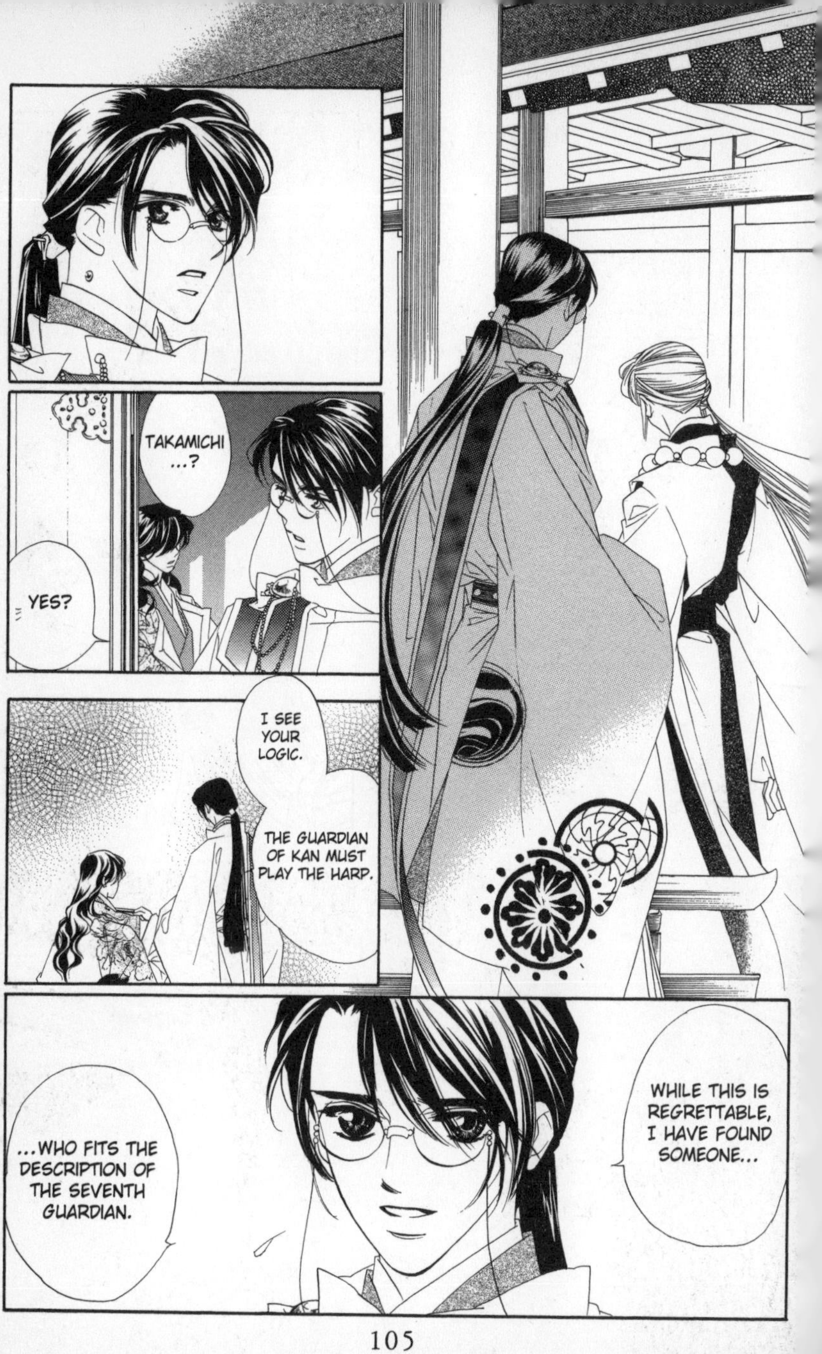
TAKAMICHI ...?
YES?
I SEE YOUR LOGIC.
THE GUARDIAN OF KAN MUST PLAY THE HARP.
WHILE THIS IS REGRETTABLE, I HAVE FOUND SOMEONE...
...WHO FITS THE DESCRIPTION OF THE SEVENTH GUARDIAN.

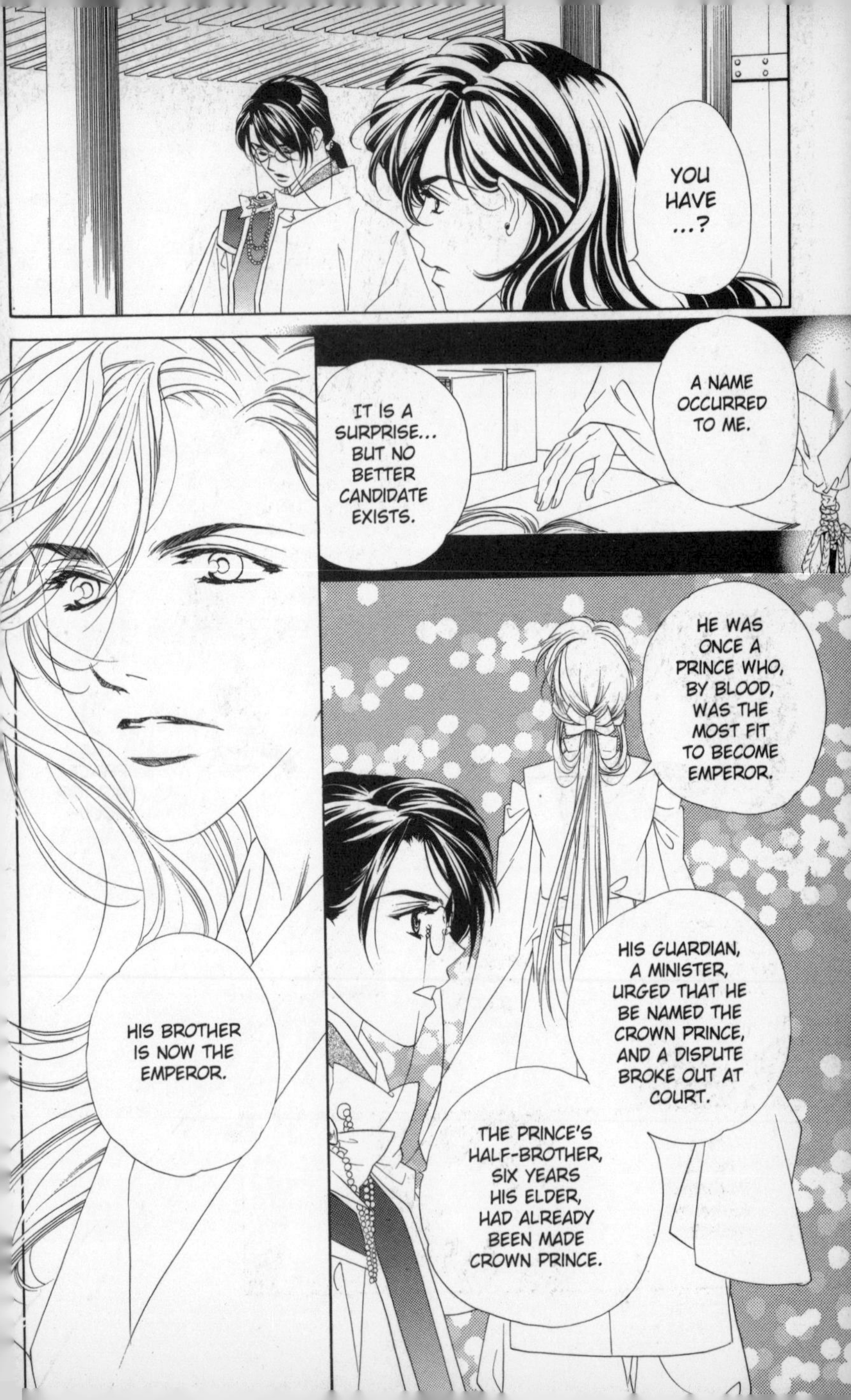
YOU HAVE ...?
A NAME OCCURRED TO ME.
IT IS A SURPRISE... BUT NO BETTER CANDIDATE EXISTS.
HE WAS ONCE A PRINCE WHO, BY BLOOD, WAS THE MOST FIT TO BECOME EMPEROR.
HIS GUARDIAN, A MINISTER, URGED THAT HE BE NAMED THE CROWN PRINCE, AND A DISPUTE BROKE OUT AT COURT.
THE PRINCE'S HALF-BROTHER, SIX YEARS HIS ELDER, HAD ALREADY BEEN MADE CROWN PRINCE.
HIS BROTHER IS NOW THE EMPEROR.

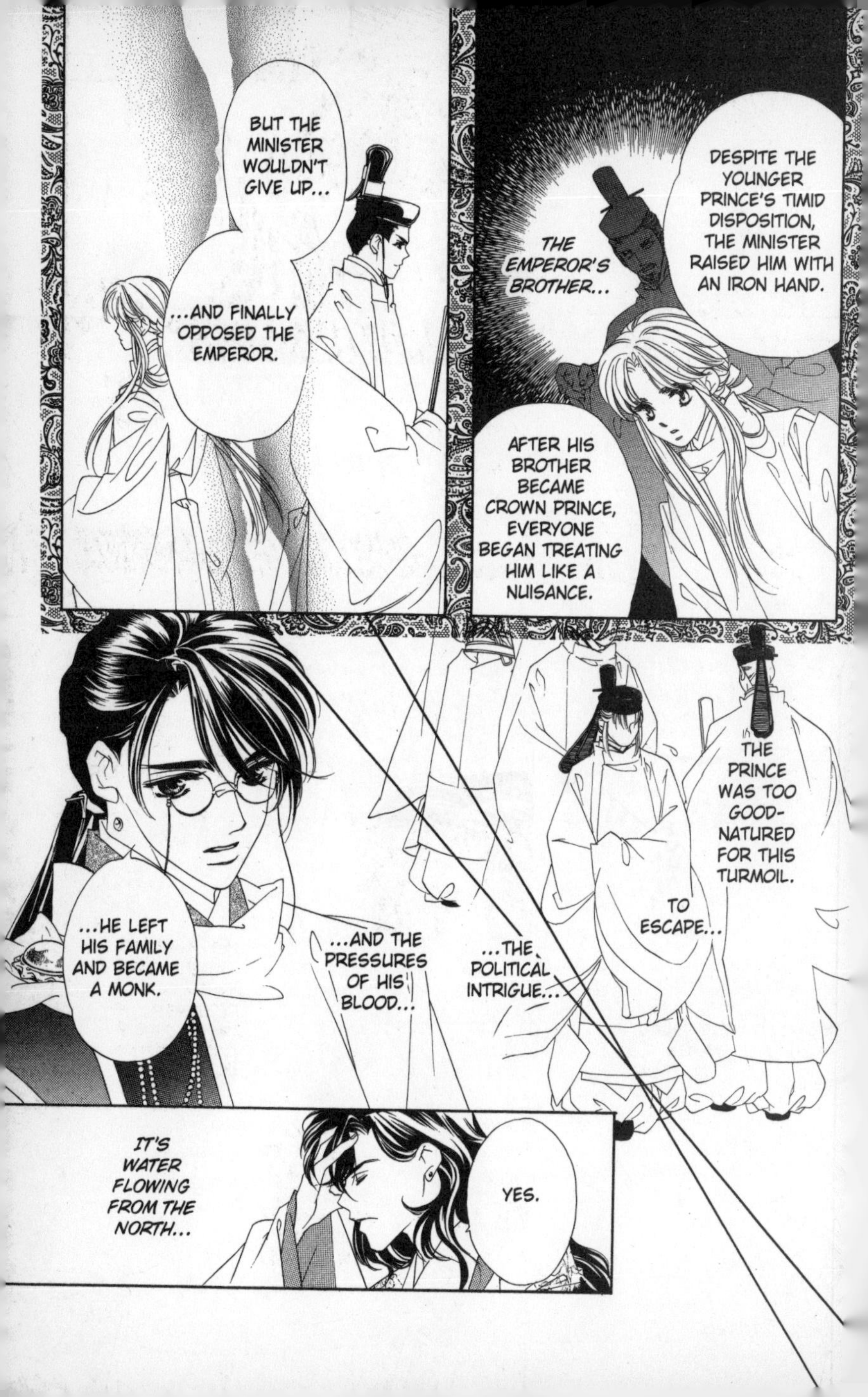
DESPITE THE YOUNGER PRINCE'S TIMID DISPOSITION, THE MINISTER RAISED HIM WITH AN IRON HAND.
THE EMPEROR'S BROTHER...
AFTER HIS BROTHER BECAME CROWN PRINCE, EVERYONE BEGAN TREATING HIM LIKE A NUISANCE.
BUT THE MINISTER WOULDN'T GIVE UP...
...AND FINALLY OPPOSED THE EMPEROR.
THE PRINCE WAS TOO GOOD-NATURED FOR THIS TURMOIL.
TO ESCAPE...
...THE POLITICAL INTRIGUE...
...AND THE PRESSURES OF HIS BLOOD...
...HE LEFT HIS FAMILY AND BECAME A MONK.
YES.
IT'S WATER FLOWING FROM THE NORTH...

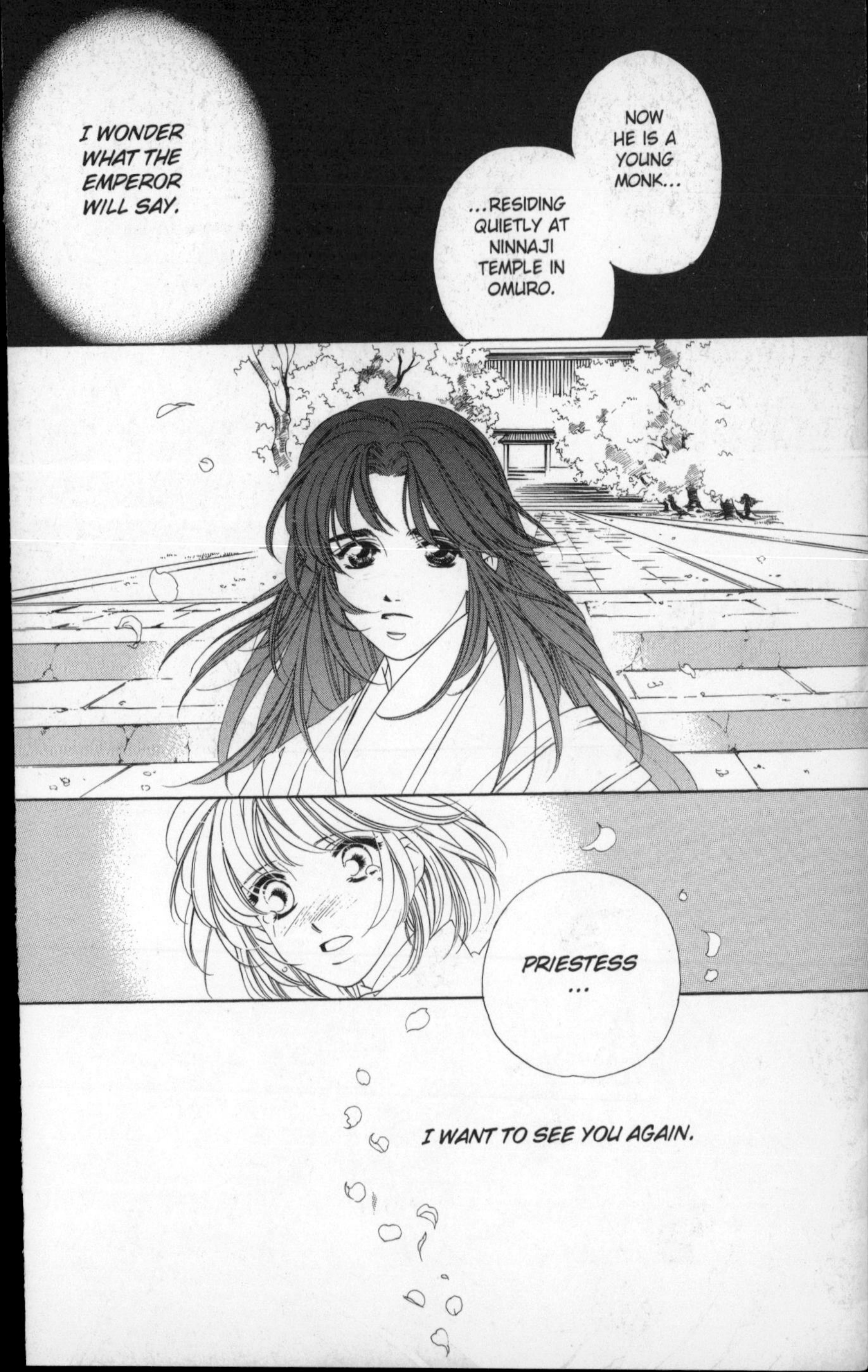
NOW HE IS A YOUNG MONK...
...RESIDING QUIETLY AT NINNAJI TEMPLE IN OMURO.
I WONDER WHAT THE EMPEROR WILL SAY.
PRIESTESS ...
I WANT TO SEE YOU AGAIN.

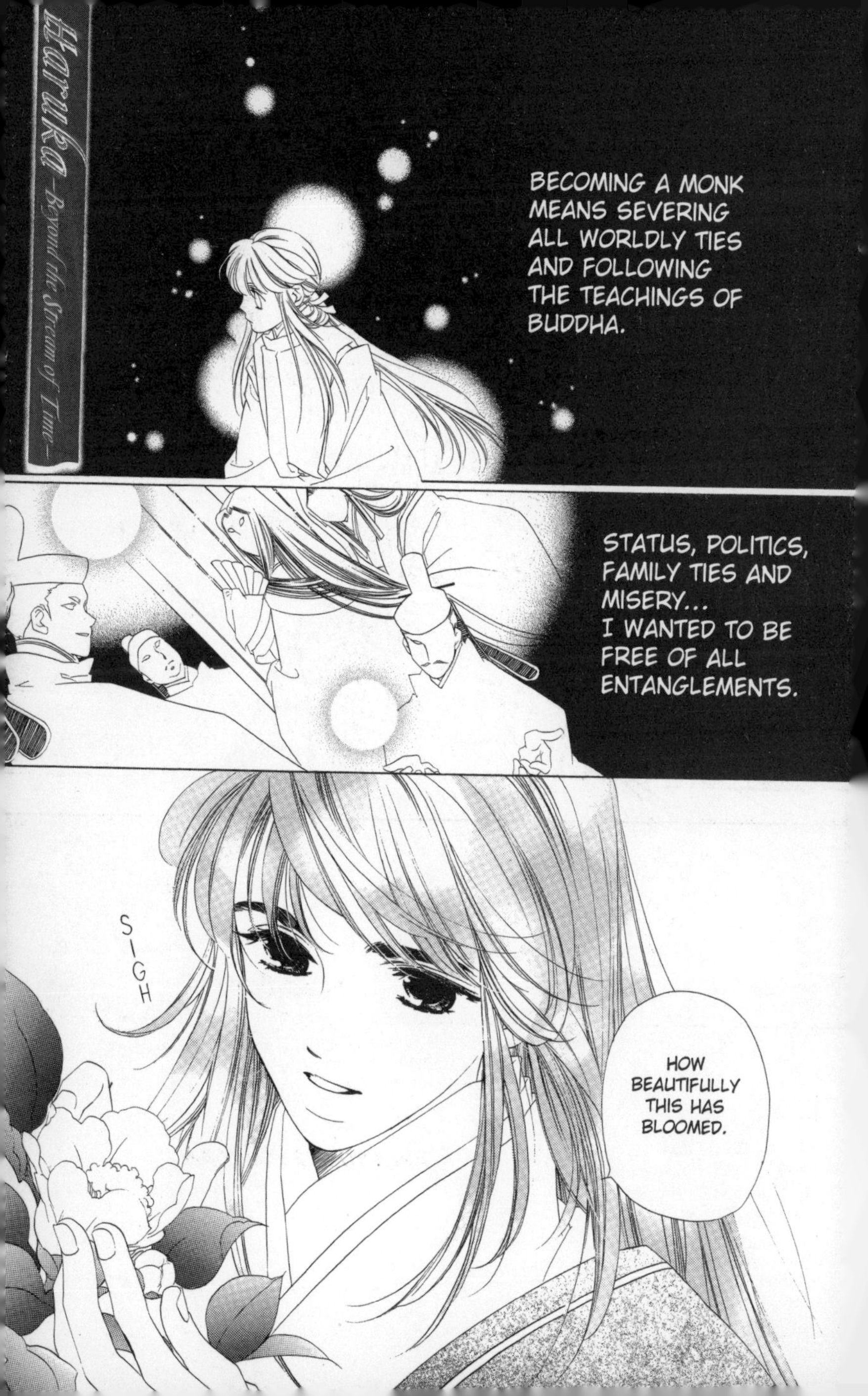
Haruka -Beyond the Stream of Time-
BECOMING A MONK MEANS SEVERING ALL WORLDLY TIES AND FOLLOWING THE TEACHINGS OF BUDDHA.
STATUS, POLITICS, FAMILY TIES AND MISERY... I WANTED TO BE FREE OF ALL ENTANGLEMENTS.
HOW BEAUTIFULLY THIS HAS BLOOMED.
SIGH

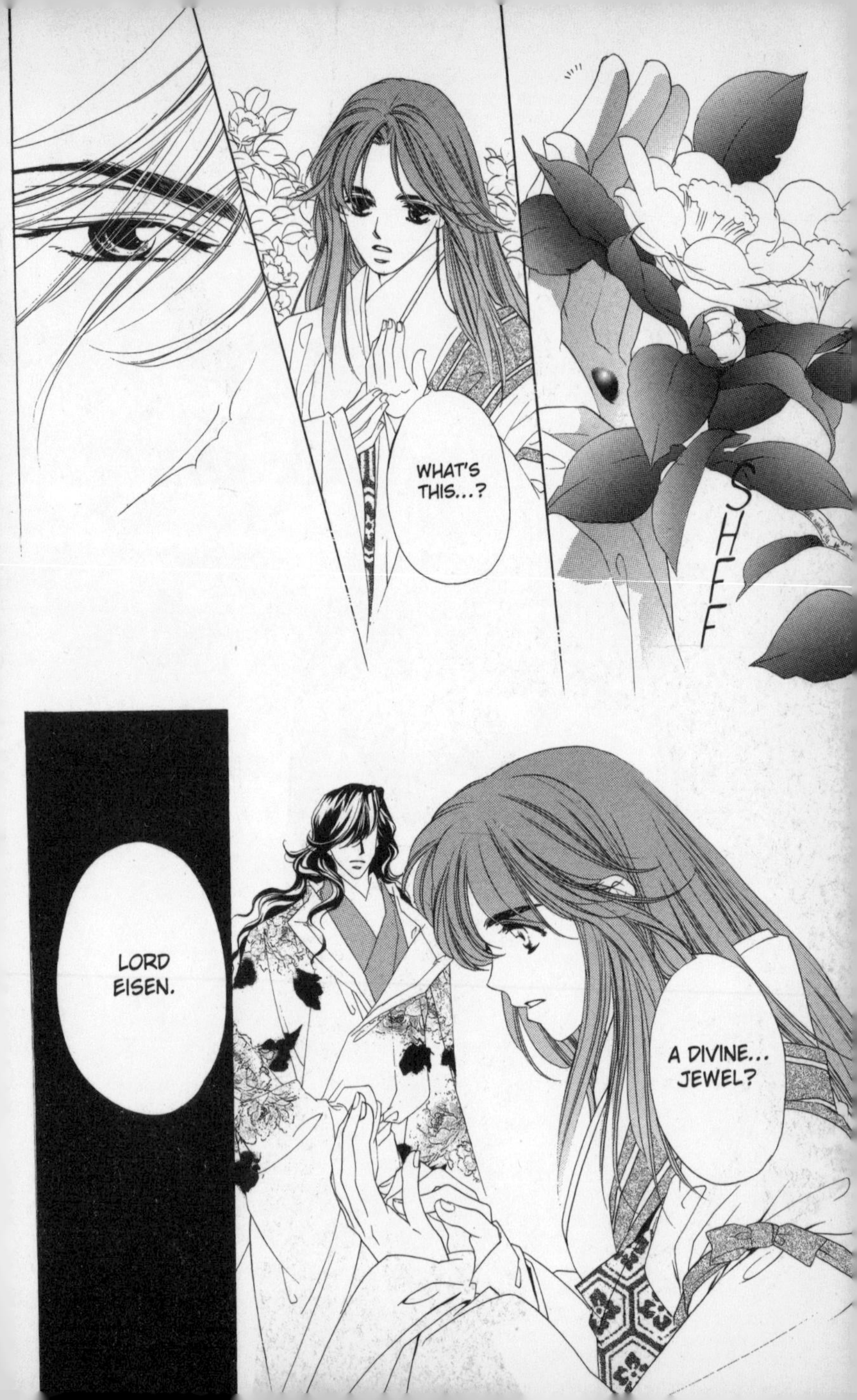
SHFFF
WHAT'S THIS...?
A DIVINE... JEWEL?
LORD EISEN.

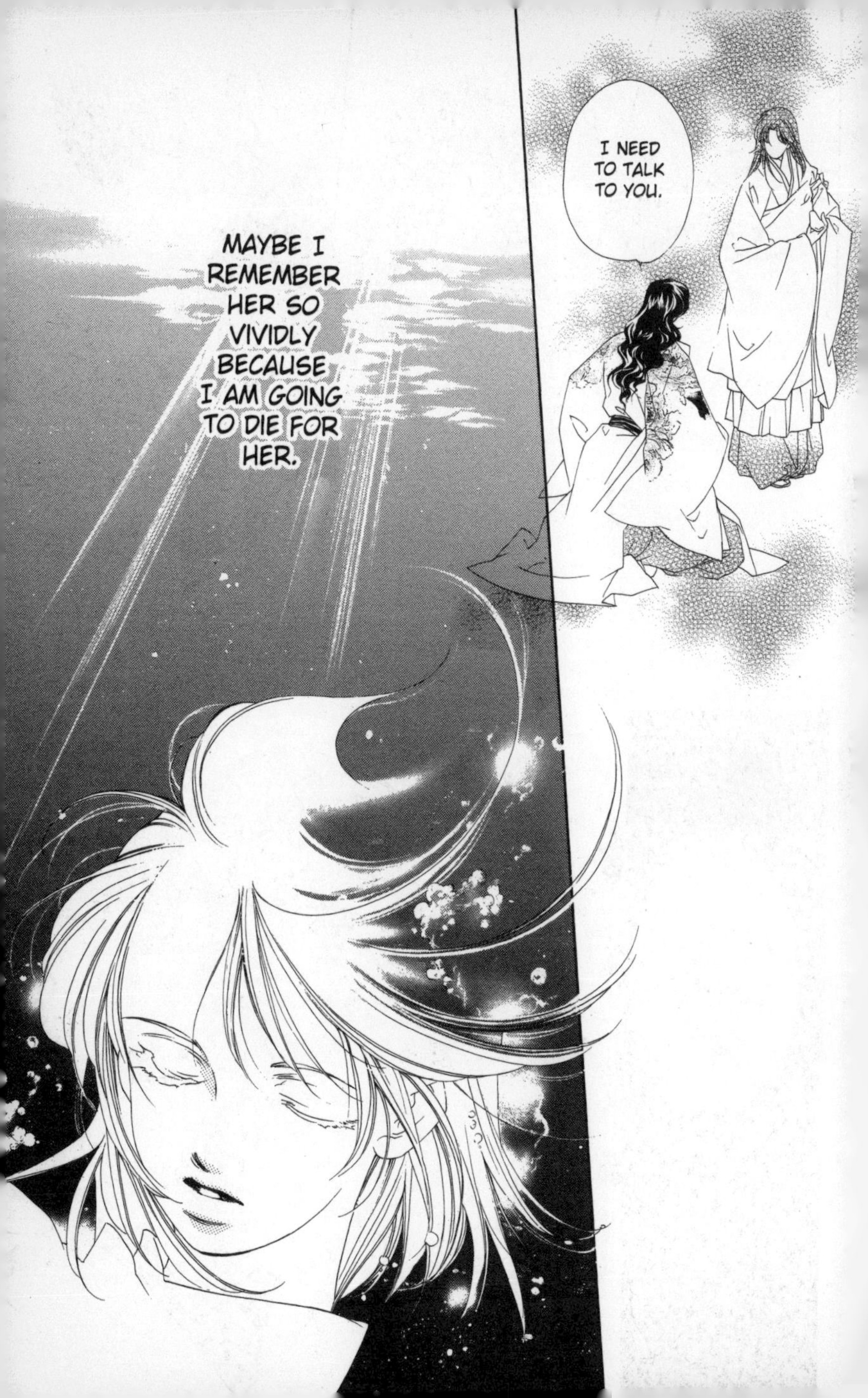
I NEED TO TALK TO YOU.
MAYBE I REMEMBER HER SO VIVIDLY BECAUSE I AM GOING TO DIE FOR HER.

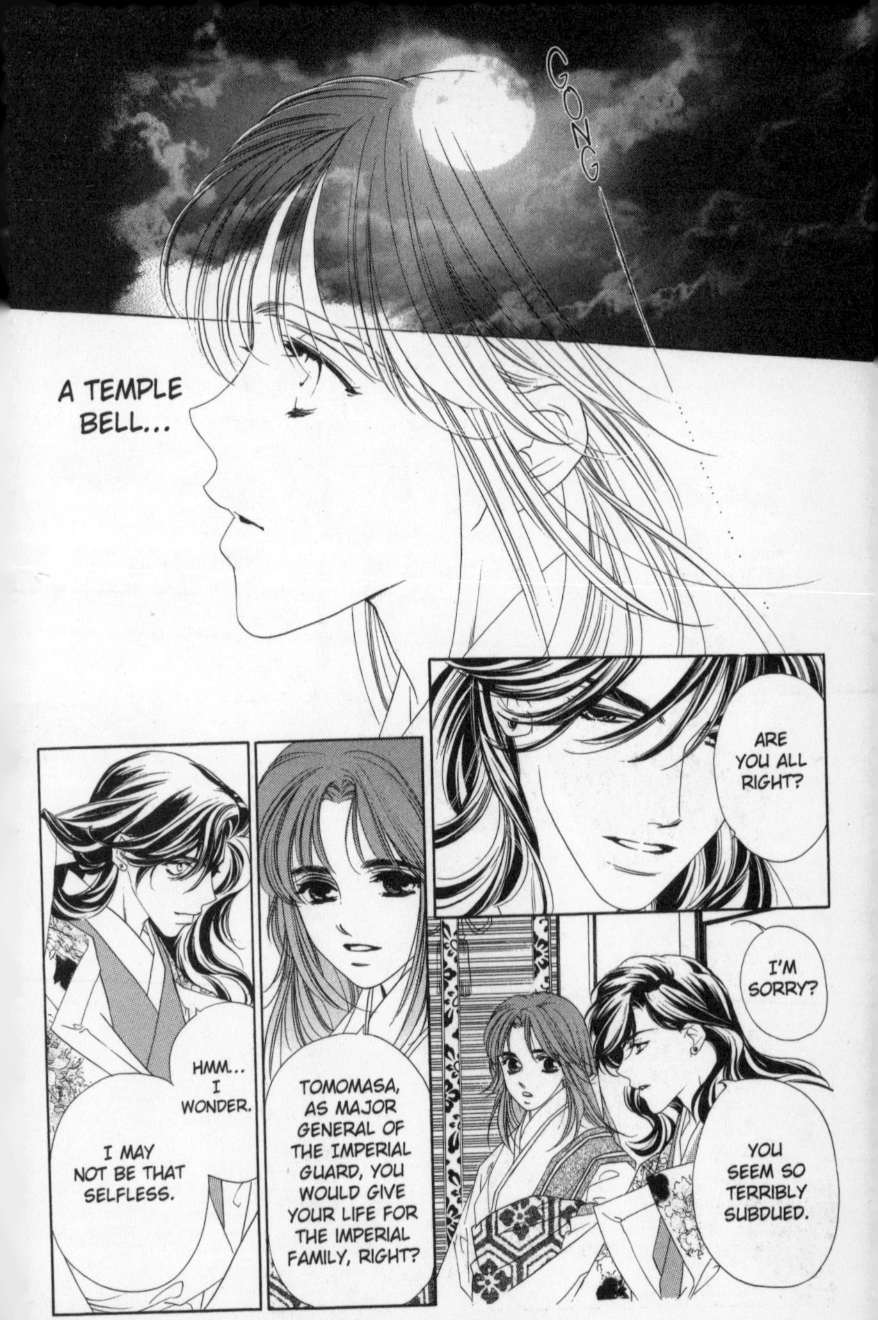

GONG
A TEMPLE BELL...
ARE YOU ALL RIGHT?
I'M SORRY?
YOU SEEM SO TERRIBLY SUBDUED.
TOMOMASA, AS MAJOR GENERAL OF THE IMPERIAL GUARD, YOU WOULD GIVE YOUR LIFE FOR THE IMPERIAL FAMILY, RIGHT?
HMM... I WONDER.
I MAY NOT BE THAT SELFLESS.

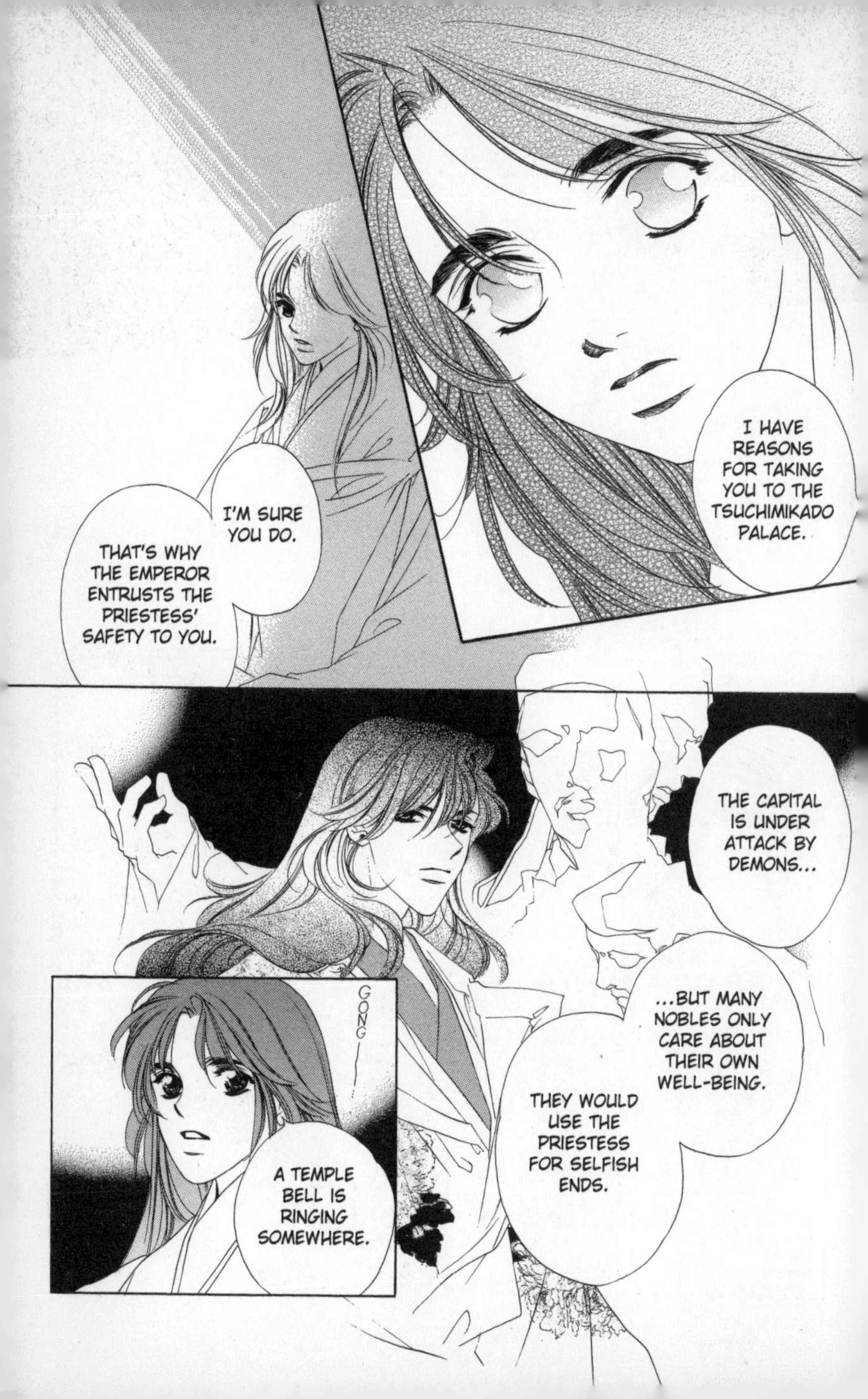
I HAVE REASONS FOR TAKING YOU TO THE TSUCHIMIKADO PALACE.
I'M SURE YOU DO.
THAT'S WHY THE EMPEROR ENTRUSTS THE PRIESTESS' SAFETY TO YOU.
THE CAPITAL IS UNDER ATTACK BY DEMONS...
...BUT MANY NOBLES ONLY CARE ABOUT THEIR OWN WELL-BEING.
THEY WOULD USE THE PRIESTESS FOR SELFISH ENDS.
GONG
A TEMPLE BELL IS RINGING SOMEWHERE.

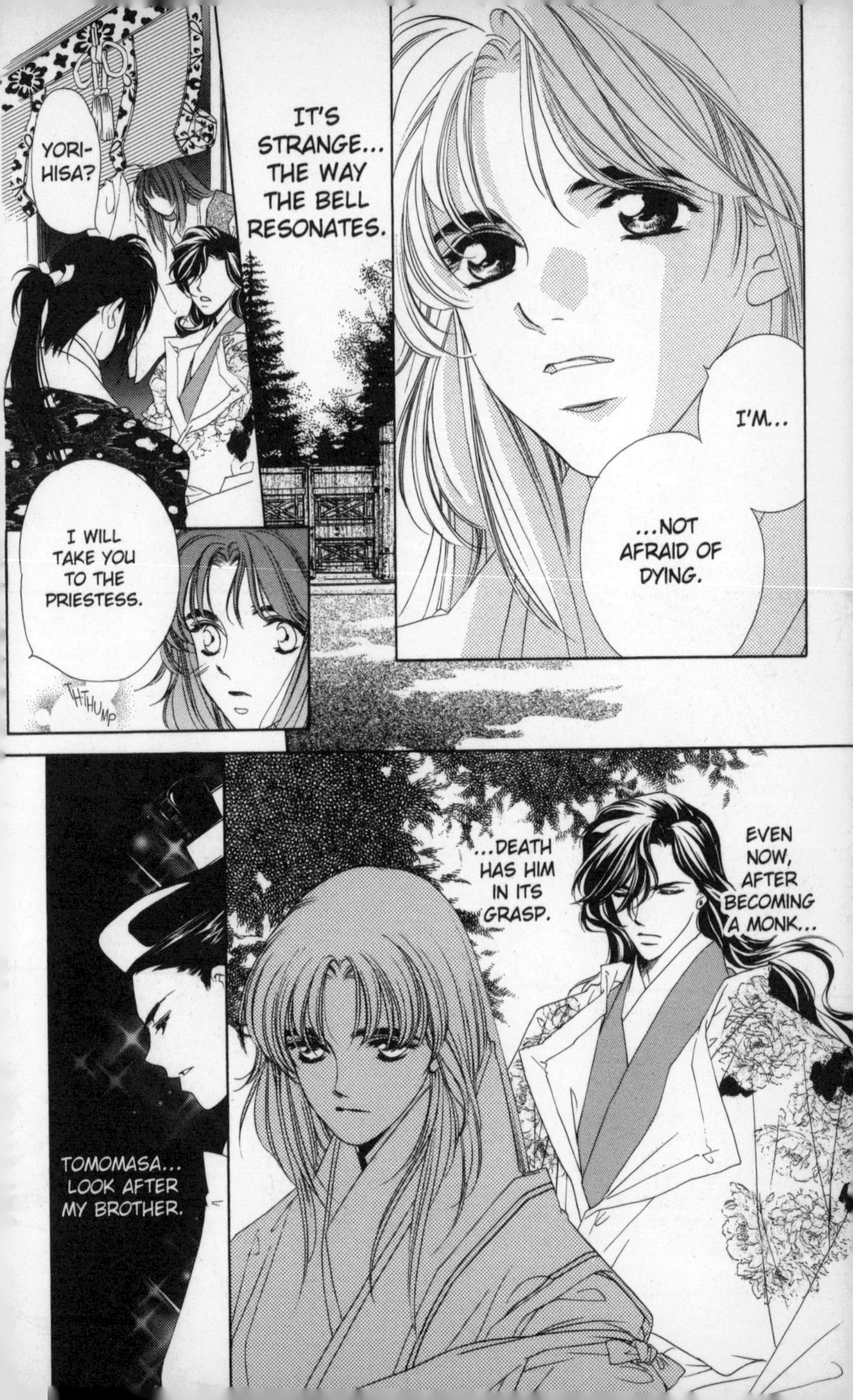
I'M...
...NOT AFRAID OF DYING.
IT'S STRANGE... THE WAY THE BELL RESONATES.
YORI-HISA?
I WILL TAKE YOU TO THE PRIESTESS.
THTHUMP
EVEN NOW, AFTER BECOMING A MONK...
...DEATH HAS HIM IN ITS GRASP.
TOMOMASA... LOOK AFTER MY BROTHER.

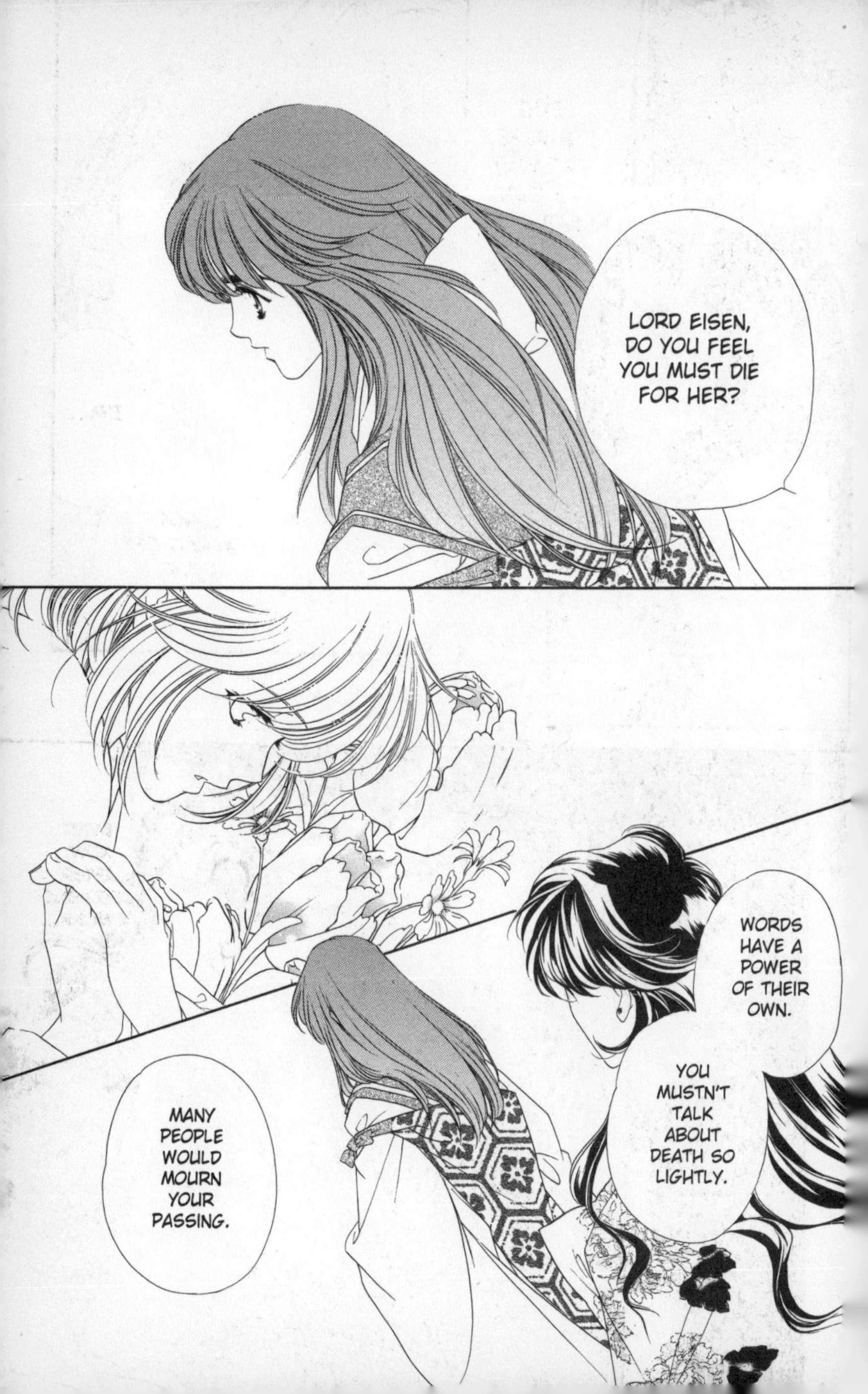
LORD EISEN, DO YOU FEEL YOU MUST DIE FOR HER?
WORDS HAVE A POWER OF THEIR OWN.
YOU MUSTN'T TALK ABOUT DEATH SO LIGHTLY.
MANY PEOPLE WOULD MOURN YOUR PASSING.

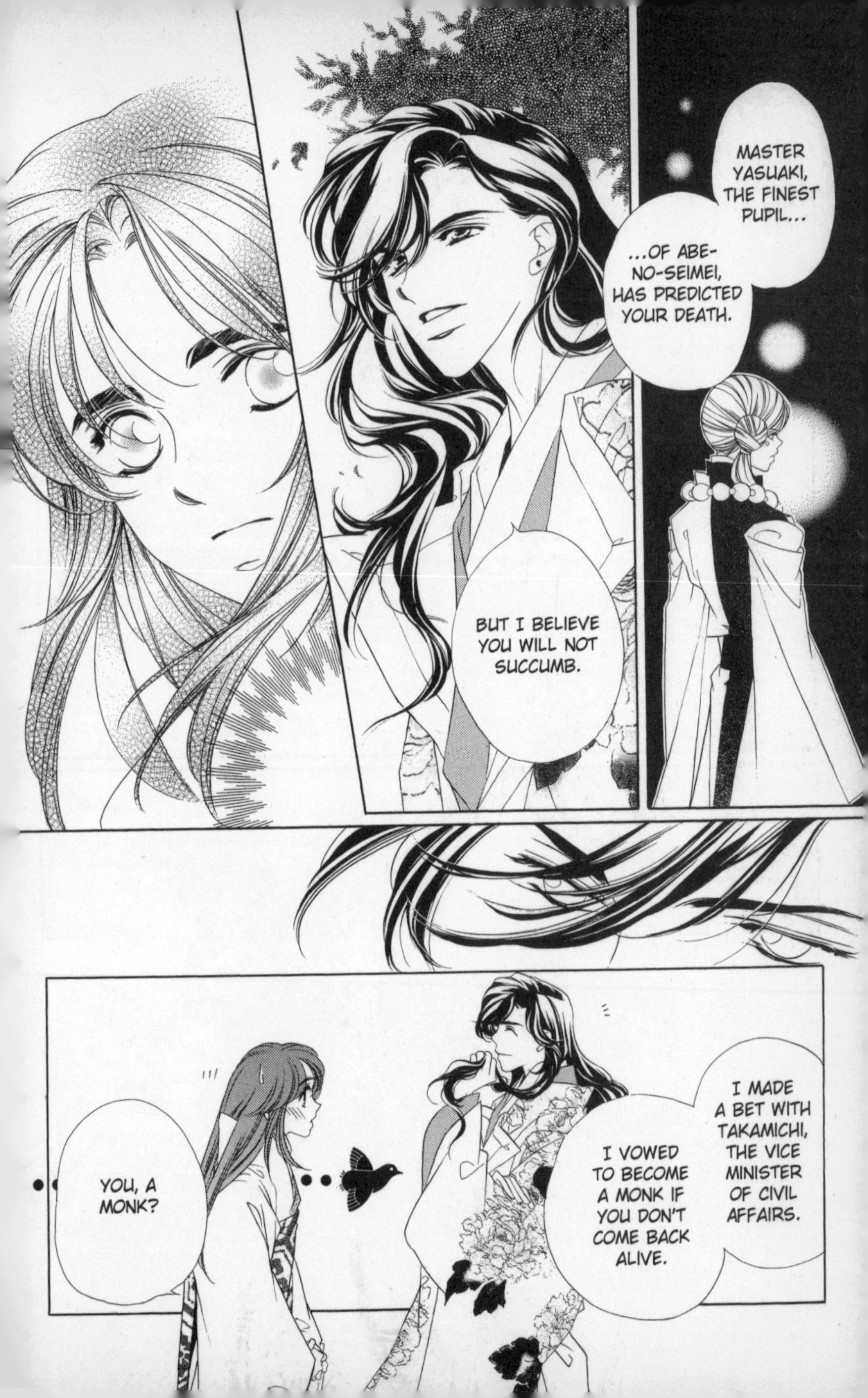
MASTER YASUAKI, THE FINEST PUPIL...
...OF ABE-NO-SEIMEI, HAS PREDICTED YOUR DEATH.
BUT I BELIEVE YOU WILL NOT SUCCUMB.
I MADE A BET WITH TAKAMICHI, THE VICE MINISTER OF CIVIL AFFAIRS.
I VOWED TO BECOME A MONK IF YOU DON'T COME BACK ALIVE.
YOU, A MONK?

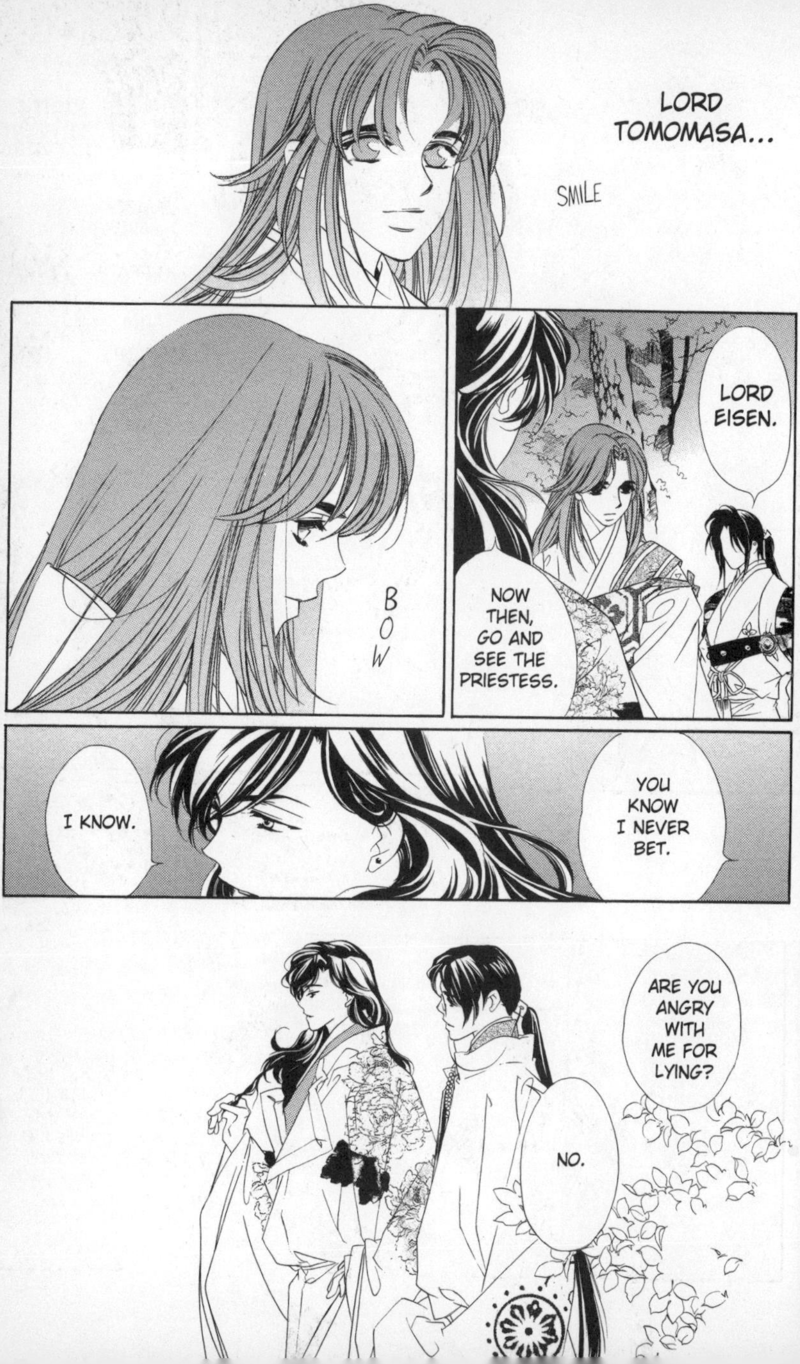
LORD TOMOMASA...
SMILE
LORD EISEN.
NOW THEN, GO AND SEE THE PRIESTESS.
BOW
YOU KNOW I NEVER BET.
I KNOW.
ARE YOU ANGRY WITH ME FOR LYING?
NO.

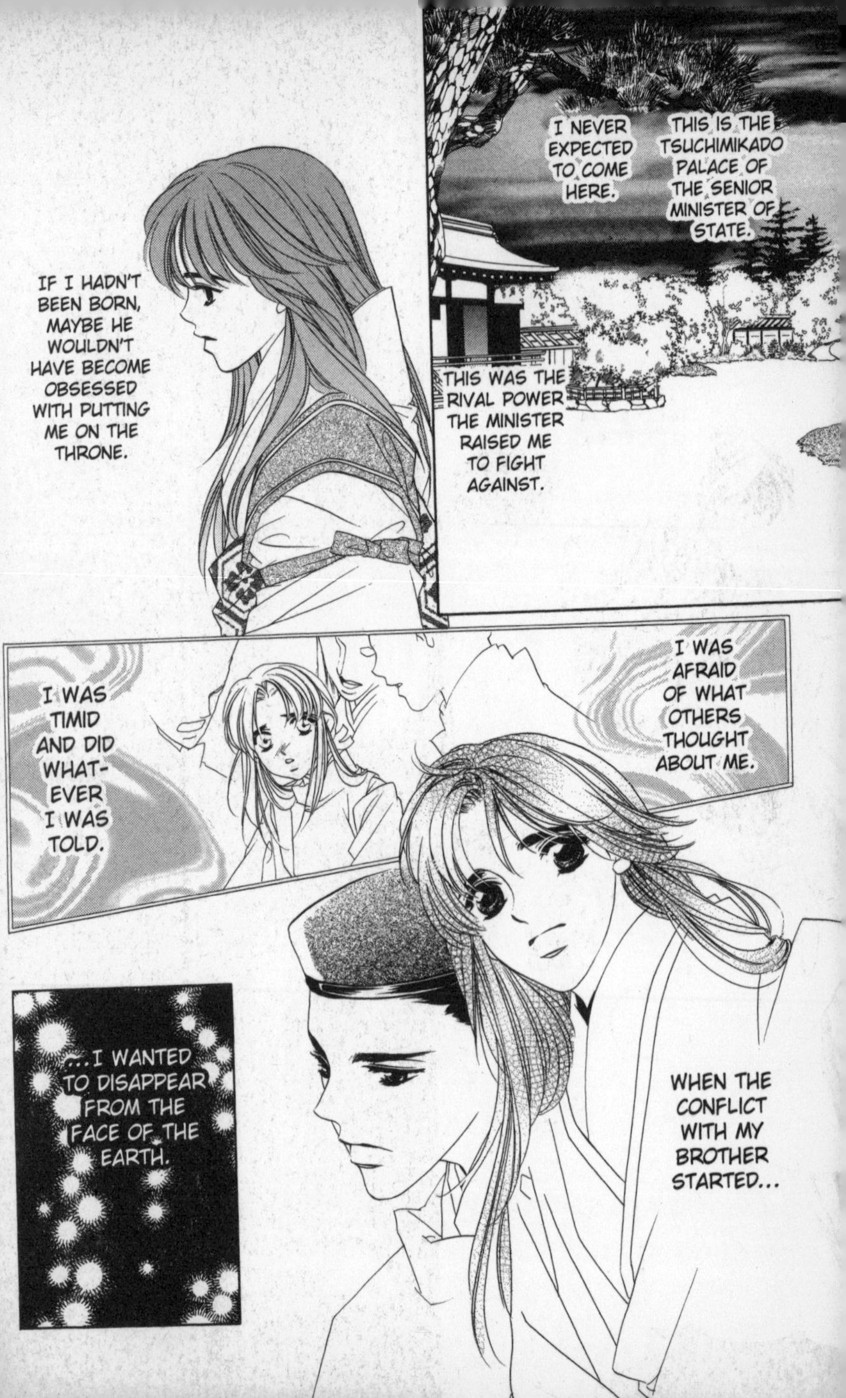
THIS IS THE TSUCHIMIKADO PALACE OF THE SENIOR MINISTER OF STATE.
I NEVER EXPECTED TO COME HERE.
THIS WAS THE RIVAL POWER THE MINISTER RAISED ME TO FIGHT AGAINST.
IF I HADN'T BEEN BORN, MAYBE HE WOULDN'T HAVE BECOME OBSESSED WITH PUTTING ME ON THE THRONE.
I WAS AFRAID OF WHAT OTHERS THOUGHT ABOUT ME.
I WAS TIMID AND DID WHAT-EVER I WAS TOLD.
WHEN THE CONFLICT WITH MY BROTHER STARTED...
...I WANTED TO DISAPPEAR FROM THE FACE OF THE EARTH.

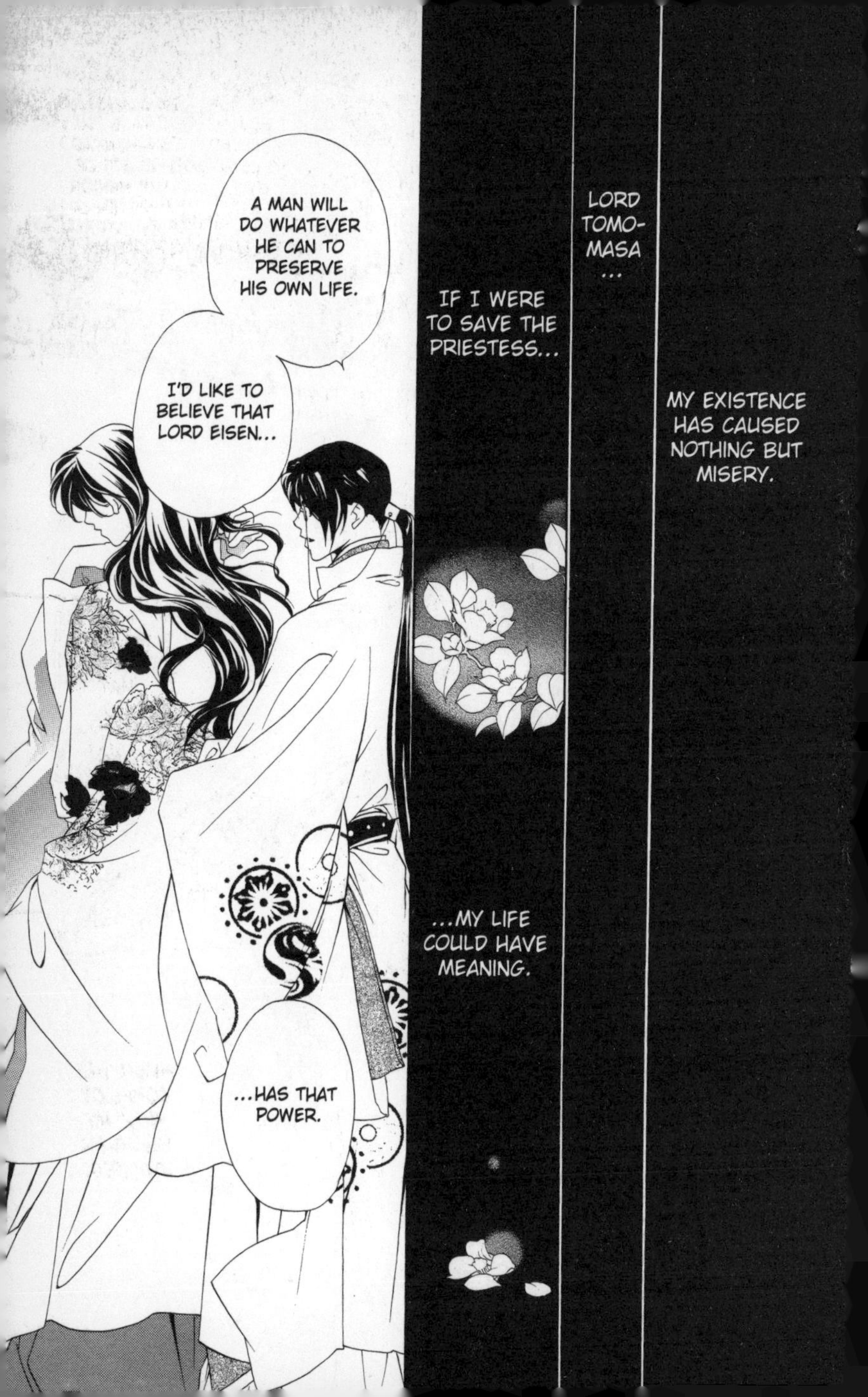
MY EXISTENCE HAS CAUSED NOTHING BUT MISERY.
LORD TOMO-MASA...
IF I WERE TO SAVE THE PRIESTESS...
...MY LIFE COULD HAVE MEANING.
A MAN WILL DO WHATEVER HE CAN TO PRESERVE HIS OWN LIFE.
I'D LIKE TO BELIEVE THAT LORD EISEN...
...HAS THAT POWER.

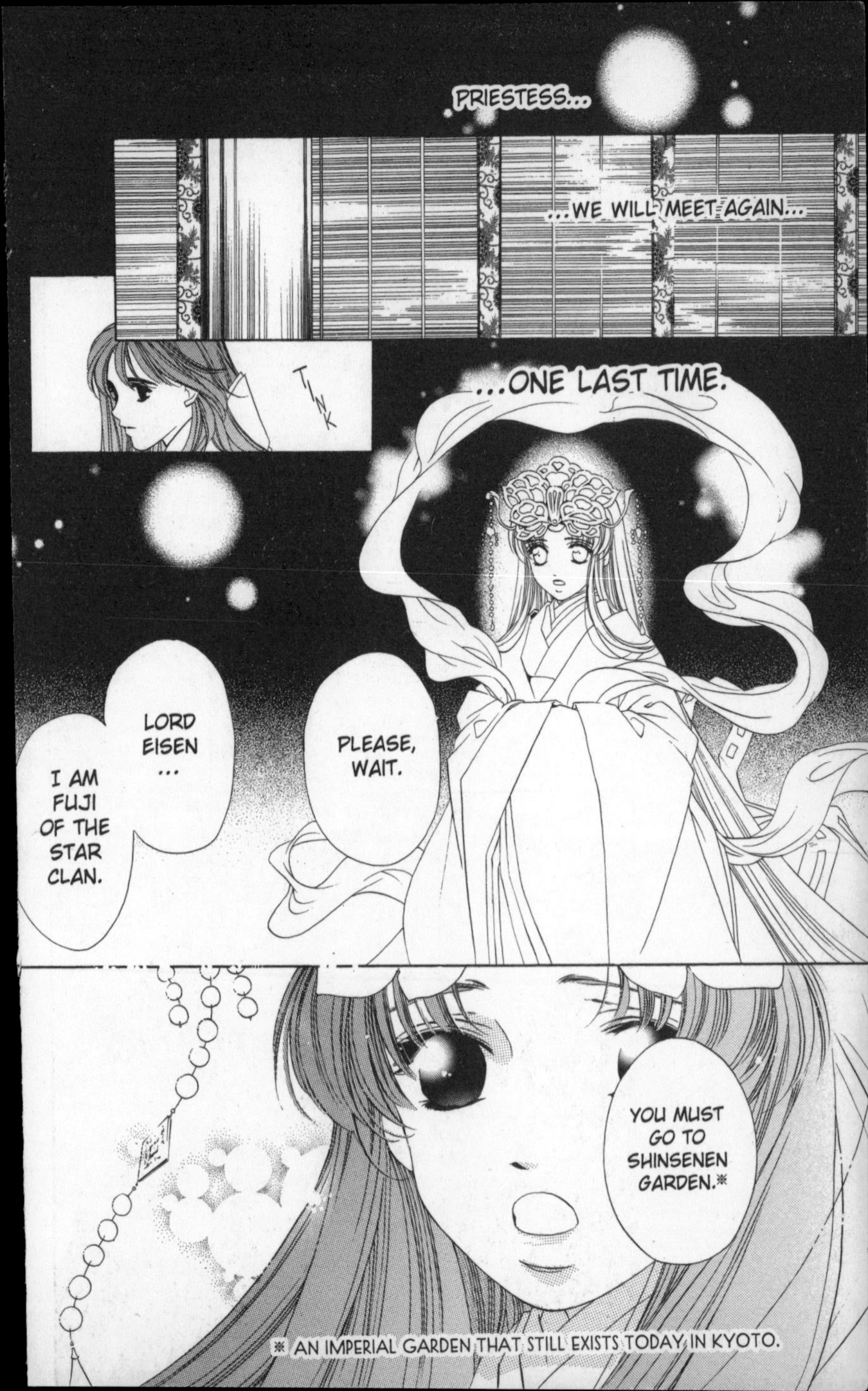
PRIESTESS...
...WE WILL MEET AGAIN...
TINK
...ONE LAST TIME.
PLEASE, WAIT.
LORD EISEN ...
I AM FUJI OF THE STAR CLAN.
YOU MUST GO TO SHINSENEN GARDEN.※
※ AN IMPERIAL GARDEN THAT STILL EXISTS TODAY IN KYOTO.

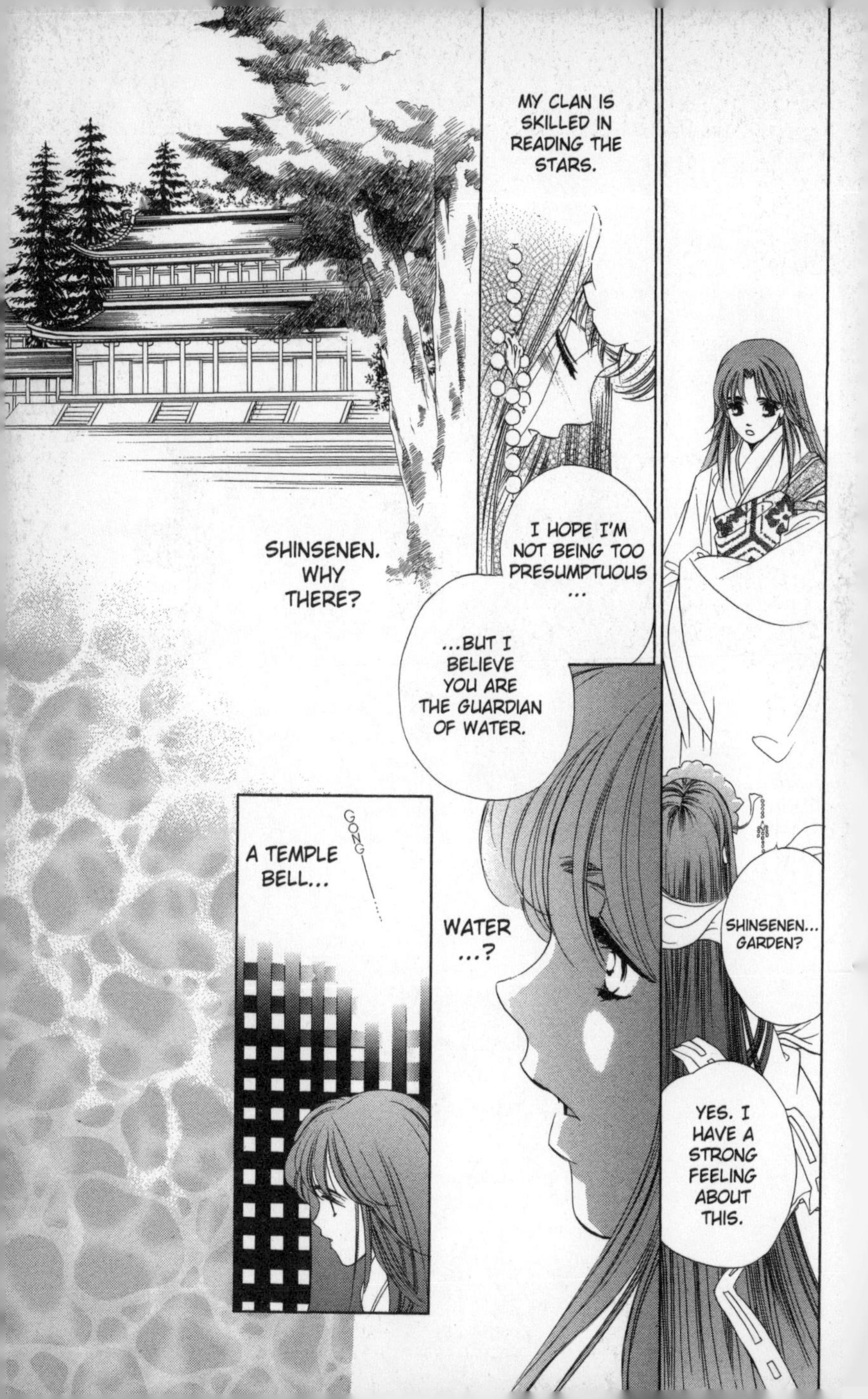
MY CLAN IS SKILLED IN READING THE STARS.
I HOPE I'M NOT BEING TOO PRESUMPTUOUS...
...BUT I BELIEVE YOU ARE THE GUARDIAN OF WATER.
SHINSENEN... GARDEN?
YES. I HAVE A STRONG FEELING ABOUT THIS.
WATER...?
SHINSENEN. WHY THERE?
GONG...
A TEMPLE BELL...

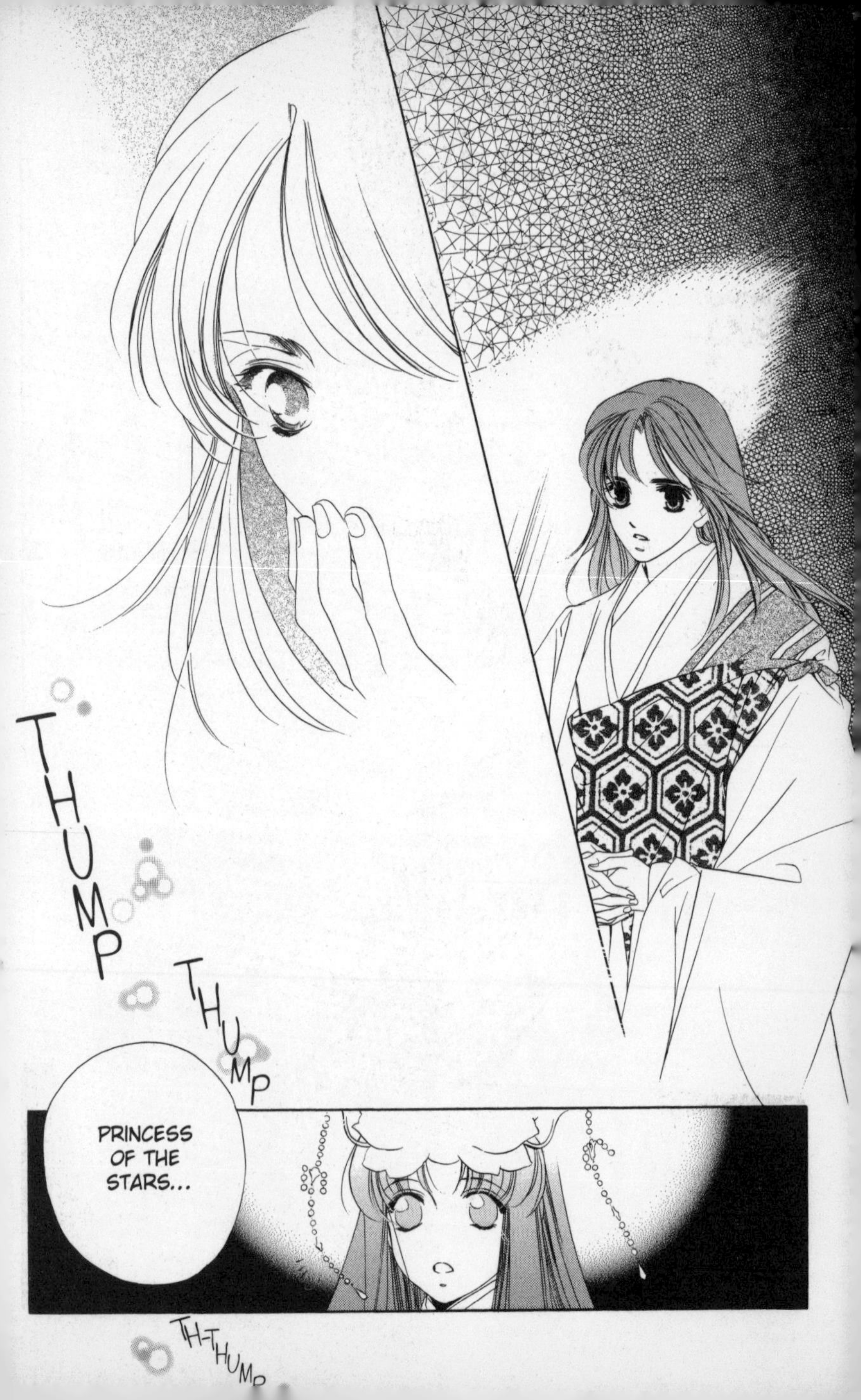
THUMP
THUMP
PRINCESS OF THE STARS...
TH-THUMP

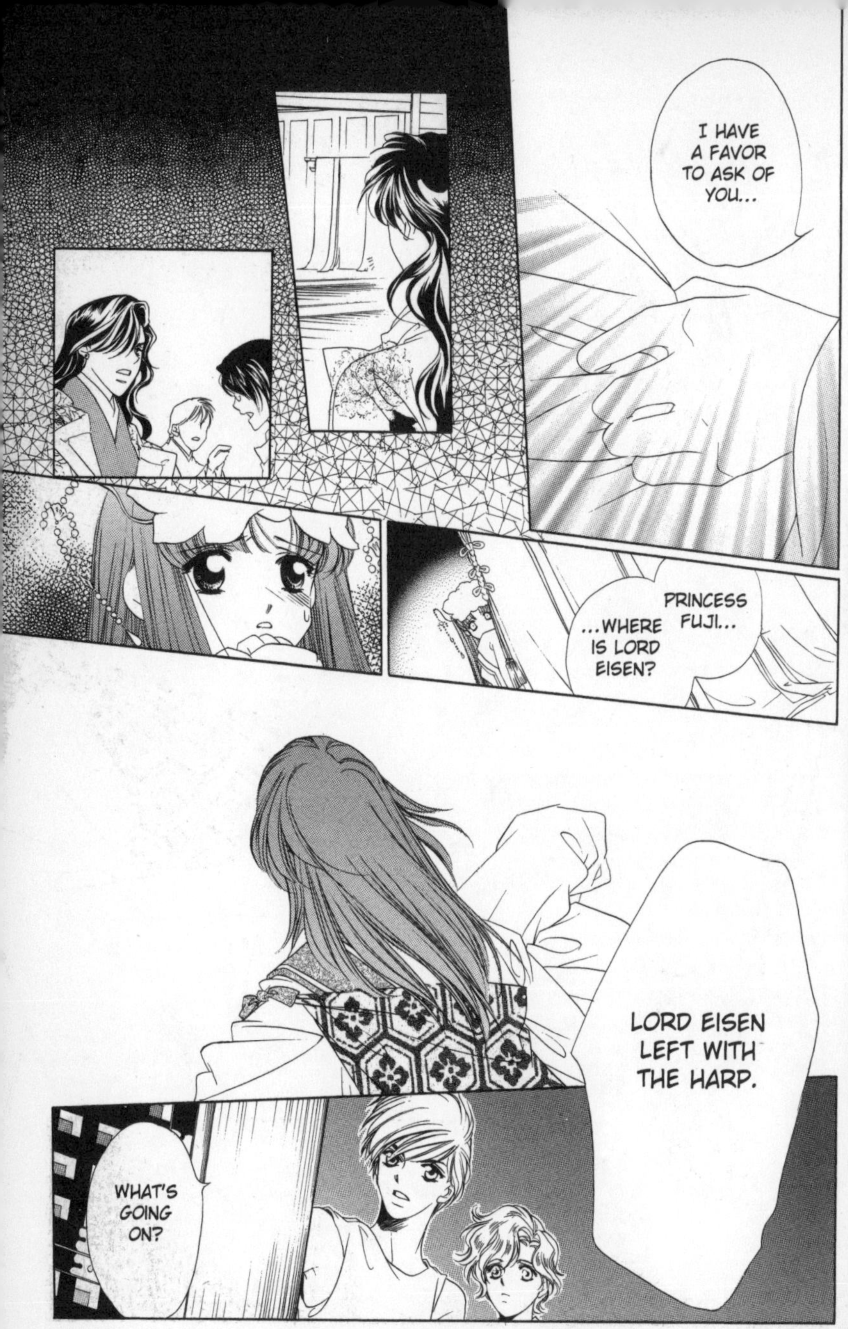
I HAVE A FAVOR TO ASK OF YOU...
PRINCESS FUJI...
...WHERE IS LORD EISEN?
LORD EISEN LEFT WITH THE HARP.
WHAT'S GOING ON?

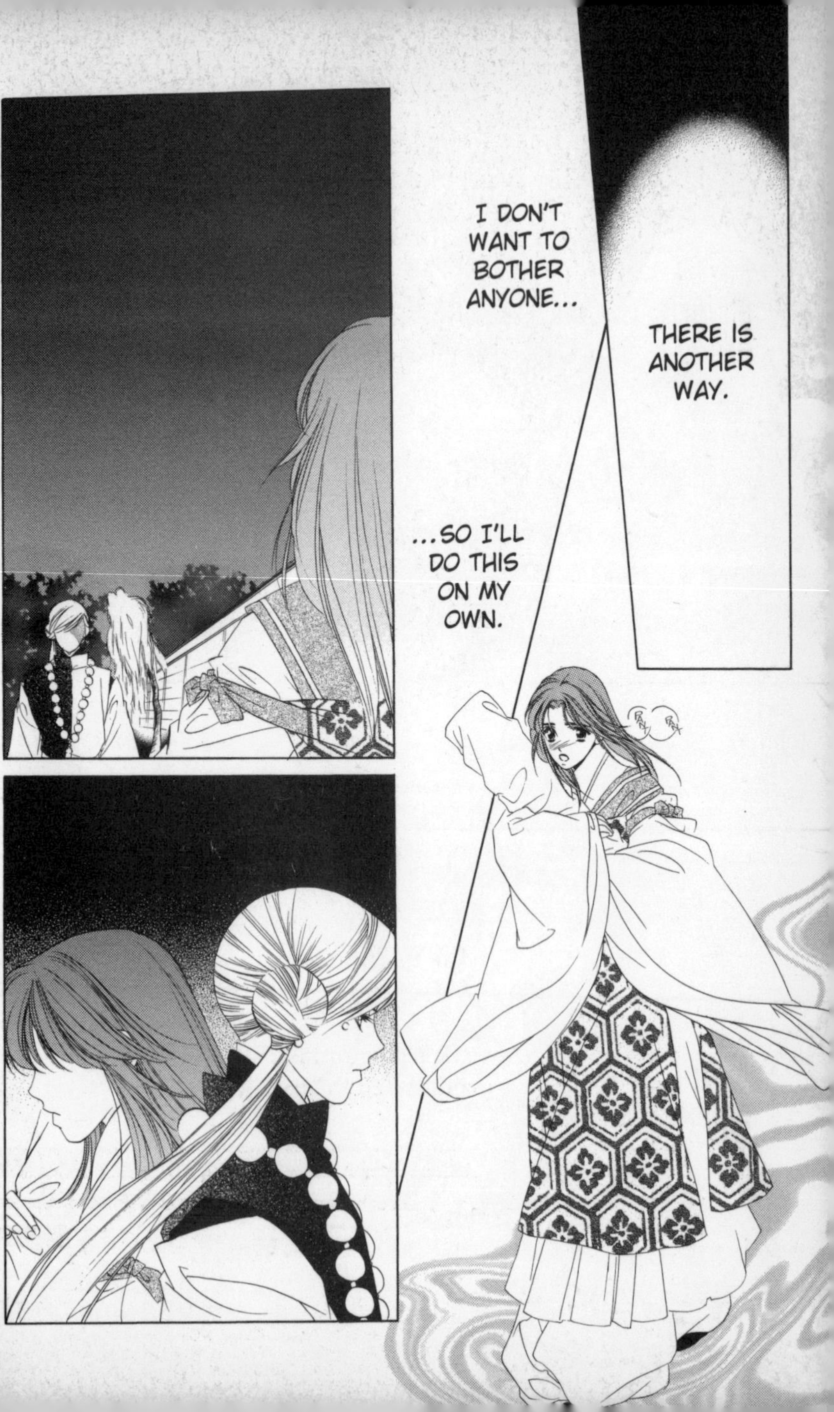
I DON'T WANT TO BOTHER ANYONE...
THERE IS ANOTHER WAY.
...SO I'LL DO THIS ON MY OWN.

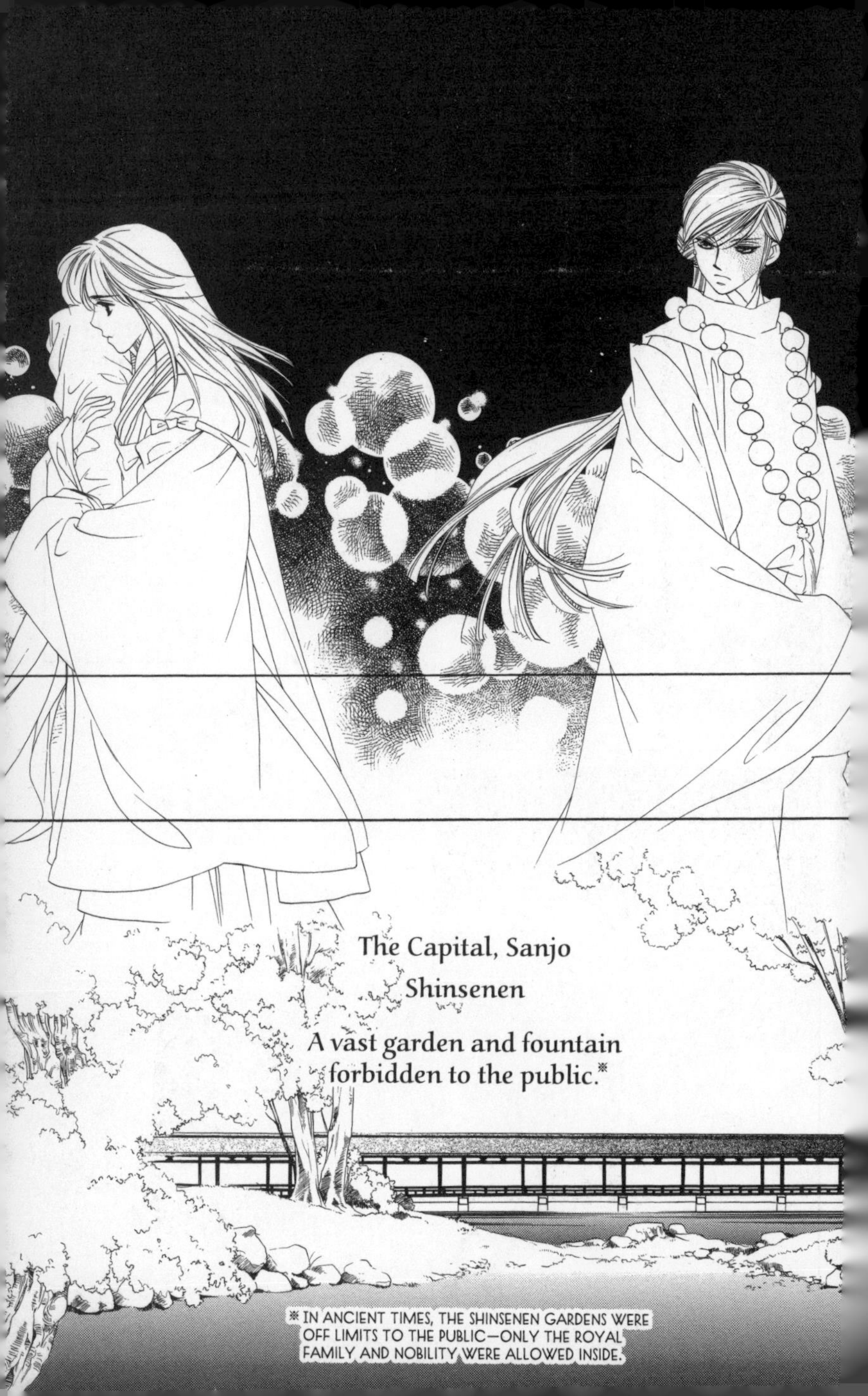
The Capital, Sanjo
Shinsenen
A vast garden and fountain forbidden to the public.※
※ IN ANCIENT TIMES, THE SHINSENEN GARDENS WERE OFF LIMITS TO THE PUBLIC—ONLY THE ROYAL FAMILY AND NOBILITY WERE ALLOWED INSIDE.

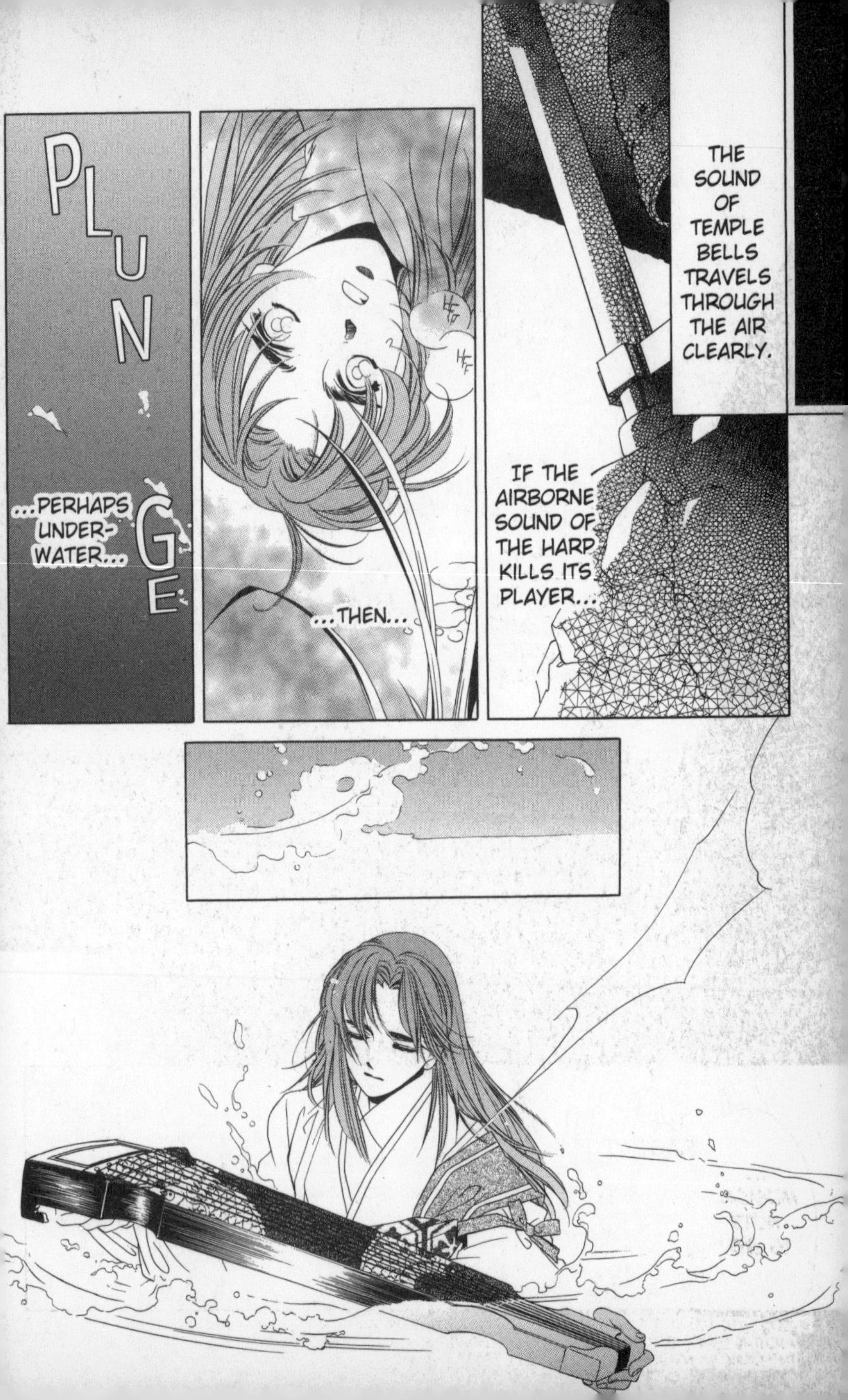
THE SOUND OF TEMPLE BELLS TRAVELS THROUGH THE AIR CLEARLY.
IF THE AIRBORNE SOUND OF THE HARP KILLS ITS PLAYER...
HEF
HEF
...THEN...
PLUNGE
...PERHAPS UNDER-WATER...

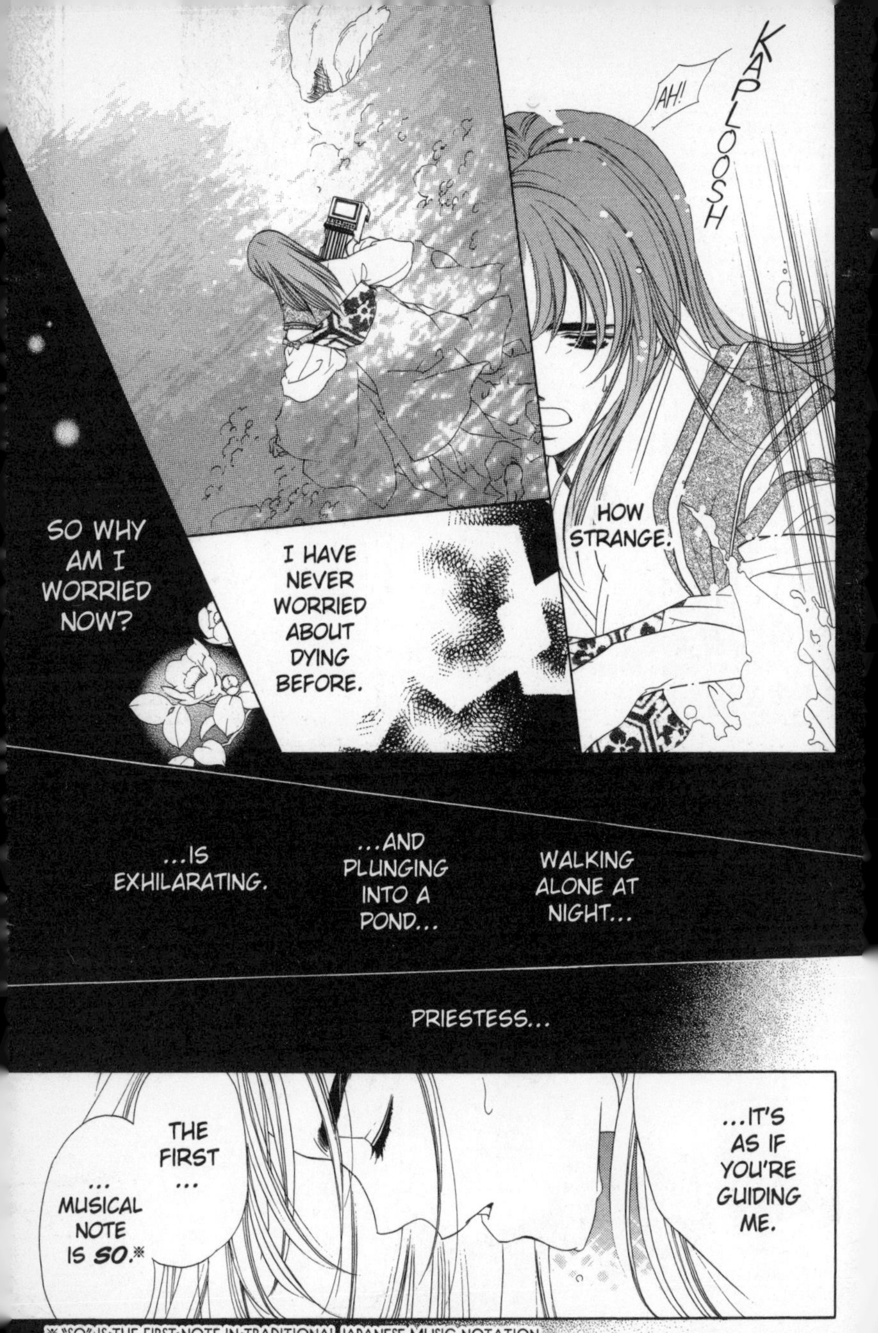
KAPLOOSH
AH!
HOW STRANGE.
I HAVE NEVER WORRIED ABOUT DYING BEFORE.
SO WHY AM I WORRIED NOW?
WALKING ALONE AT NIGHT...
...AND PLUNGING INTO A POND...
...IS EXHILARATING.
PRIESTESS...
...IT'S AS IF YOU'RE GUIDING ME.
THE FIRST ... MUSICAL NOTE IS *SO*.※

※"SO" IS THE FIRST NOTE IN TRADITIONAL JAPANESE MUSIC NOTATION, AND THE SAME FREQUENCY AS "SO" IN THE DO-RE-MI SCALE. IN AMERICAN MUSICAL NOTATION, IT'S E.

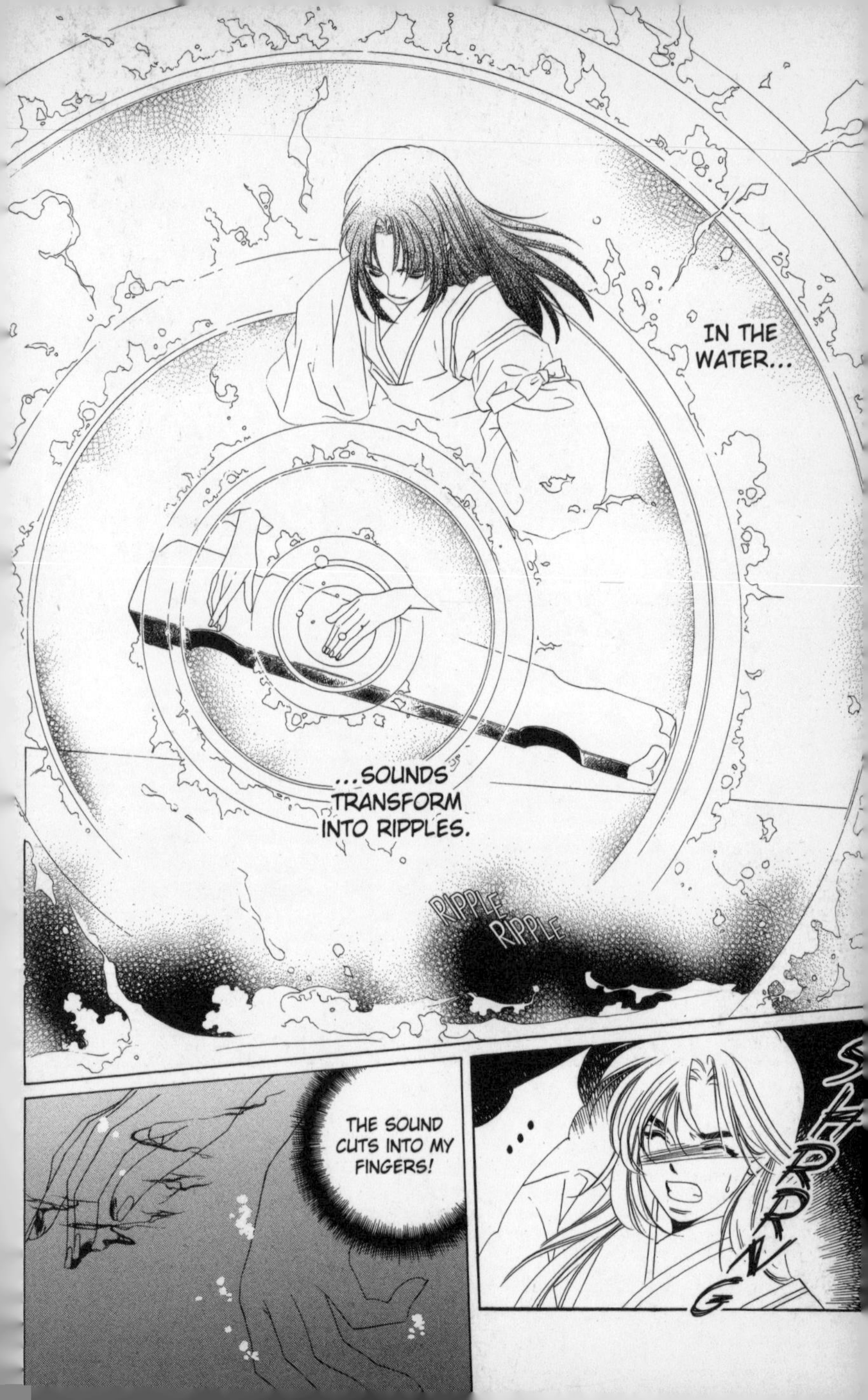
IN THE WATER...
...SOUNDS TRANSFORM INTO RIPPLES.
RIPPLE RIPPLE
SHRRRING
...
THE SOUND CUTS INTO MY FINGERS!

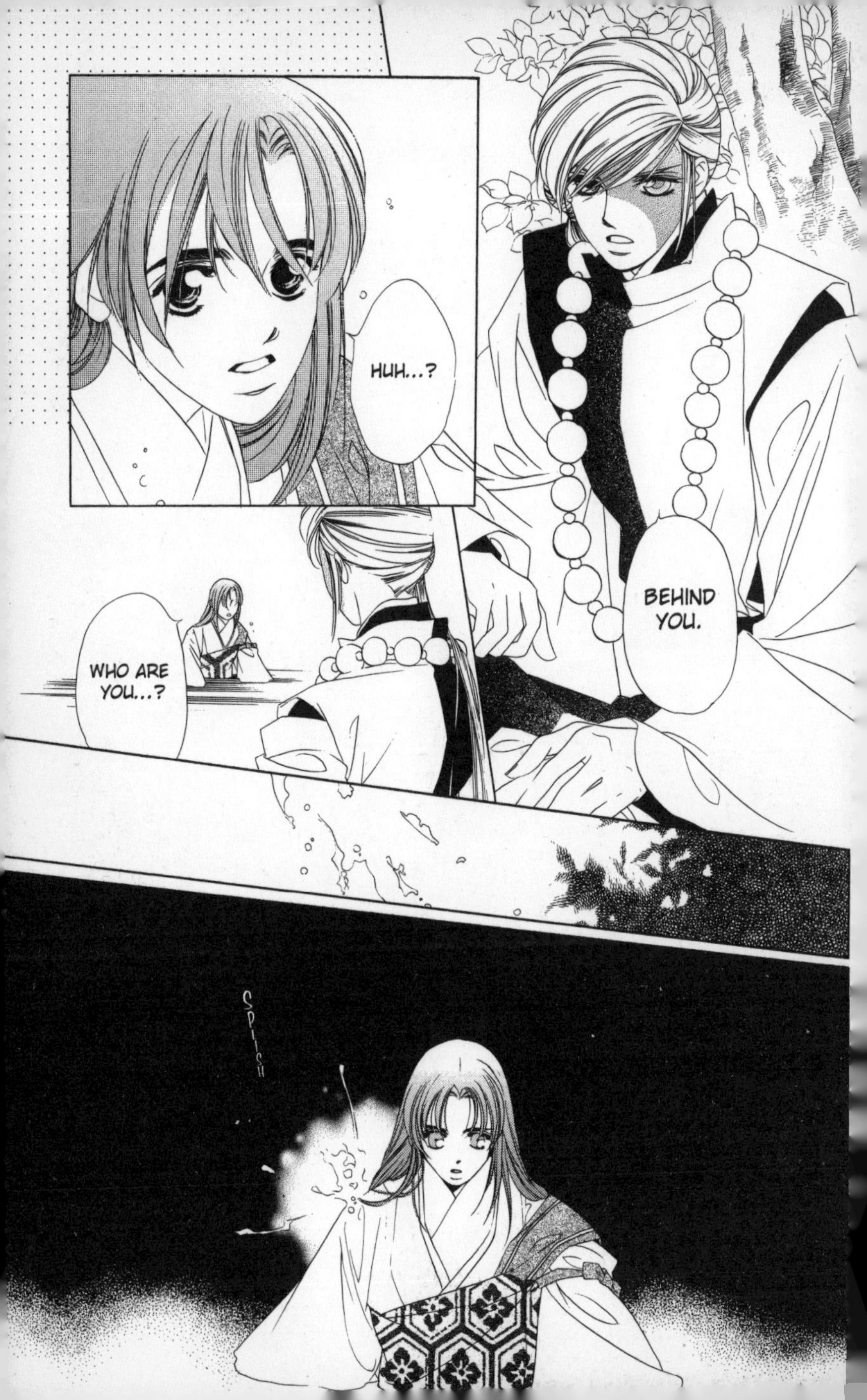
BEHIND YOU.
HUH...?
WHO ARE YOU...?
SPLISH

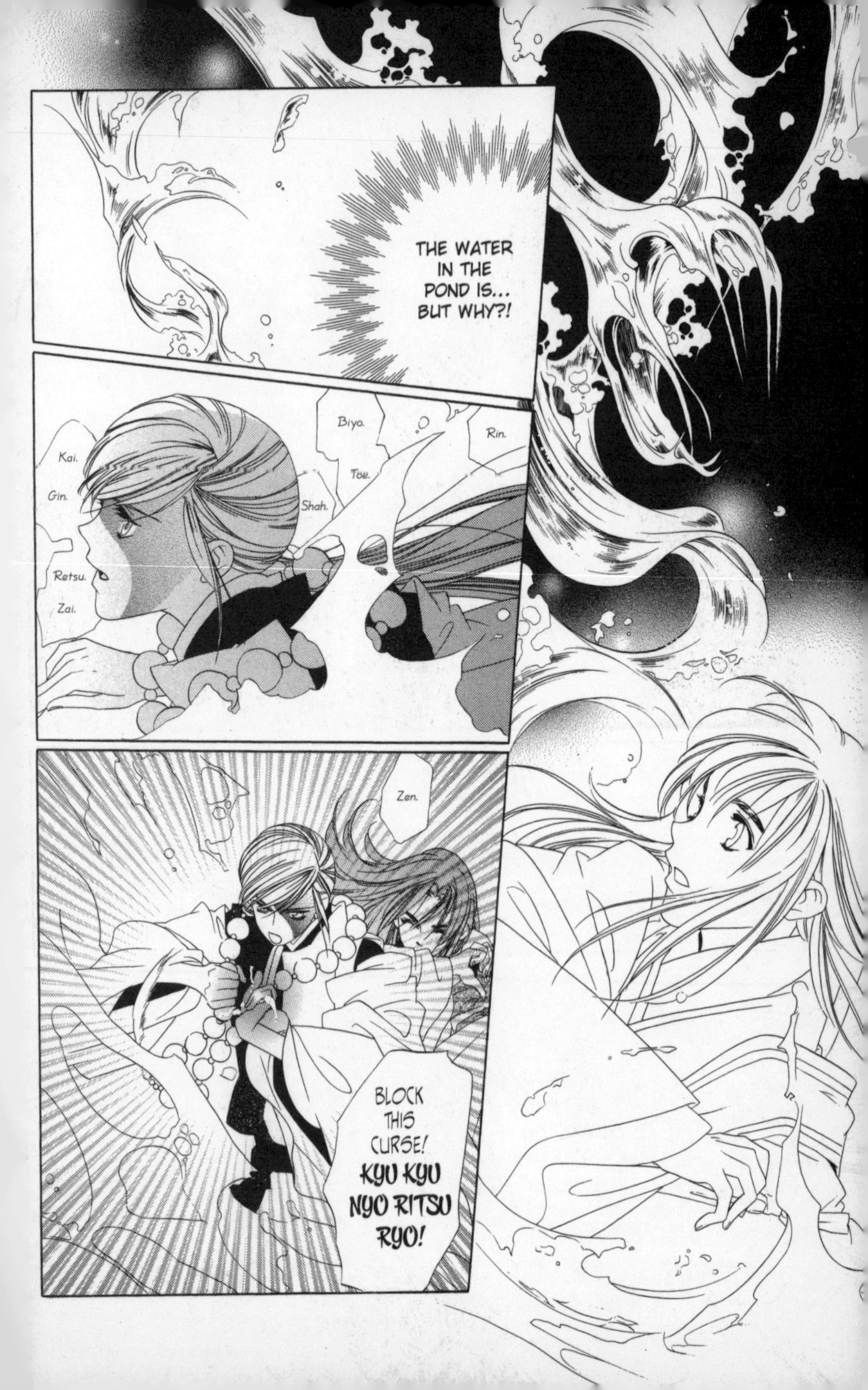
THE WATER IN THE POND IS... BUT WHY?!
Rin.
Biyo.
Toe.
Shah.
Kai.
Gin.
Retsu.
Zai.
Zen.
BLOCK THIS CURSE! KYU KYU NYO RITSU RYO!

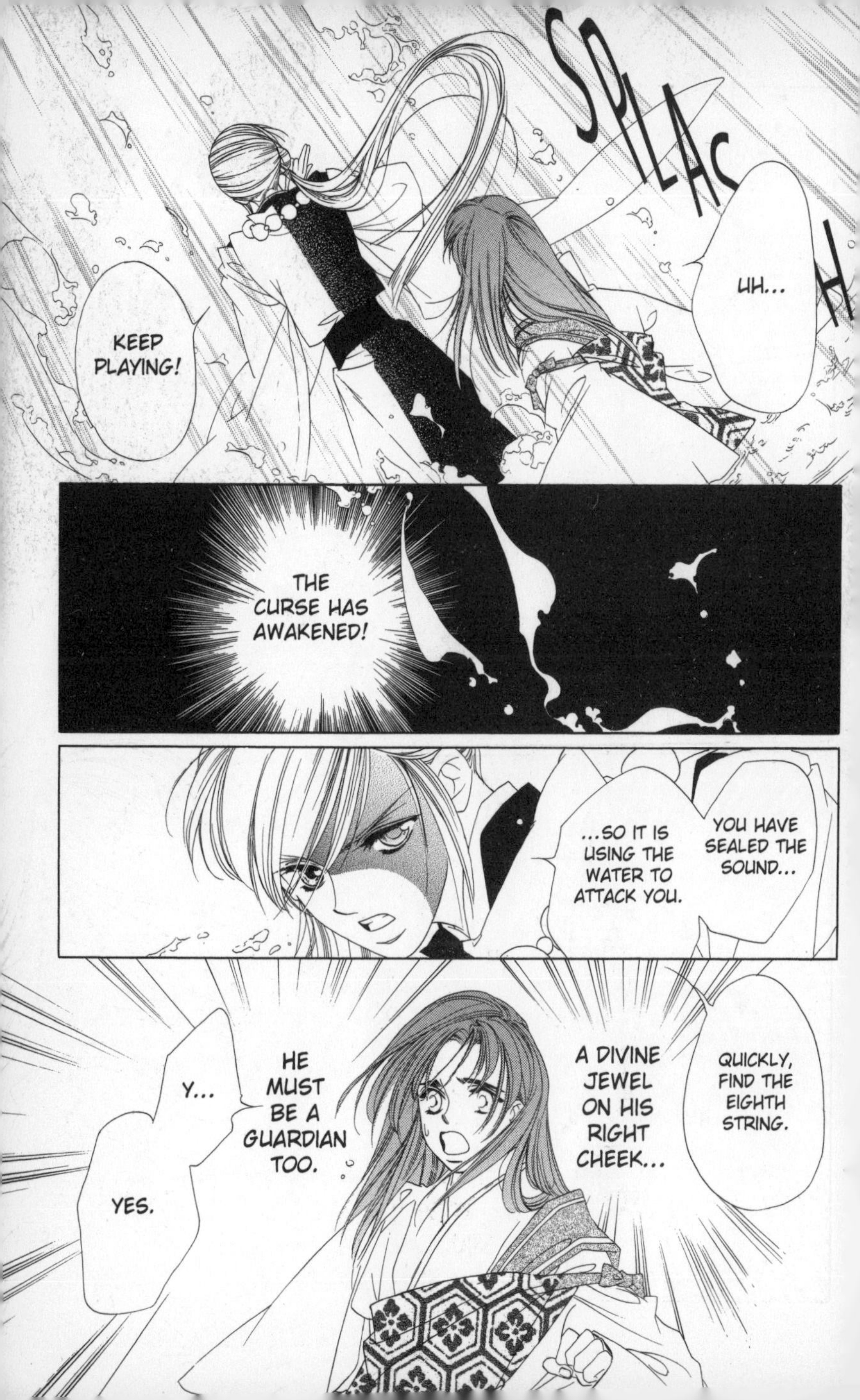
SPLASH
UH...
KEEP PLAYING!
THE CURSE HAS AWAKENED!
YOU HAVE SEALED THE SOUND...
...SO IT IS USING THE WATER TO ATTACK YOU.
QUICKLY, FIND THE EIGHTH STRING.
A DIVINE JEWEL ON HIS RIGHT CHEEK...
HE MUST BE A GUARDIAN TOO.
Y...
YES.

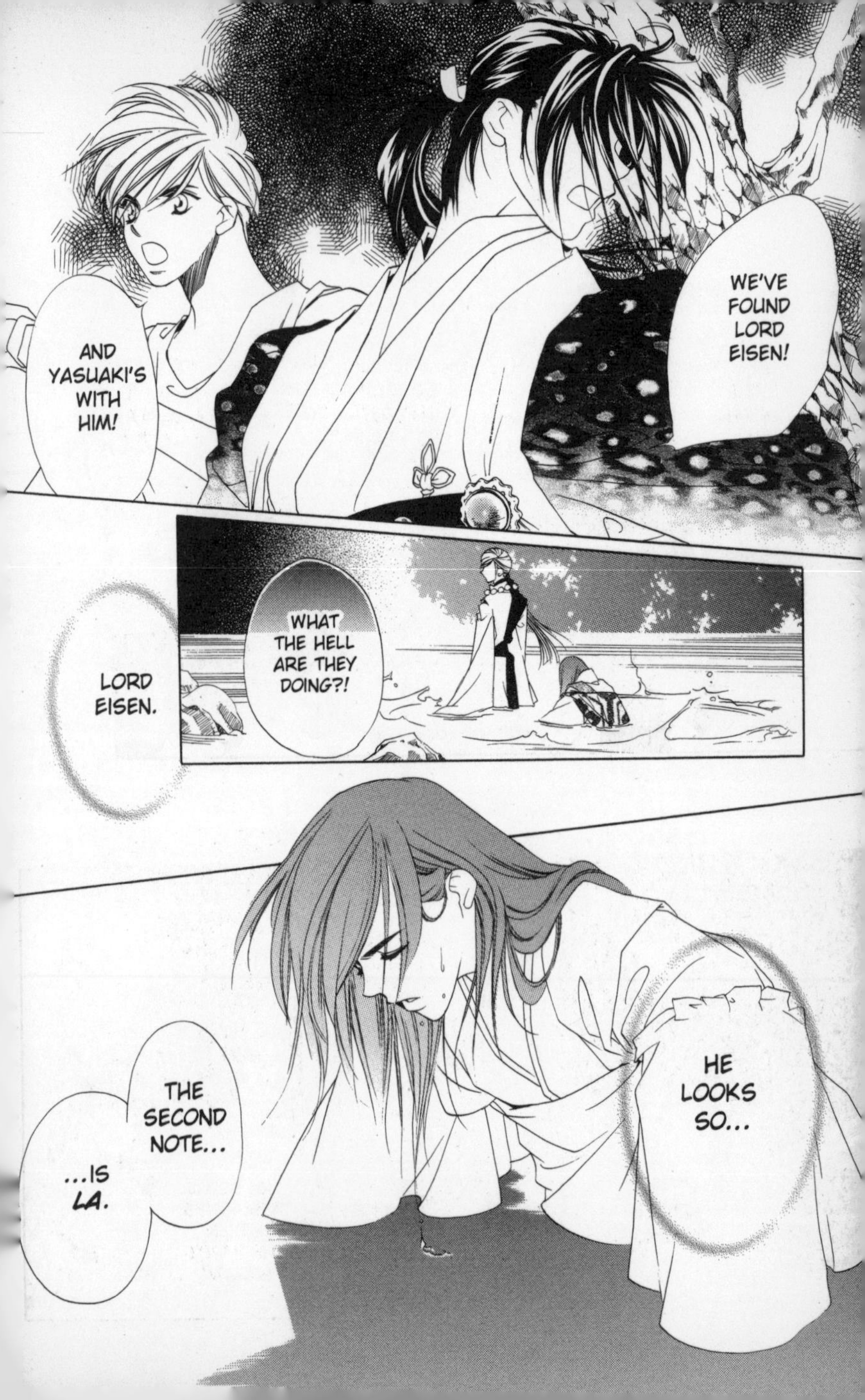
WE'VE FOUND LORD EISEN!
AND YASUAKI'S WITH HIM!
WHAT THE HELL ARE THEY DOING?!
LORD EISEN.
HE LOOKS SO...
THE SECOND NOTE...
...IS *LA*.

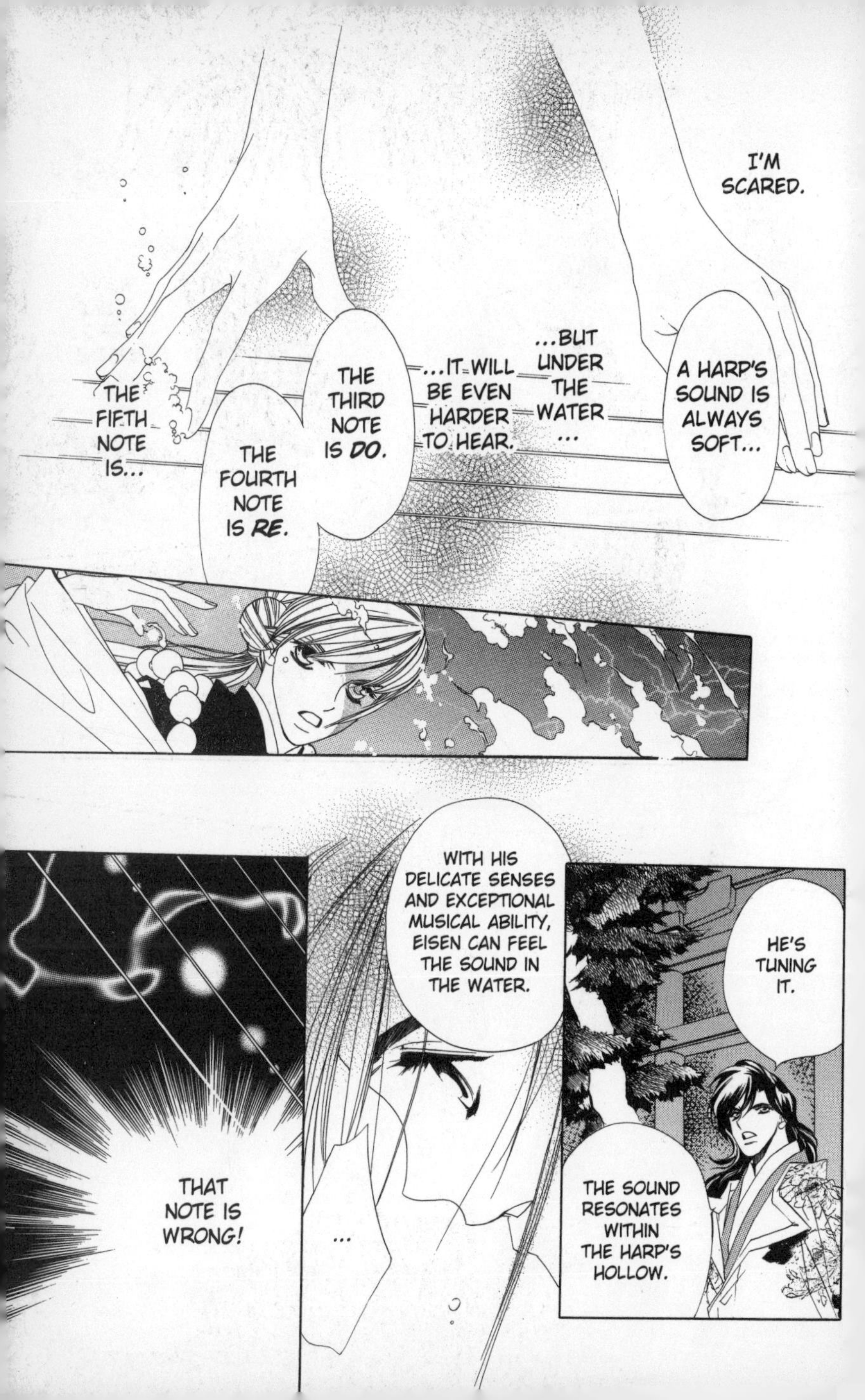
I'M SCARED.
A HARP'S SOUND IS ALWAYS SOFT...
...BUT UNDER THE WATER...
...IT WILL BE EVEN HARDER TO HEAR.
THE THIRD NOTE IS *DO*.
THE FOURTH NOTE IS *RE*.
THE FIFTH NOTE IS...
HE'S TUNING IT.
THE SOUND RESONATES WITHIN THE HARP'S HOLLOW.
WITH HIS DELICATE SENSES AND EXCEPTIONAL MUSICAL ABILITY, EISEN CAN FEEL THE SOUND IN THE WATER.
...
THAT NOTE IS WRONG!

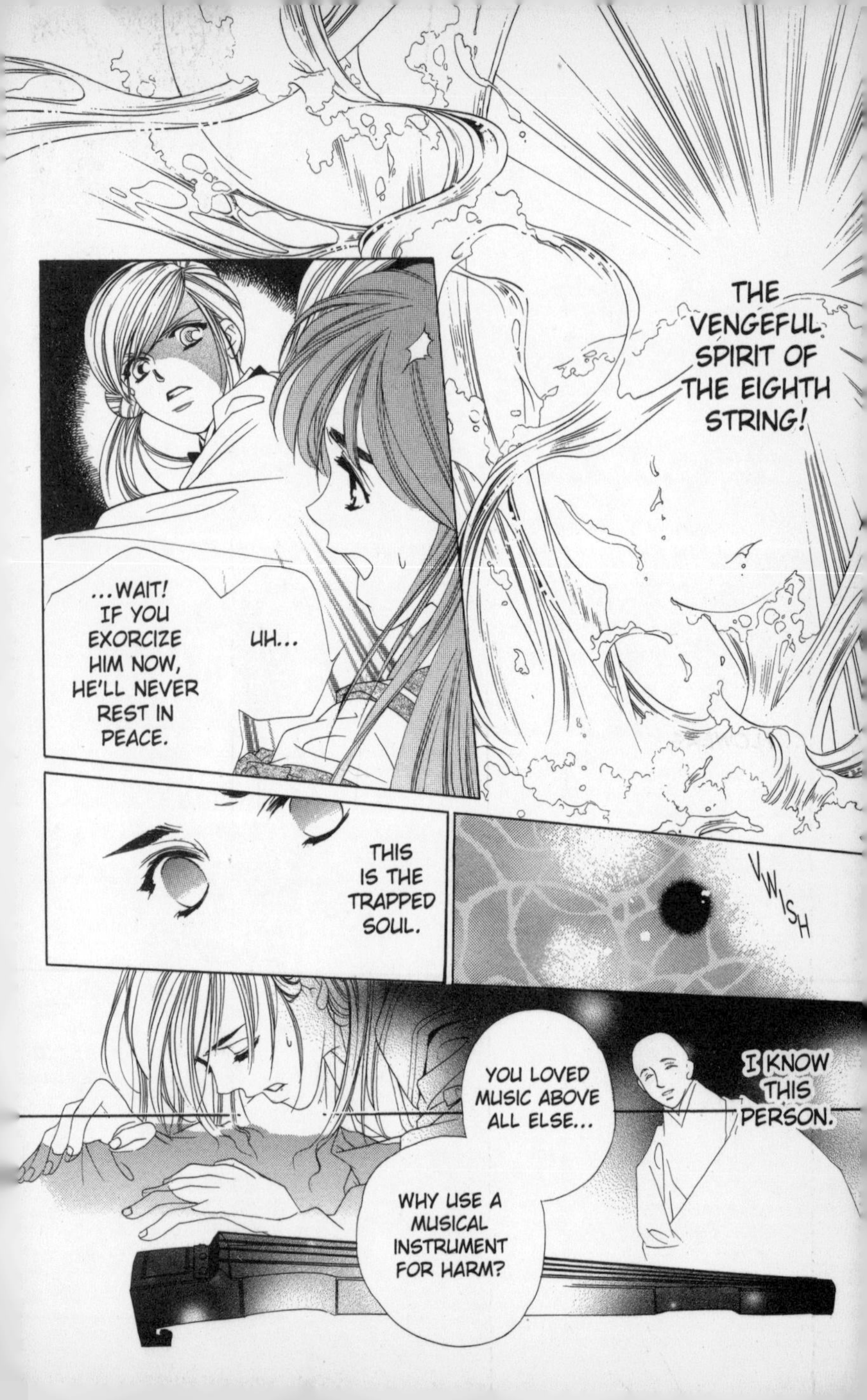
THE VENGEFUL SPIRIT OF THE EIGHTH STRING!
UH...
...WAIT! IF YOU EXORCIZE HIM NOW, HE'LL NEVER REST IN PEACE.
VWISH
THIS IS THE TRAPPED SOUL.
I KNOW THIS PERSON.
YOU LOVED MUSIC ABOVE ALL ELSE...
WHY USE A MUSICAL INSTRUMENT FOR HARM?

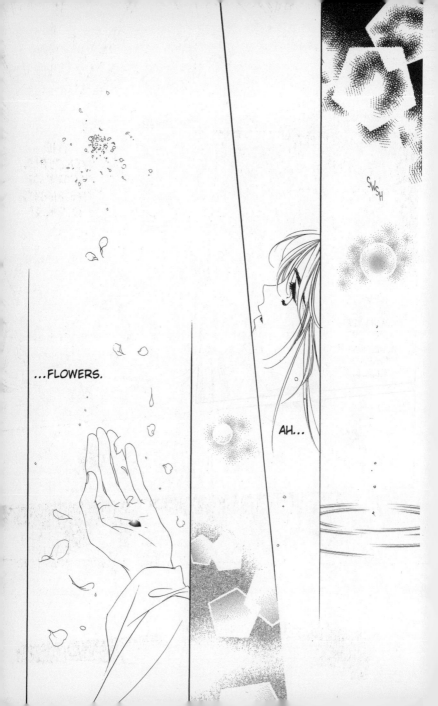

...FLOWERS.

AH...

SWSH

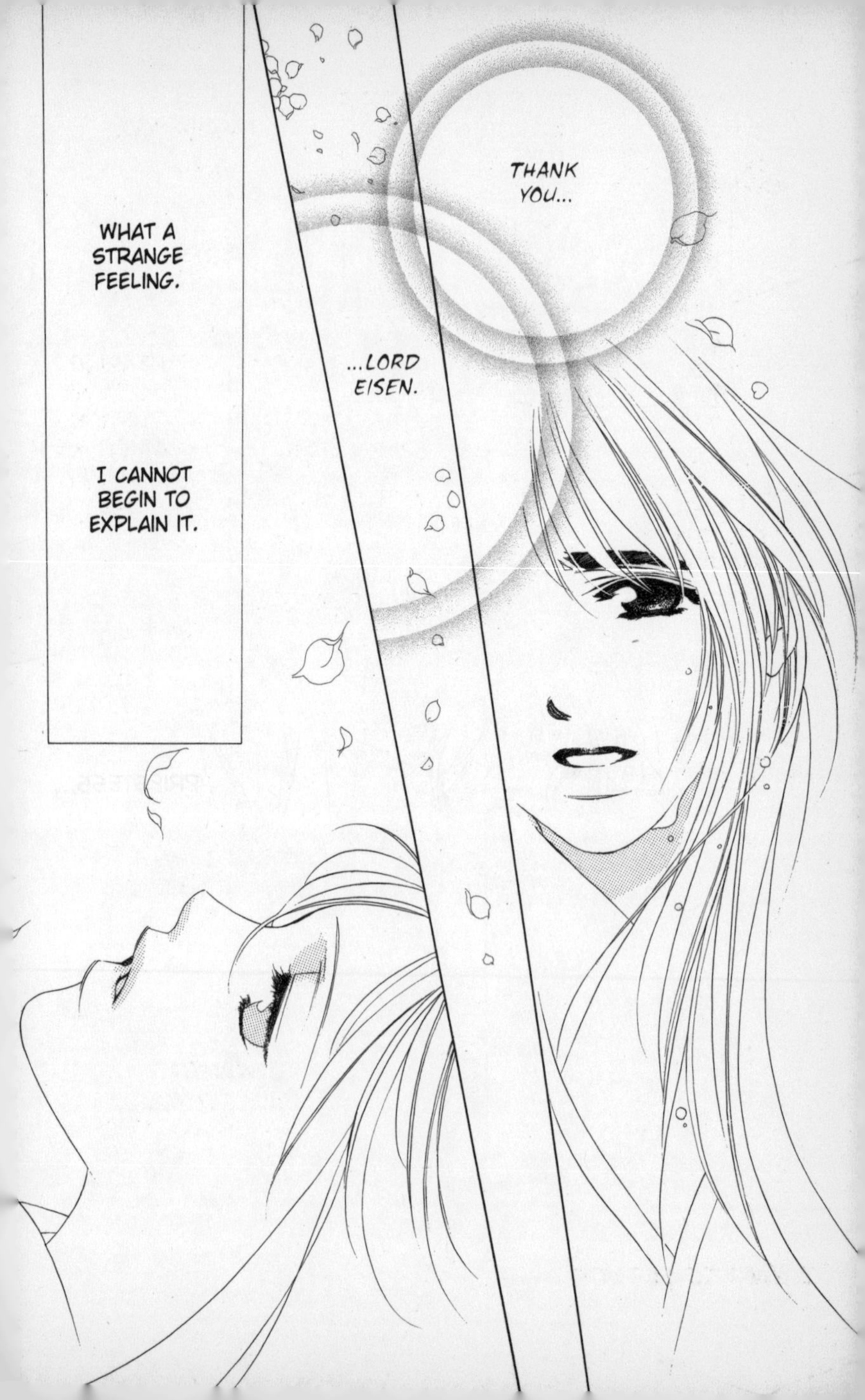
THANK YOU...
...LORD EISEN.
WHAT A STRANGE FEELING.
I CANNOT BEGIN TO EXPLAIN IT.

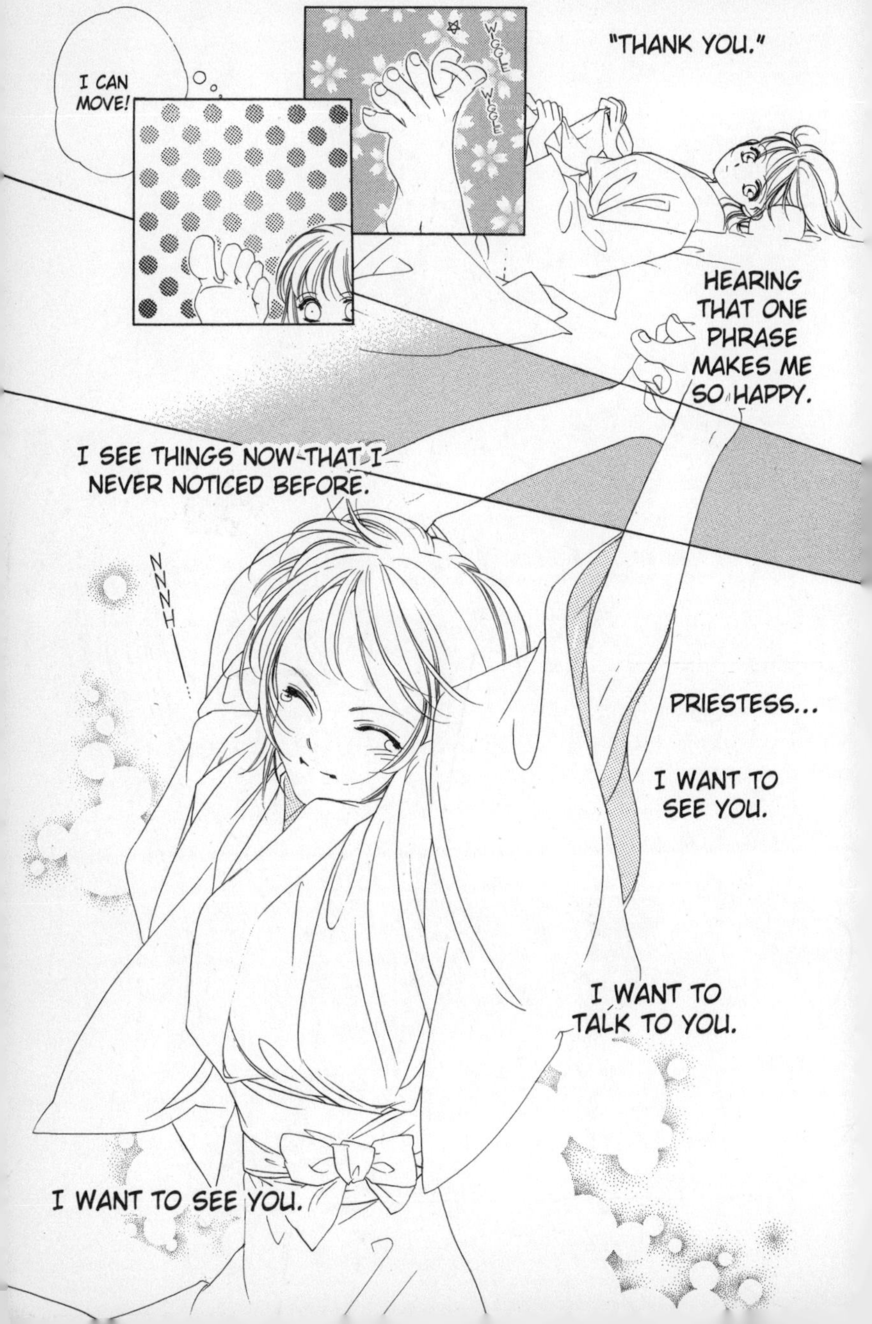
"THANK YOU."
WIGGLE WIGGLE
I CAN MOVE!
HEARING THAT ONE PHRASE MAKES ME SO HAPPY.
I SEE THINGS NOW THAT I NEVER NOTICED BEFORE.
PRIESTESS...
I WANT TO SEE YOU.
I WANT TO TALK TO YOU.
NNNH
I WANT TO SEE YOU.

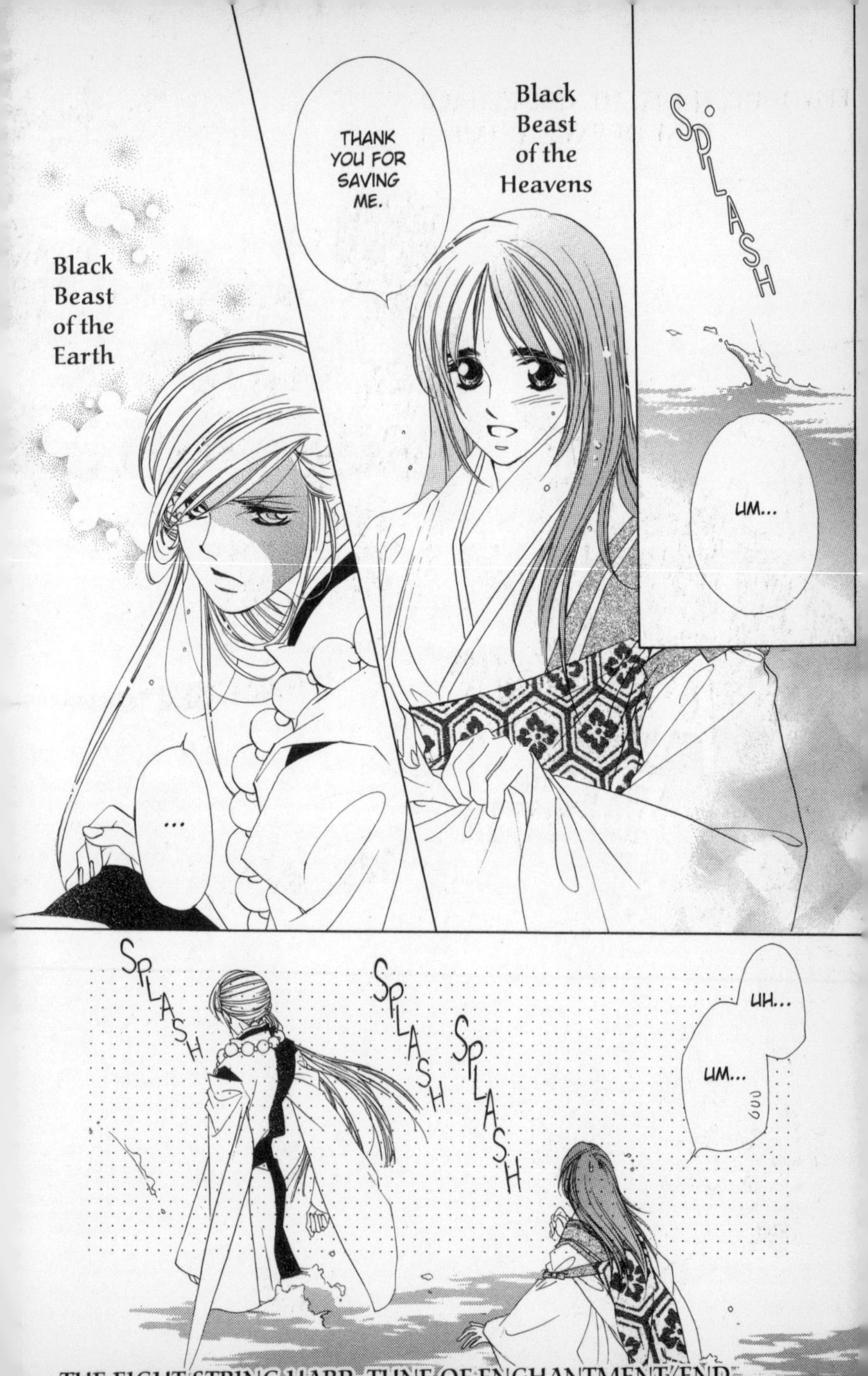
SPLASH
UM...
THANK YOU FOR SAVING ME.
Black Beast of the Heavens
Black Beast of the Earth
...
UH...
UM...
SPLASH
SPLASH
SPLASH

THE EIGHT STRING HARP—TUNE OF ENCHANTMENT/END

EPILOGUE: THE EIGHT STRING HARP–TUNE OF ENCHANTMENT

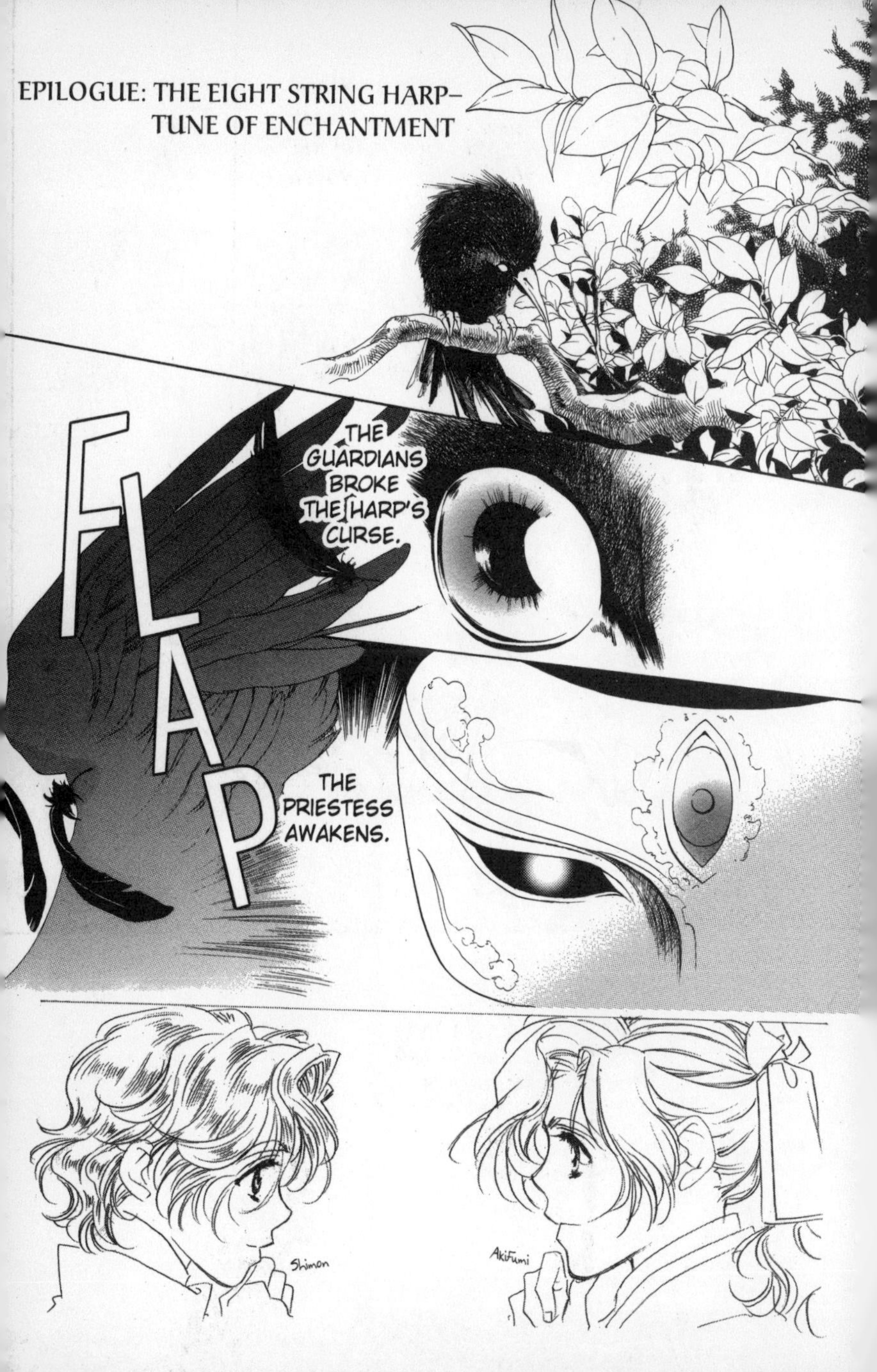
THE GUARDIANS BROKE THE HARP'S CURSE.
FLAP
THE PRIESTESS AWAKENS.
AkiFumi
Shimon

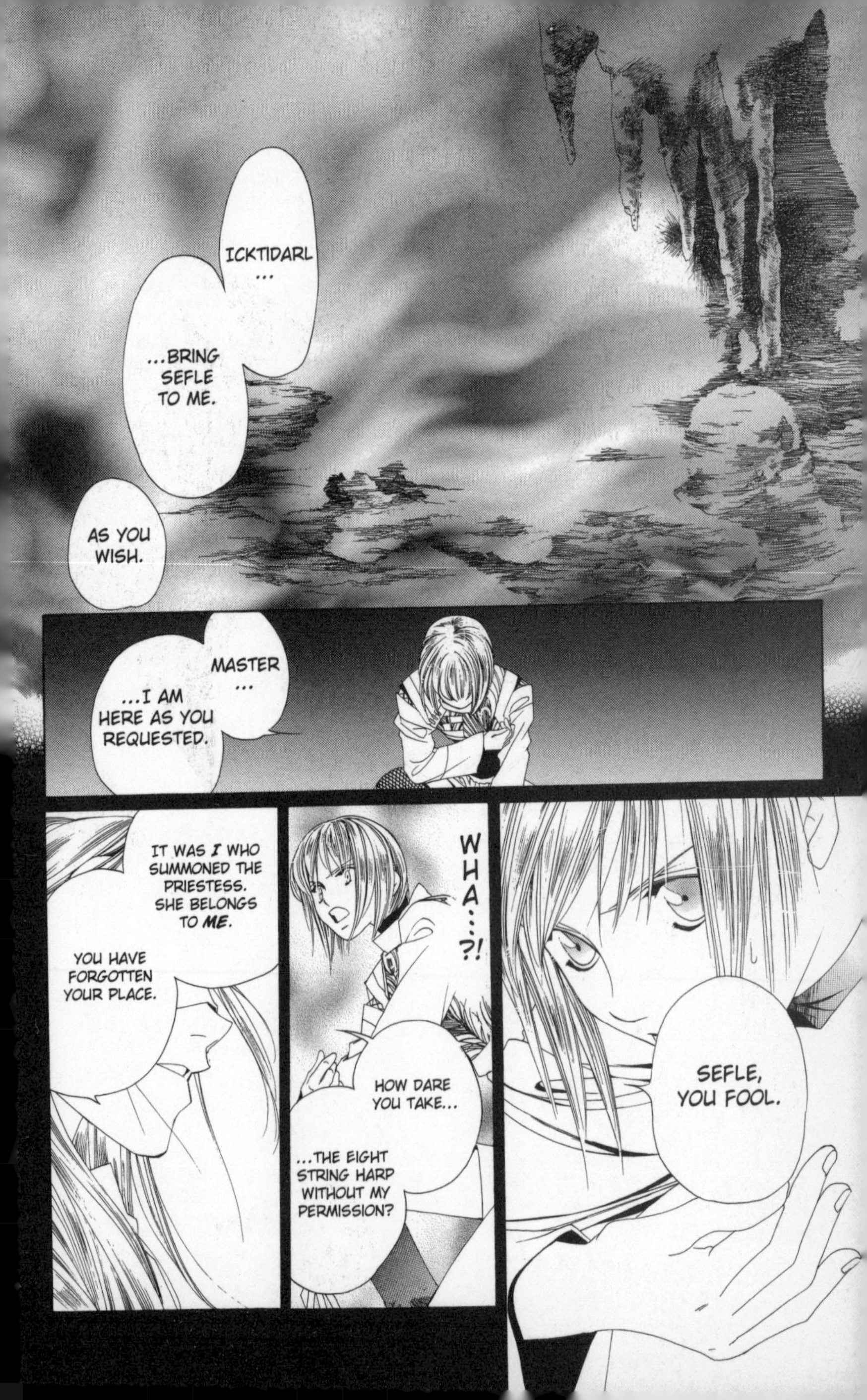
ICKTIDARL ...
...BRING SEFLE TO ME.
AS YOU WISH.
MASTER ...
...I AM HERE AS YOU REQUESTED.
SEFLE, YOU FOOL.
WHA...?!
HOW DARE YOU TAKE...
...THE EIGHT STRING HARP WITHOUT MY PERMISSION?
IT WAS *I* WHO SUMMONED THE PRIESTESS. SHE BELONGS TO ***ME***.
YOU HAVE FORGOTTEN YOUR PLACE.

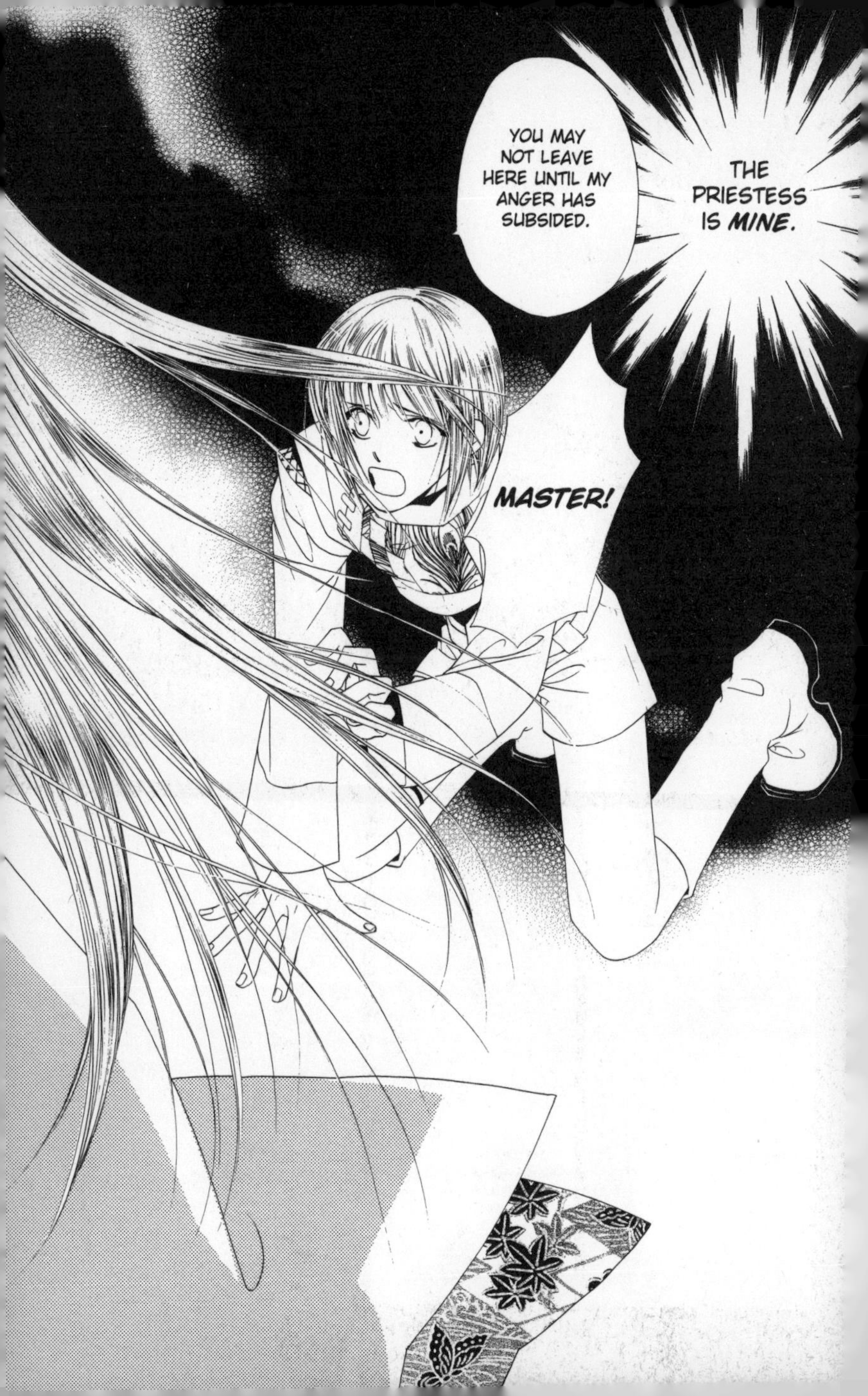
THE PRIESTESS IS *MINE.*
YOU MAY NOT LEAVE HERE UNTIL MY ANGER HAS SUBSIDED.
MASTER!

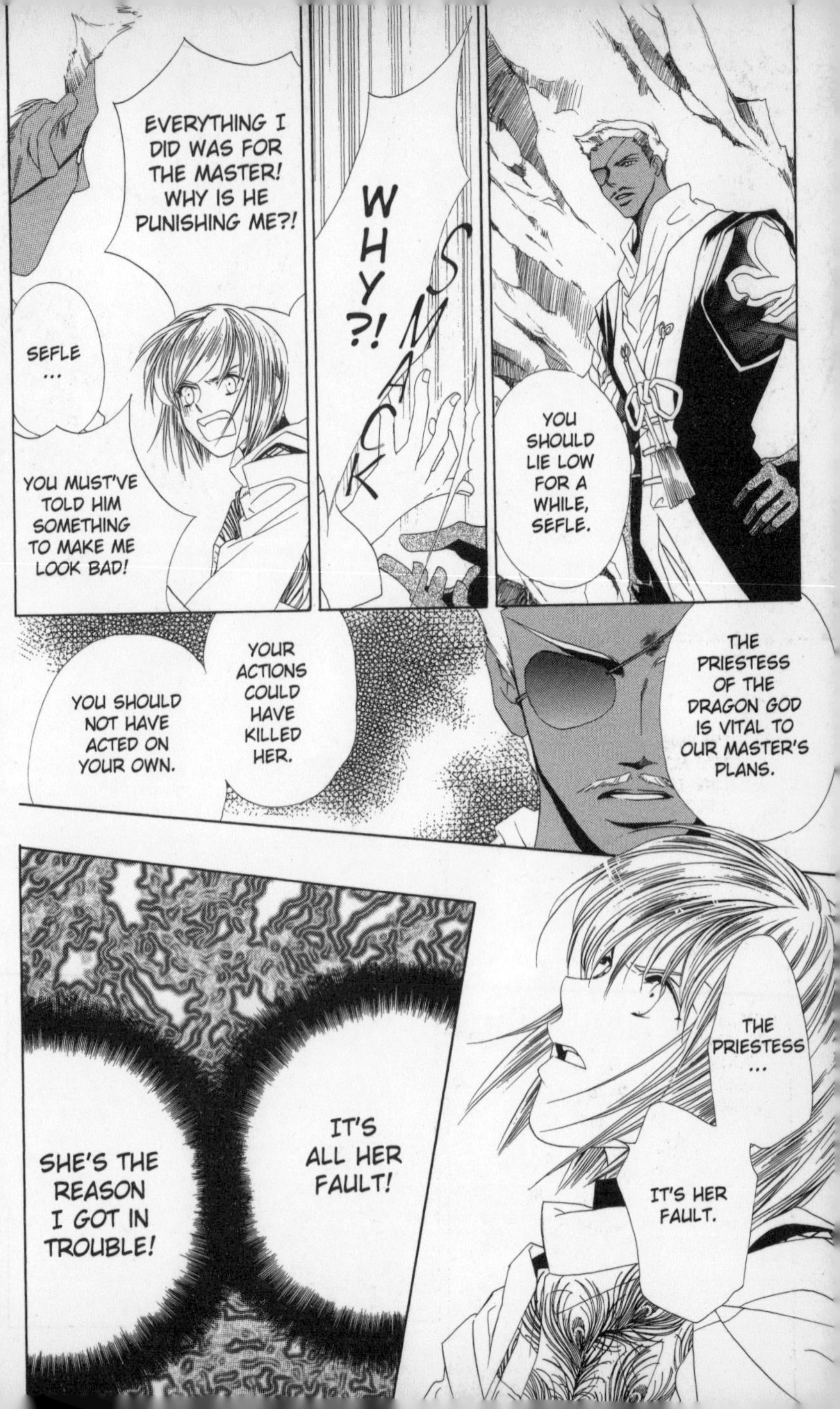
YOU SHOULD LIE LOW FOR A WHILE, SEFLE.
WHY?!
SMACK
EVERYTHING I DID WAS FOR THE MASTER! WHY IS HE PUNISHING ME?!
SEFLE...
YOU MUST'VE TOLD HIM SOMETHING TO MAKE ME LOOK BAD!
THE PRIESTESS OF THE DRAGON GOD IS VITAL TO OUR MASTER'S PLANS.
YOUR ACTIONS COULD HAVE KILLED HER.
YOU SHOULD NOT HAVE ACTED ON YOUR OWN.
THE PRIESTESS...
IT'S HER FAULT.
IT'S ALL HER FAULT!
SHE'S THE REASON I GOT IN TROUBLE!

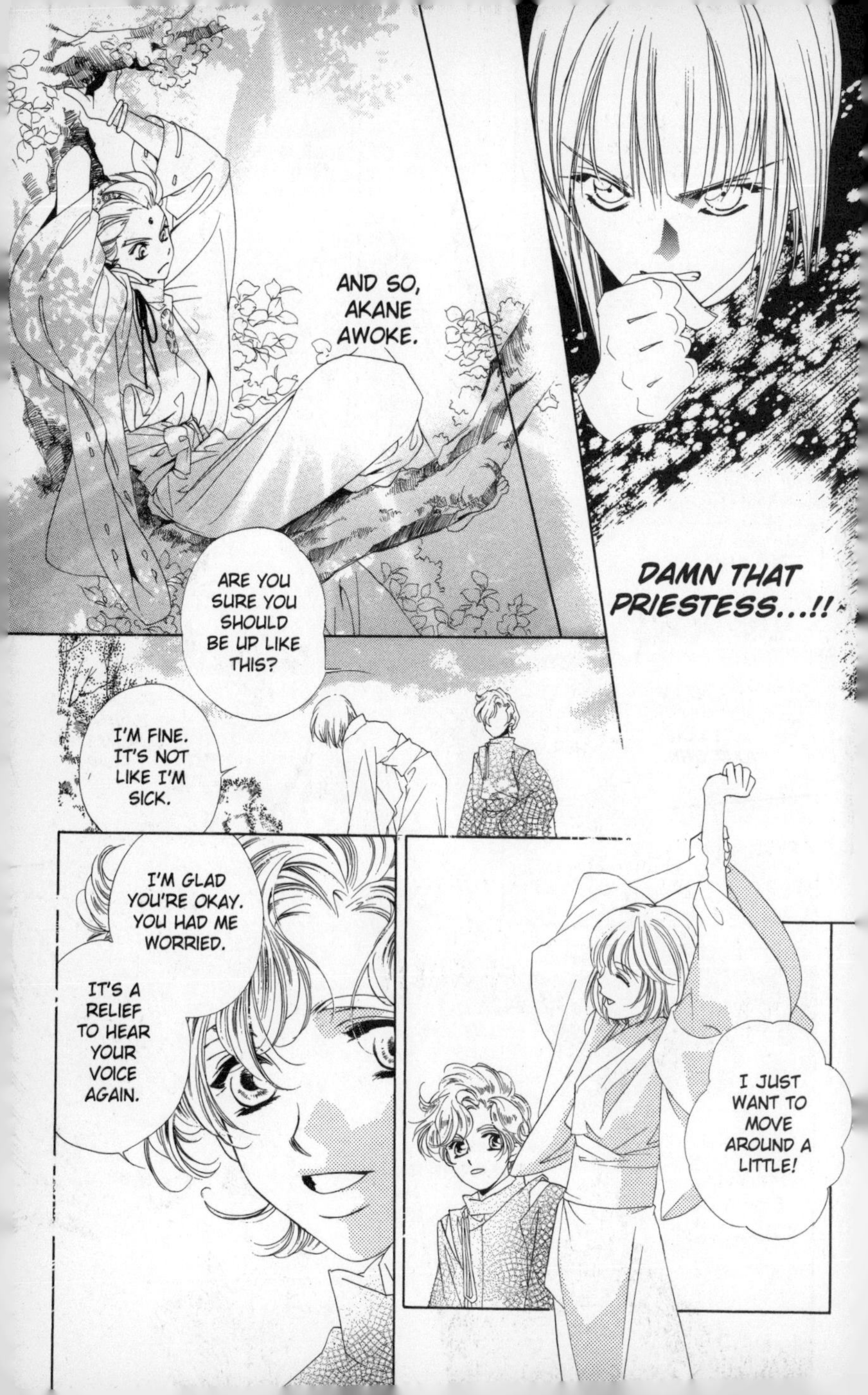
DAMN THAT PRIESTESS...!!
AND SO, AKANE AWOKE.
ARE YOU SURE YOU SHOULD BE UP LIKE THIS?
I'M FINE. IT'S NOT LIKE I'M SICK.
I JUST WANT TO MOVE AROUND A LITTLE!
I'M GLAD YOU'RE OKAY. YOU HAD ME WORRIED.
IT'S A RELIEF TO HEAR YOUR VOICE AGAIN.

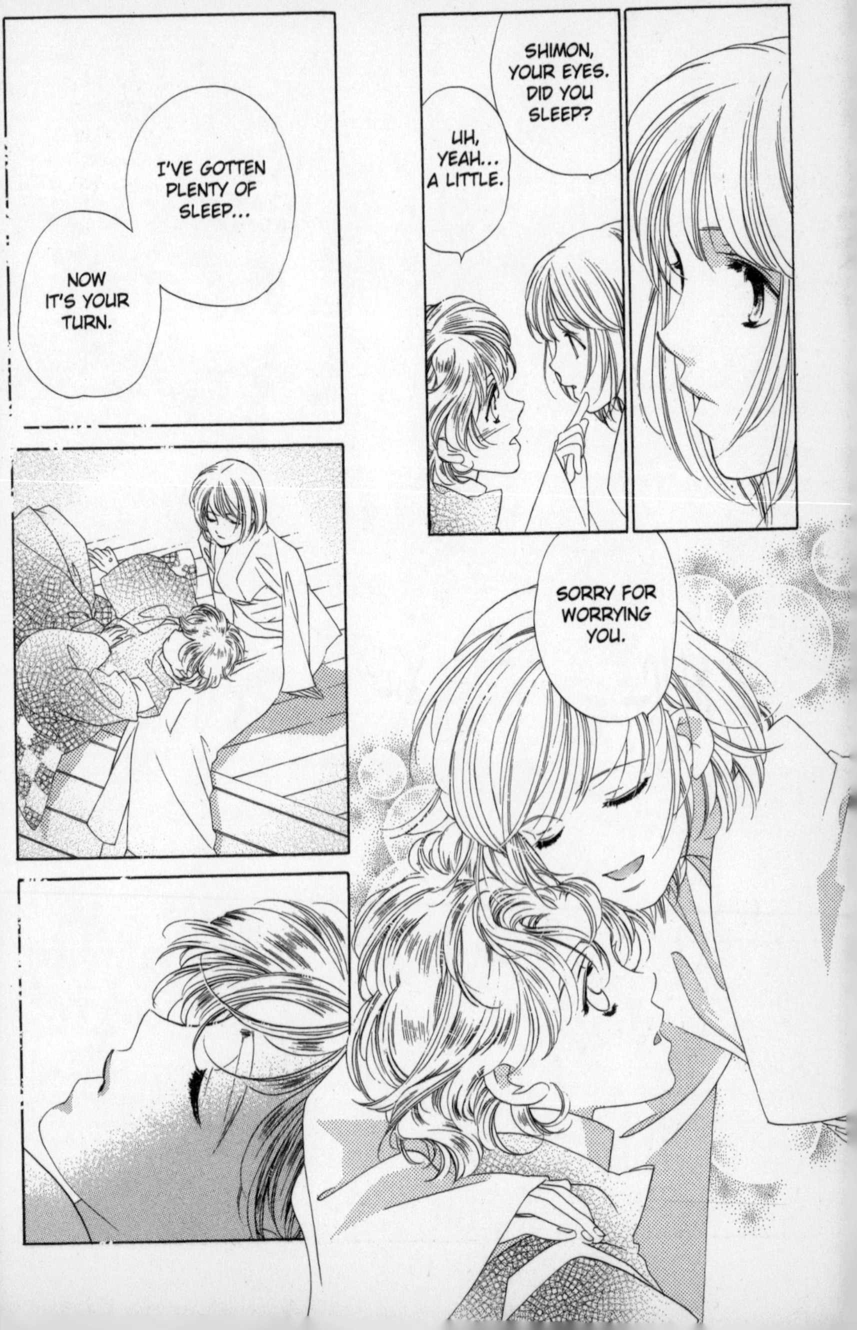
SHIMON, YOUR EYES. DID YOU SLEEP?
UH, YEAH... A LITTLE.
I'VE GOTTEN PLENTY OF SLEEP...
NOW IT'S YOUR TURN.
SORRY FOR WORRYING YOU.

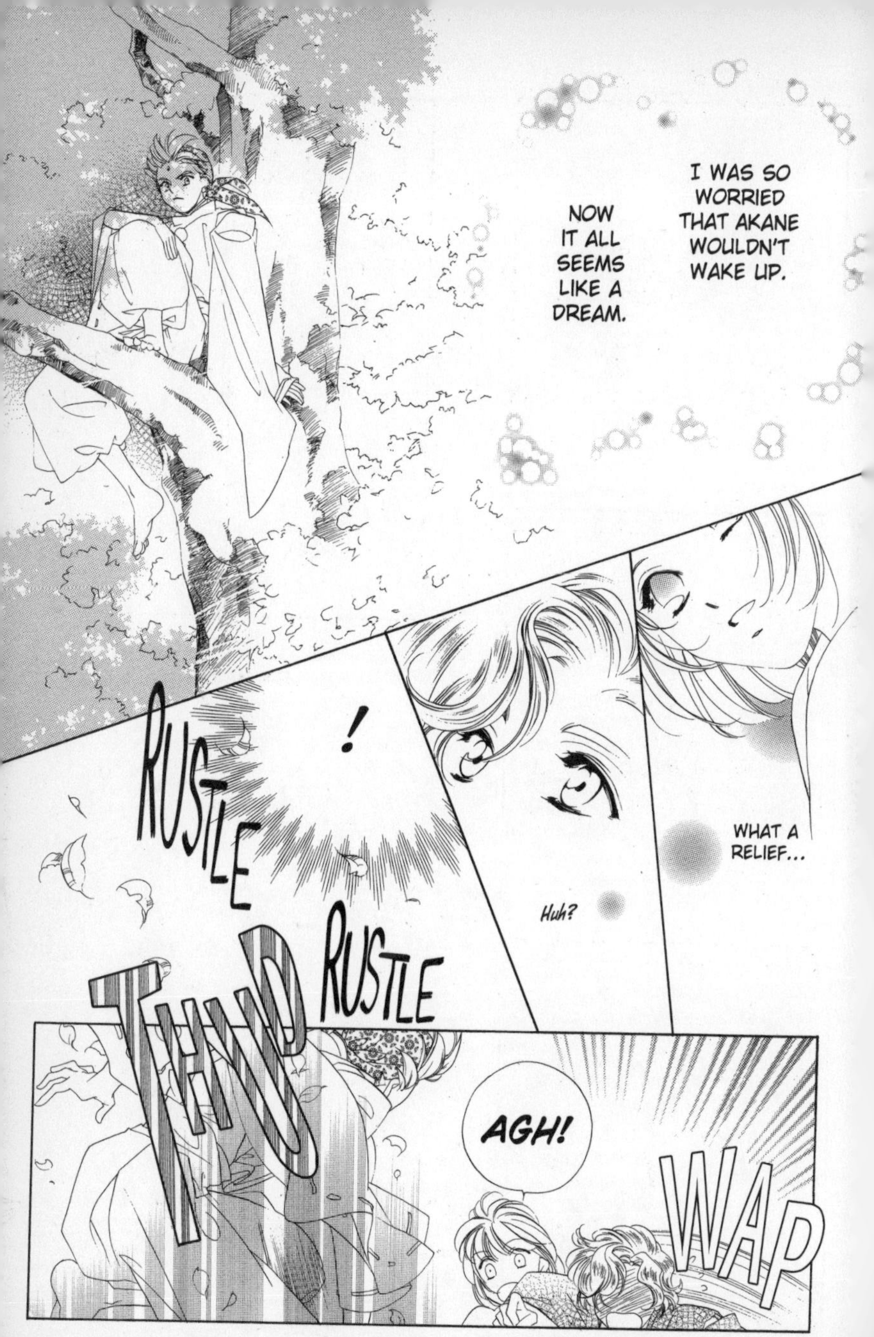
I WAS SO WORRIED THAT AKANE WOULDN'T WAKE UP.
NOW IT ALL SEEMS LIKE A DREAM.
WHAT A RELIEF...
Huh?
!
RUSTLE
RUSTLE
WAP
AGH!
THUD

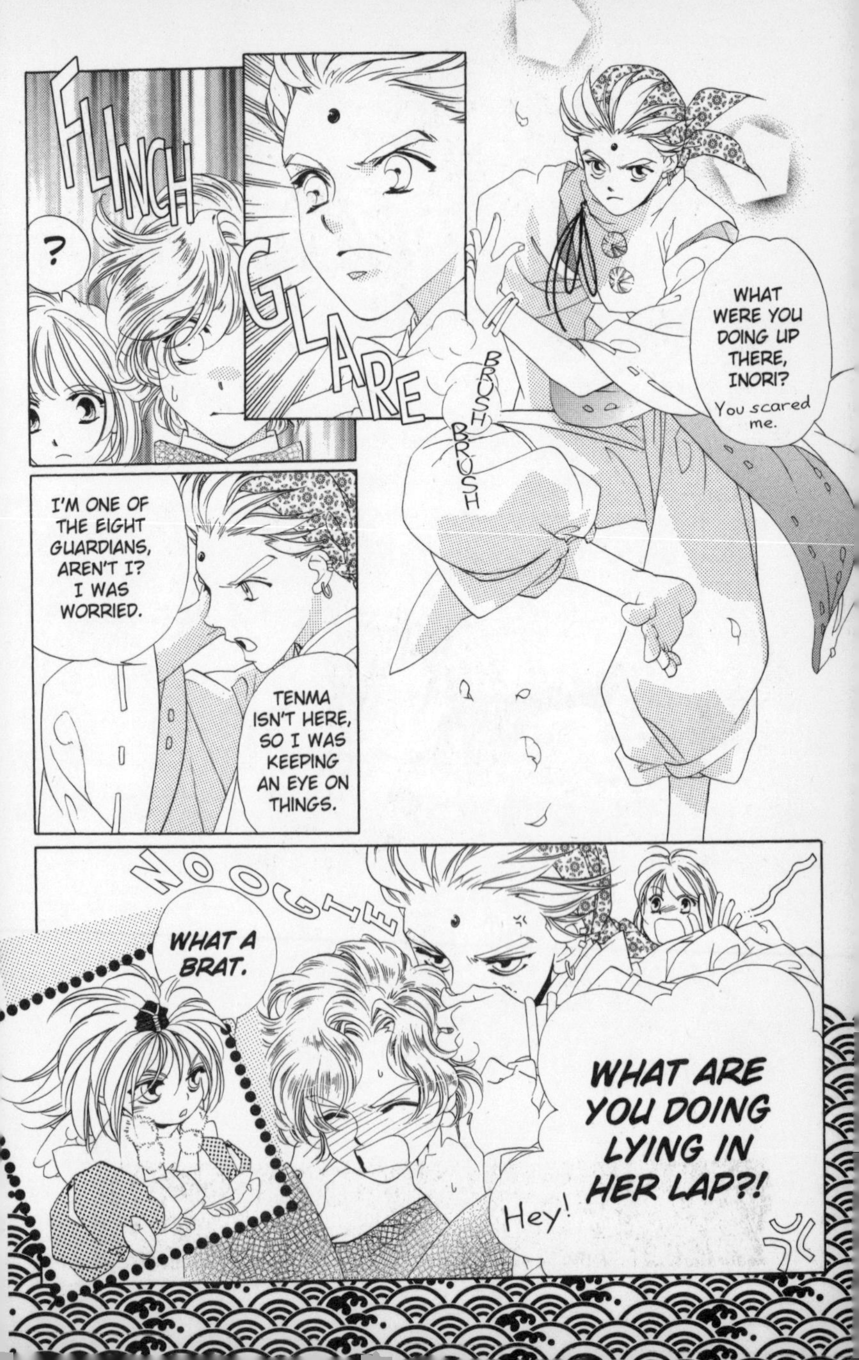
WHAT WERE YOU DOING UP THERE, INORI?
You scared me.
BRUSH BRUSH
GLARE
FLINCH
?
I'M ONE OF THE EIGHT GUARDIANS, AREN'T I? I WAS WORRIED.
TENMA ISN'T HERE, SO I WAS KEEPING AN EYE ON THINGS.
WHAT ARE YOU DOING LYING IN HER LAP?!
Hey!
NOOGIE
WHAT A BRAT.

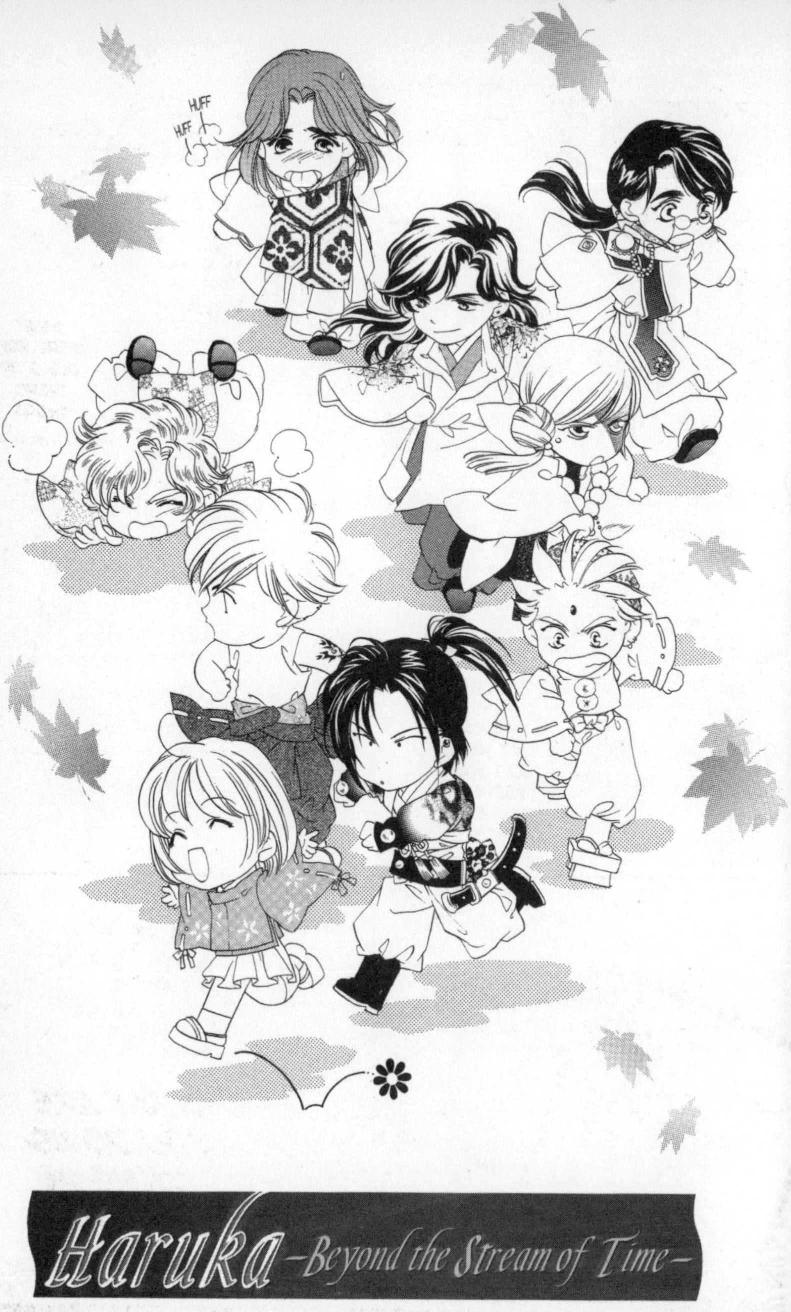
HUFF
HUFF

Haruka -Beyond the Stream of Time-

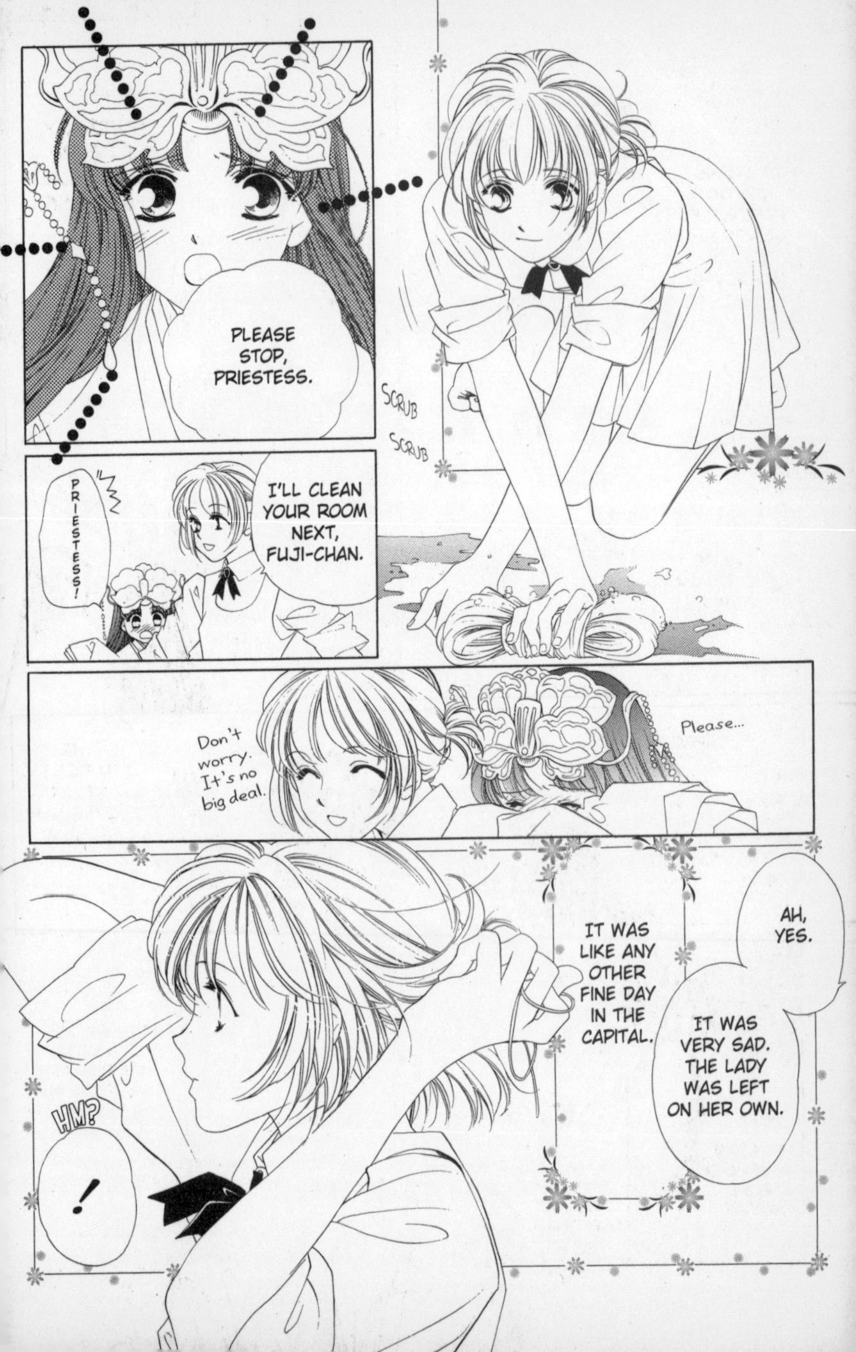
SCRUB
SCRUB
PLEASE STOP, PRIESTESS.
I'LL CLEAN YOUR ROOM NEXT, FUJI-CHAN.
PRIESTESS!
Please...
Don't worry. It's no big deal.
AH, YES.
IT WAS VERY SAD. THE LADY WAS LEFT ON HER OWN.
IT WAS LIKE ANY OTHER FINE DAY IN THE CAPITAL.
HM?
!

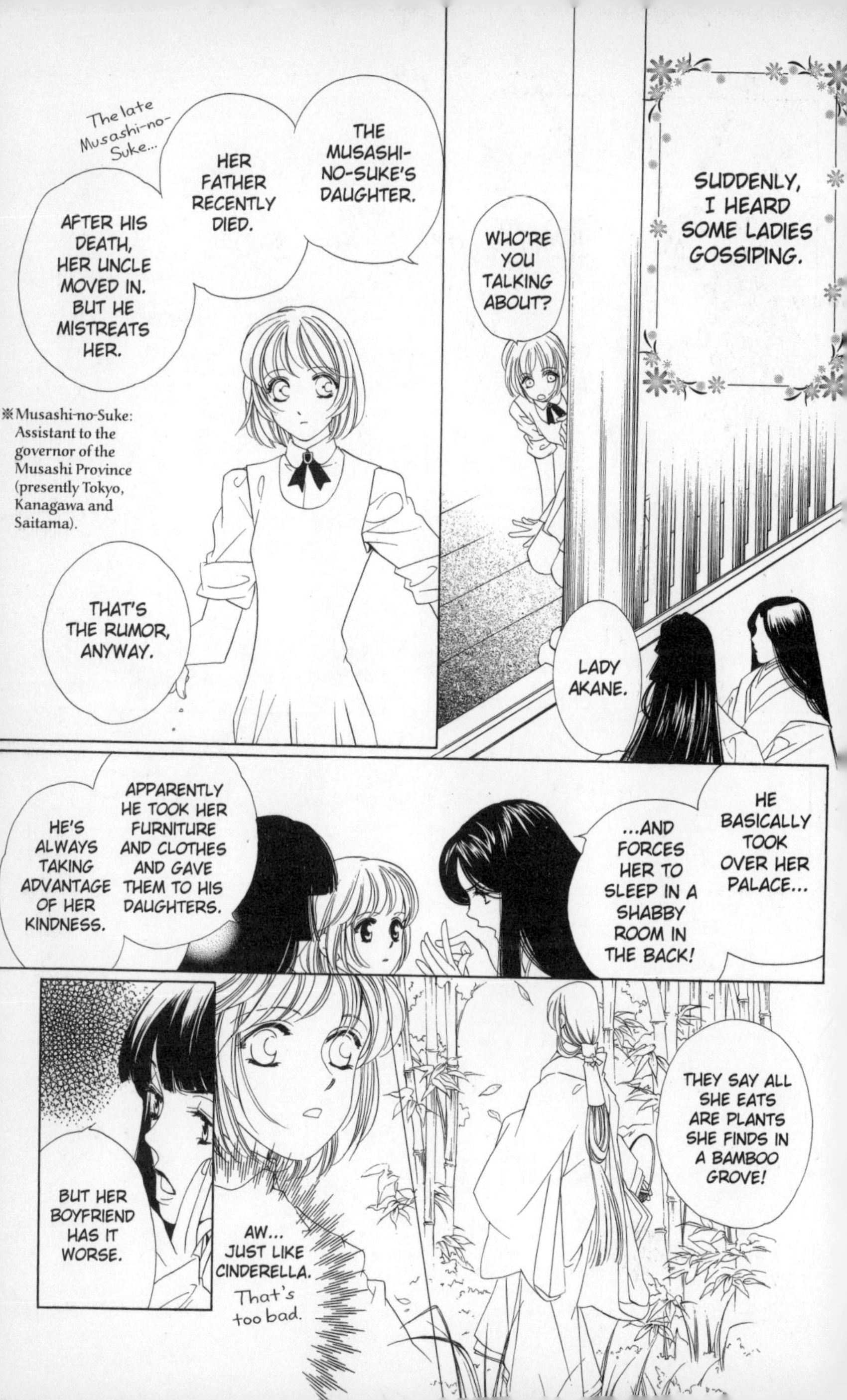
SUDDENLY, I HEARD SOME LADIES GOSSIPING.
WHO'RE YOU TALKING ABOUT?
LADY AKANE.
THE MUSASHI-NO-SUKE'S DAUGHTER.
HER FATHER RECENTLY DIED.
The late Musashi-no-Suke...
AFTER HIS DEATH, HER UNCLE MOVED IN. BUT HE MISTREATS HER.
※Musashi-no-Suke: Assistant to the governor of the Musashi Province (presently Tokyo, Kanagawa and Saitama).
THAT'S THE RUMOR, ANYWAY.
HE BASICALLY TOOK OVER HER PALACE...
...AND FORCES HER TO SLEEP IN A SHABBY ROOM IN THE BACK!
APPARENTLY HE TOOK HER FURNITURE AND CLOTHES AND GAVE THEM TO HIS DAUGHTERS.
HE'S ALWAYS TAKING ADVANTAGE OF HER KINDNESS.
THEY SAY ALL SHE EATS ARE PLANTS SHE FINDS IN A BAMBOO GROVE!
AW... JUST LIKE CINDERELLA.
That's too bad.
BUT HER BOYFRIEND HAS IT WORSE.

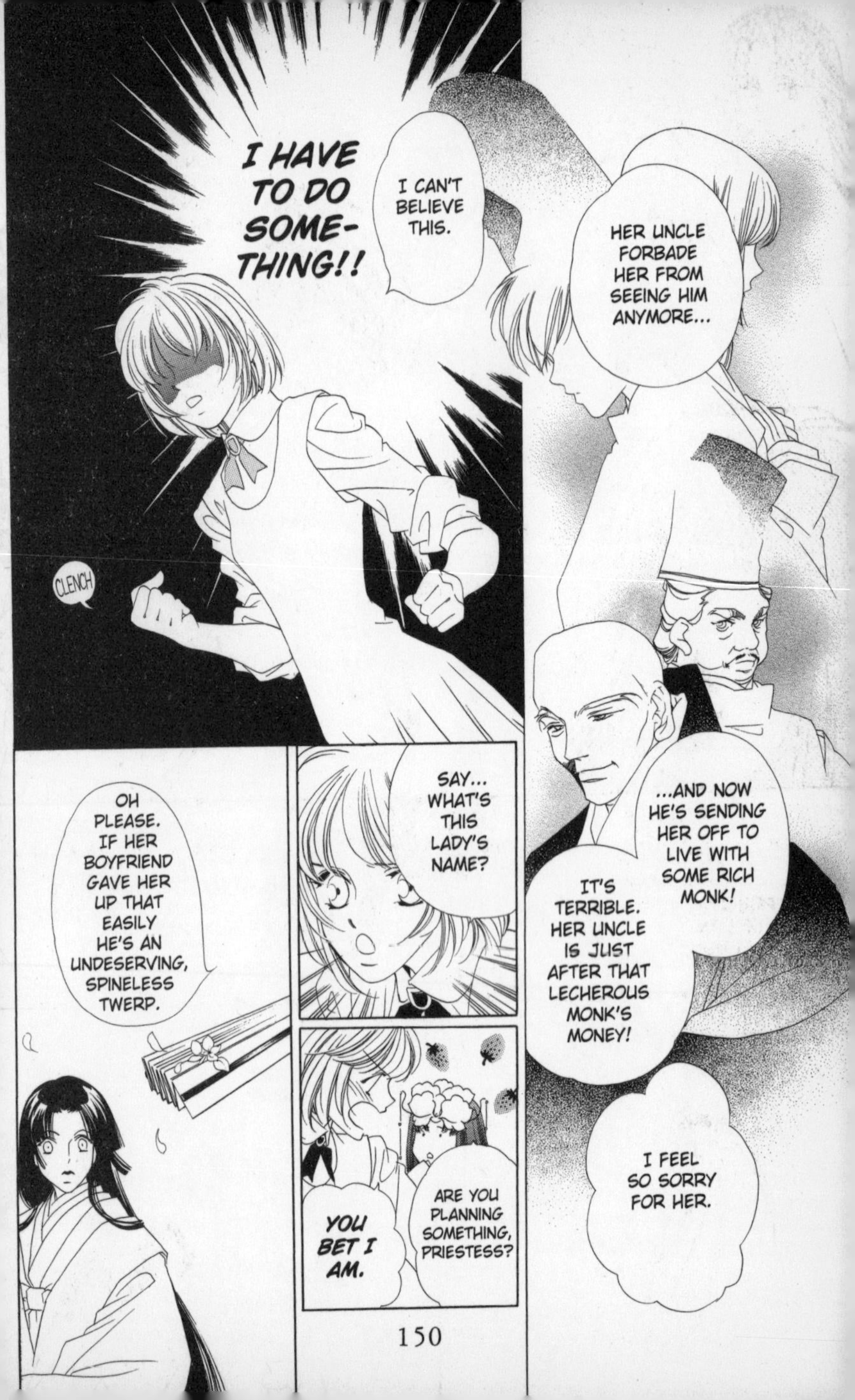
I CAN'T BELIEVE THIS.
HER UNCLE FORBADE HER FROM SEEING HIM ANYMORE...
...AND NOW HE'S SENDING HER OFF TO LIVE WITH SOME RICH MONK!
IT'S TERRIBLE. HER UNCLE IS JUST AFTER THAT LECHEROUS MONK'S MONEY!
I FEEL SO SORRY FOR HER.
I HAVE TO DO SOME-THING!!
CLENCH
SAY... WHAT'S THIS LADY'S NAME?
ARE YOU PLANNING SOMETHING, PRIESTESS?
YOU BET I AM.
OH PLEASE. IF HER BOYFRIEND GAVE HER UP THAT EASILY HE'S AN UNDESERVING, SPINELESS TWERP.

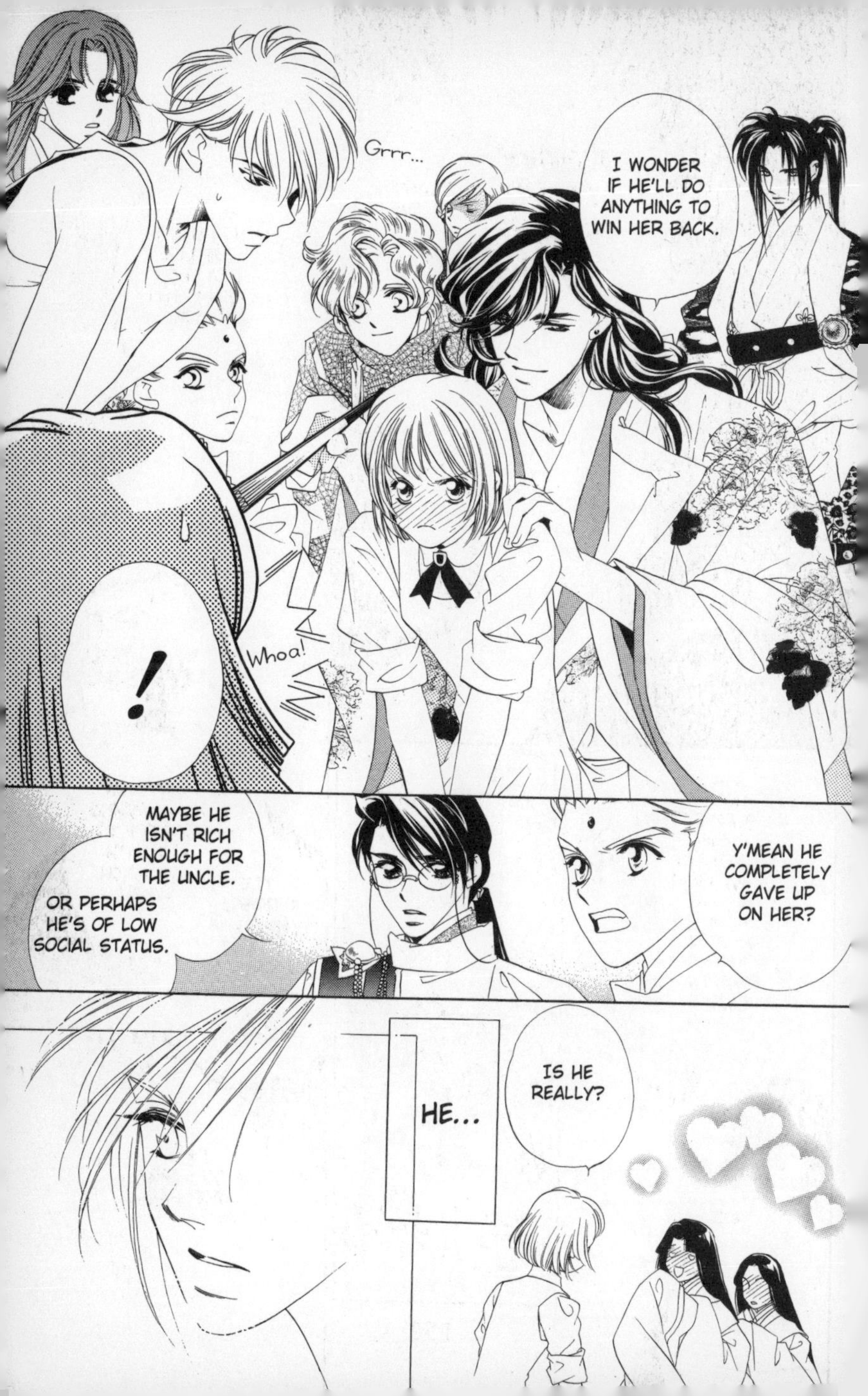
I WONDER IF HE'LL DO ANYTHING TO WIN HER BACK.
Grrr...
Whoa!
!
Y'MEAN HE COMPLETELY GAVE UP ON HER?
MAYBE HE ISN'T RICH ENOUGH FOR THE UNCLE.
OR PERHAPS HE'S OF LOW SOCIAL STATUS.
IS HE REALLY?
HE...

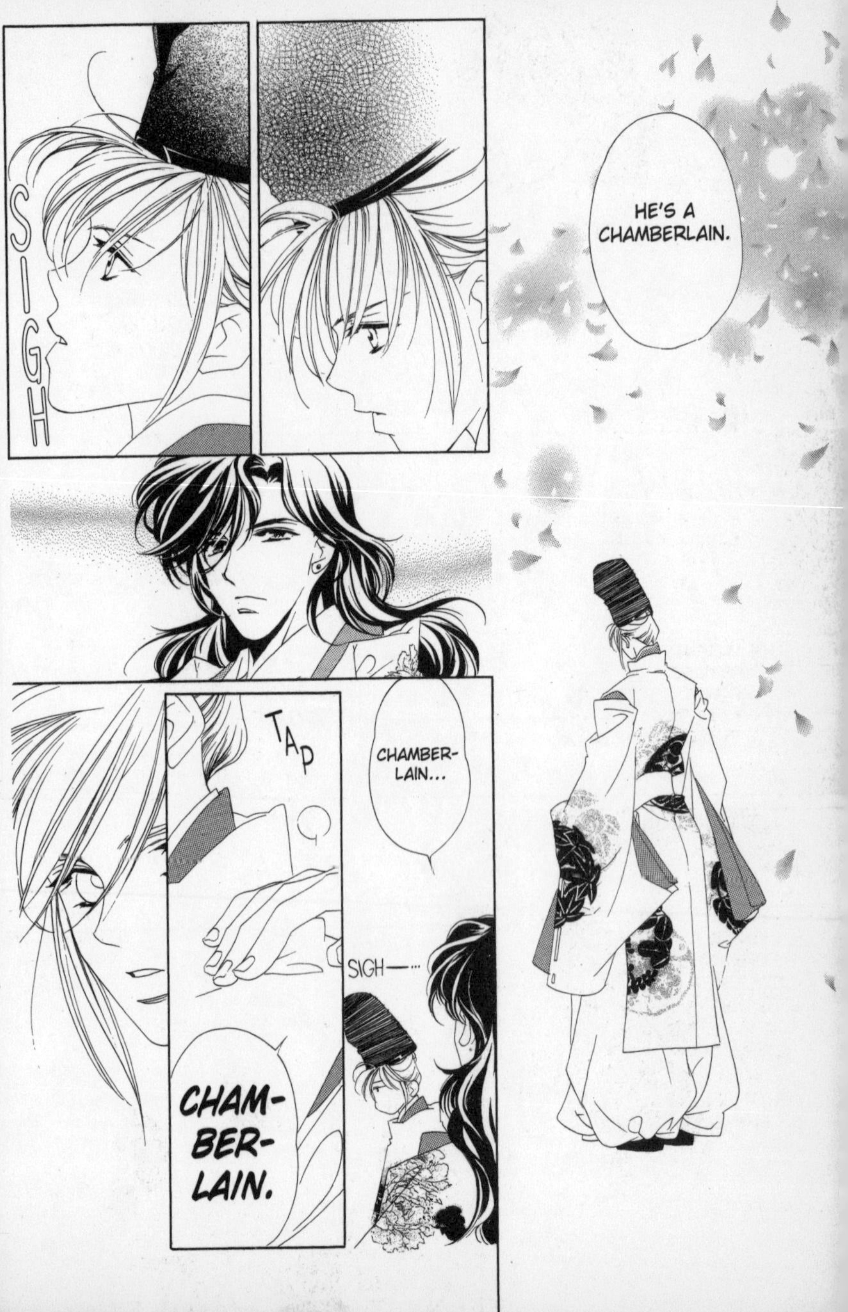

HE'S A CHAMBERLAIN.
SIGH
CHAMBER-LAIN...
SIGH—...
TAP
CHAM-BER-LAIN.

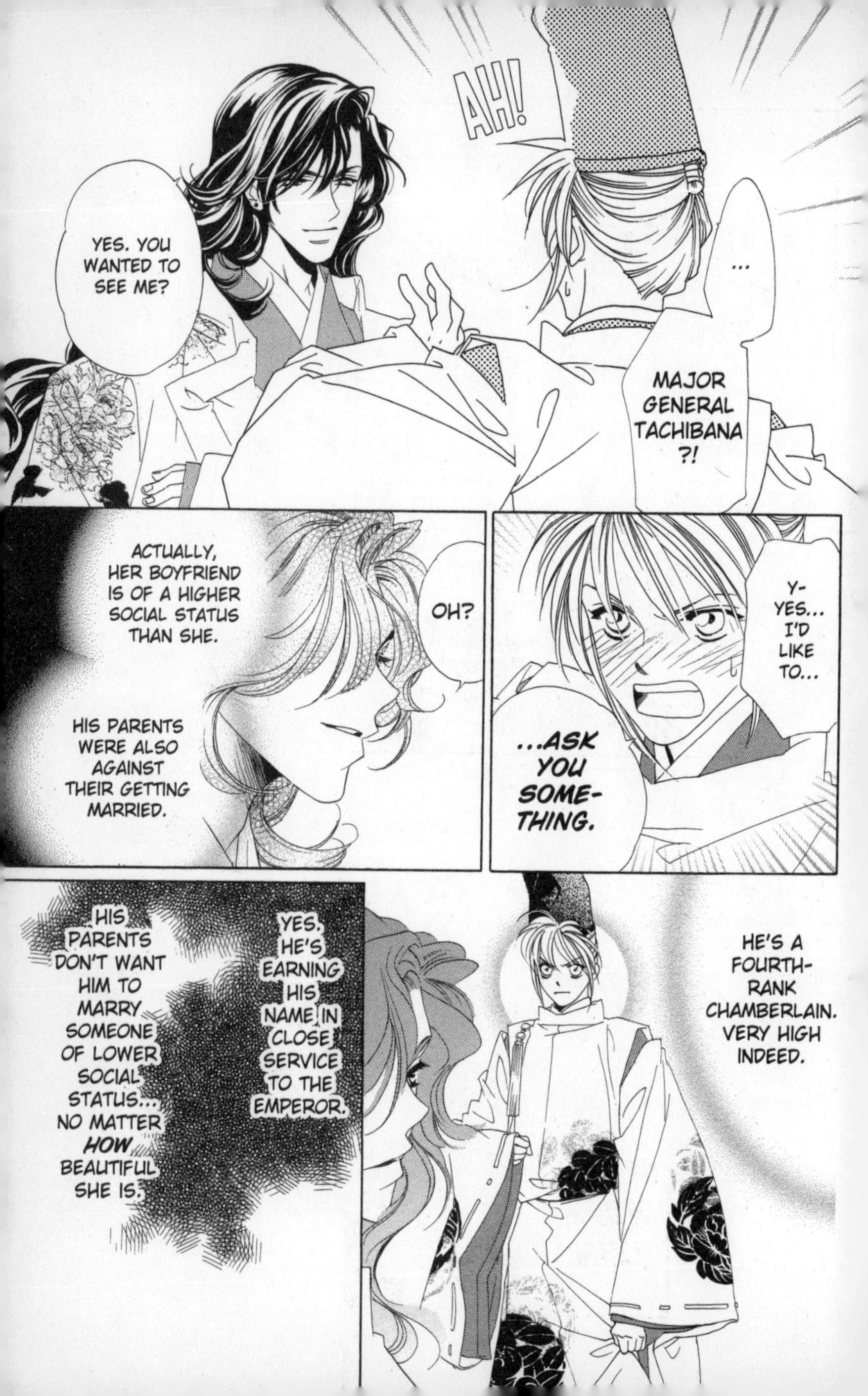
AH!
...
MAJOR GENERAL TACHIBANA ?!
YES. YOU WANTED TO SEE ME?
Y-YES... I'D LIKE TO...
...ASK YOU SOME-THING.
OH?
ACTUALLY, HER BOYFRIEND IS OF A HIGHER SOCIAL STATUS THAN SHE.
HIS PARENTS WERE ALSO AGAINST THEIR GETTING MARRIED.
HE'S A FOURTH-RANK CHAMBERLAIN. VERY HIGH INDEED.
YES. HE'S EARNING HIS NAME IN CLOSE SERVICE TO THE EMPEROR.
HIS PARENTS DON'T WANT HIM TO MARRY SOMEONE OF LOWER SOCIAL STATUS... NO MATTER *HOW* BEAUTIFUL SHE IS.

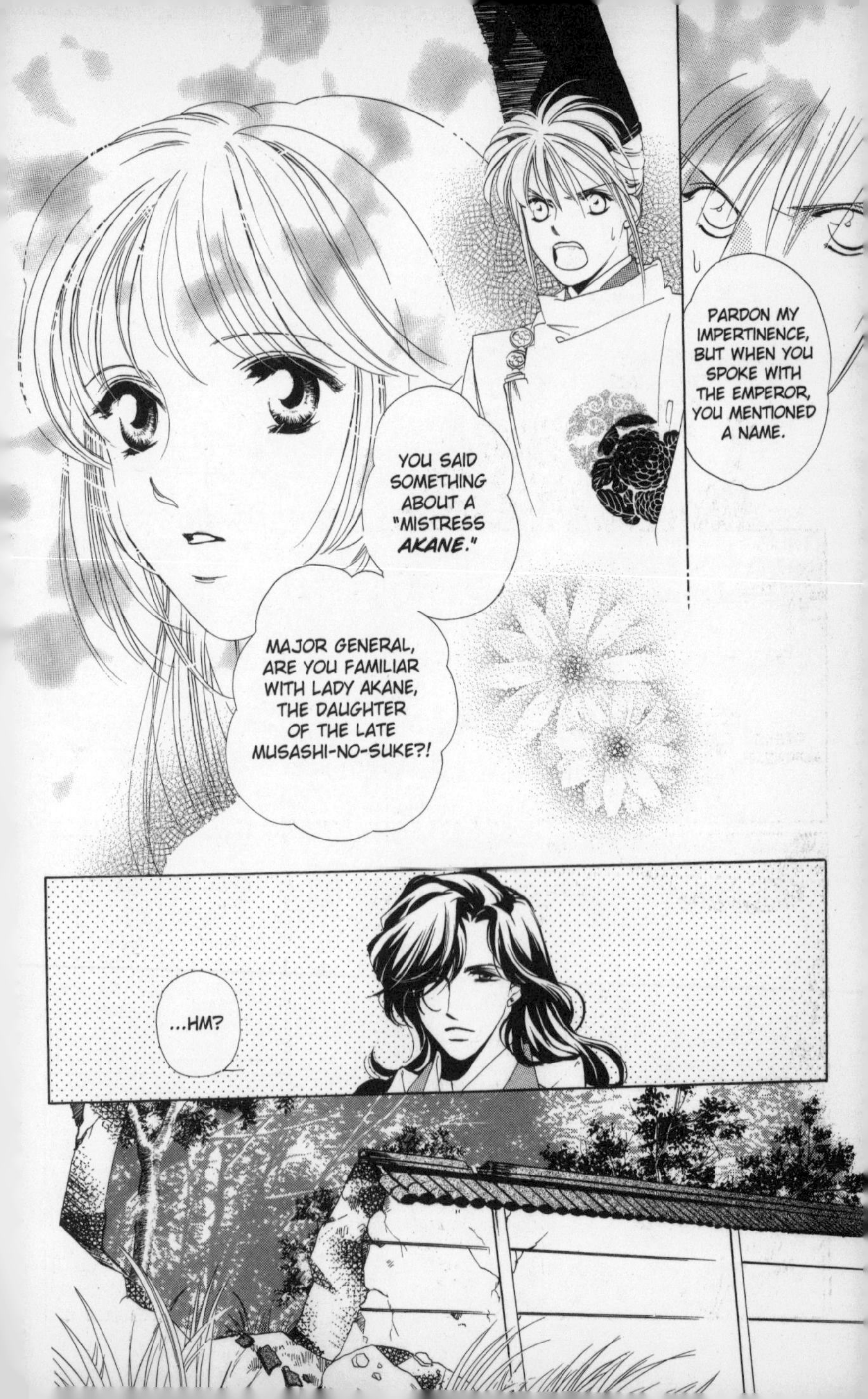
PARDON MY IMPERTINENCE, BUT WHEN YOU SPOKE WITH THE EMPEROR, YOU MENTIONED A NAME.
YOU SAID SOMETHING ABOUT A "MISTRESS AKANE."
MAJOR GENERAL, ARE YOU FAMILIAR WITH LADY AKANE, THE DAUGHTER OF THE LATE MUSASHI-NO-SUKE?!
...HM?

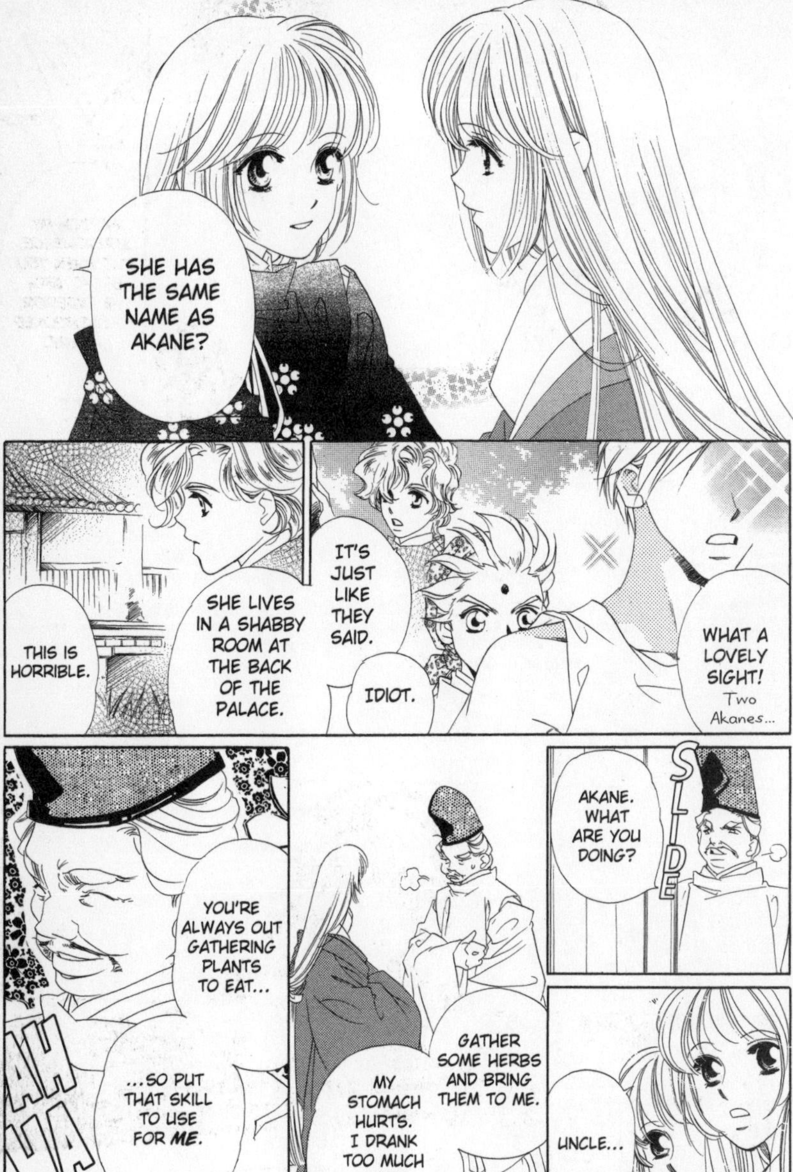
SHE HAS THE SAME NAME AS AKANE?
WHAT A LOVELY SIGHT!
Two Akanes...
IT'S JUST LIKE THEY SAID.
IDIOT.
SHE LIVES IN A SHABBY ROOM AT THE BACK OF THE PALACE.
THIS IS HORRIBLE.
SLIDE
AKANE. WHAT ARE YOU DOING?
UNCLE...
GATHER SOME HERBS AND BRING THEM TO ME.
MY STOMACH HURTS. I DRANK TOO MUCH LAST NIGHT.
YOU'RE ALWAYS OUT GATHERING PLANTS TO EAT...
...SO PUT THAT SKILL TO USE FOR *ME*.
AH HA HA HA

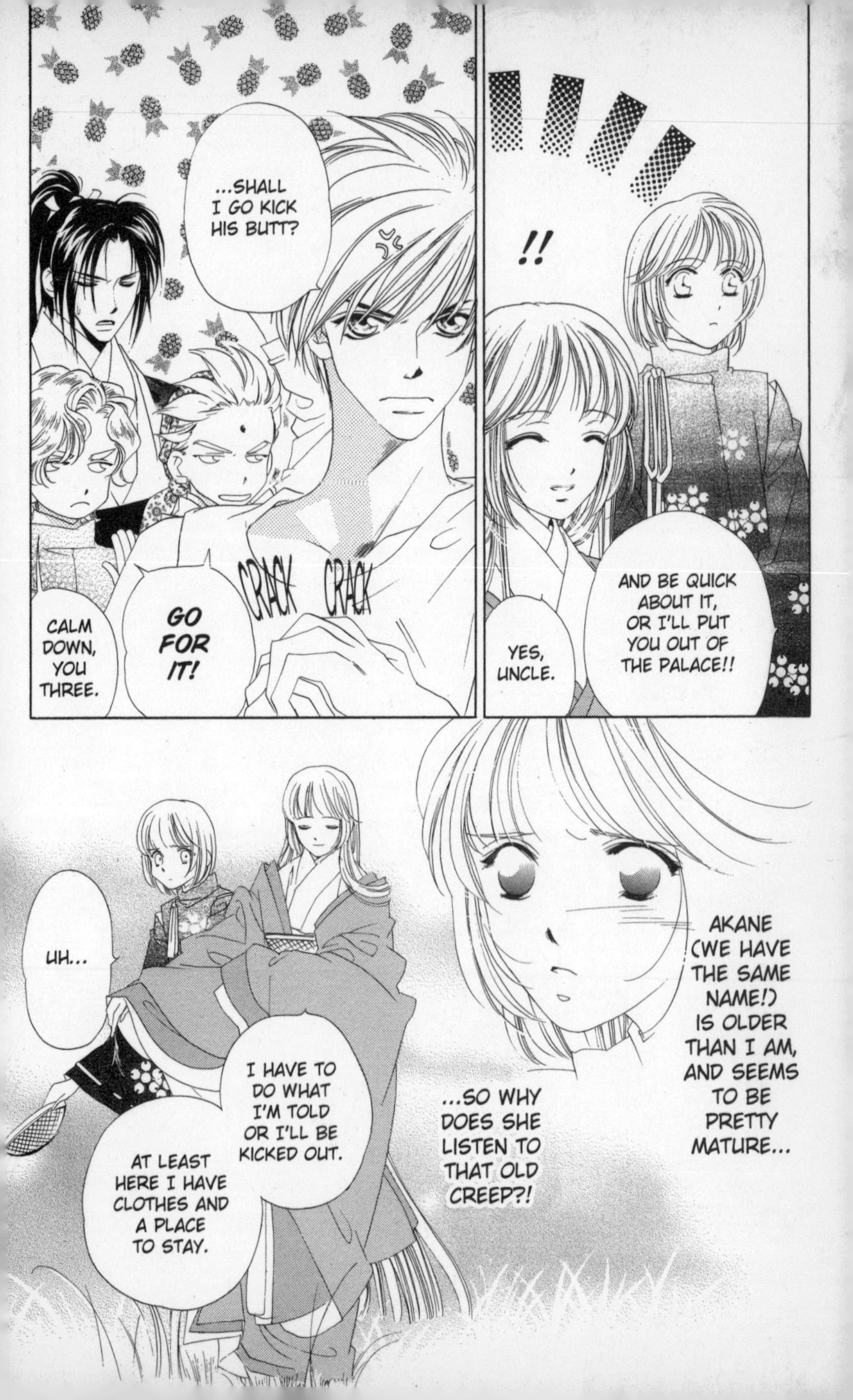
!!
AND BE QUICK ABOUT IT, OR I'LL PUT YOU OUT OF THE PALACE!!
YES, UNCLE.
...SHALL I GO KICK HIS BUTT?
CRACK CRACK
GO FOR IT!
CALM DOWN, YOU THREE.
AKANE (WE HAVE THE SAME NAME!) IS OLDER THAN I AM, AND SEEMS TO BE PRETTY MATURE...
...SO WHY DOES SHE LISTEN TO THAT OLD CREEP?!
I HAVE TO DO WHAT I'M TOLD OR I'LL BE KICKED OUT.
AT LEAST HERE I HAVE CLOTHES AND A PLACE TO STAY.
UH...

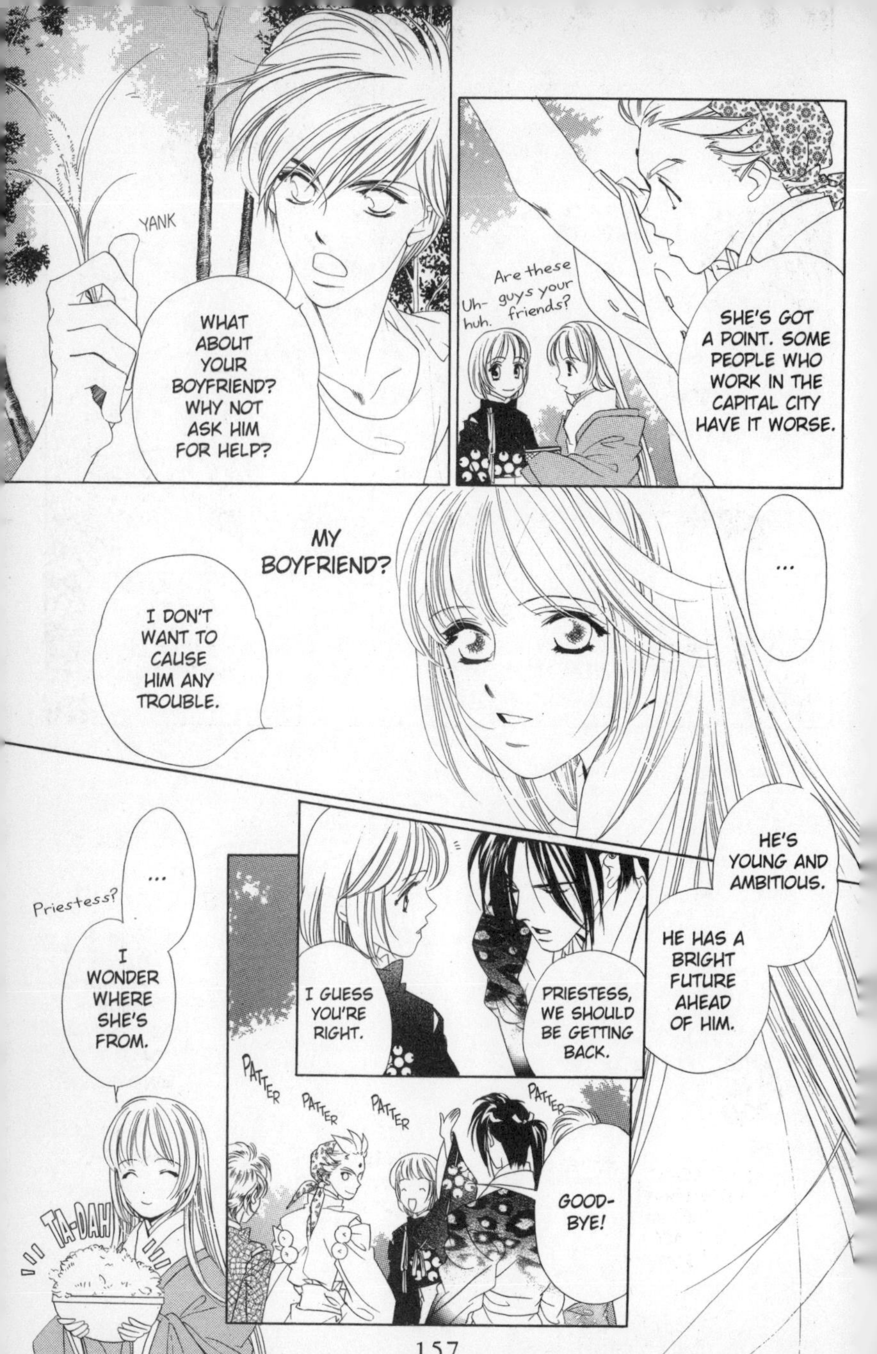
SHE'S GOT A POINT. SOME PEOPLE WHO WORK IN THE CAPITAL CITY HAVE IT WORSE.
Are these guys your friends?
Uh-huh.
YANK
WHAT ABOUT YOUR BOYFRIEND? WHY NOT ASK HIM FOR HELP?
...
MY BOYFRIEND?
I DON'T WANT TO CAUSE HIM ANY TROUBLE.
HE'S YOUNG AND AMBITIOUS.
HE HAS A BRIGHT FUTURE AHEAD OF HIM.
PRIESTESS, WE SHOULD BE GETTING BACK.
I GUESS YOU'RE RIGHT.
PATTER
PATTER
PATTER
PATTER
GOOD-BYE!
...
Priestess?
I WONDER WHERE SHE'S FROM.
TA-DAH

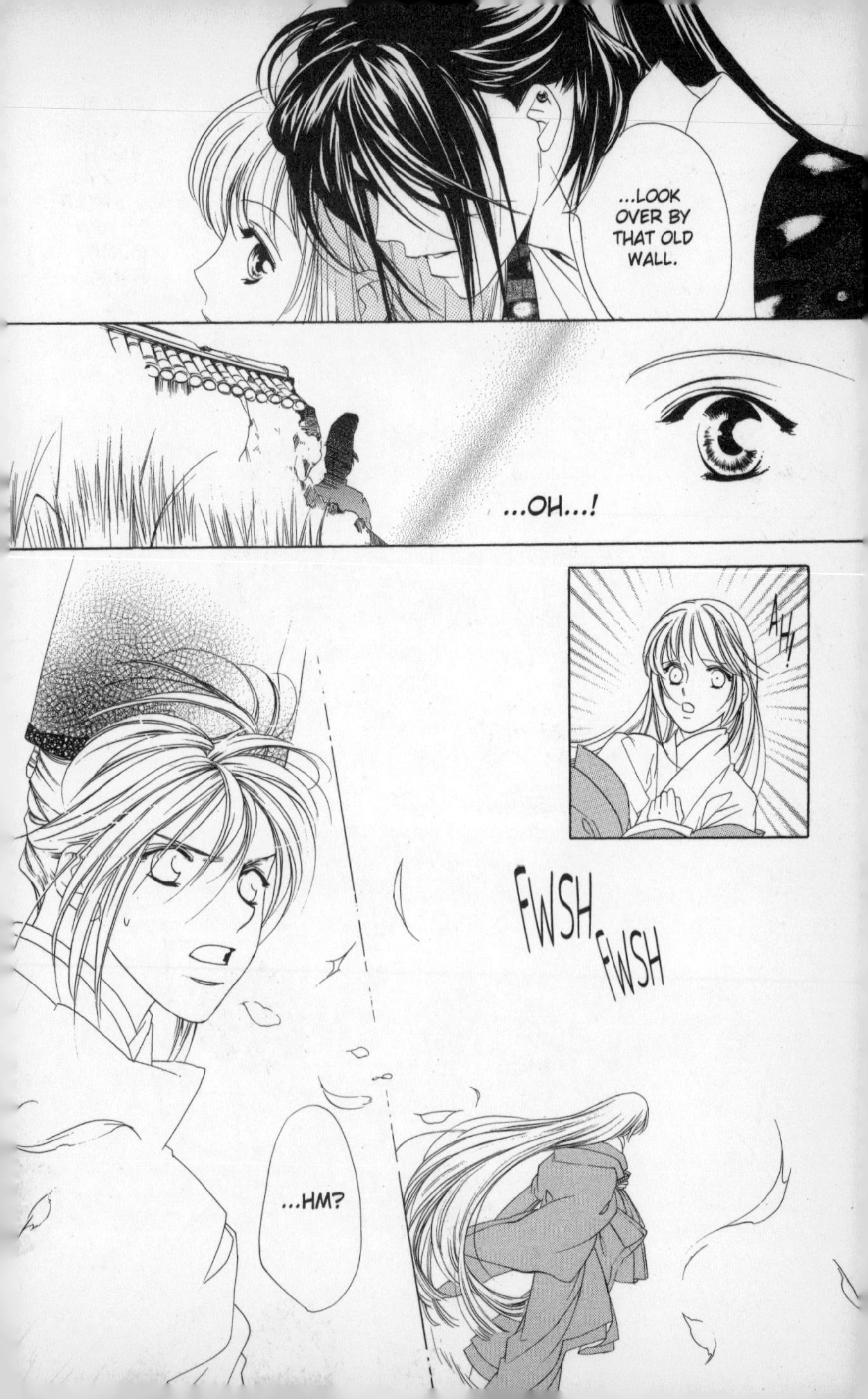
...LOOK OVER BY THAT OLD WALL.
...OH...!
AH!
FWSH FWSH
...HM?

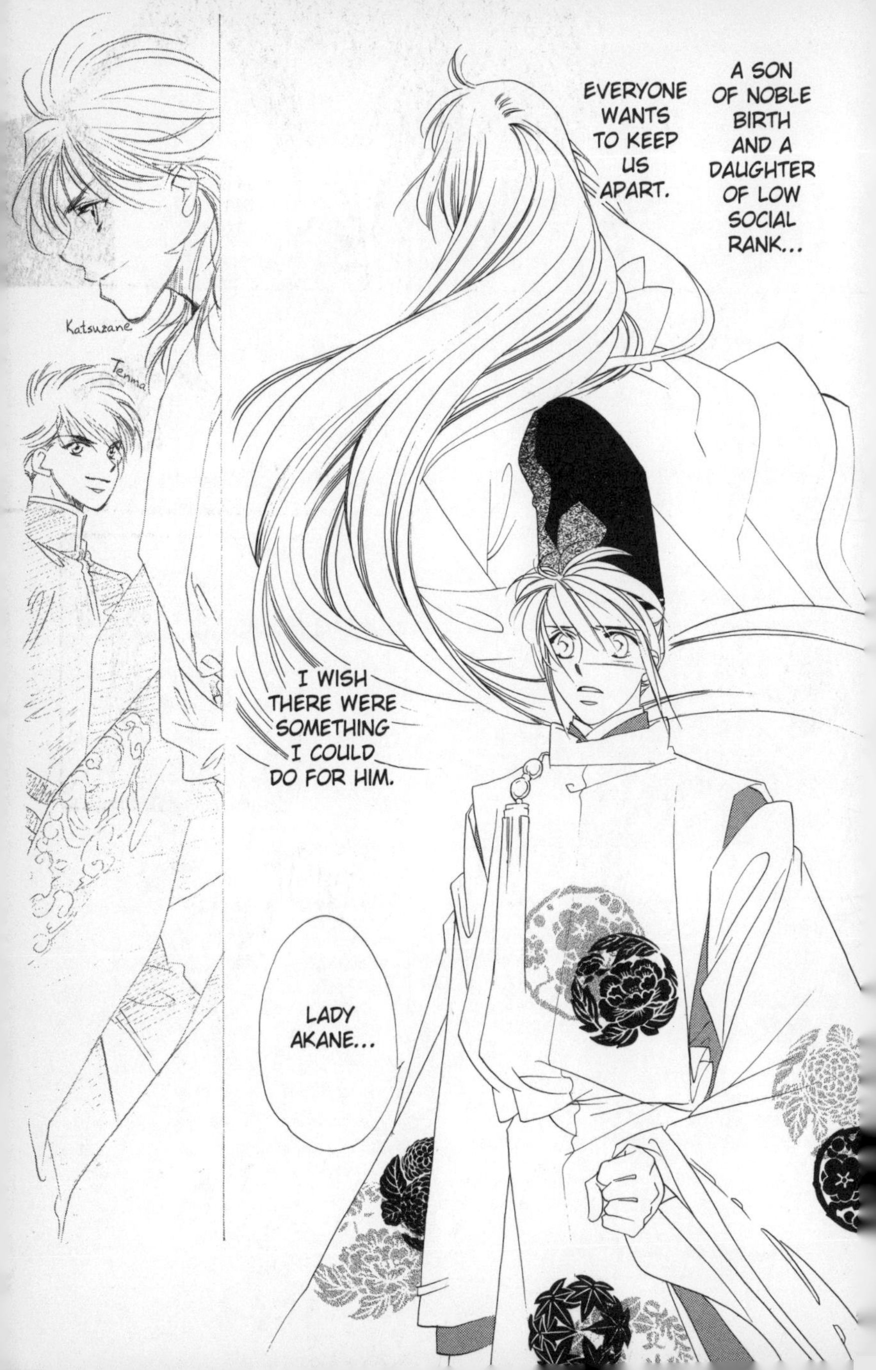
A SON OF NOBLE BIRTH AND A DAUGHTER OF LOW SOCIAL RANK...
EVERYONE WANTS TO KEEP US APART.
I WISH THERE WERE SOMETHING I COULD DO FOR HIM.
LADY AKANE...
Katsuzane
Tenma

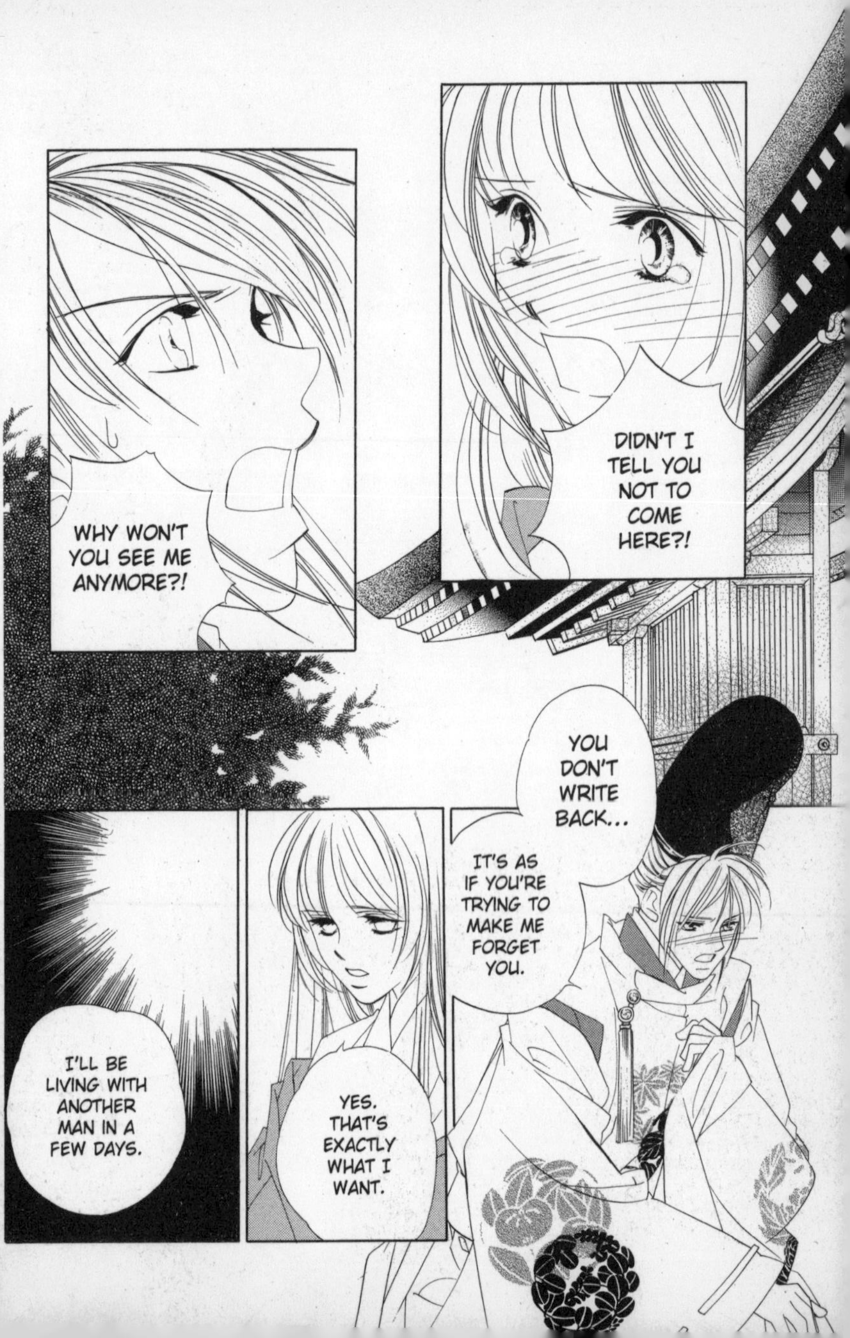
DIDN'T I TELL YOU NOT TO COME HERE?!
WHY WON'T YOU SEE ME ANYMORE?!
YOU DON'T WRITE BACK...
IT'S AS IF YOU'RE TRYING TO MAKE ME FORGET YOU.
YES. THAT'S EXACTLY WHAT I WANT.
I'LL BE LIVING WITH ANOTHER MAN IN A FEW DAYS.

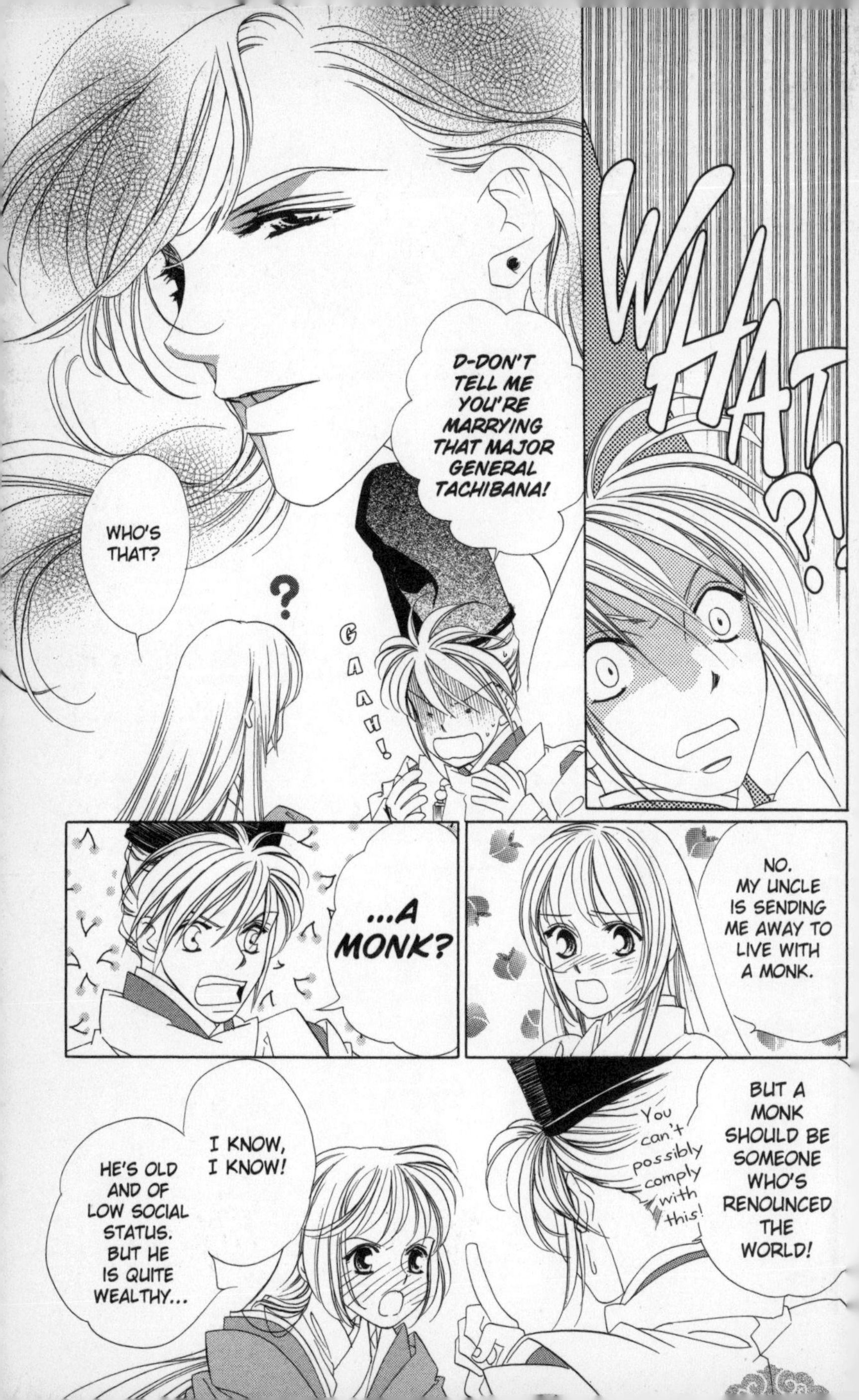
WHAT?!
D-DON'T TELL ME YOU'RE MARRYING THAT MAJOR GENERAL TACHIBANA!
WHO'S THAT?
?
GAAAH!
NO. MY UNCLE IS SENDING ME AWAY TO LIVE WITH A MONK.
...A MONK?
BUT A MONK SHOULD BE SOMEONE WHO'S RENOUNCED THE WORLD!
You can't possibly comply with this!
I KNOW, I KNOW!
HE'S OLD AND OF LOW SOCIAL STATUS. BUT HE IS QUITE WEALTHY...

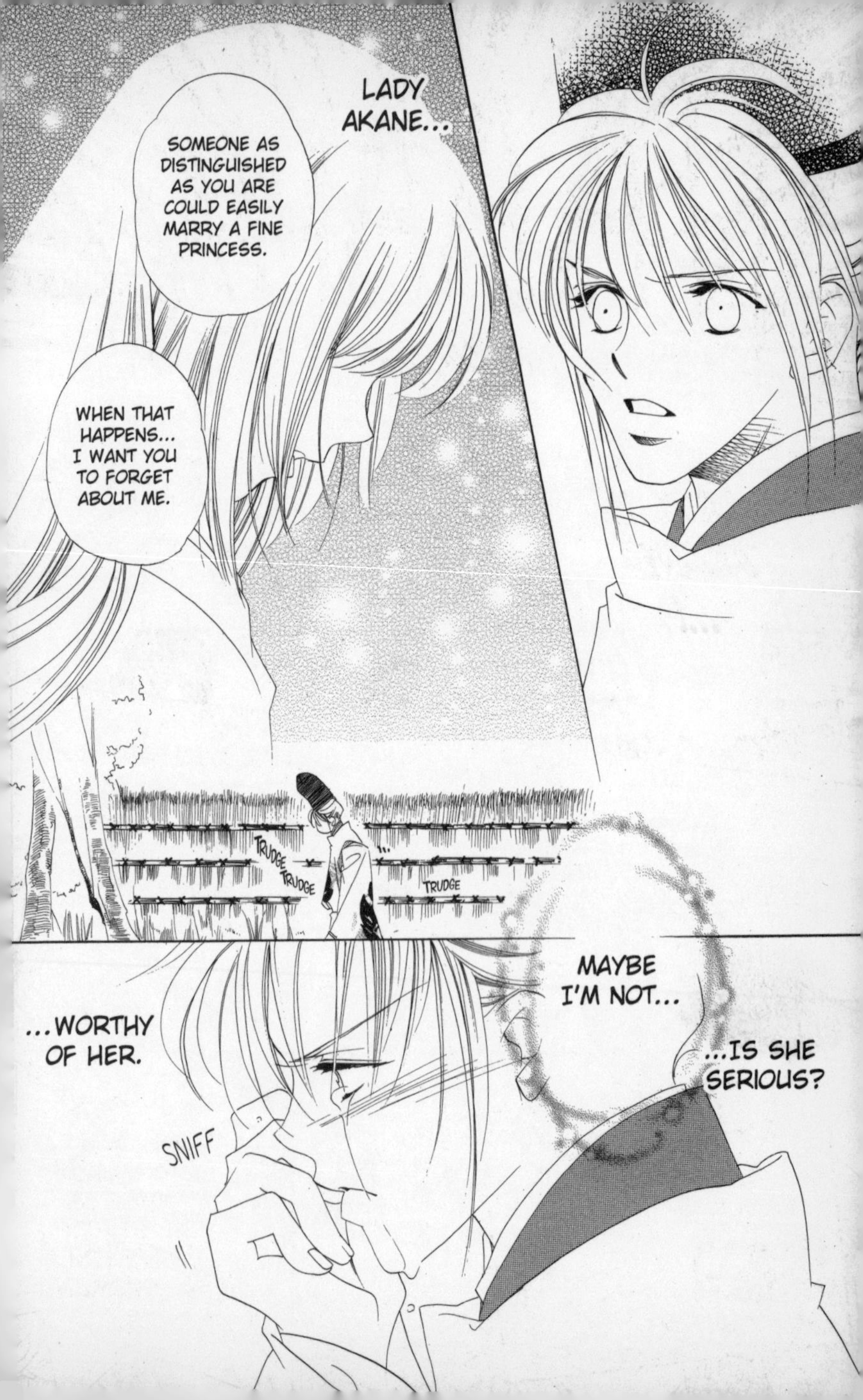
LADY AKANE...
SOMEONE AS DISTINGUISHED AS YOU ARE COULD EASILY MARRY A FINE PRINCESS.
WHEN THAT HAPPENS... I WANT YOU TO FORGET ABOUT ME.
TRUDGE
TRUDGE TRUDGE
...IS SHE SERIOUS?
MAYBE I'M NOT...
...WORTHY OF HER.
SNIFF

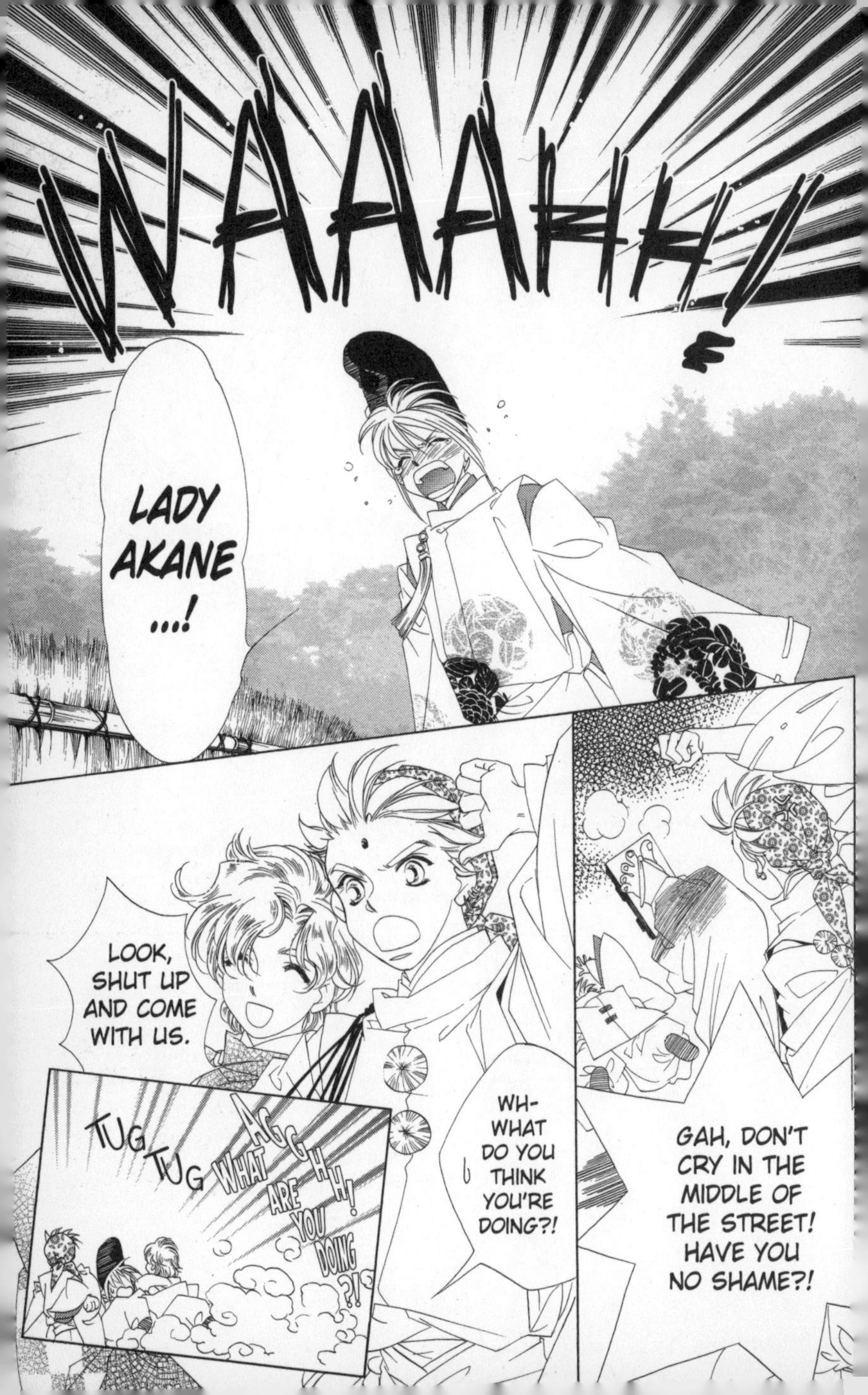
WAAAHH!
LADY AKANE ...!
GAH, DON'T CRY IN THE MIDDLE OF THE STREET! HAVE YOU NO SHAME?!
WH- WHAT DO YOU THINK YOU'RE DOING?!
LOOK, SHUT UP AND COME WITH US.
TUG TUG
AGGHHH!
WHAT ARE YOU DOING?!

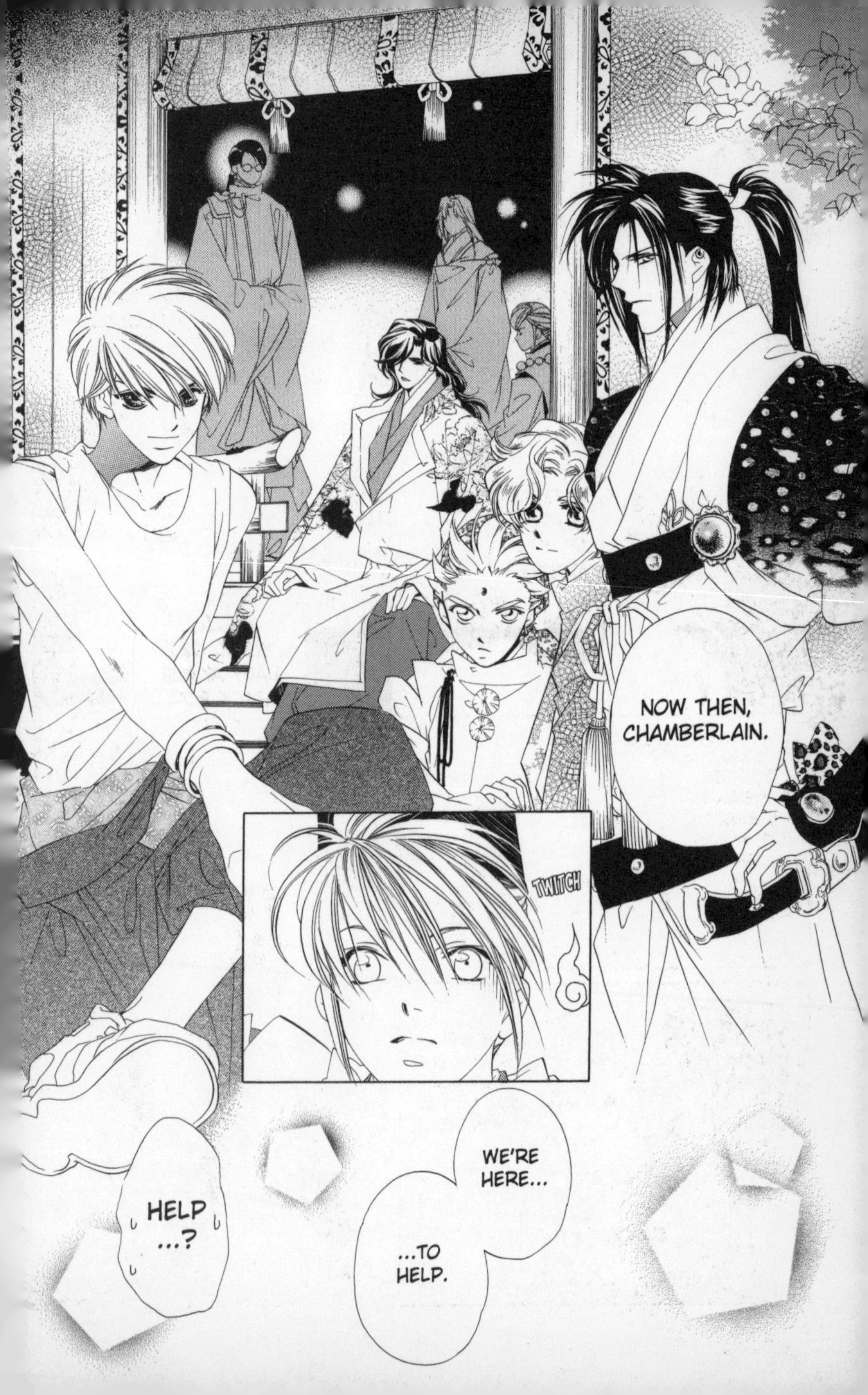
NOW THEN, CHAMBERLAIN.
TWITCH
WE'RE HERE...
...TO HELP.
HELP ...?

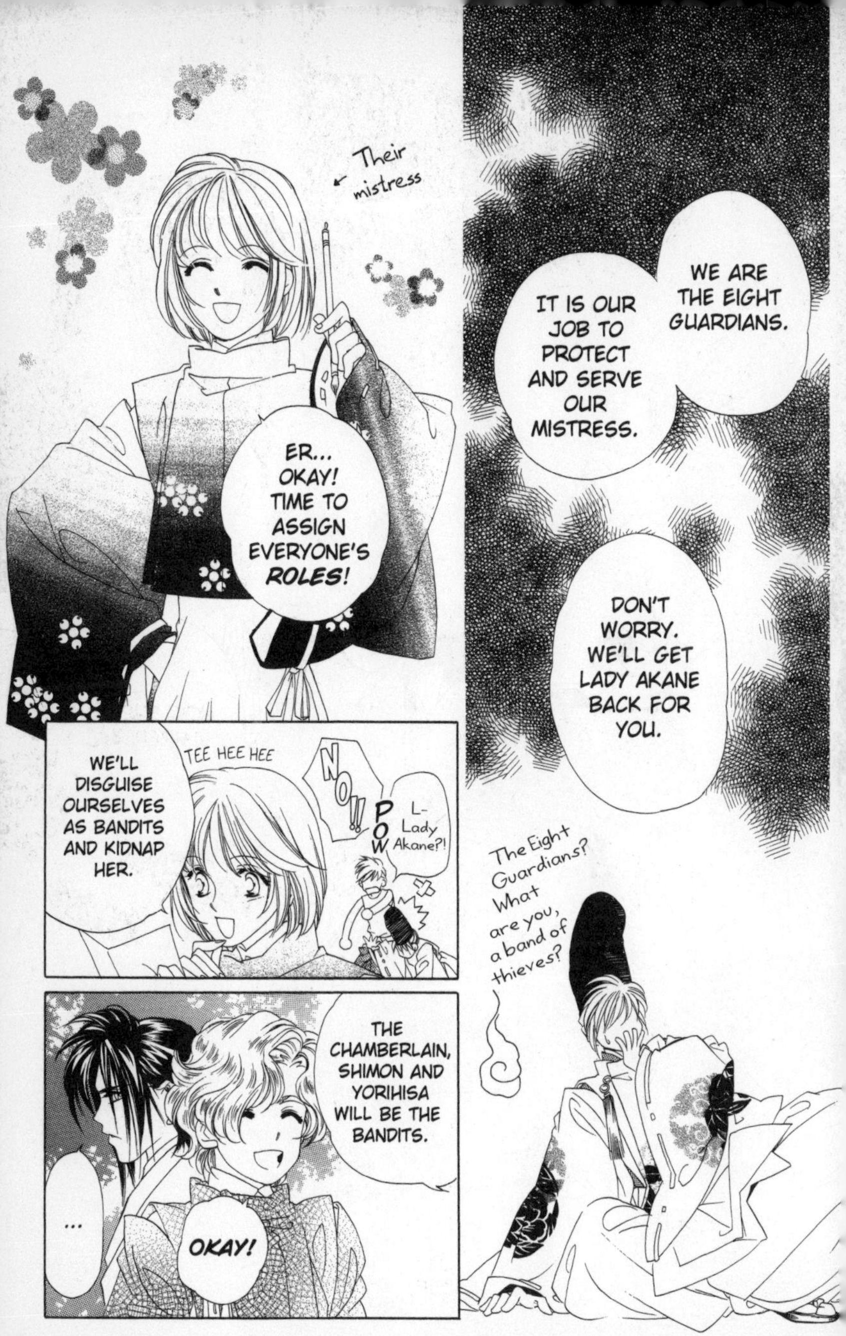
WE ARE THE EIGHT GUARDIANS.
IT IS OUR JOB TO PROTECT AND SERVE OUR MISTRESS.
DON'T WORRY. WE'LL GET LADY AKANE BACK FOR YOU.
The Eight Guardians? What are you, a band of thieves?
Their mistress
ER... OKAY! TIME TO ASSIGN EVERYONE'S ROLES!
NO!!
POW
L- Lady Akane?!
TEE HEE HEE
WE'LL DISGUISE OURSELVES AS BANDITS AND KIDNAP HER.
THE CHAMBERLAIN, SHIMON AND YORIHISA WILL BE THE BANDITS.
OKAY!
...

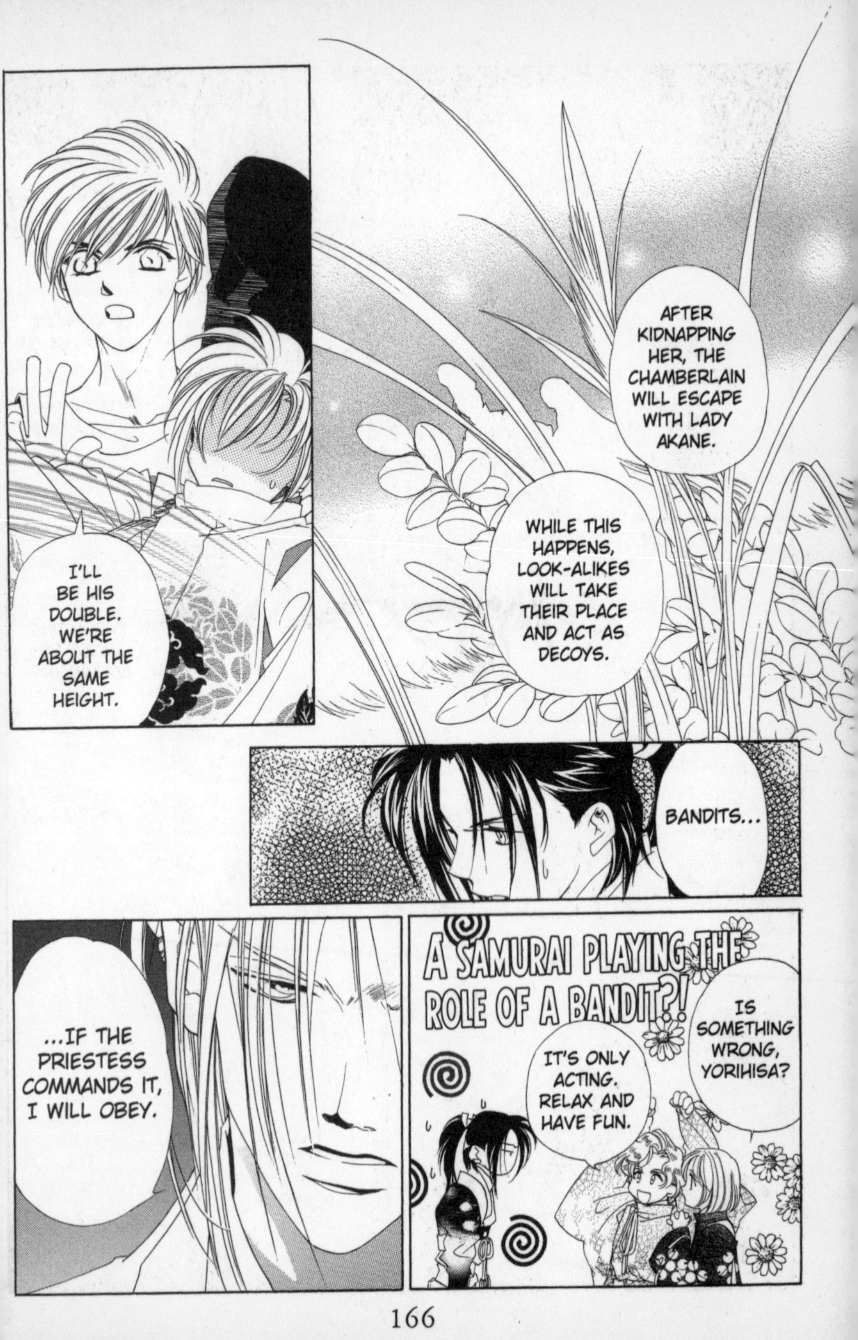
AFTER KIDNAPPING HER, THE CHAMBERLAIN WILL ESCAPE WITH LADY AKANE.
WHILE THIS HAPPENS, LOOK-ALIKES WILL TAKE THEIR PLACE AND ACT AS DECOYS.
I'LL BE HIS DOUBLE. WE'RE ABOUT THE SAME HEIGHT.
BANDITS...
A SAMURAI PLAYING THE ROLE OF A BANDIT?!
IS SOMETHING WRONG, YORIHISA?
IT'S ONLY ACTING. RELAX AND HAVE FUN.
...IF THE PRIESTESS COMMANDS IT, I WILL OBEY.

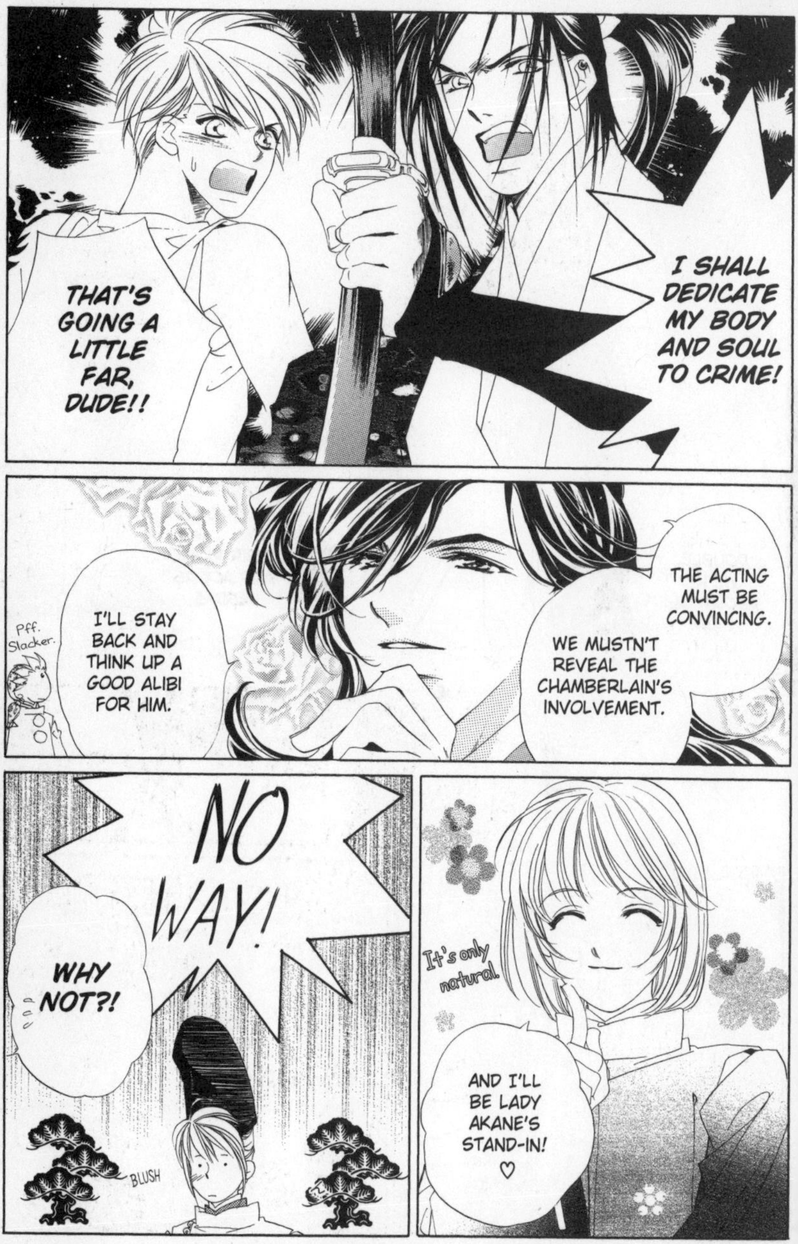
I SHALL DEDICATE MY BODY AND SOUL TO CRIME!
THAT'S GOING A LITTLE FAR, DUDE!!
THE ACTING MUST BE CONVINCING.
WE MUSTN'T REVEAL THE CHAMBERLAIN'S INVOLVEMENT.
I'LL STAY BACK AND THINK UP A GOOD ALIBI FOR HIM.
Pff. Slacker.
It's only natural.
AND I'LL BE LADY AKANE'S STAND-IN! ♡
NO WAY!
WHY NOT?!
BLUSH

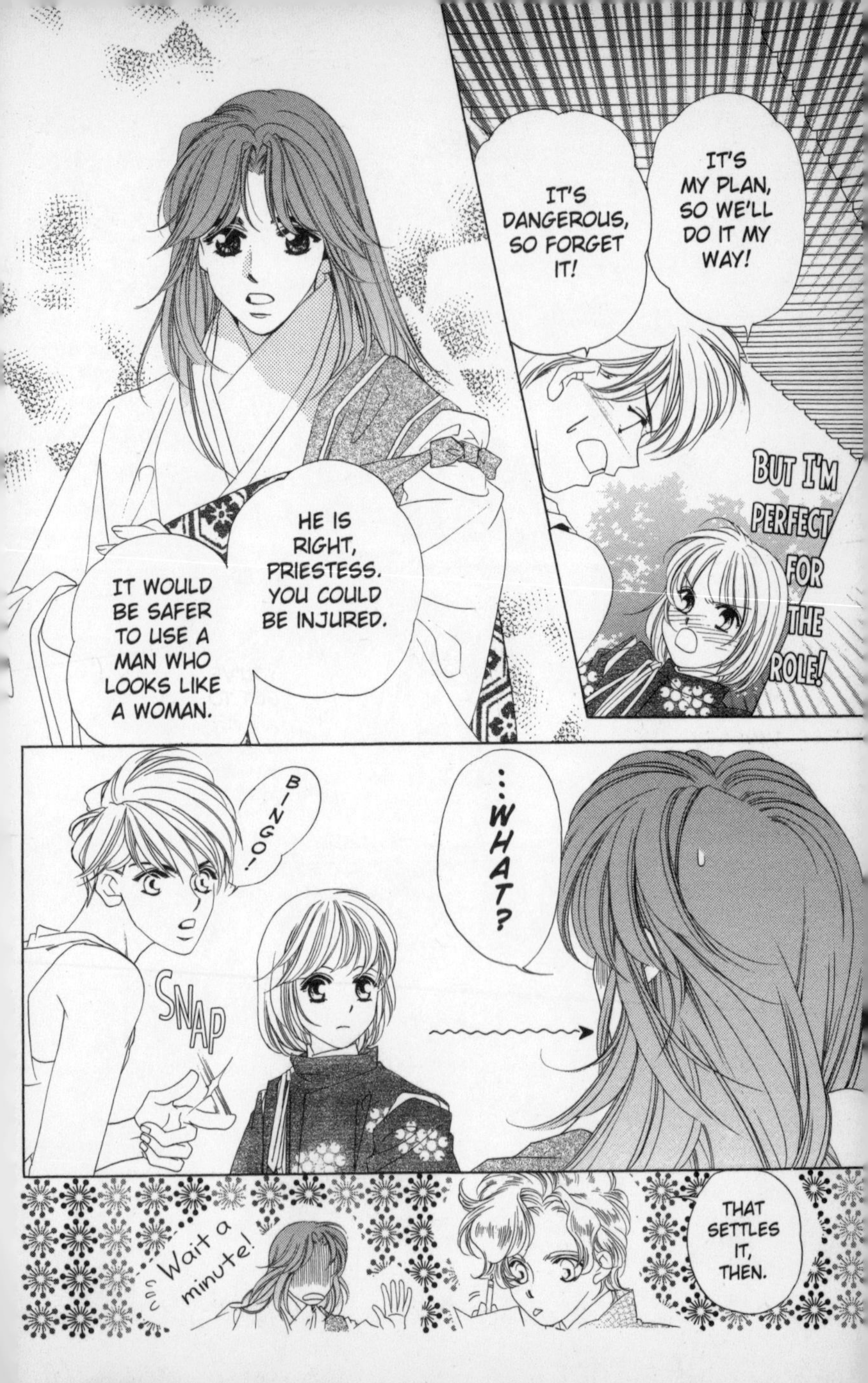
IT'S MY PLAN, SO WE'LL DO IT MY WAY!
IT'S DANGEROUS, SO FORGET IT!
BUT I'M PERFECT FOR THE ROLE!
HE IS RIGHT, PRIESTESS. YOU COULD BE INJURED.
IT WOULD BE SAFER TO USE A MAN WHO LOOKS LIKE A WOMAN.
...WHAT?
BINGO!
SNAP
THAT SETTLES IT, THEN.
Wait a minute!

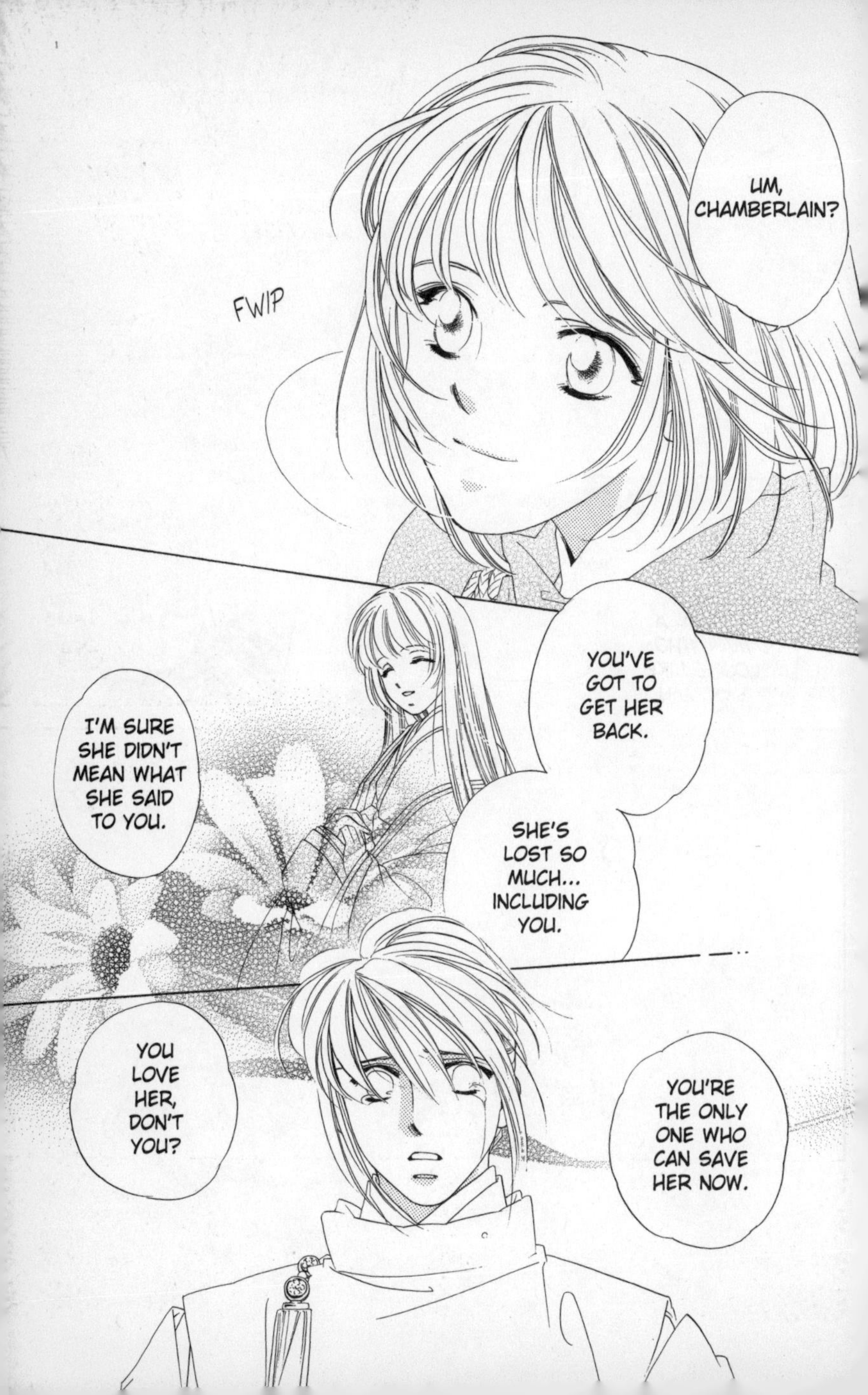
UM, CHAMBERLAIN?
FWIP
YOU'VE GOT TO GET HER BACK.
I'M SURE SHE DIDN'T MEAN WHAT SHE SAID TO YOU.
SHE'S LOST SO MUCH... INCLUDING YOU.
YOU'RE THE ONLY ONE WHO CAN SAVE HER NOW.
YOU LOVE HER, DON'T YOU?

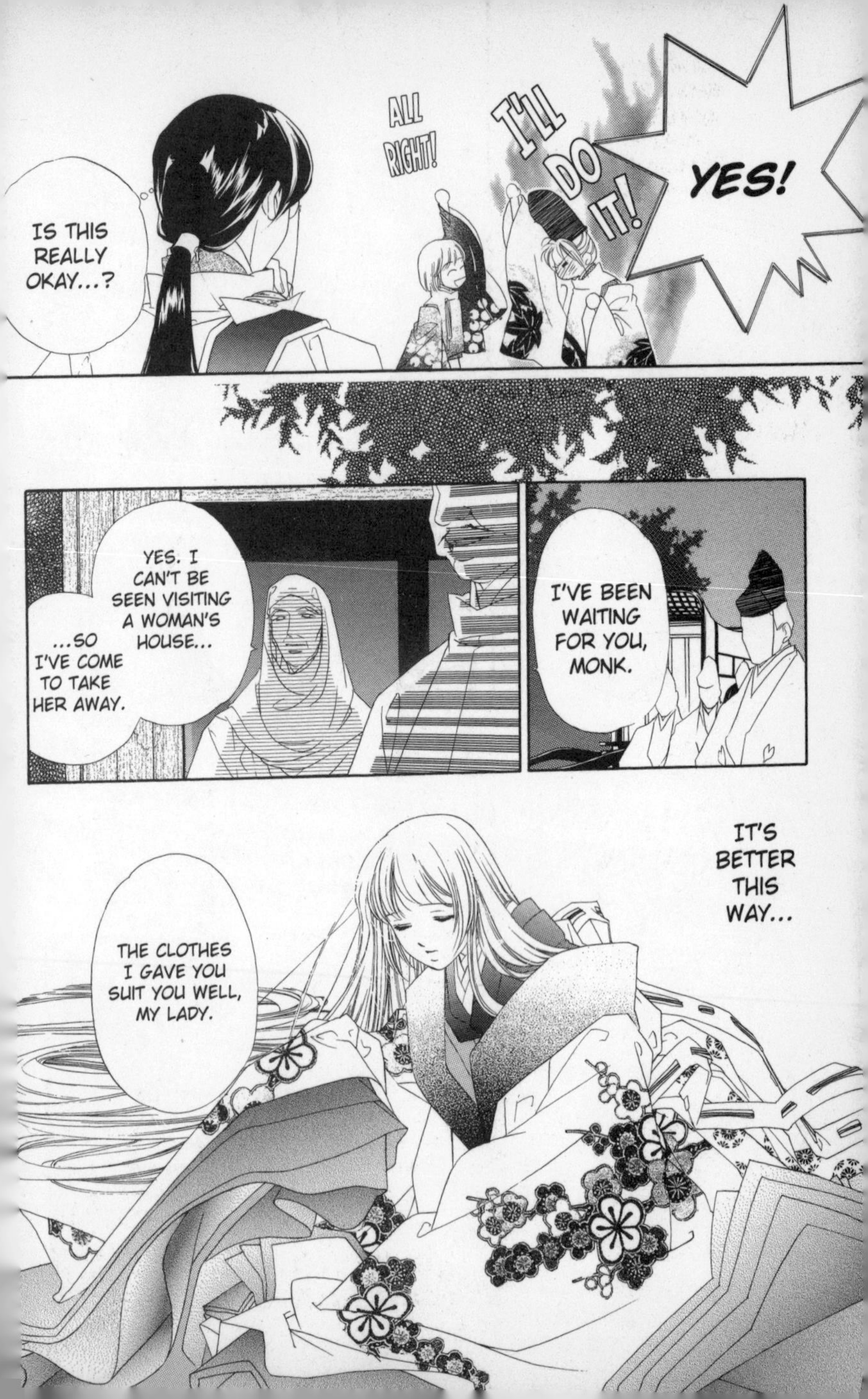
YES!
I'LL DO IT!
ALL RIGHT!
IS THIS REALLY OKAY...?
I'VE BEEN WAITING FOR YOU, MONK.
YES. I CAN'T BE SEEN VISITING A WOMAN'S HOUSE...
...SO I'VE COME TO TAKE HER AWAY.
IT'S BETTER THIS WAY...
THE CLOTHES I GAVE YOU SUIT YOU WELL, MY LADY.

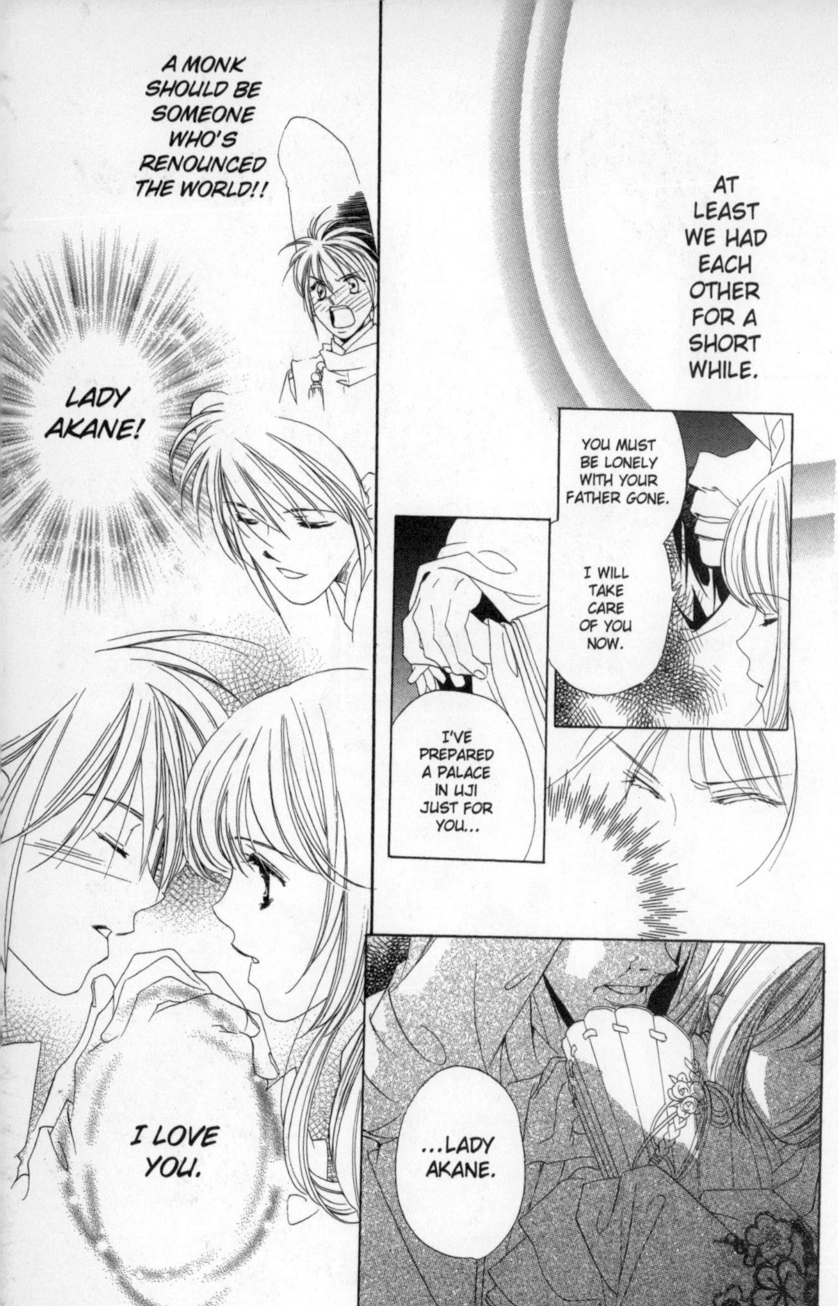
AT LEAST WE HAD EACH OTHER FOR A SHORT WHILE.
YOU MUST BE LONELY WITH YOUR FATHER GONE.
I WILL TAKE CARE OF YOU NOW.
I'VE PREPARED A PALACE IN UJI JUST FOR YOU...
...LADY AKANE.
A MONK SHOULD BE SOMEONE WHO'S RENOUNCED THE WORLD!!
LADY AKANE!
I LOVE YOU.

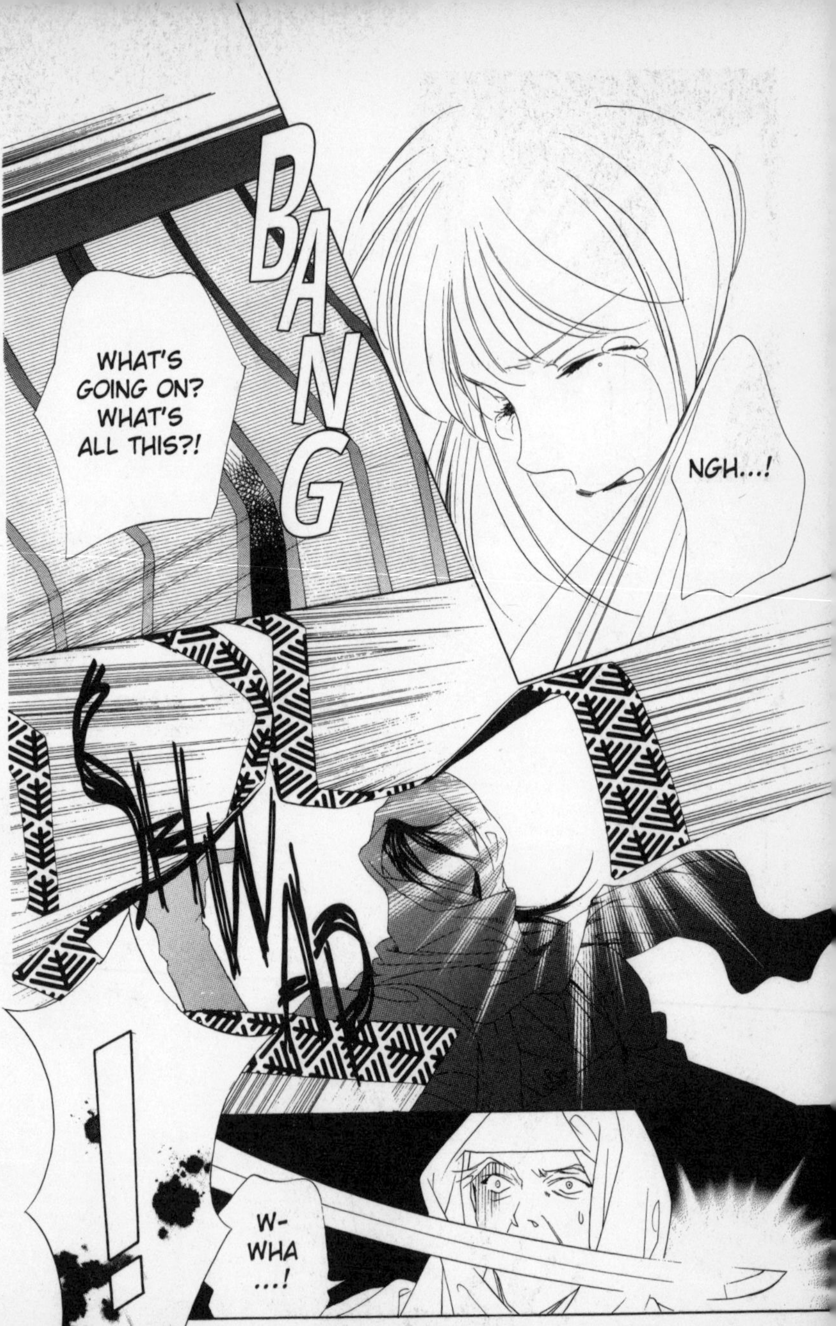
NGH...!
BANG
WHAT'S GOING ON? WHAT'S ALL THIS?!
SHWAP
W-WHA ...!
!

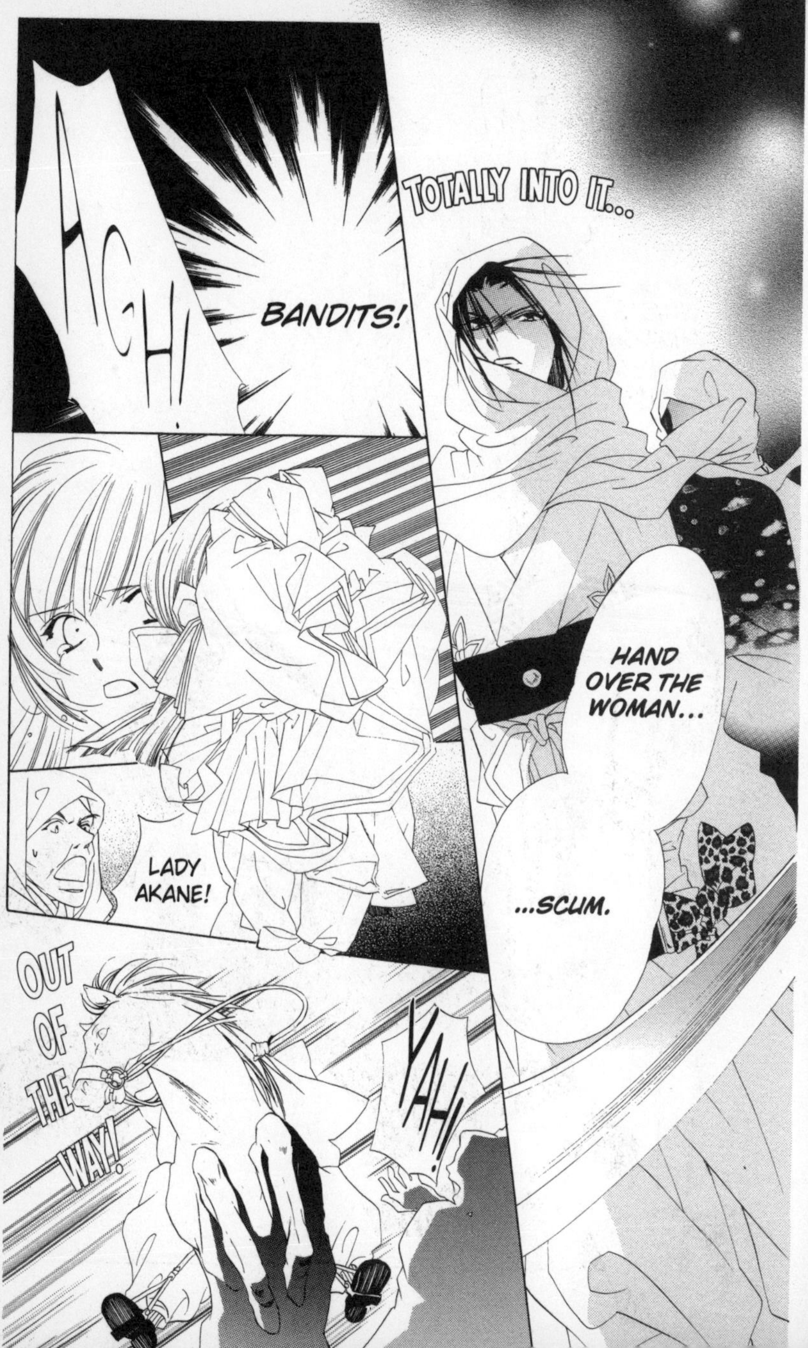
TOTALLY INTO IT...
HAND OVER THE WOMAN...
...SCUM.
AGH!
BANDITS!
LADY AKANE!
YAH!
OUT OF THE WAY!

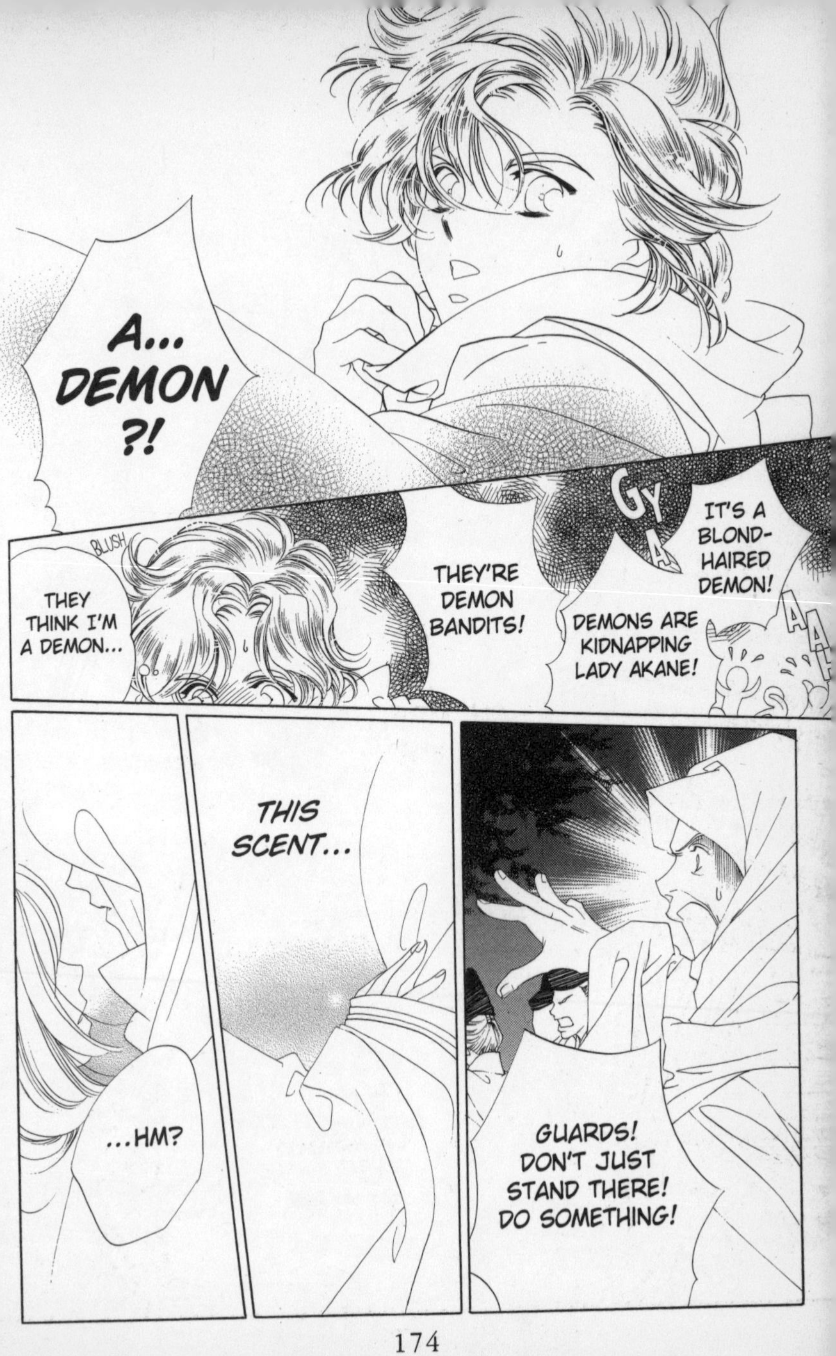
A... DEMON ?!
GYA
IT'S A BLOND-HAIRED DEMON!
DEMONS ARE KIDNAPPING LADY AKANE!
THEY'RE DEMON BANDITS!
BLUSH
THEY THINK I'M A DEMON...
GUARDS! DON'T JUST STAND THERE! DO SOMETHING!
THIS SCENT...
...HM?

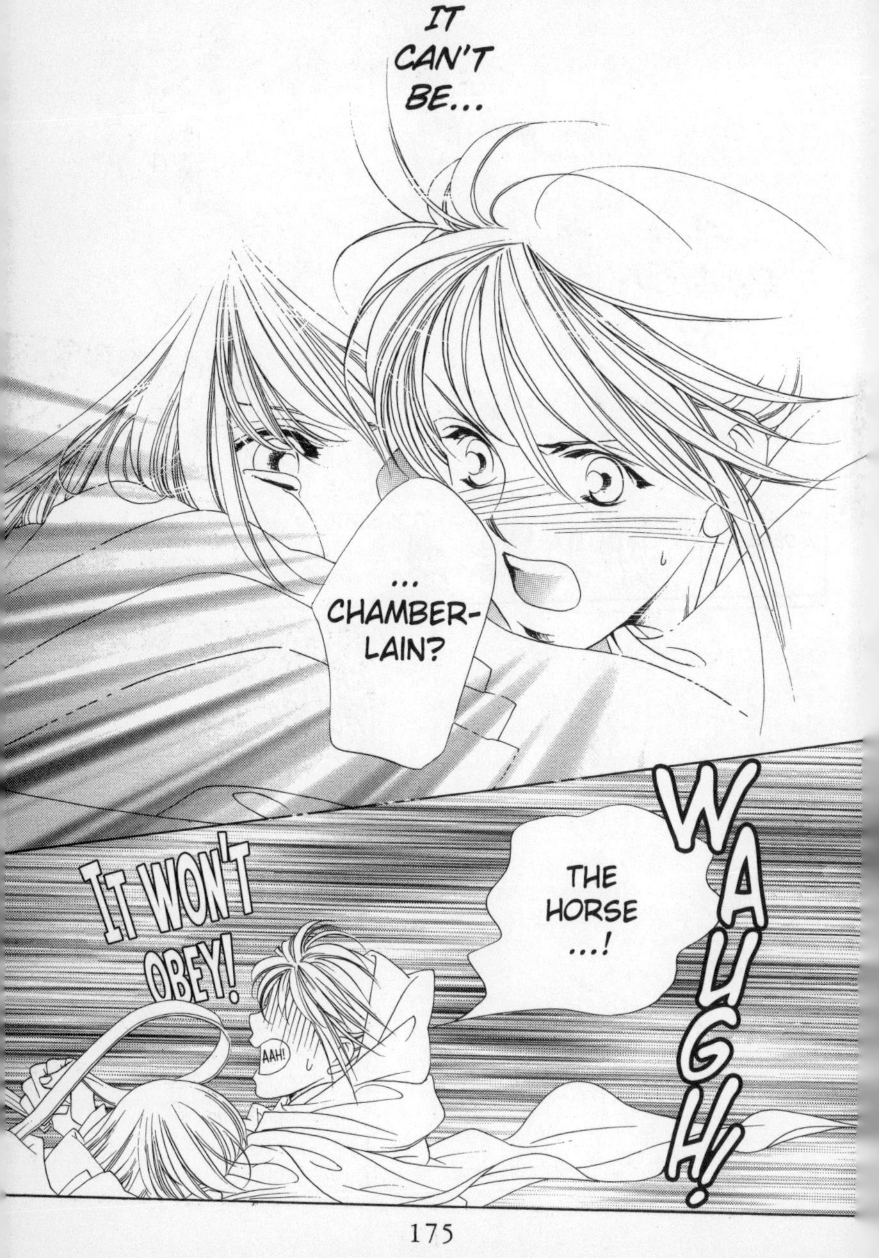
IT CAN'T BE...
... CHAMBER-LAIN?
WAUGH!
THE HORSE ...!
IT WON'T OBEY!
AAH!

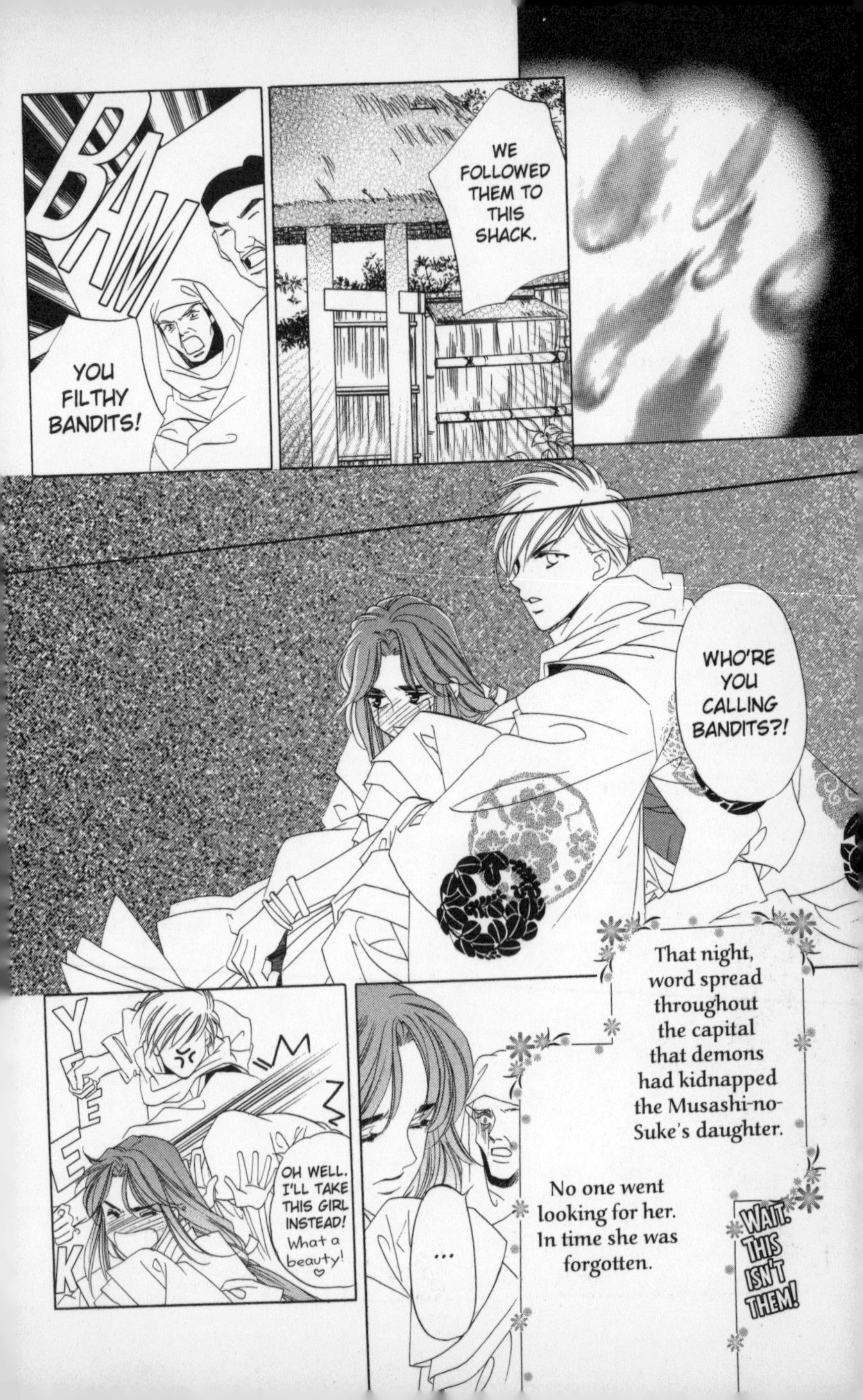
WE FOLLOWED THEM TO THIS SHACK.
BAM
YOU FILTHY BANDITS!
WHO'RE YOU CALLING BANDITS?!
That night, word spread throughout the capital that demons had kidnapped the Musashi-no-Suke's daughter.
WAIT. THIS ISN'T THEM!
No one went looking for her. In time she was forgotten.
...
YEEEK
OH WELL. I'LL TAKE THIS GIRL INSTEAD! What a beauty! ♡

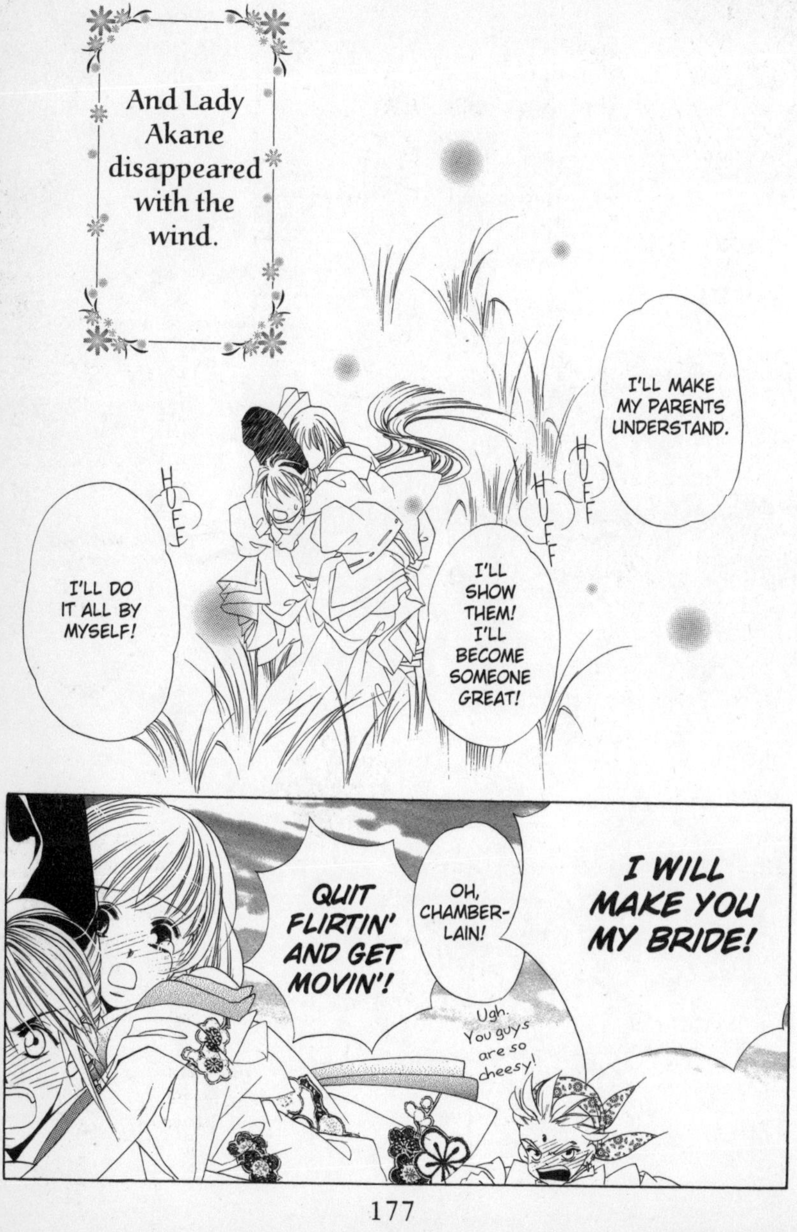
And Lady Akane disappeared with the wind.
I'LL MAKE MY PARENTS UNDERSTAND.
HUFF
HUFF
I'LL SHOW THEM! I'LL BECOME SOMEONE GREAT!
HUFF
I'LL DO IT ALL BY MYSELF!
I WILL MAKE YOU MY BRIDE!
OH, CHAMBER-LAIN!
QUIT FLIRTIN' AND GET MOVIN'!
Ugh. You guys are so cheesy!

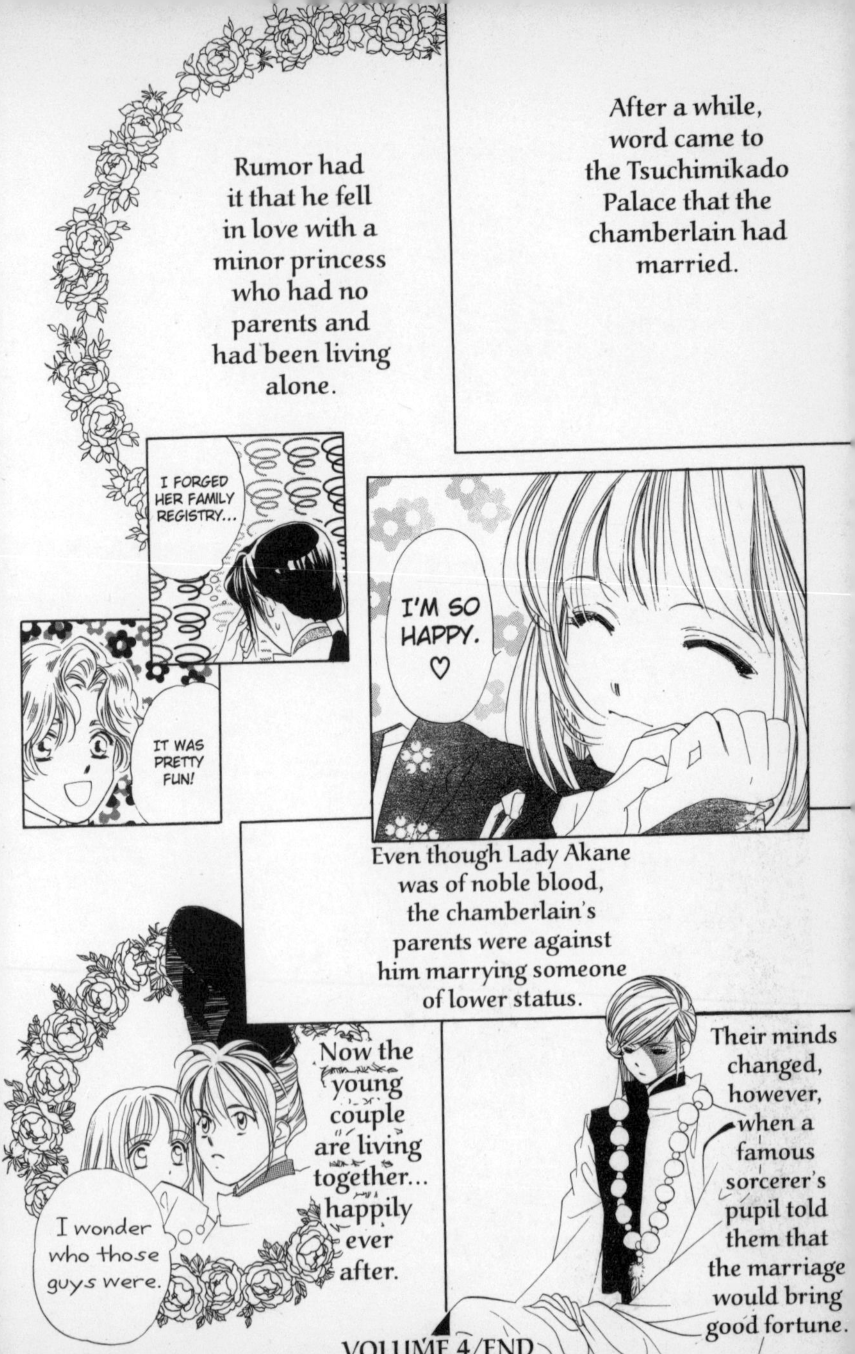
After a while, word came to the Tsuchimikado Palace that the chamberlain had married.
Rumor had it that he fell in love with a minor princess who had no parents and had been living alone.
I'M SO HAPPY. ♡
I FORGED HER FAMILY REGISTRY...
IT WAS PRETTY FUN!
Even though Lady Akane was of noble blood, the chamberlain's parents were against him marrying someone of lower status.
Their minds changed, however, when a famous sorcerer's pupil told them that the marriage would bring good fortune.
Now the young couple are living together... happily ever after.
I wonder who those guys were.

VOLUME 4/END

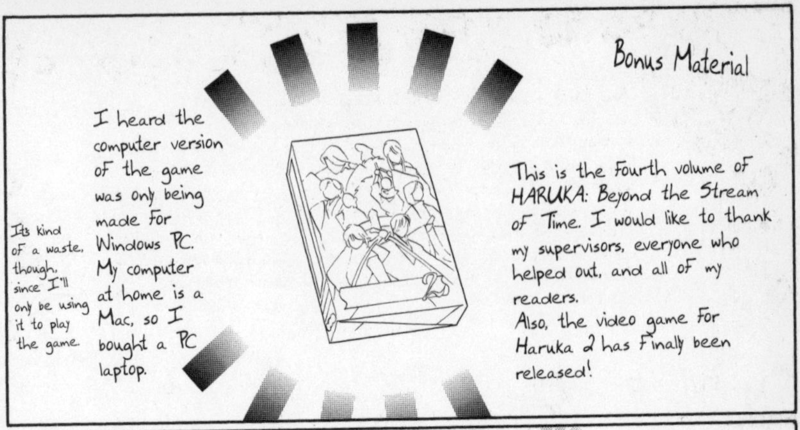
Bonus Material
This is the fourth volume of HARUKA: Beyond the Stream of Time. I would like to thank my supervisors, everyone who helped out, and all of my readers.
Also, the video game for Haruka 2 has finally been released!
I heard the computer version of the game was only being made for Windows PC. My computer at home is a Mac, so I bought a PC laptop.
It's kind of a waste, though, since I'll only be using it to play the game.

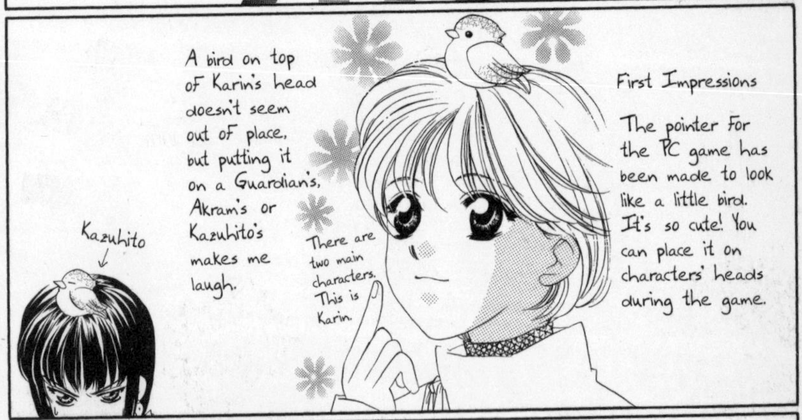
First Impressions
The pointer for the PC game has been made to look like a little bird. It's so cute! You can place it on characters' heads during the game.
There are two main characters. This is Karin.
A bird on top of Karin's head doesn't seem out of place, but putting it on a Guardian's, Akram's or Kazuhito's makes me laugh.
Kazuhito

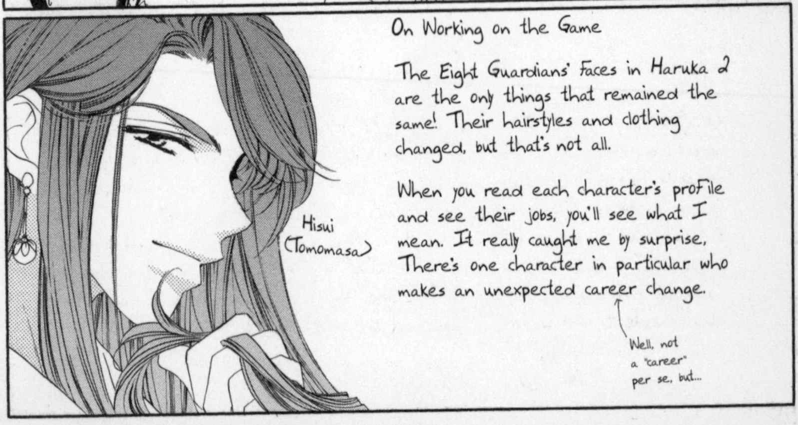
On Working on the Game
The Eight Guardians' faces in Haruka 2 are the only things that remained the same! Their hairstyles and clothing changed, but that's not all.
When you read each character's profile and see their jobs, you'll see what I mean. It really caught me by surprise. There's one character in particular who makes an unexpected career change.
Well, not a "career" per se, but...
Hisui (Tomomasa)

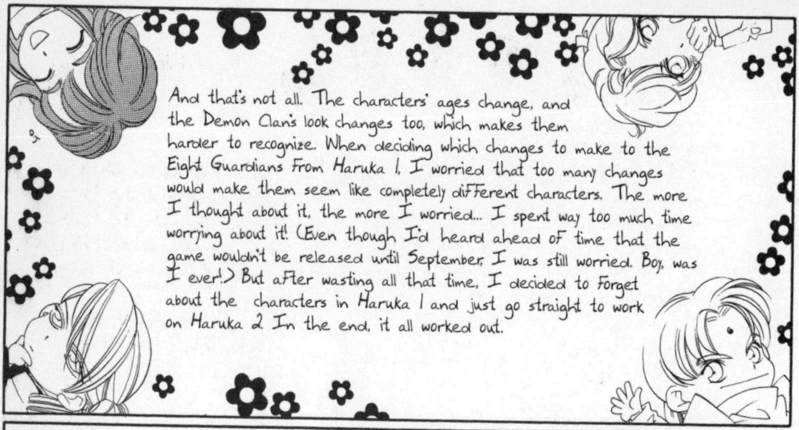
And that's not all. The characters' ages change, and the Demon Clan's look changes too, which makes them harder to recognize. When deciding which changes to make to the Eight Guardians from Haruka 1, I worried that too many changes would make them seem like completely different characters. The more I thought about it, the more I worried... I spent way too much time worrying about it! (Even though I'd heard ahead of time that the game wouldn't be released until September, I was still worried. Boy, was I ever!) But after wasting all that time, I decided to forget about the characters in Haruka 1 and just go straight to work on Haruka 2. In the end, it all worked out.

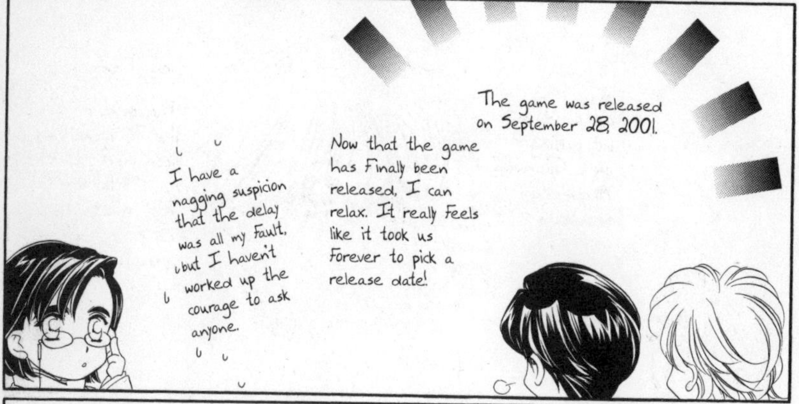
The game was released on September 28, 2001.
Now that the game has finally been released, I can relax. It really feels like it took us forever to pick a release date!
I have a nagging suspicion that the delay was all my fault, but I haven't worked up the courage to ask anyone.

Something Interesting That Happened to Me

On the way back from a recent trip to Yokohama, while my luggage was being checked at Haneda Airport, I was pulled aside by a security guard. He asked me what I had in the bag, which caught me by surprise. I had forgotten that my utility knife was still in my bag! I took it out and handed it to the guard. I felt so embarrassed... I always use a utility knife while making manga, so I'd thought nothing of packing it. But one thing still bothered me after that incident: why wasn't I checked on my flight to Yokohama?

Sorry for all the fuss!

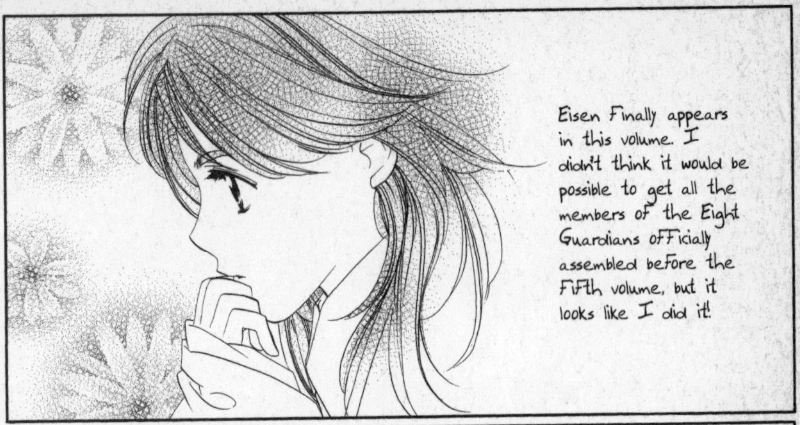
Eisen Finally appears in this volume. I didn't think it would be possible to get all the members of the Eight Guardians oFFicially assembled beFore the FiFth volume, but it looks like I did it!

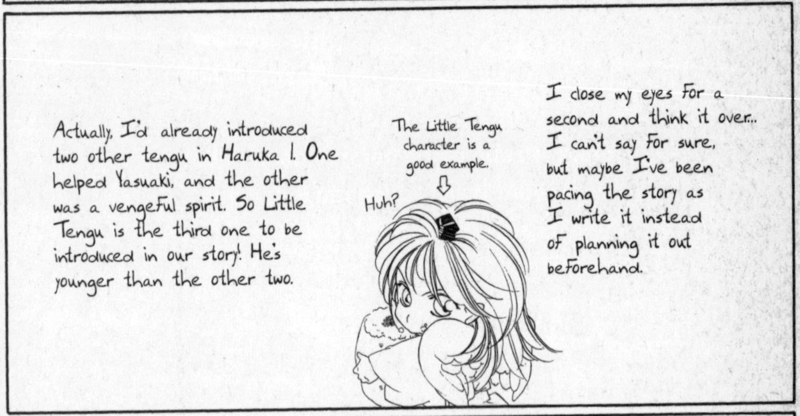
I close my eyes For a second and think it over... I can't say For sure, but maybe I've been pacing the story as I write it instead of planning it out beForehand.
The Little Tengu character is a good example.
Huh?
Actually, I'd already introduced two other tengu in Haruka 1. One helped Yasuaki, and the other was a vengeFul spirit. So Little Tengu is the third one to be introduced in our story! He's younger than the other two.

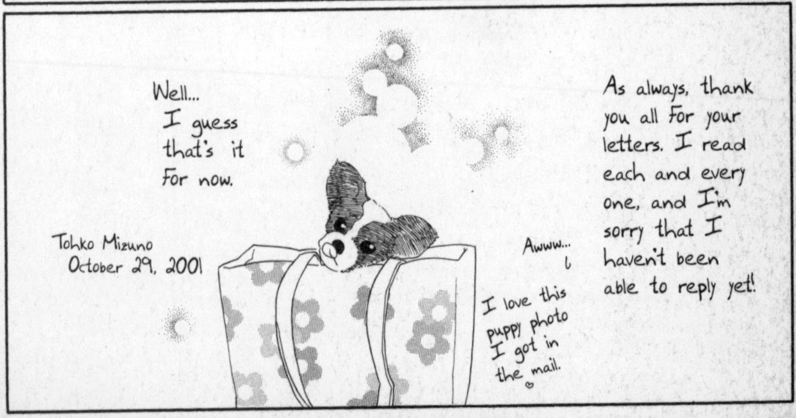
As always, thank you all For your letters. I read each and every one, and I'm sorry that I haven't been able to reply yet!
Awww...
I love this puppy photo I got in the mail.
Well... I guess that's it For now.
Tohko Mizuno
October 29, 2001

BONUS MATERIAL/END

Tohko Mizuno made her mangaka debut
with *Night Walk*, which ran in *Lunatic
LaLa* magazine in 1995. Showcasing
her delicate line work and use of rich
textures and patterns, the quasi-
historical *Haruka* is Mizuno's first
serialized manga and is based on a video
game of the same name. It has spawned
several books, including a fanbook, a
super guidebook, and a collection of
illustrations. Mizuno is also the author of
Mukashi, Oboronaru Otoko Arikeri (Once
Upon a Time, There Was a Hazy Man).

HARUKA
VOL. 4
The Shojo Beat Manga Edition

STORY AND ART BY
TOHKO MIZUNO
ORIGINAL CONCEPT BY RUBY PARTY

Translation/Stanley Floyd, HC Language Solutions
Touch-up Art & Lettering/James Gaubatz
Design/Yuki Ameda
Editor/Carol Fox

Editor in Chief, Books/Alvin Lu
Editor in Chief, Magazines/Marc Weidenbaum
VP, Publishing Licensing/Rika Inouye
VP, Sales & Product Marketing/Gonzalo Ferreyra
VP, Creative/Linda Espinosa
Publisher/Hyoe Narita

Harukanaru Toki no Nakade by Tohko Mizuno
© Tohko Mizuno, KOEI Co., Ltd. 2001
All rights reserved.
First published in Japan in 2002 by HAKUSENSHA, Inc., Tokyo.
English language translation rights arranged
with HAKUSENSHA, Inc., Tokyo.
The stories, characters and incidents mentioned
in this publication are entirely fictional.

Printed in Canada

Published by VIZ Media, LLC
P.O. Box 77010
San Francisco, CA 94107

Shojo Beat Manga Edition
10 9 8 7 6 5 4 3 2 1
First printing, April 2009

www.viz.com

store.viz.com

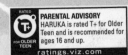

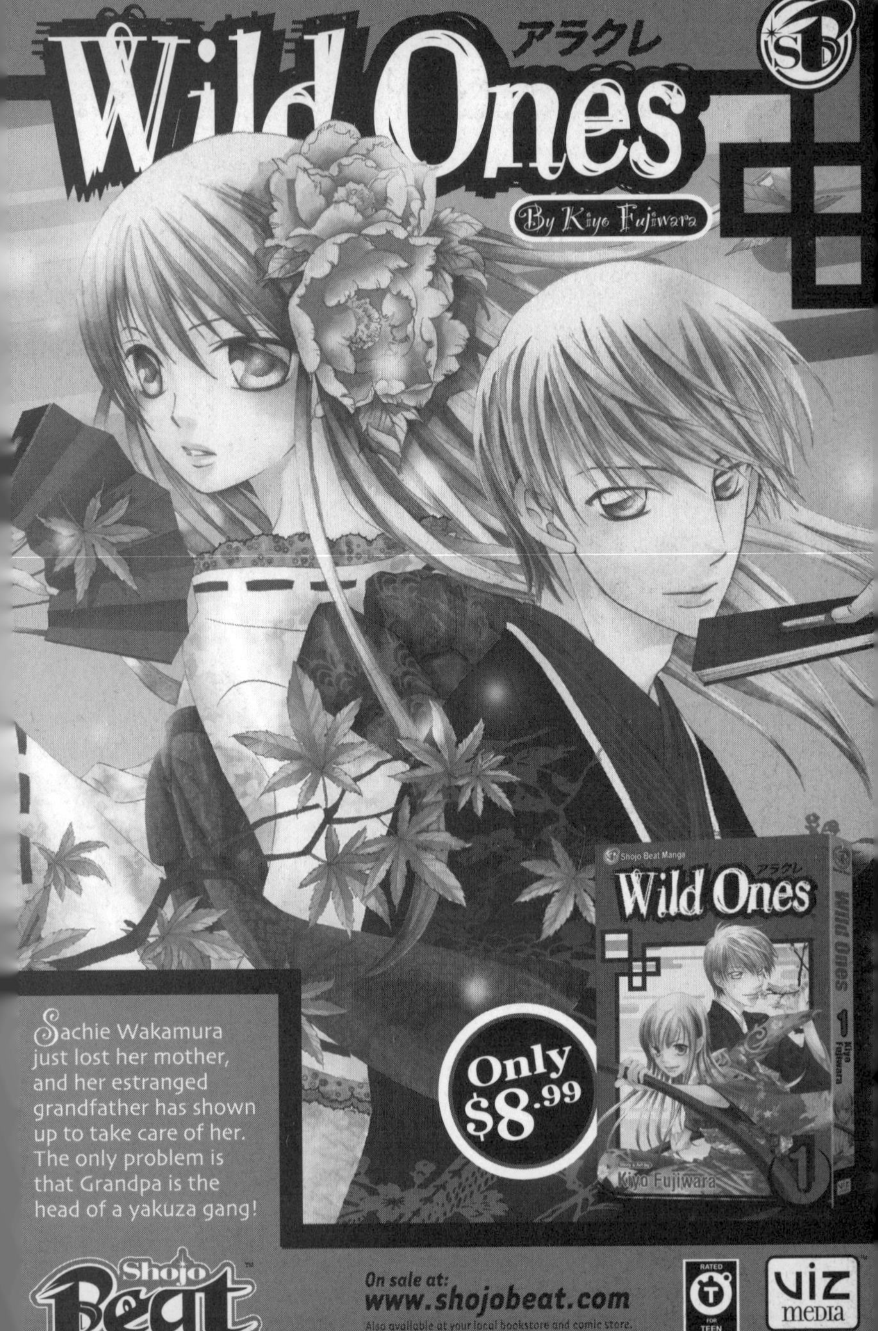
Wild Ones
アラクレ
By Kiyo Fujiwara
Shojo Beat Manga
Wild Ones
アラクレ
Kiyo Fujiwara
Only $8.99
Sachie Wakamura just lost her mother, and her estranged grandfather has shown up to take care of her. The only problem is that Grandpa is the head of a yakuza gang!
Shojo Beat
MANGA from the HEART
On sale at:
www.shojobeat.com
Also available at your local bookstore and comic store.
Arakure © Kiyo Fujiwara 2004/HAKUSENSHA, Inc.
RATED T FOR TEEN
ratings.viz.com
viz media
www.viz.com

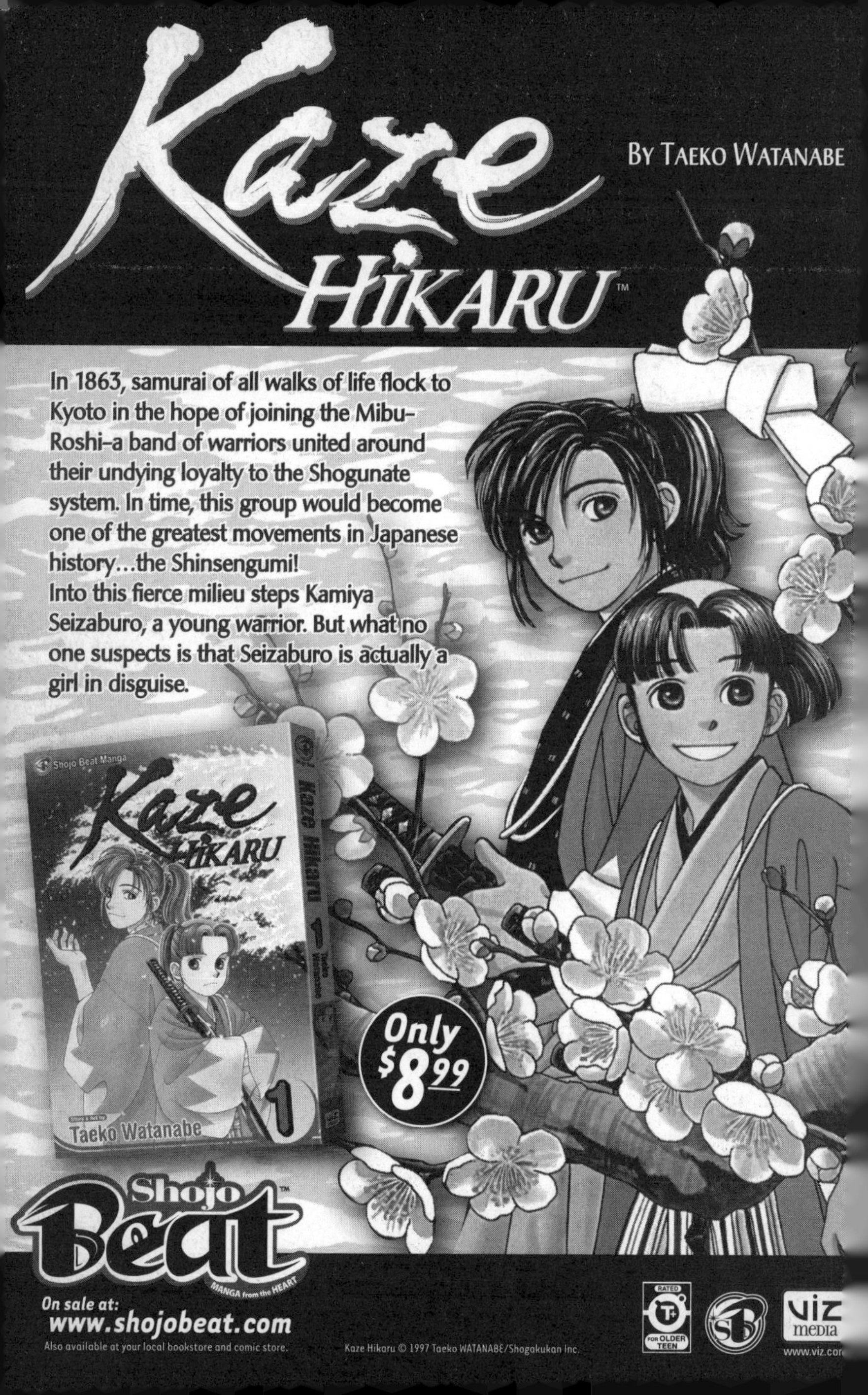
Kaze Hikaru™
By Taeko Watanabe
In 1863, samurai of all walks of life flock to Kyoto in the hope of joining the Mibu-Roshi–a band of warriors united around their undying loyalty to the Shogunate system. In time, this group would become one of the greatest movements in Japanese history…the Shinsengumi!
Into this fierce milieu steps Kamiya Seizaburo, a young warrior. But what no one suspects is that Seizaburo is actually a girl in disguise.
Shojo Beat Manga
Kaze Hikaru
1
Taeko Watanabe
Only $8.99
Shojo Beat™
MANGA from the HEART
On sale at:
www.shojobeat.com
Also available at your local bookstore and comic store.
Kaze Hikaru © 1997 Taeko WATANABE/Shogakukan Inc.
RATED T+ FOR OLDER TEEN
viz media
www.viz.com

Shojo Beat™

MANGA from the HEART

The Shojo Manga Authority

The most **ADDICTIVE** shojo manga stories from Japan **PLUS** unique editorial coverage on the arts, music, culture, fashion, and much more!

12 GIANT issues for ONLY $34⁹⁹*

That's 51% OFF the cover price!

Subscribe NOW and become a member of the 🅑 Sub Club!

- **SAVE** 51% OFF the cover price
- **ALWAYS** get every issue
- **ACCESS** exclusive areas of www.shojobeat.com
- **FREE** members-only gifts several times a year

Strictly VIP!

3 EASY WAYS TO SUBSCRIBE!

1) Send in the subscription order form from this book OR
2) Log on to: www.shojobeat.com OR
3) Call 1-800-541-7876

Save [...] price!

Shojo Beat

MANGA from the HEART

The Shojo Manga Authority

This monthly magazine is injected with the most **ADDICTIVE** shojo manga stories from Japan. PLUS, unique editorial coverage on the arts, music, culture, fashion, and much more!

☑ **YES!** Please enter my one-year subscription (12 GIANT issues) to *Shojo Beat* at the LOW SUBSCRIPTION RATE of **$34.99!**

Over **300 pages** per issue!

NAME

ADDRESS

CITY   STATE   ZIP

E-MAIL ADDRESS   P7GNC1

☐ MY CHECK IS ENCLOSED (PAYABLE TO *Shojo Beat*)   ☐ BILL ME LATER

CREDIT CARD: ☐ VISA   ☐ MASTERCARD

ACCOUNT #   EXP. DATE

SIGNATURE

CLIP AND MAIL TO →   SHOJO BEAT
Subscriptions Service Dept.
P.O. Box 438
Mount Morris, IL 61054-0438